Inuen, et Sculp.

GARDENS AND GARDENING
IN EARLY MODERN ENGLAND AND WALES
1560–1660

11

Jill Francis

GARDENS AND GARDENING

IN EARLY MODERN ENGLAND AND WALES

1560–1660

PUBLISHED FOR THE PAUL MELLON CENTRE FOR STUDIES IN BRITISH ART
BY YALE UNIVERSITY PRESS • NEW HAVEN AND LONDON

ISBN 978-0-300-232080 HB
Library of Congress Control Number: 2017954634

Designed by Emily Lees
Printed in China

Endpapers   Detail of the title page from John Gerard's *Herball,* 1597 (see fig. 39)
Frontispiece   Jacques le Moyne, *French Rose and Privet Hawk Moth, c.*1585
p. vi   Gardener at work from Thomas Hyll's *The Gardeners Labyrinth,* 1577
p. viii   Red gooseberry from *Tradescant's Orchard, c.*1620 (see fig. 154)
p. x   Gardens at Conwy Castle, *c.*1600 (see fig. 96)

For Louisa, Nathaniel and Elin

CONTENTS

Note to the reader ix

Acknowledgements xi

Introduction 1

1 The 'Arte of Gardening': The Books 22

2 'Profits and Pleasures': The Social Context 42

3 Setting the Scene: Elizabethan Gardens 54

4 Continuities: Early Seventeenth-century Gardens 92

5 The Gardeners 126

6 New Aspirations: 'A Garden of Pleasant Flowers' 150

7 The Knotty Problem of Knots 182

8 Artificial Ornament in the Garden 210

9 War and Peace: Gardening in the Mid-seventeenth Century 236

10 The Plants 276

11 Conclusions: 'A ffitt place for any Gentleman' 316

Appendices

1 Bibliography of gardening literature published in English, c.1558–1660 330

2 Transcript of Sir Thomas Hanmer's essay on gardening 338

Abbreviations 342

Notes 344

Select bibliography 368

List of illustrations 376

Index 383

The red Gousberry
Ripe June 15

NOTE TO THE READER

Old-style dating has been retained where it appears in manuscript sources, the year beginning on 25 March.

Where possible, spelling and punctuation have been reproduced as they appear in original documents, with the exception that modern forms of u/v and i/j have been used and the 'thorn' replaced with 'th'. Contractions of 'your', 'with', 'which', 'that' and 'then' have been silently expanded. Book titles and the names of authors appear as in the original editions.

Numbers appear in Roman and Arabic forms, as in the original.

ACKNOWLEDGEMENTS

It takes many people to write a book, and I take this opportunity to express my gratitude to everyone – both within and outside academia – who has helped me bring this one to fruition. I would like to acknowledge specifically the generous financial assistance received from the Arts and Humanities Research Council, which enabled me to take up my post-graduate studies in the first place. At that time, the holders of the public purse strings appeared to understand the importance and value of research in the arts and humanities – we can only hope that, in the future, such priorities may once again come to the fore. Also acknowledged is the valuable help I have received from archives and libraries around the world and in particular, the many hours I have spent surrounded by friends, colleagues and books at the University of Birmingham's Shakespeare Institute Library. I am much obliged too for the support I have received from the Paul Mellon Centre in bringing this work to publication.

Generous input from academic colleagues has been gratefully received, and I am truly indebted to Professor Richard Cust for guiding me expertly and wisely through my initial research and the writing up of my thesis. His invaluable advice and encouragement stayed with me as I worked through the later stages of this project.

Many thanks also go to family and friends who have helped with illustrations, proof-reading, endless cups of tea and a sympathetic ear: to Jonathan, Matthew, Lyndon, Robert, Bettina, Lorna, my beloved cat Henry, and especially to my husband Manuel for his unfailing support, encouragement and love that have seen me through all the highs and lows of this process. Finally, for providing an abundance of respite and joy, and for constantly reminding me that there are more important things in life than work, my love goes to my beautiful grandchildren, to whom I dedicate this book. Perhaps one day you will even read it!

INTRODUCTION

Although many men must be content with any plat of ground, of what forme or quantity soever it bee, more or lesse, for their Garden, because a more large or convenient cannot bee had to their habitation: Yet I perswade my selfe, that Gentlemen of the better sort and quality, will provide such a parcell of ground to bee laid out for their Garden, and in such convenient manner, as may be fit and answerable to the degree they hold. To prescribe one forme for every man to follow, were too great presumption and folly: for every man will please his owne fancie.[1]

These words, from the opening of John Parkinson's *Paradisi in Sole, Paradisus Terrestris*, 'The Ordering of the Garden of Pleasure', written in 1629, encapsulate at once the subject of the pages that follow: an investigation into the gardens, gardeners and gardening practices of the gentlemen of early modern England. At the same time, they locate Parkinson in a perfect position to act as our commentator, because as well as writing this remarkable gardening book for which he is now best known, John Parkinson presents a full list of credentials which establish him as a fitting observer of contemporary gardening practice. First and foremost, he was a gardener himself and his book is full of intensely practical advice based on his own experience of growing and cultivating plants on a large two-acre plot in Long Acre, near Covent Garden in London. He lived for all his long working life in the city, earning his living as an apothecary. Although plants were the tools of his trade and Parkinson saw the growing of plants as an essential element in the pursuance of his profession, for him, gardening was more than just an extension of his work. He was passionate about plants, revelling in their beauty and growing hundreds of new and exotic varieties in his garden of pleasant flowers.[2]

He was an important figure on the London gardening scene – he knew John Gerard, the author of *The Herball* and gardener to the Elizabethan statesman Lord Burghley; he was a life-long friend of John Tradescant, the renowned plant hunter of the age; he was a mentor to young botanists such as Thomas Johnson; he was ranked by the Flemish botanist Dr Matthias de l'Obel as one of the most important gardeners of his time in London and by 1640 he had been appointed to the position of *Botanicus Regius*, Herbalist to Charles I.[3]

Much about John Parkinson can be seen reflected in the portrait that appears in the front of his book (fig. 1). The text declares him as an apothecary of London. The family coat of arms in the bottom left corner of the woodcut, the Latin text, his mode of dress and the shield of the Worshipful Society of Apothecaries in the bottom right corner all reveal him as a man of learning and some substance, defining his status as both a gentleman and a respected member of his profession. But the portrait also reveals him as a gardener. In his hand he is holding a single flower stem – a Sweet John, or Sweet William as it is now known. Apart from the obvious play on his name, it is significant that at a time when plants

were mainly valued for their medicinal and other uses, this particular plant had, by Parkinson's own definition, no use in 'physycke', but instead was noted for the colour and variety of its flowers.[4] As will be shown, Parkinson not only recommends flowers for the garden purely as objects of beauty and delight but also, as demonstrated in his words quoted at the head of this introduction, he regards a garden in which to display them as a fitting statement of wealth and status.

In addition to the abundance of gardening advice and his considerable knowledge of plants and flowers being grown in seventeenth-century England, Parkinson also provides a personal commentary on the society in which he lived and worked. He offers his own views on current trends – what people 'now adais' are doing in their gardens – some of which he approves and some of which he does not.[5] He despairs over idle and ignorant gardeners who do not know how to deal with the new 'outlandish' plants arriving from overseas, and untrustworthy nurserymen who do not know their 'Arch-Dukes' cherry from their 'Flanders'.[6] He grapples with moral issues, such as gardeners who presume to control nature, trying to change the colour, scent and form of plants, doing 'as much as God himselfe that created them'.[7] And although he purports to be addressing 'most men', his constant references to the gentlemanly status of his readers reflects his own concern with this, one of the major preoccupations of the age.[8]

Within the pages of *Paradisi in Sole* then, John Parkinson provides one of the most comprehensive overviews of early modern gardening available to us, highlighting precisely the kinds of questions to be taken up in the pages that follow. What form exactly did a man's 'plat of ground' take and how did that change over the period? Who was gardening? Why were they gardening and how, ultimately, did they view the spaces they had created?

This book sets out to explore what early modern gardeners were doing in their gardens. Specifically, it looks beyond the well-researched but unrepresentative and extravagant showpieces of the nobility into the more ordinary gardens of the rural county gentry, in order to piece together a picture of what was actually happening in the generality of gardens during the period. It identifies and traces a change from the essentially utilitarian nature of gardening at the beginning of the period to the development of the ornamental flower garden in the seventeenth century and the gradual acceptance over that time of the activity of gardening as a leisure pursuit worthy of the gentry. At the same time, it explores the contexts – social, cultural, intellectual, geographical – that allowed these changes to occur, facilitating new understanding and insight into both the aspirations of contemporary gardeners as well as the everyday practicalities of gardening in early modern England.

2 Attributed to Ambrosius Bosschaert,
*Large Bouquet in Gilt-Mounted Wan-Li Vase, c.*1620

What follows is more than just another history of gardens. Rarely, if ever, has this subject been examined from the viewpoint of the contemporary gardener or garden-owner and it is this omission that is addressed here. Thus far, garden history has been considered from a wide variety of disciplines including art history, literary history, architectural history, landscape architecture and more recently, archaeology. While this interdisciplinary approach is to be applauded, it has nevertheless had the effect of subjecting much of garden history to its theoretical aspects, examining aesthetics, iconography, symbols and meaning, but rarely dealing with practical issues. In other words, the concentration has been on the history of gardens, and specifically on garden styles, as opposed to the history of gardening itself.[9] It is somewhat surprising, for instance, that the science of horticulture has barely impinged on garden history at all. This book therefore offers a new approach, looking at gardening as did the people of the time, as an essentially practical activity in which a broad spectrum of society was engaged.

At the same time, the book identifies this period as one of tremendous change, charting the concerns and preoccupations of the age which affected all areas of life including gardens and gardening practice, and it is possible to see how these both contributed to, and reflected, wider changes in society. At the beginning of the period, in the opening years of the reign of Elizabeth, gardens were essentially the same as they had been for centuries. They were enclosed spaces whose primary function was the utilitarian one of providing food, medicines, flavourings and scent for the household. To grow plants and flowers purely for their ornamental value was an indulgence reserved for the wealthy few. However, the new century and the new Jacobean regime brought rapid change. Adventurers returned from across the seas with untold exotic delights for the garden. The number of plants and flowers available increased dramatically, bringing not just new varieties to be grown and admired but also extending the possibilities of the ornamental garden (fig. 2). Spring-flowering bulbs, and later an extended range of tender evergreen plants, revolutionised the way gardeners could plan their gardens, because it became possible to have colour from plants in the garden all year round. Planting had to be carefully planned so as to allow each specimen to reach its full potential and be suitably displayed. As well as these practical considerations, new attitudes to luxury and pleasure engendered new ways of thinking, allowing gardeners who possessed the means to do so to cultivate purely ornamental gardens. They became avid collectors, paying large sums for desirable plants and, in the new spirit of conspicuous consumption, gardens were viewed by some not just as a personal pleasure but as a new context in which to display wealth and status. Analysis of all these factors will demonstrate the vital role that gardens and gardening have to play in enhancing our understanding of early modern culture.

To begin at the beginning: what exactly is meant by a 'garden' and how is the activity of 'gardening' to be defined? Parkinson describes a garden as a 'plat' or 'parcell' of ground, but specifies quickly that in order to protect the herbs, flowers and early fruit, it must be defended against cold winds and frost with brick or stone walls, ideally on one side by the house, or with large trees 'to keepe it the warmer'.[10] The sixteenth-century garden writer Thomas Hyll quotes the Roman horticulturalist Columella as observing that once people had been introduced to the delights of gardening, they then became skilful in the ordering and dressing of garden plots 'by well fensing and comely furnishyng of their grounde, with sundry needefulle & delectable trees, plantes and herbes'.[11] In the newly translated editions of the Bible, contemporaries would have read in the book of Genesis that 'the Lord God took the man and put him into the garden of Eden to dress it and to keep it', but then, the eating of an apple later, 'the Lord God sent him forth from the garden of Eden, to till the ground'.[12] Adam's expulsion from the Garden implies a defined space from which he was sent to the wider world outside. Furthermore, once Adam was sent away from the Garden, the nature of his work changed from that of a gardener – dressing and keeping the garden – to that of an agricultural labourer, tilling the ground, against which it is set in contrast. In his systematic overview of medieval gardens, the historian Frank Crisp explains that in the selection of illustrations which form the basis of his book, many were excluded because although they showed flowers growing, 'they were not enclosed and therefore could not be said to represent a true garden'.[13]

From these examples, it seems that the defining characteristics of a garden include the fact that it is an enclosed space, that it will contain cultivated plants, whether fruit, flowers or trees, and that it is separate from whatever other activities may be going on outside its boundaries. This definition still holds even in the most controversial of examples, such as the modern-day 'garden of movement', designed by Gilles Clément and opened in the Parc Citroën in Paris in September 1992. It is an area of fallow land, where the processes

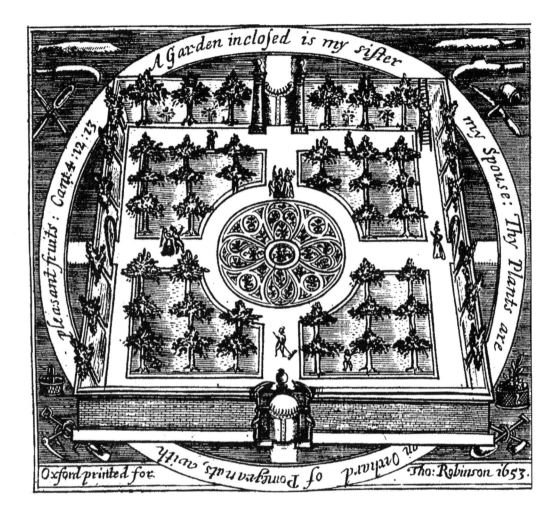

of colonisation and migration typical of plants that inhabit such environments are apparently allowed to take their natural course. There is much debate therefore as to whether or not it can be called a garden at all. But despite appearances, Clément has revealed that the plants in this space are carefully managed to maintain plant diversity and that it is, in fact, 'a privileged enclosure carefully watched over by the gardener'.[14] Set as it is within the boundaries of the park and surrounded by other, different and separate gardens, it seems to conform exactly to the definition described earlier – enclosed, managed by a gardener and separate from everything around it.

All this seems reasonably unequivocal, but there are some terms which blurred the boundaries. One in particular was the concept of the orchard, an apparently ubiquitous element of all but the smallest of early modern gardens. In 1653, Ralph Austen wrote that it would be of great benefit to all 'If men would plant fruit-trees, not only in Gardens, but also in many of their fields and hedges'.[15] The frontispiece of his book shows an illustration of a totally enclosed garden, planted entirely, apart from a small ornamental bed in the centre, with fruit trees (fig. 3).

For William Lawson, another contemporary garden writer, who was also an active gardener, it seems that the orchard *was* the garden and he uses the terms almost interchangeably. His book is primarily concerned with the planting and maintaining of an orchard, including explicit instructions on how it should be 'fenced'.[16] But, as well as fruit trees, this area could also include many features that we would associate with gardens – flowers, mounts, walks, mazes and any manner of 'ornaments'. Lawson includes a plan of an ideal garden, in which the orchard areas are well within the bounds of the garden walls (see fig. 47).[17] Again, it seems that what defines an orchard as distinct from fruit trees simply planted in fields is that it is enclosed, therefore making it part of the garden. From other archival evidence it seems that the pruning and care of fruit trees was the responsibility of the gardener, so throughout this book the definition of a garden will include the orchard and, following on from this, gardening will refer to any activity relating to the cultivation of plants within these enclosed areas.[18]

The final word on this, however, should perhaps go to another contemporary observer, William Harrison, who offered a more pragmatic definition: 'I comprehend, therefore, under the word "garden" all such grounds as are wrought with the spade by man's hand'.[19] This reminds us that, at the end of the day, gardening involves a great deal of hard work and, throughout everything that follows, it is vital to bear in mind the role of gardener as labourer, although he – or she – may not always be visible.[20] Much garden history attributes the making of gardens to the designers and owners, but it must never be forgotten who it is that really does the back-breaking toil of digging, ditching, manuring and weeding (fig. 4).

This book aims to enhance our understanding of gardens and gardening during the early modern period, more specifically in the years 1560–1660. But why this particular time? And how is it to be defined?

First and foremost, there is still an enormous amount of research to be carried out on the gardens of this era: this episode in the story of the English garden has yet to be told in any detail and it is not difficult to see why that should be. In the first instance, there are few gardens to look at because the evidence on the ground is simply not there: almost no

gardens have survived extant from this period, the vast majority having either disappeared
altogether or been subject to such change and renovation over the centuries that little or
nothing remains of their original state. There are a few rare exceptions, the garden of Sir
Thomas Tresham at Lyveden New Bield in Northamptonshire providing a notable example.
Here, recent archaeological excavations of the site have revealed the layout of the garden
as almost untouched since Sir Thomas's death in 1605 and it is possible for the modern-day
visitor to experience the garden in something of the same way as Tresham's contemporaries may have done (fig. 5).[21]

In other cases, fragments remain of original gardens, such as the sixteenth-century terraces and ponds at Llantrithyd in south Wales or the seventeenth-century garden features

at Wotton House and Albury Park in Surrey (see figs 138, 142). Archaeological remains of another early seventeenth-century garden can still be seen at Campden Manor in Gloucestershire, as well as two extant banqueting houses (see figs 128, 175). But these are rare examples. Other gardens of course have survived, but not as they were in the seventeenth century: those at Trentham Hall and Stowe, for instance, are now exemplars of the English landscape garden laid out in the eighteenth century by Capability Brown, but leaving no trace of what came before.[22]

   Adding to this paucity of evidence on the ground, the available documentary evidence relating to this period is equally disparate and scant. Given the essentially practical and inherently ephemeral nature of gardening, it is perhaps not surprising that relatively little information about this activity was ever written down in the first place, and much of what was written lies buried within archives rarely examined for this kind of data. Thus far, most studies dealing with this period have concentrated on the few well-documented gardens of royalty and the aristocracy, because records are still extant for these showy extravaganzas. However, while offering an appealing picture of these exceptional gardens, they tell us little about what the ordinary garden might have looked like, because this, of course, was not their subject.[23] The aim of this book, therefore, is to extend this somewhat limited view-point and to build a picture of the more modest gardens of the late sixteenth and early seventeenth century, looking at the 'ordinary' gardens of the county gentry as opposed to the 'extraordinary' gardens of the aristocracy and the courtly elite.

In addition, the appearance in the mid-sixteenth century of the first horticultural manuals to be written in English and dedicated solely to the 'arte' of gardening provides a useful starting point for the current investigation. Not only does the fact of this newly available material indicate that gardening had come to be perceived by contemporaries as a subject worthy of consideration in its own right, it also provides a body of accessible material which offers a particular insight into the world of the early modern gardener. The changes and developments in gardens and gardening over the following hundred years can then be traced to their establishment as legitimate areas of scientific and intellectual debate by the gentlemen of the Royal Society in 1660. Although this provides as useful a point in time as any other at which to end this book, the restoration of Charles II in the same year also appears to represent a turning point in garden history that is recognised by contemporaries and historians alike. John Aubrey noted in his *Natural History of Wiltshire* (written between 1656 and 1691) that 'in the time of King Charles the Second gardening was much improved and became common'. He also observed that the pleasure of gardens was 'unknown to our great-grandfathers'.[24] A little later, in the early 1700s, Daniel Defoe comments on 'the strange passion, for fine gardens, which has so commendably possessed the English gentlemen of late years'.[25] Obviously, these are subjective judgements, but nevertheless a shared impression of noticeable changes within the living memory of these writers can be detected. With the benefit of hindsight, modern historians have frequently cited the Restoration as a significant juncture in garden history, as it self-evidently provided, as in many other areas of life, a fresh starting point. And a recent overview of gardens in London in 1660 concludes that before this time, England 'had no great pride in gardens, and no identifiable national style'.[26] While these may be arguable points, they nonetheless add weight to the idea that there is a general perception of a sea-change around this time. So if this is the case, it begs the question of what was happening in gardens before 1660. This book sets out to answer that question.

In contrast to the traditional paradigm routinely employed in garden history, which attempts to categorise gardens into a progression of chronological garden styles according to a set of common features appertaining to a particular period, this book acknowledges that it is, in fact, extremely difficult to make distinct divisions between one period and the next: such an approach inevitably results in an over-simplification that can hide the complexities of what was actually happening on the ground. It has been observed that this traditional methodology has much in common with the history of art and indeed, much of the defining terminology used in garden history is borrowed from art history: renaissance, mannerist, baroque, picturesque, landscape and so on.[27] However, while it is undeniable that aesthetics have a place in gardens and gardening, there are a host of other factors which have to be taken into account when trying to determine a gardening 'style'. Many are mundane and practical: topography, climate, available land, pre-existing gardens, cost, the balance between the utilitarian uses of the gardens and the ornamental aspects all have to be considered, as well as the less tangible factors such as the purpose of the garden, how it reflected the owner's social standing and how it was intended to be viewed by others. In other words, it is essential to consider the context within which a garden was made and the outside influences that had to be taken into account.

For most people, the idea of building a new garden from scratch was out of the question: even Sir Richard Leveson, who spent a considerable amount of time and money on the rebuilding of his house and gardens at Trentham Hall in Staffordshire in the 1630s, was basically remodelling what was already there, reusing materials and existing layouts, but introducing some new elements into the garden such as fashionable steps, terraces and a fountain.[28] This example well illustrates that whatever the owner's aspirations, at any one time their garden would inevitably have contained a mixture of both old and new elements, traditional and more fashionable features. Given that this piecemeal approach was likely to have been employed in many gardens, the difficulties of trying to correlate a particular style with a particular period become obvious.

Rather than trying to shoehorn gardens into a series of neat but misleading progressional styles then, this book will start, as it were, at the other end: looking at actual gardens and the contexts within which they were created to try to understand the reasons why they were fashioned as they were. In order to do this, a wide range of primary sources will be examined including contemporary gardening literature, diaries, correspondence, household accounts and other scraps of information from gentry manuscript collections, together with contemporary paintings, drawings, maps and plans. It will attempt to view gardens and gardening as contemporaries did by examining the records they left behind them, rather than relying on subsequent interpretations which often simply perpetuate errors, myths

6 The garden at Shakespeare's New Place, Stratford-upon-Avon, where the pitfalls of historical reconstruction have been avoided by laying out instead a modern re-imagining of Shakespearean themes

and traditions in such a way that they eventually become transmuted into fact. The scarcity of evidence regarding gardens of this period has already been noted, but it appears that, despite lack of concrete data in this area, a picture of Elizabethan and early Stuart gardens nevertheless seems firmly fixed in the modern mind, being perpetuated through historical garden re-creations and reconstructions which, regrettably, do not always stand up to close scrutiny. Garden re-imaginings and restorations are of course an excellent way of bringing the past back to life, but we must approach them with caution. Not only is there often little actual evidence on which to base the re-creation, but we must also be wary of the way in which evidence has been interpreted and re-interpreted over the years. It has been noted that as 'each generation tries its hand at restoring the past, in due course, the result looks more characteristic of the generation of restorers than it does of the period aimed at'.[29] Returning to contemporary sources, as this book aims to do, is one way in which traditional and occasionally fanciful notions can be challenged and reappraised.

A major primary source for this study has been the range of contemporary practical gardening manuals which began to appear during the middle of the sixteenth century, the first gardening book to be written in English, Thomas Hyll's *A most briefe and pleasaunte treatise, teachyng how to dresse, sowe, and set a garden*, being published c.1558. Previous to this, the body of what we would now call horticultural literature was generally limited to herbals and books on husbandry, mostly published in Latin. At the beginning of the century, copies of classical Roman texts on agriculture, first printed on the Continent, began to appear in England.[30] Although works in the English language did not appear until later in the century, these Latin texts were nevertheless accessible to educated Englishmen and as such formed the basis of a number of books to be written and published in the vernacular, including John Fitzherbert's *Boke of Husbandry* (1534), Thomas Tusser's *A hundreth good pointes of husbandrie* (1557) and Barnabe Googe's translation of Conrad Heresbach's *Foure Bookes of Husbandry* (1577). However, as their titles suggest, these early books were concerned essentially with farming and agriculture rather than gardening, and were aimed at the husbandman rather than the gardener.

At the same time, herbals – specifically concerned with the naming of plants and their 'uses' and 'vertues' – which had been composed in manuscript form by scholars and monks for centuries, were now being printed and distributed in England. Again, the first examples were in Latin, with William Turner's *New Herbal* (1551) the first to be published in English. The end of the century saw the publication of Gerard's immensely popular *The Herball, or Generall Historie of Plantes* (1597), which was reprinted, substantially updated and improved by Thomas Johnson in 1633, again proving so popular that it was reprinted as soon as 1636. This was surpassed only by Parkinson's *Theatrum Botanicum* of 1640, probably the most detailed and accurate herbal ever printed in the English language, which was to hold its place as a textbook for doctors and apothecaries for more than a hundred years.[31] However, as this indicates, herbals, concerned as they were with the uses of plants, were far more likely to have been read by medical practitioners – either professionally or by housewives in the home – than by gardeners, as they offered little in the way of practical instruction on how actually to grow them. So, although some of these texts will occasionally be referred to in this book, it is on the new genre of gardening manuals that attention will be specifically focussed.

Following the publication of Thomas Hyll's book in about 1558, the subsequent hundred years saw the publication of approximately twenty new gardening books, many of which appeared in numerous editions and reprints. They essentially took the form of practical manuals, and as such offer a valuable insight into the activity of gardening in early modern England, reflecting continuities and changes in both practice and attitudes to gardening throughout the period.

Further to this, they also reveal, either implicitly or explicitly, much about the concerns of the society within which they were written. From the outset, a link between the language of the books and the cultural ideals and discourses of the time is established. For instance, the ubiquitous rhetoric of an ordered and hierarchical society which pervaded every aspect of the Tudor world was demonstrated, as well as anywhere else, in gardens and writing about gardens. Hyll 'teacheth the skilful ordering of the garden', Reynolde Scot describes 'The Reformation of a Disordered Garden' and Gervase Markham urges the necessity for keeping the earth in good order, so as to avoid a 'Chaos of confusednesse'.[32] And the gardens themselves reveal that order in their enclosed symmetry of straight lines and geometric shapes, clearly indicated in the simple woodcut drawings which illustrated the garden manuals (fig. 7).

At the same time, as has already been noted, this was a period of change, and the traditional notion of a static social hierarchy – in which everyone knew their place and was content with their lot – was in fact being constantly challenged as people at all levels of society seized opportunities to increase their wealth and improve their status. As will be explored extensively through the chapters that follow, the cultivation of an ornamental pleasure garden, the traditional preserve of the elite, was by the early seventeenth century becoming an acceptable cultural activity right across the social strata, particularly, as Parkinson observes, for 'Gentlemen [and gentlewomen] of the better sort and quality'.[33] His language here is an acknowledgement of one of the pre-eminent concerns of society at the time, the necessity to assert and display status and particularly, perhaps, to assert new-found status.

However, while this literature provides an invaluable starting point for examining the practices and aspirations of the early modern gardener, it has its limitations. A number of historians have used contemporary gardening manuals as a basis for their analysis of early modern gardens and garden practices, but this can result in a somewhat one-sided view.[34] Given that the advice and information contained within these manuals will always be prescriptive rather than descriptive, thus reflecting ambition rather than actuality, it is not always easy for the historian to judge the distance between the ideal and actual practice.[35] Just as today's lavishly illustrated 'coffee-table' books offer a glorious picture of how the perfect garden should look but in fact bear little resemblance to the plot that all but the most avid of gardeners attempt to cultivate, we must be aware of the possibility that early modern texts similarly represented aspirations rather than reality. However, by supplementing the evidence from these texts with a range of other documentary sources, including evidence of actual gardening practice, this book aims to discover what 'real' gardeners were doing in 'real' gardens at this time.

Another area of difficulty that can arise in attempting to read early modern texts through the eyes of contemporary readers lies in the use of technical language that is associated specifically with gardening. Some terms – such as grafting, sowing, planting – are still used today and thus present no problem. Other words, such as 'table' or 'proportion' which are used in several contemporary texts to describe various parts of the garden, are now rarely used, so we have to make our best guess at their meanings from the context in which they appear. Other terms have changed their meaning, and we must be wary of attributing modern meanings to seemingly unproblematic words such as 'fence' (in fact, meaning any method of enclosing a garden), or 'herb' (meaning any flowering plant). Yet other words can prove extremely problematic, the word 'knot' being a pertinent example. Although the term is used constantly throughout the period and in various contexts, it is nevertheless difficult to know what contemporaries actually understood by it, and the design for early garden knots, therefore, continues to be a matter of conjecture among garden historians. This particular example is taken up for fuller discussion in Chapter 7.

Finally, perhaps the greatest potential confusion arises over plant names. Before the current system of binomial plant classification was introduced by Carl Linnaeus in 1753, there was no standard naming of plants, so one cannot always identify exactly what plants are being referred to by early modern writers and gardeners. Again, where possible, an attempt is always made here to identify plants and flowers from contemporary sources – Parkinson's book, with its many helpful illustrations, has proved an invaluable guide. For instance, a woodcut illustration (fig. 8) confirms that gilliflowers, a ubiquitous summer flowering plant of the period, were what we would now call carnations or pinks.[36]

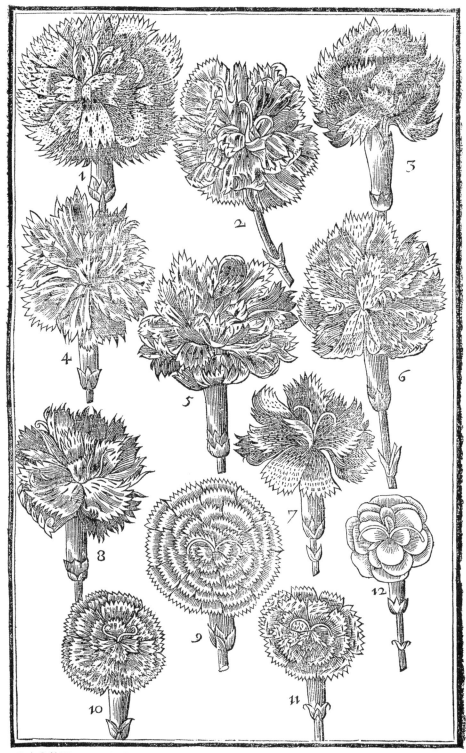

1 Heroina Radolphi florum Imperatoris Principssa dictus. Master Tuggie his Princesse. 2 Caryophyllus Oxoniensis. The French or Oxford Carnation. 3 Caryophyllus Westmonasteriensis. The Gallant or Westminster Gilloflower. 4 Caryophyllus Bristoliensis. The Bristow. 5 Caryophyllus Chrystallinus. The Chrystall or Chrystalline. 6 Caryophyllus Sabaudicus striatus. The stript Sauadge. 7 Caryophyllus Granatensis maximus. The Granpere or greatest Granado. 8 Caryophyllus peramœnus. The Dainty. 9 Caryophyllus Silesiacus maximus lagenti Ioanni Iohn Witty his great tawny Gilloflower. 10 Caryophyllus Silesiacus striatus. The stript Tawny. 11 Caryophyllus marmor amœlus. The marbled Tawny. 12 Caryophyllus roseus rotundus magistri Tuggie. Master Tuggie his Rose Gilloflower.

D d

Parkinson uses these terms as well, but *Dianthus*, the Latin name which now identifies them, does not appear in his book at all. Similarly, the names 'saffron' and 'crocus' were both used to identify the many varieties of this flowering bulb, but we now tend to use the term 'crocus' for the plant and reserve the term 'saffron' for the expensive spice obtained exclusively from the autumn-flowering variety *Crocus sativa*. 'Pompions', 'melons' and 'cucumbers' are also names that seem to be used interchangeably, posing yet another source of possible confusion.[37] And so on. We must constantly be wary of assuming that words with which we may be familiar mean what we think they do.

Early modern printed sources underpin much of this book, but they also form the main focus of Chapter 1, which provides an introduction to the gardening literature of the period. It examines these books within the wider culture of the printed works that were coming thick and fast since the first volumes had left Gutenberg's printing presses in Germany more than a century before, looking at both the physical make-up of the books and the role of the reader in the use of these texts. Chapter 1 explores how the nature of the literature itself evolved, reflecting both changes in gardening and changes in wider society, covering a range of works, from the publication of Hyll's *Briefe and pleasaunte treatise* in about 1558 to John Evelyn's first penning of his magnum opus on gardening, the manuscript for *Elysium Britannicum*, initially compiled in the 1650s. Chapter 2 sets the social and intellectual background to the story that follows. The subsequent chapters then concentrate on the gardens and gardeners that form the backbone of this book and which now require some introduction.

Having resolved to leave aside the well-documented gardens of the aristocracy, the gardens that will be examined are, in the main, those that were owned by the rural county gentry, the 'gentlemen' to whom John Parkinson frequently refers. The gentry are a notoriously difficult group to define and, according to contemporaries, could include anyone from the titular nobility to those 'that are simply called gentlemen'.[38] While bearing in mind the pragmatic conclusion that 'flexible definitions of gentility were a necessary feature of ... early modern England', the gentlemen encountered in this book comprise not members of the aristocracy, but those from the broader ranks of the gentry, from knights and esquires, such as Sir Thomas Temple and John Evelyn, to the lesser parish gentry, such as the clergyman William Lawson.[39] These gentlemen owned substantial houses and gardens and attended to their own estates. They are clearly still a select group, their status generally articulated by their land-ownership, their holding of unpaid public office such as Justice of the Peace, county sheriff or Member of Parliament, as well as by their income and, more importantly, their expenditure – a vital demonstration of their wealth and social standing. Although there will be occasional forays into more modest plots, it is on the gardens of this social group that this book will focus.

Much of the evidence to be presented here is based on a range of seventeenth-century gentry manuscript collections, shedding light on the gardens and gardening activity of that period. However, in order to set the scene, Chapter 3 focuses on sixteenth-century gardens, using a range of more disparate sources to piece together a picture of what an Elizabethan gentleman's garden may have looked like. At the same time, the chapter establishes that this period was beginning to see signs of change.

The next five chapters continue to explore continuities, changes and developments into the seventeenth century, a task greatly aided by the availability of significantly more extant primary material. Gardening literature continued to be produced, including the landmark publication of Parkinson's *Paradisi in Sole* in 1629, more family portraits with glimpses of gardens in the background began to appear and garden plans such as that of Evelyn's Sayes Court all contribute to the picture. But it is the household accounts, memoranda and correspondence mentioned earlier which, although often fragmentary, offer the most useful insight into what was actually going on in gardens across the land. These documentary sources have proved particularly valuable as, unlike much of the evidence previously utilised by garden historians of this period, they do not represent aristocratic households or the gardens of elite courtiers, but instead offer contemporary and complementary evidence of gardens and gardening in more modest households.

Although examples of this kind of evidence have been used in several recent case studies, these have tended to focus on specific gardens in isolation, without necessarily placing them in any wider context.[40] This book aims to broaden that view, by looking at a range of gardens across the country, comparing and contrasting evidence from a variety of sources, in order to build a picture of – if such a thing ever existed – the generality of gardens. The manuscript collections examined cover a wide geographical area, from Devon to Yorkshire, from Wales to Hertfordshire, and documents include detailed and not so detailed household accounts as well as more personal memorandum books and correspondence.

While there may be only an occasional glimpse of some of the gardens mentioned here, others will feature frequently, as will their owners. Two gentlemen in particular we shall often meet are Sir John Oglander, who inherited his father's estate at Nunwell on the Isle of Wight in 1609, and Sir Thomas Temple, who, after his retirement from public life in 1624, became increasingly engaged with creating a new garden at his childhood home at Burton Dassett in Warwickshire.[41] Both these men demonstrate an active interest in gardens and gardening and in the plants and flowers within them. Through Oglander's six commonplace books and Temple's copious correspondence with his estate manager, we gain a particular insight that allows us to move significantly beyond simply how their gardens may have looked, important as that is, to gain some understanding of the attitudes, priorities and preferences that influenced the shaping of their gardens.

Other gentry gardens for which there is more limited but still useful evidence in the form of account book entries, include those of Sir Thomas Pelham of Halland House in Sussex, Sir Richard Leveson of Trentham Hall in Staffordshire, Sir Thomas Puckering of Warwick Priory and Sir Thomas Aubrey of Llantrithyd in south Wales, to introduce just a few.[42] In contrast to Oglander and Temple, evidence relating to these gardens concentrates more on the ornamental features of the gardens, the accounts from Trentham Hall in particular offering a comprehensive account of the laying out of a new fashionable gentry garden. It appears, from this evidence at least, that these gentlemen were perhaps more interested in creating gardens for show than they were in the cultivation of plants. Examined alongside relevant contemporary literature, material relating to all these gardens will form the basis of the middle chapters of this book, which will consider in turn various aspects of gardening during this period including the practicalities of gardening, the place of the ornamental flower garden and in particular the knot garden, other ornamentation in the garden and a chapter on the vital role of the gardeners who actually did the work.

Chapter 9 represents the final two decades of the period, looking back over the preceding century and forward to the post-Restoration era. The story of this period is told through the eyes of men who lived through the tumultuous years of the Civil War and the uneasy peace that followed it. Many were gentlemen who found themselves either voluntarily or compulsorily exiled to the Continent but who on their return, with no role to play in public life, turned to cultivating their gardens. The two most significant figures here are the diarist and gardener John Evelyn and his friend and correspondent Sir Thomas Hanmer, who gardened at Bettisfield in north Wales. During his long life, Evelyn produced a voluminous body of work that has assured his place as a ubiquitous figure in garden history – any book on the subject is bound to mention him somewhere within its pages. However, given that the majority of his life and work fall outside the period covered by this book, discussion here will be confined to his contribution to garden writing and his gardening activities during the early years of his life, concentrating in particular on the maps, plans and correspondence surrounding the creation of gardens at the family home in Wotton belonging to his elder brother George in the 1640s and at his own home at Sayes Court in Deptford in 1653.[43] Sir Thomas Hanmer is perhaps less familiar. As well as the garden at Bettisfield, he also created and maintained at least two other gardens in the 1650s, one at his mother's home in nearby Haulton and the other at his London home in Lewisham. He is best known for producing the manuscript of *The Garden Book*, only published after a chance discovery in 1933, but which now takes its rightful place in the canon of seventeenth-century gardening literature. In addition to this, Hanmer left behind him a wealth of other material, including notebooks, correspondence and memoranda which also repay close attention.[44] The contribution made by these two men to this consideration of seventeenth-century gardening is particularly valuable because, as well as being well-known writers, they were both, like Parkinson and Lawson, active gardeners themselves.

Chapter 10 turns its attention to one of the central, but ephemeral and therefore somewhat elusive, elements of the garden: the plants themselves. It explores how new plants were actually obtained by gardeners for their gardens. Where were they being bought? How were they being exchanged and transported? How much did they cost? It examines the development of the nursery trade in England, as interest in and demand for rare and exotic plants from the New World and the Continent increased. As the development of a fully fledged commercial nursery trade began to take hold only in the middle of the seventeenth century, much of the focus of this chapter will be on the nascence of this trade as seen through the practices of gardeners of the late sixteenth and early seventeenth century. At the same time, another less well-documented aspect of these exchanges is revealed, namely, the inevitable dissemination of information and ideas that must have accompanied it. We are reminded that it was not just plants but also horticultural knowledge and experience, gathered at home and abroad, that were being exchanged in networks of fellow garden-enthusiasts, whether friends, acquaintances, correspondents or nurserymen.

The final chapter draws on the themes explored in this book in an attempt to establish what these gardens, however they may have looked, actually meant to the gardeners and garden-owners who created them. Beyond their undoubted utilitarian functions, how else were these gardens being used by those that enjoyed them? How were they utilised as a backdrop for hospitality and display and how were they viewed by visitors? Which parts of the garden were kept private and why? Consideration will be given to how, in tune with the changing times, gardens became fitting symbols of wealth and status among the gentry.

Before moving on, however, there is one final salutary note to sound: in an area as subjective as gardening and one in which, at a practical level, most elements can be changed relatively easily on a whim, the place of individual taste must never be forgotten. A garden is not like a house, which may stand testament to its builders and owners for centuries. Gardens can be – and often are – different from year to year, reflecting much more short-term changes both in planting and structure. So, while the arrival of a new 'must-have' tulip may for some have meant the digging of a new bed or the rearranging of an old one to accommodate it, others may have preferred old-fashioned roses and gilliflowers to ornament their beds; while the writer and garden connoisseur Francis Bacon advocated leaving plants growing into the paths so that they would be crushed underfoot and release their scents, Parkinson advised wide paths to be kept clean by weeders; some saw no place for statues in the garden while others made them a central feature; Evelyn's garden at Sayes Court was an eclectic mix of many influences and styles reflecting his travels around Europe, not necessarily designed into a coherent whole but included because he liked them. Unless a garden is designed by an 'outside' designer, this element of personal taste will always be an important factor. Across a void of four hundred years, Sir Robert Sidney sounds this warning to the garden historian: in April 1605, he wrote to his estate steward, Thomas Golding: 'The little garden, since it is so forewards, may goe on for this yeare: if I doe not like it, I can alter it the next.'[45]

1

THE 'ARTE OF GARDENING'

The Books

Thomas Hyll's *A most briefe and pleasaunte treatise, teachyng how to dresse, sowe, and set a garden* published c.1558 was the first book written in English exclusively dedicated to the subject of gardening (fig. 9). 'The lyke hitherto hath not bin published in the English tongue', Hyll declared, but it is 'nowe Englished by me, for the commoditie of many'.[1]

Reynolde Scot, who published a book on the subject of hop gardening in 1574, claimed that 'I rather chuse to incurre the daunger of derision in speaking homelye, than the fault of ingratitude in saying nothing' and he would therefore 'write plainly to playne men of the country'.[2] Hyll and his contemporaries, many of whom published books on a wide range of subjects, of which gardening was just one, clearly viewed the emerging print culture in England as an opportunity to pass on information to a new and growing audience for small and relatively inexpensive books, written in the vernacular. It also seems that by the time Hyll's book was published, the subject was acquiring a status of its own: 'Bycause thys Arte of Gardening is of it selfe very profitable, and bringeth most necessarie commodities…it deserveth no small commendation'.[3] Gardening, Hyll was saying, is now a subject worthy of a book in its own right.

Following the publication of Hyll's initial treatise, six more gardening manuals were written and published in the remainder of the sixteenth century and about twice that number by 1660. As can be seen from the bibliographical details provided in Appendix 1, many were issued and reissued as new editions numerous times after their initial publication. Hyll's *The Gardeners Labyrinth*, for instance, was reprinted no less than eight times between its first publication in 1577 and 1660 and by that same year, William Lawson's highly popular *A New Orchard and Garden* (1618) had not only been reprinted nine times but had also been incorporated in full into sixteen editions of another contemporary work written by Gervase Markham, *A Way to Get Wealth*. The constant reissuing of these works, often heralded by the printers as newly revised or augmented, when in fact they may simply have been given a new title page or frontispiece, clearly points to their widespread popularity and perceived marketing potential.

While it is undeniable that the advent of printing dramatically accelerated the distribution of information written in the vernacular, England, geographically cut off from the mainstream Continental book trade, was somewhat on the fringes of the European print revolution and in fact the number of works printed in English during the sixteenth century was limited.[4] Nevertheless, among those that were published, one popular genre was that of what might today be called 'how-to manuals', that is, texts specifically written to instruct the

A MOST BRIEFE

and pleasaunte treatise, teaching how to dresse, sowe, and set a garden: and what remedies also may be had and vsed agaynst suche beastes, wormes, flies, and suche like, that noye Gardens, gathered oute of the principallest Auethors which haue writté of gardening, as Palladius, Columella, Varro, Ruellius, Dyophanes, learned Cato, and others manye moe. And nowe englished by Thomas Hyll Londiner.

9   Title page from Thomas Hyll's *A most briefe and pleasaunte treatise*, c.1558
10   'The booke unto the Reader' from Leonard Mascall's *The Arte and maner,*
howe to plant and graffe, 1572

reader on a wide variety of subjects – household matters such as cookery, family medicine, preserving, brewing and distilling or dying cloth, as well as outdoor activities such as beekeeping, animal husbandry, horse-training and, of course, gardening. All these didactic texts provided an accessible link between theoretical and practical knowledge and formed a substantial proportion of the printed material produced during this period. A 'new body of readers' had been identified by printers as requiring such practical instruction – but who these readers were has proved more difficult to establish.[5] The kind of subjects covered in many of these publications can be compared to those found in popular magazines today and, in the same way that magazines offer a window into 'how the other half lives', these publications were appealing to those who aspired to raise their status. Not only did they offer insight into a way of living that was desirable because people of status already lived that way, they also offered practical advice on how that status could be achieved and appropriately displayed.[6] William Lawson's *New Orchard and Garden* provides an excellent example of this. Lawson devotes the first chapter of his practical book to advice on how to employ the right gardener but concludes: 'If you be not able, nor willing to hire a gardener, keep your profits to yourself, but then you must take all the pains: and for that purpose…to instruct you, have I undertaken these labours, and gathered these rules'.[7] His book is apparently addressed to the householder who would garden, rather than the gardener by trade, indicating that gardening, as well as reading about gardening, was becoming established as an acceptable activity for a new 'middling' group who were turning to these books for just such instruction.[8]

That all the titles in this new genre were in English implies a wider readership of such material than the educated gentleman who may have read the earlier classical works on which they were based, which brings us back to the question of for whom these 'how-to-do gardening' books were being written. Who was buying them, who was reading them and how were they being used by their owners? The authors themselves offer some clues: Leonard Mascall, for instance, addresses the 'poore man', the 'riche man' and 'the noble man' in his opening 'booke unto the Reader' (fig. 10); Reynolde Scot similarly addresses both the poor and the rich, but also includes 'the learned' and 'the unlearned', helpfully providing illustrations to assist the understanding of 'him who cannot read at all'.[9] Hyll, as noted, published his book for 'the commoditie of many'.

The titles of the books, their prefaces and dedications can also give at least an indication as to whom the author perceived as his potential audience: *The English Husbandman*, 'The Country Housewife', 'all those that delight in gardening'.[10] Others were even more specific: Richard Gardner addressed his 1599 book on kitchen gardening 'to his loving neighbours and friends, within the towne of Shrewsbury'.[11] At first sight, it might appear that such books were aimed not just at readers across the social spectrum but at both men and women. However, although a few publications were apparently addressed to women, they tended to be short, simple and lacking in any detailed instruction. Advice on growing vegetables and herbs was generally offered as an adjunct to the woman's role as cook and physician within the household and the rare specific mention of women in these titles suggests that this was in fact unusual, implying that normally these books were aimed at male readers. For instance, Lawson's *Country Housewifes Garden* comprised a slim booklet which, when published, was appended to the much more lengthy and detailed *New Orchard and Garden*, which was clearly, although not explicitly, aimed at the gentleman gardener.

It also seems unlikely that these books would have been widely used by labourers, workmen or the 'poorer' sort. In the first instance, even these relatively cheap manuals were too expensive for most people. According to a study of contemporary book sales, an unbound copy of Hyll's *Gardeners Labyrinth* was sold in 1578 for 1s 8d, the average price for new books such as this being about ½d per sheet.[12] However, given that the average wage for a labourer varied between around 6d to 1s per day, this would still have been beyond the reach of many.[13] Secondly, there was also the question of literacy. Markham, for instance, explicitly differentiates between the husbandman, or 'Master of the Family', to whom his book is addressed and who he considers should be able to read and write, and 'the Servants in Husbandrie', such as the bailiff or the under-farmer, of whom he says it really does not matter whether they are acquainted with reading and writing or not, as other qualities are more important.[14] Obviously, if these people cannot read, they are unlikely to be using his book (although they may of course be benefitting from their master's reading of it), but the implication is that this manual is aimed at the literate husbandman.

In attempting to identify readers, literacy is of course a crucial factor, but it is one which is, unfortunately, extremely difficult to establish, as the situation was far more complex than might at first appear. Literacy in early modern England had a variety of meanings, none of which necessarily matches our modern understanding of the word, that is, being able to read and write. In the first instance, ability to read was much more prevalent than ability to write: children of labourers and people who worked on the land, for instance, may well have attended 'petty' school for a few years before being old enough to work. During this time, they would have been taught the basics of reading, but only those who remained at school for longer were eventually taught to write as well.[15]

It is also possible to draw distinctions between different types of reading skills which related directly to different types of written material: for instance, print was much easier to read than handwritten script. In fact, the likelihood is that only the privileged few who could themselves write would also have been able to read script. Even then, there were those who did not consider anyone literate unless they could read Latin, the language of scholarship – a skill necessarily limited to the educated social elite.[16] Given these variations, 'From the most able, to him that can but spell',[17] it is difficult to know how, and in what sense, many of the population were 'literate'. Also, actually measuring this proportion of the population is almost impossible, because the only evidence we have is of people who could write, clearly a much lower number than the 'invisible' readers who have left no mark of their abilities.[18]

Having said this and as evidenced by recent work on the history of the book, there is much more to the use of a book than simply being able to read it. In material terms, the item that the printer sold to his customer was in a number of senses incomplete: it is likely to have been sold as an unbound text (a premium was charged for binding) and may well have included errata sheets, encouraging the reader to find and correct any errors.[19] Also, in the particular case of didactic literature such as gardening manuals, it is clear from the texts themselves that 'they lacked utility until put into practice'.[20] In other words, until a reader interacts in some way with a book, uses the book, whether through reading it, correcting and amending it or acting on its advice, it cannot fulfil its potential or purpose.

Nevertheless, the most obvious use of a book is that it is to be read, whether in private for the benefit of the reader or out loud for others to listen and learn. As Scot writes in his preface, 'I desire of the learned, patience in reading, or the unlearned, diligence in hearing'. Similarly, Mascall hopes his reader will find 'something to help his need', to 'reape some fruit where earst he had but weede'.[21] What is clear is that these were not books which the authors intended to be left on the shelf. As noted earlier, the texts often included simple illustrations, usually added by the printer, to aid understanding: Lawson mentions in his preface that the Stationer has provided woodcuts of 'Knots and Models...to satisfie the curious desire of those that would make use of this book'.[22] In broader terms, too, it has been argued that these texts and images were open to interpretation by their readers, to be shaped according to their own needs.[23] To say that the same text may mean different things to different people is hardly a radical contention, but questions of how far the meaning is determined by the author and how far it is attributed to the reader, whether a text has any meaning at all without a reader or whether there is a 'correct' reading of a text are much more open ones and, although this is not the place to explore these issues, it reminds us again that there is more to a book than the words printed on the page.[24]

One recent and fruitful line of enquiry in trying to establish how people used books has been to study the annotations and marginalia left by readers of the time.[25] Unlike today, when great value is placed on a pristine, clean copy of a text and any kind of marking or annotation in the margin is frowned on, in the early modern world – in the early days of the printed text – readers were positively encouraged to read with a pen in hand to make notes, add aide-mémoires and generally use – as opposed to just read – the book. The contemporary writer Henry Peacham advises that while care should be taken to keep books handsome and well-bound, 'Yet for your owne use spare them not for noting or interlining'.[26] Schoolboys were taught to make notes on and in their books, to mark 'difficult words, or matters of special observation'.[27] In an age when paper was an expensive commodity, this was a judicious use of resources and one which greatly aided the acquisition and retention of knowledge – actually reading the book was just one part of this process. Bearing in mind that handwritten marginalia were necessarily limited to the few readers who not only could write but also possessed the means to buy substantial books in which to do so, examination of such annotations gives some clues as to the uses and ownership of such volumes. They link the reader directly to the book.

An example of such a book is John Parkinson's major contribution to gardening literature of the time, his sumptuous folio volume *Paradisi in Sole, Paradisus Terrestris* published in 1629. This book runs to a total of 628 folio pages of plant descriptions and gardening instruction and includes three indexes – one of Latin plant names, one of their English equivalents and one categorising the plants by their uses. It is illustrated throughout with many full-page woodcuts. It has not been possible to ascertain an exact price for Parkinson's *Paradisi*, but it is known that a copy of his herbal, *Theatrum Botanicum*, was purchased by John Goodyear for 36s plus 3s for binding, that an unbound copy of the 1633 revised edition of Gerard's *Herball* was purchased for 42s 6d, while a bound copy sold for 48s.[28] As already noted, the average price for a new book at this time was about a halfpenny a sheet, so these illustrated volumes, at well over a penny a sheet and with many more pages, were clearly expensive. Although these two herbals ran to twice as many pages as *Paradisi in Sole*, this still gives a good indication of the high prices commanded for these lavish volumes, as well as suggesting some clues as to their presumed readership.

In the particular case of *Paradisi in Sole*, the annotations, inscriptions and marginalia found in surviving copies of this substantial volume are highly revealing. It is known, for example, that John Tradescant, the renowned plant-hunter and gardener of his age, owned a copy of Parkinson's book (now housed in the Bodleian Library, Oxford): in the blank pages at the back, Tradescant kept his own extensive plant list, including all those 'Reseved [received] from forrin parts…since the impression of this Book'. As well as the names of the plants he acquired, he also noted his suppliers, including renowned nurserymen such as the French king's gardeners Jean and Vespasien Robin and the Parisian brothers René and Pierre Morin. Sir John Reresby, who gardened at his home at Thrybergh in Yorkshire, also kept an extensive record of the 402 plants in his garden, frequently cross-referenced to pages in Parkinson's book, presumably so that he could look them up to obtain more information on their cultivation. In his *Garden Book*, Sir Thomas Hanmer describes a plant as being 'the same with the Figure in Parkinson', suggesting the possibility at least that he was writing his own manuscript with a copy of *Paradisi in Sole* alongside to guide him.[29] John Evelyn also owned this book – there is a copy in the British Library inscribed in 1650 with a Latinised version of his name and the words 'Meliora Retinete', part of Evelyn's motto 'Explore everything: keep the best'. In 1643, another copy was given as a gift to her 'dear sister, Anne Purefoy' by Lady Franklin, the wife of Sir John Franklin, a member of the Long Parliament. Whether or not Anne read it is unrecorded, but that copy, now in the Folger Shakespeare Library, Washington, DC, reveals that she coloured in some of the illustrations. And as well as gardeners and garden-writers, it is also clear from the footnotes that accompany Abraham Cowley's *Plantarum Libri Sex* of 1662 that, as the poet sat writing his extensive lines of Latin verse about herbs and flowers, he too had a copy of Parkinson's *Paradisi in Sole* at his side as a guide to plant names and their qualities.[30]

Even from this small sample, then, there is evidence of its readers using this particular book in a variety of ways. Hanmer, Reresby and Cowley left annotations and marks which indicate their active reading, Purefoy received it as a gift, Tradescant and Evelyn noted their ownership and Tradescant also used the empty leaves in the volume as available paper on which to record his plant acquisitions. The back of a well-used gardening book seems a sensible place to keep such a list: it is unlikely to get lost. Evidence such as this, rare as it is, gives some concrete answers to the question of who was reading and using this book and it is clear that, compared to the didactic manuals already discussed, Parkinson clearly had a different reader, and gardener, in mind.

As well as being considerably more expensive, *Paradisi in Sole* stands out from its predecessors as a new kind of gardening book because it describes for the first time the creation of a garden in which flowers and plants take centre stage, recommending many 'beautifull flower plants, fit to store a garden of delight and pleasure'.[31] At the same time, it was a practical book, containing much advice for gardeners on how to lay out their gardens and cultivate the plants within them, and the specific information we have about particular owners gives substance to the kind of reader at whom this book was aimed: someone who could afford to buy such an expensive volume, who was educated enough to be able to read and write in it, who had the leisure and resources to read such a book sitting at his or her desk, as it was clearly far too heavy to be carried about as a reference manual – in short, the 'gentleman [and gentlewoman] of better sort and quality' to whom Parkinson addresses his book. While Hyll's *Briefe and pleasaunte treatise* can rightly take its place as the first gardening book to be written in English, Parkinson's *Paradisi in Sole* represents the first gardening book aimed specifically, despite his occasional nod in the direction of 'most men', at the wealthy gentleman and gentlewoman.

Given this illuminating evidence regarding the owners and readers of Parkinson's book, it is regrettable that among the surviving copies of the smaller, cheaper, practical gardening manuals mentioned so far, there is, by contrast, little or no evidence of annotations or other marks. There is an irony in the fact that the more these books were used for their intended purpose – as instruction books – the less likely they are to have survived for us to examine today. Gardening manuals in particular will have been pocketed, taken out and consulted in the field, subjected to the vagaries of the prevailing weather conditions, handled with muddy fingers, dropped in puddles and so on, and in fact are far less likely to have survived than many other types of practical books. Those that have remained intact were probably not used as intended but left on the shelf, to be perused by the early modern equivalent of 'armchair' gardeners. Even so, just looking at the format of these books can give us some idea as to ownership. Typically, they were small, plain, octavo volumes, about the size of a modern-day paperback, that could be cheaply reproduced.[32] They ran to a hundred or so pages and as such they would have been accessible both to the practical gardener, in that they could be easily carried around, and to the less wealthy, as the price may well have been within their reach. Given, as already mentioned, the lack of material evidence of 'invisible' readers, we can only speculate as to the users of these cheaper, practical manuals and perhaps the best we can do is to suggest, from the evidence presented so far, that the readers of these books were the literate 'middling' sort, the professional estate gardener or, as Lawson suggests, the householder who could not afford to pay a gardener and must therefore do the work themselves. They appear to be aimed at practitioners, albeit practitioners who could read. The intended readers, then, were those who were going to be engaged in these activities, and the range of gardening literature available by this time reveals the subject as worthy of the attention of gardeners across the social strata.

As discussed in the Introduction, the use of this kind of literature as a guide to actual practice has its limitations: that it is prescriptive rather than descriptive, that it represents aspirations rather than reality, are two significant factors which must constantly be borne in mind. One further limitation, however, which represents a particular problem when it comes to gardening literature, arises from the fact that much of the material in print was, in one way or another, derivative. The classical texts of the Greeks and Romans, which included many agricultural and horticultural works, formed the basis of the intellectual legacy of the period and to compile new works from known sources was perfectly acceptable. It is therefore not surprising to find that the first English gardening books published in the sixteenth century relied heavily on both the received wisdom of the ancients as well as contemporary Dutch and French Renaissance writers. In 1572, Mascall declared: 'I have taken out of diverse authors this simple work into our Englishe tongue', although in fact the greater part of the book is simply a translation of a popular French publication, Davy Brossard's *L'Art & maniere de semer, faire pepiniers des sauvageaux* (?1551).[33] In 1594, the anonymous author of *The Orchard, and the Garden* 'gathered' his information from the Dutch and French and Hyll in 1579 stated with no apology that 'I have not given thee any labour of mine owne, but rather have collected the sayinges and writings of many auncient authours'.[34] Little is known about Hyll but it is apparent that he earned his living as a compiler and translator of books and pamphlets on a wide range of subjects including astronomy, surgery, medicine, arithmetic, physiognomy and philosophy as well as gardening, so the likelihood is that he was no gardener himself, and indeed he never claims to be.[35] The point here is that he based his authority for what he wrote in the classics and that, in line with prevailing intellectual thinking, was authority enough. At the same time, it is interesting that gardening is included among the subjects that Hyll and his printers clearly viewed as popular for a growing readership.

Other books were simply direct translations. Richard Surflet's *Countrie Farme* (1600) had originally been published in French in 1564 by Charles Estienne as *L'agriculture et Maison Rustique*, a popular work reprinted numerous times between 1564 and 1598: Surflet's was a direct translation into English of the 1598 edition. Even John Evelyn's first foray into horticultural publishing in 1658 was a translation of Nicolas Bonnefons's *The French Gardiner*. Many of these books were reprinted over the years, sometimes under the same author, albeit often after his death or sometimes with a changed name and title. On other occasions, texts were simply reprinted under a different author's name. Whatever the other implications, we must note again the obvious popularity of this genre of gardening literature.

This general practice of translating works from Italian and French sources was thus both acceptable and desirable, but it leaves us not knowing to what extent these earliest books reflected actual contemporary practice in England. In the particular case of gardening literature, the uncertainty is even more pronounced because advice and practices could not simply be transplanted from Mediterranean climates to England: the conditions were different and the directions did not necessarily apply. This is not to say that the advice in these books was never valid, but simply that it has not been 'Englished' – other than translated – in the light of experience.

During the seventeenth century, there came a marked change in the way gardening writers approached their work, reflecting a tendency to question the place of traditional philosophies and eternal truths in the early modern world, and instead to pursue knowledge through practical experiment. This view was first popularised in print by Francis Bacon (fig. 11) who disparagingly viewed the current perceptions of natural history – particularly within the court circles in which he moved – as entertaining but untrustworthy knowledge; he set out to prove that science was a subject that civil society should take seriously. His aim was to elevate the study of natural history, the utility of which was becoming more apparent as people travelled further and further away from familiar shores, to a publicly useful form of science. He challenged traditional views on a number of fronts. In his *Novum Organum* of 1620, he proposed a new framework for the study of natural history, 'the foundation of all', based on empirical knowledge, openly criticising the classical approach of writers such as Aristotle and Pliny. He wrote, for instance, of the latter's *Natural History* that there was 'Nothing duly investigated, nothing verified, nothing counted, weighed or measured...what in observation is loose and vague, is in information deceptive and treacherous.' The problem articulated here was that knowledge was gathered indiscriminately, without any verification on the part of the author, but it was presented – and accepted – as authoritative. In Bacon's view, however, knowledge was born of experience, not authority. Similarly, Bacon also rejected alchemy, magic and the occult, not because they did not offer any insight into nature – he conceded that they did – but because secrecy was an essential element of their art and this aspect was completely at odds with Bacon's aim to create and disseminate a public knowledge.[36] Such ideas were not entirely new but Francis Bacon was the first person to rationalise and systematise these notions in print, and posterity has duly credited him with laying the foundations of modern scientific method.

There is, however, plenty of evidence that such ideas were already in circulation and being practised by natural scientists, apothecaries, medical practitioners and gardeners throughout this period. It has been shown, for example, that a thriving community of natural scientists living and working in sixteenth-century London was already establishing a new empirical culture based on scientific experiment. Concerned with the study of the natural world in an active and practical way, these men were 'simply getting on with

MO TITI MELLO RA

MEDIO FIRMA CRIA

Honᵐᵒ Franciscᵒ Baconᵒ Baro de Veru:
lam Vice-Comes Sᶜᵗⁱ Albani mortuus 9 Aprilis,
Anno Dⁿⁱ 1626. Annoꝗ Aetat 66.

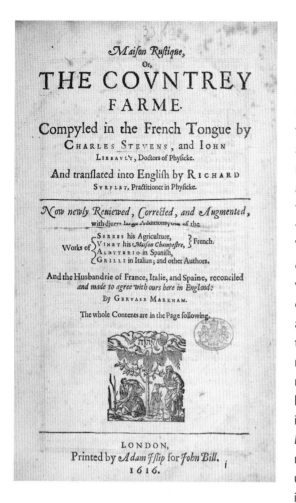

Maifon Ruftique,
Or,

THE COVNTREY
FARME.

Compyled in the French Tongue by
CHARLES STEVENS, and IOHN
LIEBAVLT, Doctors of Phyficke.

And tranflated into Englifh by RICHARD
SVRFLET, Practitioner in Phyficke.

Now newly Reviewed, Corrected, and Augmented,
with divers large Additions, out of the

Works of { SERRES his Agriculture,
VINET his Maifon Champeftre, } French.
ALBYTERIO in Spanifh,
GRILLI in Italian; and other Authors.

And the Husbandrie of France, Italie, and Spaine, reconciled
and made to agree with ours here in England:
By GERVASE MARKHAM.

The whole Contents are in the Page following.

LONDON,
Printed by Adam Iflip for John Bill.
1616.

it', their work contrasting sharply with that of court and university intellectuals such as Bacon, who were still fiercely debating the authority of ancient texts.[37] And as Bacon was theorising this new system of knowledge based on observation and experience, so too early seventeenth-century gardeners and garden writers were reflecting these ideas in their practice and in their books. While Hyll ensured that his readers were aware of his authoritative classical sources and that their work was not diminished by any advice of his own,[38] later authors such as Markham, Lawson and Parkinson were at pains to point out that they were writing from their own experience and not relying on ancient authorities for their information. Their advice was more practical and the knowledge they were imparting pertained specifically to the English climate and conditions. In *The English Husbandman*, Markham states: 'I saw one man translate and paraphrase most excellently upon Virgil's Georgickes, a worke only belonging to the Italian clime',[39] and he resolves rather to 'set downe the true manner and nature of our right English Husbandry', including a chapter on the 'Art of planting, Grafting and Gardening after our latest and rarest fashion. A worke never before written by any Author'.[40] This book was published in 1613, swiftly followed in 1616 by *The Countrey Farme*, an edited edition of Surflet's 1600 translation but which Markham, as the title page states, has 'Now newly Reviewed, Corrected and Augmented...the Husbandrie of France, Italie and Spain, reconciled and made to agree with ours here in England' (fig. 12).

This book also contains a chapter on gardens but, despite his claims, Markham did not actually change any of the original text: he simply added to it, with the result that the reader is often faced with confusing and contradictory information. For instance, he writes that, among other varieties, pepper trees, 'Apples of Paradise' (tomatoes) and olive trees should be included in a good hedge for the garden – advice perhaps appropriate for a Mediterranean garden. Yet, a few lines later, he suggests that brambles, whitethorn and blackthorn are suitable for a quickset hedge – advice which, as will be seen, is in line with other English contemporary writers and far more suited to prevailing English conditions.[41] It seems that despite his own practical knowledge and his respect for the experience and wisdom of his fellow husbandmen, first and foremost, Markham was still working under the 'powerful influence of the classical message', using conventional genres and traditional models on which to base his notions of advice and experience.[42] This may well be the case but, whether he was successful or not, Markham's stated aim was to give the reader new and relevant information and his desire to declare that this is what he was doing suggests that this was now a popular course of action. Markham, like Hyll, was a prolific author, successfully publishing books on an astonishing variety of subjects and, again, although it is unlikely that Markham was necessarily an expert in gardening, the fact that someone so sensitive to the market chose this subject for a practical manual based on English empirical experience suggests a new audience for such publications – one which could both afford and read books but which was also interested in actually engaging in practical gardening.

While it is possible to argue that Markham's books were the result of an amalgam of classical and contemporary influences, this was not the case for Lawson's *New Orchard and Garden*. This book, published in 1618, was devoted entirely to gardening, and was written 'by long experience...of...my Northerne Orchard and Country Garden'.[43] Lawson lived and worked in the parish of Ormsby in Yorkshire on the banks of the River Tees and his long experience is defined on the title page as 'forty eight years' (see fig. 78).[44] Although he admires the work of classical authors, Lawson will leave them to 'their times, manner and several countries', recognising that their advice does not appertain to the English garden. Instead, he has 'of my mere and sole Experience, without respect to any former written Treatise, gathered these Rules and set them down in writing'.[45] The truth of this is borne out in the text, where Lawson frequently refers to his own particular knowledge of gardening in the north of England. He gives advice, for instance, as to which fruit trees are 'most common, and meetest for our Northern countries', suggesting the planting of apples, pears, plums and damsons rather than the more tender fruits such as apricots and peaches which 'will not like in our cold parts'.[46] And he not only fails to refer to received wisdom but also knowingly contradicts it: 'And herein I am of a contrary opinion to all them which practise or teach the planting of trees, that ever yet I knew, read or heard of'. He confidently goes on to explain and justify his own thoughts on the correct spacing of trees in an orchard, based on his own observations over nearly fifty years.[47] In this respect, then, *A New Orchard and Garden* indeed lives up to its title, representing a new approach to gardening and to gardening advice.

John Parkinson bases his *Paradisi* equally firmly on his own experience of plants and gardening. He reiterates again and again in the opening pages that his authority is based purely on his own knowledge gained through experiment, observation and practice. Unlike Lawson, who simply leaves the work of classical authorities aside, Parkinson, in line with Bacon, positively rejects them. He is confident in the new scientific method as the key to knowledge: 'This I doe affirm upon good knowledge and certaine experience, and not as many others doe, tell of wonders of another world, which themselves never saw nor ever heard of, except some superficiall relation, which they themselves have augmented according to their owne fansie and conceit'.[48]

Here Parkinson's comments are directed both at earlier authors of herbals – who were writing about a different place and time when many of the plants known to him were unheard of, thereby making their information both out of date and irrelevant to English conditions – and at more recent writers for whom he reserves his more scathing criticism. According to Parkinson, these writers presumed a knowledge of the new plants that began flooding into the capital at the end of the previous century, often as little more than seeds, roots or dead twigs, without having seen for themselves or understood the nature of the plant. As he writes, 'some of these errours are ancient, and continued by long tradition, and others are of later invention'.[49] It is difficult not to see his specific target here as John Gerard, whose *Herball* of 1597 was widely condemned as being plagiarised and inaccurate for these very reasons.[50] While it seems that Gerard had been prepared to accept whatever he was told about new plants from abroad, Parkinson actually took the seeds, bulbs and roots arriving from the ships and planted them in his garden to observe how they grew. In 1608, he commissioned Guillaume Boel, a plant-hunter, to seek out rare plants in Spain on his behalf. Boel came back with more than two hundred different kinds of seeds, of which Parkinson later wrote: 'by sowing them [I] saw the faces of a great many excellent plants'.[51] That is how he built up his extensive knowledge of plants and flowers – by growing them in his garden and observing their nature. This was no mere intellectual theorising: he was actively putting into practice what he preached. He was dismissive of what he called 'idle tales and fancies' – practices such as adding pike's blood to a graft in an apple tree to make the fruits red or honey to make them sweet – the kind of advice perpetuated by Hyll, Mascall and Scot. Instead, Parkinson challenges head on the idea that the nature of plants can be altered by human intervention, categorically asserting that there is nothing we can do that is not already found in nature: God is the only creator and all that we, or the gardener, can do is to nurture and improve that which is already provided in nature, working in harmony with it in order to bring it to perfection.[52] Therein, for Parkinson, lay the 'arte of gardening'.

Far from setting a new standard for gardening literature, however, the innovations identified in Parkinson's *Paradisi in Sole* were not, it seems, taken up by new writers but were overlooked in the gardening publications of the following thirty years. These instead followed much the same format as they always had, reverting to the earlier derivative models based on herbals and gardening treatises first published in the previous century. Indeed, a closer examination of even these newly published materials, detailed in Appendix 1, reveals that almost all were either reprints or compilations of earlier publications and were not new at all. Why this should have happened is a moot point: perhaps in unsettled times gardeners were not ready to tackle new and radical notions but took refuge in the familiar, or perhaps, as noted previously, the high cost of this particular book may have limited its readership and therefore its influence. That said, the marked gap in the publication of new material was not limited to gardening literature but appears to have been a general phenomenon relating to all household books.[53] It could be argued that the first major and original work to take up Parkinson's legacy was John Rea's *Flora: De Florum Cultura*, which was not published until 1665. Rea himself claimed that he had considered revising his predecessor's work but – again, probably with an eye on his potential market – he decided instead to write a completely new book.[54] However, the resulting tome did not differ markedly from Parkinson's. It had the advantage of including new plant discoveries that had been made during the intervening years, but the disadvantage of having no illustrations. He dismissed their inclusion as being 'altogether needless…good for nothing', but the truth of the matter was that he could not afford them.[55]

The fact is that probably the two most important works of gardening literature produced during this later period were never printed at all but were only ever circulated in manuscript form. The first of these, written by Sir Thomas Hanmer of Bettisfield, was entitled, in one version at least, 'Of a Flower Garden', of which at least three copies are known to have survived. This work did not appear in printed form until 1933, when one of the manuscript copies was discovered and published by Ivy Elstob as *The Garden Book of Sir Thomas Hanmer*.[56] The second was the monumental work by John Evelyn, *Elysium Britannicum*, begun in the 1650s but never completed in his lifetime – the unfinished manuscript was published only in 2000. Although these works were not available in the public domain in the same way as the printed gardening books discussed so far, there is evidence to suggest that Evelyn's and probably also Hanmer's work were circulating as manuscripts among contemporary gardeners.

Recent scholarship has shown that the publication of unprinted, or scribal, texts occupied an important place in early modern culture.[57] Contemporary understanding of the words 'print' and 'publish' were varied and broader than our understanding now: in the sixteenth and seventeenth centuries, scribal publication could be, and often was, chosen over printed communication. Far from being viewed as a substandard precursor to print, scribal publication – that is, the writing, copying and distribution of a text in manuscript form – remained common practice until at least the end of the seventeenth century, retaining its position alongside printed materials as a viable means of communication. There was no sense of it being either inferior or incomplete.[58]

To this on-going scholarly debate we can now bring the examples of Hanmer's *Garden Book* and Evelyn's *Elysium Britannicum*. What these works have to tell us about contemporary gardening practice will be dealt with extensively in Chapter 9, while discussion here will be limited to the nature of their contribution to the body of contemporary gardening literature.

Sir Thomas Hanmer produced at least three manuscript versions of his garden book: the National Library of Wales (NLW) holds an unbound folio entitled 'Of Flowers' and a bound quarto version entitled 'Of a Flower Garden'. Neither of these manuscripts is dated and neither of them appears to be the version used by Ivy Elstob for the eventual publication of the book in 1933, which it seems has now disappeared.[59] Elstob states that her transcription is from a manuscript volume of 1659 and, although the manuscript at which she was looking is no longer available to us, there is no reason to assume that this information is not accurate.[60] She describes the manuscript as a thick quarto, bound in plain brown calf, which sounds remarkably similar to the extant copy in the NLW archive, although there are enough differences in the content to be certain that this is a different version.[61] What is less easy to establish is whether or not Hanmer ever intended to publish this work as a printed book, and knowledge of the existence of at least two similar bound manuscript copies lends weight to the idea that in fact he did not. It has long been assumed that an essay on the current state of gardening, found among the pages of Hanmer's unbound manuscript, was written as a preface, apparently indicating his intention to publish his work as a printed text.[62] However, it is equally possible that this was never Sir Thomas's intention at all and that he simply produced a small number of manuscripts to be circulated among friends and acquaintances with whom he shared a common enthusiasm for gardening, and it was as an introduction to this limited publication that he wrote the essay.

Hanmer was clearly regarded by his contemporaries as an authority on plants and gardening, as knowledge of his work appears to have been disseminated during his lifetime to his peers. John Evelyn, whom Hanmer had met in France and again in London, sought his advice in planting his garden at Sayes Court, as well as inviting Hanmer's contributions to his own *Elysium Britannicum*. Hanmer contributed three full pages on tulips, as well as pages on anemones, irises, ranunculus and daffodils, all of which were simply inserted as they were, in Hanmer's handwriting, into Evelyn's manuscript. Other information on auriculas, gilliflowers and hyacinths was incorporated by Evelyn into his text, either fully or as marginal notes.[63] John Rea, the Shropshire nurseryman and acquaintance of Hanmer, referred to his superior knowledge in his *Flora: De Florum Cultura* (1665): 'I know your Judgement in things of this nature to be Transcendent', he writes in one of two dedicatory epistles that open this book. Hanmer himself writes in a letter to John Evelyn that in Wales 'many gentlemen...have upon my instigation and perception, fallen to plant both flowers and trees and have pretty handsome little grounds'.[64] All this adds weight to the idea that Hanmer may have been writing for this small, defined group of fellow garden enthusiasts rather than for a more general readership. The extant finished manuscripts seem complete and, although none is identical, the content is basically the same. They are all written in Hanmer's own hand with neat interlinear revisions that are unlikely to have been made by anyone but the author.[65] Hanmer lived in north Wales, far from London's printing presses, and it may also be relevant that he was writing these texts during the Interregnum when, as a Royalist, he may have preferred to keep a low profile. It is not difficult therefore to identify a number of reasons why Hanmer may have chosen to publish his book in manuscript form. So, perhaps, as well as providing an invaluable source of early modern gardening knowledge, Sir Thomas Hanmer's *Garden Book* represents another candidate to add to the growing list of seventeenth-century scribal publications.

Whatever his intentions, however, what we see from these manuscripts is that Sir Thomas was writing an informed book based on his own considerable experience of gardening in north Wales. His manuscript books are compiled from notes made in two small memorandum books during the 1650s. Some of the notes relate to his own experience and observations, others to those collected from gardening contemporaries. These notebooks will be examined in detail later but suffice it to say here that they clearly formed the basis of knowledge in Hanmer's book: like Lawson and Parkinson before him, Hanmer is writing from his own experience. It is intensely practical and personal: he only writes about what he knows and what he is interested in, namely, the flower garden and how to grow and nurture the plants that will be cultivated in it. It is interesting that by the time Hanmer was writing in 1659, the importance of the ornamental flower garden – first brought to the fore in print by John Parkinson – seems established and accepted.

Finally in this chapter, we turn to the work of John Evelyn. Although his first gardening book was published in 1658 (a translation, *The French Gardiner*[66]) and despite the fact that he went on during his long life to produce a string of other extremely popular works on the practicalities of growing trees, vegetables and salads – which no doubt contributed to his reputation both then and now as a horticultural expert – Evelyn's major work during the mid-1600s was his draft of *Elysium Britannicum*. The nature and purpose of this manuscript have been, and continue to be, the subject of much debate but the consensus is that it was first compiled around 1657–9: Evelyn mentions it in his dedication to *The French Gardiner* and his correspondence reveals that he was distributing drafts of the text to friends and colleagues in 1660.[67] John Ingram, the editor who finally brought Evelyn's draft into print in 2000, observes that there is no doubt that much of the material contained within the *Elysium Britannicum* was compiled from a wide variety of sources, both ancient and modern and included contributions from Evelyn's wide network of colleagues. He notes that in some cases, pages written in other hands, such as those from Thomas Hanmer, are simply inserted as loose leaves into the text.[68] The scope of *Elysium Britannicum* was monumental. Beginning with Adam and Eve and the loss of Eden, Evelyn shows how the 'Arte of Gardening' can re-create this paradise. His themes range from the practical, including sections on soil and compost, medicinal plants, decorative flowers, the design of parterres and groves; to the scientific or pseudo-scientific, including the cosmic processes that influence the seasons and the generation and growth of plants; and to the philosophical, including enquiry into the perfection of nature and the dignity of gardening and the gardener.

In his preface to *The French Gardiner*, Evelyn writes: 'I have long since had inclinations, and a design of communicating some other things of this nature from my own experience: and especially concerning the Ornaments of Gardens, etc.'[69] So, like other gardening authors, Evelyn intended to base his book on experience, and we know he was well equipped to do this because by this time he had gained plenty of practical experience in the creation of new gardens both at the Evelyn family seat in Wotton, Surrey, and at his own home at Sayes Court in Deptford. However, what was different about Evelyn was his wish to combine the dissemination of practical information with his higher literary aspirations. Therefore he presented his information, not 'plainly to playne men' as Reynolde Scot did, but embellished with classical allusions and quotations from ancient and more recent authors, demonstrating, in addition to his experience, his wide and learned reading. Evelyn's approach brings us back full circle to the idea, rejected by Parkinson (and Bacon), that classical texts can be a basis for modern scientific knowledge and his frequent use of Latin prose once more necessarily restricted the readership of his book to the educated few. His frequent lapses into Latin and Greek not only emphasised his desire to establish the credentials of his subject matter by grounding it in ancient authority, but also set his book apart from earlier English gardening books which, as has been seen, had a tendency towards practicality and accessibility. This led to some contemporary criticism that such an approach was distancing the work from its proper audience: 'the countryman must go learn Latin and the poets to understand our author', wrote the Yorkshire doctor Nathaniel Johnson in 1666, but this writer did at the same time recognise that perhaps this was Evelyn's point, that in writing 'scholar and gentleman like of this subject' the purpose was 'to make gentlemen in love with the study'.[70] The elevated literary style of *Elysium Britannicum* suggests an elevated subject and is perhaps indicative of the high status to which Evelyn wished to raise the discourse of gardening.[71]

In his quest, however, to produce the most up-to-date statement of the gardener's art and science, Evelyn continually altered and annotated the text of *Elysium Britannicum* throughout his life, introducing thousands of changes and additions over more than four decades. Unlike Hanmer's *Garden Book*, then, and despite the fact that it was clearly circulated to a wide range of friends and colleagues over the years, Evelyn's *Elysium* remained unpublished in any sense of the word. Evelyn himself never felt that his manuscript was complete, instead stating his intention to 'correct, improve and adorn' his text as new information came to hand. Twenty years after the production of the first draft, Evelyn wrote that 'I am almost out of hope that I shall ever have strength and leasure to bring it to maturity'.[72] And he was right, of course: a further twenty years of revision still did not result in a completed manuscript or publication. However, finished or not, now that this opus has finally been edited and published, it maintains its place as one of the most important horticultural works of the seventeenth century.

The wide range of gardening literature examined here, from the small, cheap and accessible manuals of Hyll and Mascall, through Parkinson's expensive *Paradisi in Sole, Paradisus Terrestris*, to the manuscript works of Hanmer and Evelyn which were necessarily limited to a restricted readership, all indicate not only a growing interest in the subject of gardening but also offer valuable insight into the aspirations and activities of the early modern gardener and garden-owner. Although the derivative nature of much of the material brings into question how much some of these books actually reflected contemporary practice, it has nevertheless been demonstrated that both Lawson's *New Orchard and Garden* and Parkinson's *Paradisi in Sole*, being original books written by experienced gardeners, stand out in terms of what they can tell us about the realities of the early modern garden.

In addition, and despite the limitations of the genre, all these works of gardening literature remain extremely valuable as guides to the social and cultural concerns of the time and to the intellectual and moral context within which the story that follows is set. It is this aspect of these books that will be the focus of the next chapter.

2

'PROFITS AND PLEASURES'

The Social Context

Within the opening lines of almost any early modern gardening text, it is inevitable that the ideas of profit and pleasure appear, usually together but juxtaposed as two separate, and at times, conflicting notions. Thomas Hyll writes that the gardener will receive 'two special commodities: The first is profit, which riseth through the increase of hearbes and floures; the other is, pleasure, very delectable through the delight of walkying in the same'; Markham announces the second part of his book as the 'Art of Planting, Grafting and Gardening, either for pleasure or profit'; Mascall declares in his opening doggerel 'Unto the Reader' that the 'The pleasure of this skill is great, The profit is not small'.[1] On the title page of Ralph Austen's *A Treatise of Fruit-trees* (fig. 13) these themes are graphically depicted: illustrated in the bottom half of the page is a perfectly enclosed and symmetrically ordered garden. It is peopled with groups of gentlemen and women walking and taking pleasure in the garden as well as three gardeners who are working in it – pruning, raking and harvesting fruit. The top of the page bears the motif of 'Profits' and 'Pleasures' portrayed as equal and together, inextricably entwined. Austen writes at length about both the profits and pleasures of gardening, concluding that 'when they runne along, hand in hand, the profit is more because of the pleasure and the pleasure is more because of the profit'.[2]

Parkinson also talks of pleasure and profit in *Paradisi in Sole*. Unlike Austen, however, who sees the two notions as 'one imbracing another, supporting, and upholding each other',[3] Parkinson separates the ideas literally into two different gardens: the garden of pleasure, full of 'all sorts of pleasant flowers',[4] and the kitchen garden, consisting of 'Herbes and Rootes, fit to be eaten of the rich and poor as nourishment'.[5] Having said that, he recognises that not everyone has the luxury of two gardens and must make one place serve for all uses, in this case 'making their profit their chiefest pleasure'.[6] It is not difficult, thus, to establish the ubiquity of the notions of profit and pleasure in early modern garden writing, but it still needs to be asked why this should be and how, exactly, these terms were understood by contemporaries.

So, why this preoccupation with profits and pleasures at all? At first sight, the answers seem as simple as they are obvious. The growing of fruits, vegetables and herbs provides food and medicines for the household while surpluses, whether given away to neighbours or sold at market, bring further benefits to the family and the community. Gardens, whether full of sweet-scented flowers, well-ordered fruit trees or precisely laid out knots, are pleasant places in which to pass the time. And to some of these writers at least, the actual activity of gardening was a pleasurable one – as Lawson says, 'there can be no human thing more excellent, either for pleasure or profit' as the tending of an orchard.[7] Despite this, while none of these writers would deny the pleasure of gardens and gardening, they appear to demonstrate a need to justify the pleasures of gardening by the profits that it

Profits.   Pleasures.

A Treatise of
FRVIT=TREES

Shewing the manner of Grafting, Setting, Pruning, and Ordering of them
in all respects : According to divers new and easy Rules of experience;
gathered in y̓ space of Twenty yeares.

Whereby the value of Lands may be much improued, in a shorttime, by
small cost, and little labour.

Also discovering some dangerous Errors, both in y̓ Theory and Practise
of y̓ Art of Planting Fruit=trees.

With. the Alimentall and Physicall vse of fruits.

Togeather with

The Spirituall vse of an Orchard: Held forth in divers Similitudes be=
tweene Naturall & Spirituall Fruit=trees: according to Scripture & Experiēce.

By RA: AUSTEN

Practiser in y̓ Art of Planting

A Garden inclosed is my sister my Spouse: Thy Plants are an Orchard of Pomegranats, with pleasant fruits: Cant: 4 :12 :13

Oxford printed for.   Tho: Robinson 1653.

brought. And therein lay the problem: in a society essentially based on and governed by Christian and humanist social and intellectual values, the very notions of profit and pleasure were troublesome.

The predominant model to which society aspired at the beginning of our period was hierarchical and prescriptive: the world was conceived as a series of static relationships, and an individual's place in this divinely created scheme was predetermined by birth and social circumstances. Ambition and social climbing were frowned upon. As Reynolde Scot observes in the preface to his *Perfite Platforme of a Hoppe Garden*, it is not 'greedye traveyle', but 'the blessing of the Lorde that maketh men riche'.[8] In other words, the individual cannot, indeed should not, do anything to improve his own status, as his place in the world is determined by God and he should be content to stay there. This concept was the cornerstone of sixteenth-century thinking on political stability and maintenance of the social order. It follows that the needs and aspirations of the individual were necessarily subordinate to the proper functioning of society as a whole.[9]

This view, in which every individual contributed towards the good of the whole – or the 'common wealth' – guided Tudor social and economic thought: the whole social order, from noblemen to merchants to husbandmen and artisans, was obliged to contribute to the common good, and individual or private profit-seeking was viewed with deep suspicion. At all levels, men were subject to the insistence on productive and profitable occupation, where profit was understood as a recognisable contribution to the health, knowledge, virtue or material well-being of the commonwealth, essential to the maintenance of a stable, ordered and just society. This stability was threatened if the private interests of the individual should take precedence over the public.[10]

These ideas of course throw up inconsistencies. In the same way that private wealth, particularly inherited wealth, was a fact of life in early modern society, so too, if hard work and industriousness were to be encouraged (as indeed they were), success would inevitably bring with it a degree of wealth and prosperity. This dichotomy between 'public' and 'private' interests was a contradiction successfully addressed by the Tudor regime: profit was legitimate if it was no detriment to the interests of others, but was viewed as implicitly harmful if retained by the individual rather than invested in the commonwealth. In other words, profit may be condoned if the interests of the commonwealth are put before the interests of the individual, the public before the private.

Despite the prevalence of this traditional rhetoric, it perhaps still comes as a surprise to find the writers of early garden manuals engaging with these same ideas, using the 'front matter' of their books to express their concerns about the social issues of the time. Mascall, for instance, introduces his book with an exhortation 'Unto the Reader':

The common weale cannot but winne,
Where eche man dothe entende:
By skill to make the food fruites mo[re]
And yll fruites to amende.[11]

Planting and grafting is seen as an occupation that can be of benefit to all because everyone is working to the same end – to bear fruit, or profit. This conflation of ideas successfully blurs the boundaries between the literal and the metaphorical, resulting in an ambiguity to be interpreted by the reader. Mascall goes on to say that his advice is 'not an exercise only to the minde, but likewise a great profit manyways, with maintenaunce of health unto the bodie'. Again, this can be interpreted literally – relating to the individual or at a wider level, incorporating the whole of society. Mascall goes on to write specifically about his own views on the state of the nation. He criticises 'the base and abject sort of the commonwealth' who are contemptuous of 'labouring of the earth': it comes as somewhat of a surprise to find that he is talking here of 'faire personages', who clearly think they do not need to dirty their hands with manual labour. Like Scot, Mascall appears to be reflecting the general unease directed at those social aspirants who were blurring the boundaries of the traditional social order by seeking to improve their place within it and become gentlemen. He urges his reader to 'leave al wanton games and idle pastimes…and be no more as children whiche seeke but their owne gaine and pleasure and seeke one of us for another in all good workes for the commonwealth'.[12] He is not saying that there is necessarily anything wrong with gain, or indeed pleasure, but it must be done for the right reasons, and that is the furtherance of the common wealth. And for Mascall, the activity of gardening was a practical way in which the individual could play his part for the benefit of the whole society.

Gervase Markham, writing at the beginning of the following century, also sees his work as 'most acceptable to men, and most profitable to the kingdome'.[13] He talks in specific terms of the 'utility and necessitie'[14] of the husbandman, for the 'filling and emptying of his barnes is the increase and prosperity of all his labours'.[15] It is interesting that the emptying of the barns – the distribution of the profits – is as important as filling them in the first place. This illustrates specifically the idea that the accumulation of wealth is acceptable as long as the ends are a contribution to the good of the community. Like his contemporaries, he clearly links the work of the husbandman and the resulting profit with stability and social order: 'it is most necessary for keeping the earth in order…which else would grow wilde…and nothing remayning but a Chaos of confusednesse'.[16]

If profit was a troublesome concept, however, the idea of personal pleasure was even more so. Seen as 'private' and selfish, the pursuit of pleasure did not sit happily with the image of Christian humanist virtue: it was associated with recreation and idleness, traits traditionally viewed with contempt and suspicion. As has been noted, for any activity not to be seen as self-indulgent, it had to be profitable and also for the common good: idleness (and by implication leisure and pleasure) produced neither. However, by the early seventeenth century, in line with changing economic conditions both within the country and abroad, these ideas were beginning to change. While moralists continued to condemn conspicuous wealth, private indulgence and the pursuit of profit and pleasure, the fact is that by the 1620s, rather than imposing tight controls over economic expansion, government policies were being designed to encourage individual profit. The resulting prosperity was recognised as a factor in maintaining social stability, and the pursuit of self-interest acknowledged as being of benefit to the whole. Increased wealth and prosperity of course brought with them the desire and the means to indulge in new luxury goods that were becoming increasingly available.[17] It has been suggested that in fact contemporary social prescription was 'wildly out of line with reality' and that new sources of wealth created new aspirations which played havoc with traditional notions of a static social order as men sought to 'get on in life'.[18] As one contemporary observed, 'the sons...not contented with their states of their fathers to be counted yeomen...must skip into his velvet breeches and silken doublet and...must ever after think scorn to be called any other than gentlemen'.[19]

It seems, then, that traditional notions regarding the pursuit of profit and pleasure were being challenged on all fronts. And, to return to the gardeners under discussion, although often still linking the pleasures of gardening to the profits to be had, none denies those pleasures. For some the pleasure was in the pleasant and ordered result: 'What joy and fruit commeth of trees:...when the trees bee planted / And set orderly and pleasantly, they give no small pleasure to man.'[20] For others, the pleasure was in the labour and skill (a solution, of course, to the idleness problem). Lawson, for instance, could stand back, once the hard work of establishing his orchard and garden was done, and take delight in the fruits of his labours: 'But as God hath given man things profitable, so hath he allowed him honest comfort, delight and recreation in all the works of his hands...For what is greedy gaine, without delight, but moyling, and turmoiling in slavery? But comfortable delight, with content, is the good of everything, and the pattern of heaven'.[21] Lawson, who, as well as being a keen gardener, was also a clergyman, then goes on to make the obvious, and convenient, comparison with Paradise: 'What was Paradise? but a Garden and Orchard of trees and hearbs, full of pleasure? and nothing there but delights'.[22] In Christian belief, when God chose the perfect situation for Man before the Fall, he placed him in a garden. The punishment for his sin was to be cast out. It is therefore not too difficult a step to justify the pleasures of a garden as ordained by God, at the same time remembering that Adam was not idle in his garden but was charged with tending and working in it. It is this pleasure that Lawson feels he can legitimately take in his garden.

The expression of notions such as these also draws attention to the idea of a garden as a place of spiritual and physical refreshment. Mascall claims that the skill of planting and grafting 'doth refresh the vital spirits of men' as they feel with their hands 'the secret works of nature'.[23] Lawson writes of those who are exhausted by the troublesome affairs of their estates, 'tyred with the hearing and judging of litigious controversies, choaken with the close ayre of their sumptuous buildings…overburthened with tedious discoursings', but who can retire to their gardens and orchards in order to renew and refresh their 'over-wea-ried spirits'.[24] Again, perhaps this is seen as a legitimate pleasure. In setting up this direct contrast between the 'sweet and pleasant aire' of the garden and the 'close ayre' of the city, Lawson is reflecting closely another prevalent social anxiety – unfavourably distinguish-ing the 'court' from the 'country'. Although there was nothing particularly new about this idea,[25] during the early years of the seventeenth century in the lead up to the Civil Wars, this ideology was becoming specific and polarised, increasingly contrasting the positive image of the morally upright 'country' with a negative image of the corrupt and dishonest 'court' and drawing on active concerns of the population over extravagance, depravity and popery manifested by the rulers of the land.[26] The very words 'court' and 'country' became synonymous with corruption on the one hand and honesty on the other. However, Lawson stops short of outright condemnation of court or city life; rather, he recognises the burdens of such a life, offering his 'delicate Garden and Orchard' as 'the remidie'.[27]

So for the garden writers of the early seventeenth century, pleasures and profits were still intricately linked: pleasure in the garden was seen in terms of the profits gained, whether by the satisfaction achieved through the hard work, the actual foodstuffs produced for the household and beyond, the benefits of spiritual and physical refreshment or simply the pleasure of seeing an ordered and comely space adorned with flowers, blossom and fruit.

Many of these arguments are reiterated by Parkinson in the opening pages of *Paradisi in Sole*. In his Epistle to the Reader, he introduces the framework within which the rest of his book will be set. First and foremost he, like Lawson, places his work in a specifically Chris-tian context, most obviously by referring to Paradise not once but twice in the title of his book (fig. 14).

His opening lines in the Epistle describe 'God, the creator of Heaven and Earth' who 'planted a garden for him [Adam] to live in, which he stored with the best and choysest Herbes and Fruits the earth could produce'. It is difficult not to miss the direct comparison with the earthly paradise which Parkinson intends to create in this book. He notes, again as Lawson did, that in this garden and 'even his innocency', Adam 'was to labour and spend

his time'. Parkinson talks too of the garden as a place of spiritual refreshment 'by comforting the mind, spirit and senses with an harmless delight' and, echoing the views of Francis Bacon, he deems it 'a thing unfit to conceal or bury knowledge God hath given and not impart it': he believes knowledge should be shared, not held as 'secrets', and this is one of the reasons that he is writing the book, in order to 'further inform the reader'. These themes are all well-rehearsed by his contemporaries, but where Parkinson stands out among them is in his attitude to the profits and pleasures of gardening. He discusses them both but, unlike his gardening contemporaries, he places a different emphasis on pleasure. Within the framework of conventional Christian rhetoric, he reiterates the pleasures of gardening again and again: 'God planted a Garden…that he [Adam] might have not onely for necessitie whereon to feede, but for pleasure also', 'God made to grow everie tree pleasant to the sight and good for meate' and so on. Even after Adam had 'lost the place for his transgression', he did not lose the knowledge that God had given him and was able to continue to 'use all things as well of pleasure as of necessitie'. According to Parkinson, delight and pleasure in gardens has been there since the beginning. It was given by God and does not therefore have to be justified in the way that his predecessors felt was necessary. As will be seen, for Parkinson, gardens, plants and flowers are to be recommended for no other reason than that they are delightful and pleasurable.

Thus the idea of the pursuit of self-interest for profit or pleasure was becoming more acceptable in early modern England. One factor which demands further consideration is the related and contemporaneous rise in conspicuous consumption. Contrasting vividly with traditional classical, humanist and biblical discourses that differentiated between needs and wants, privileging the first and condemning the second, the idea of luxury and acquisition of luxury goods was, by the early seventeenth century, also beginning to lose its overtones of moral disapproval. New aspirations, fuelled by the ever-increasing number of rare and exotic goods arriving in the ports of London, increased opportunities for travel, increased awareness of new possibilities arising from the continued spread and accessibility of books and print, even royal encouragement of luxury trades such as James I's enthusiastic endorsement of a domestic silk industry: all these were making available and creating a demand for exotic and luxury goods which in turn engendered a growing culture of conspicuous consumption, which was becoming both acceptable and desirable.[28] While wealth had always been recognised as a necessity required to meet the obligations of living in a style appropriate to an elevated position in society, it seemed that now the display of luxury and the acquisition of goods not only indicated status but could also *confer* status on their owners.[29] This posed yet another challenge to traditional notions of hierarchy, as alongside the expanding range of luxury goods available was an expanding section of the population who felt both entitled to use them and were prosperous enough to acquire them.

As new desires were engendered and satisfied, the old distinctions between needs and wants were eroded, until luxuries gradually became relabelled as necessities. Whereas early in the seventeenth century Thomas Mun condemned 'silks, sugars and spices' as 'unecessary wants' leading to 'idleness and pleasure contrary to the law of God', by 1667 Bishop Thomas Sprat could write that goods were to be welcomed because they brought 'pleasure' and 'greater delight'. The quest for wealth and possessions was becoming an acceptable goal for human endeavour and the pursuit of self-interest, profit or pleasure was no longer morally condemned.[30]

It is within this environment and as a response to the changing times that Parkinson produced his outstanding book on gardening in which he unequivocally extols the virtues of the ornamental pleasure garden for its own sake. Under cover of an apparently conventional veneer, the publication of *Paradisi in Sole* in 1629 in fact represented a revolution in horticultural writing. This is a bold statement to make, but closer study of the text reveals a radical new approach by the author to his subject: *A Garden of all Sorts of Pleasant Flowers*. This supplementary English title given to *Paradisi in Sole* is both remarkable and revealing: not only is this the first book to take the beauty of plants and flowers as its principal subject, it is also the first to describe the creation of a garden in which the flowers and plants take centre stage. Parkinson himself declares that this is a new kind of book: 'having perused many herbals...none of them have particularly severed those that are beautifull flower plants, fit to store the garden of delight and pleasure, from the wilde and unfit' and this is what he sets out to remedy: he has 'here selected and set forth a Garden of all the chiefest for choyce and fairest for show'.[31] In contrast to the gardening books that preceded it, this book devotes the first and by far the longest chapter to the 'Ordering of the Garden of Pleasure', in which Parkinson advocates gardens, plants and gardening for no other reason than that they are pleasurable. He recommends plants and flowers as ornaments, delights, objects of beauty or curiosity. He feels no obligation, as for instance Gerard had done, to attribute 'uses' and 'vertues' to plants, any more than he feels the necessity to regard the pleasure as some kind of 'reward' for hard work, as appears to have been the case with Lawson. While acknowledging that 'the delight is great', Gerard insists in his *Herball* that 'the use [of plants] is greater, and joyned often with necessitie'.[32] Parkinson, in contrast, relegates the description of uses and virtues of plants to the bottom of his list of reasons for writing his book: 'Fourthly [and lastly], I have also set down the Vertues and Properties of them in a briefe manner'.[33] The first plant he describes in his

book is the Crown Imperial, 'for his stately beautifulness deserveth the first place in this our Garden of delight'. He devotes a full folio page to a description of how it looks and another to an exquisite woodcut drawing of the flower (fig. 15). Parkinson dismisses its virtues with 'I know of none'.[34]

In the same way that the consumption of luxury goods was becoming accepted, so too was the display of rare and costly plants in the garden, so we should perhaps not be surprised at Parkinson's timely advice on how to plant them and show them off to their best advantage. In the late sixteenth and early seventeenth century, plant collectors travelled the world in search of exotic plants to stock the gardens of the nobility, gardens that were, in themselves, showpieces of wealth, status and fashion. Books such as Parkinson's *Paradisi in Sole* were also luxury items and the popularity of such works brought the rare and exotic to the attention of a wider public. Through its pages, Parkinson hopes to guide his readers in what plants to choose, in order 'to satisfie therefore their desires that are lovers of such Delights'.[35] Parkinson has no problem with those who seek their own pleasure and indeed positively encourages them to do just that. It seems that no longer does the pursuit of pleasure have to be justified by 'profits': it can be actively sought in its own right.[36]

The first two chapters of this book have highlighted some of the fundamental shifts in the way the people of early modern England viewed their world – an acceptance of the emerging concept of science slowly displacing the unchallenged wisdom of ancient authorities; the dichotomy between concepts of public good and private prosperity gradually veering in favour of the individual; and previously frowned upon notions such as consumption, luxury and pleasure no longer being moral issues. All this contributed to creating a new social context in which wealth and status could be displayed, and which could be displayed in gardens as well as anywhere else.

Having established this intellectual background, it is now time to step outside in order to explore how the theory presented in the manuals matches actual practice in the gardens of early modern England.

3

SETTING
THE SCENE

Elizabethan Gardens

The Elizabethan age, it has been seen, was one preoccupied with the maintenance of good order and stability in society. This desire was reflected in many areas of life, including in its gardens. It was a commonplace analogy of the time to view the household as a microcosm of the state, conceived as a miniature commonwealth, where patriarchal authority was seen as a manifestation of the divinely ordered hierarchy.[1] The male head of the household ruled his wife, children and servants, just as a monarch ruled his people: if good order could be kept in the family, then it followed that good order would be kept in the state. In his 1577 translation of Conrad Heresbach's *Foure Bookes of Husbandry*, Barnabe Googe wrote: 'Herein were the old husbands very careful and used always to judge, that where they found the garden out of order, the wyfe of the house (for unto her belonged the charge thereof) was not good huswyfe.'[2] Here Googe implicitly links the notion of the well-run patriarchal household with the outward signs of this: the state of the garden was a visible indication of the state of the household and, by inference, the morality of the household members and the authority of the husband within that household.

This obsession with good order was revealed explicitly in the gardens themselves, which were characterised by an enclosed symmetry of straight lines and geometric shapes, such as those depicted in the woodcut drawings which illustrated contemporary garden manuals. One image which appears in a number of Elizabethan gardening books (fig. 16) depicts a symmetrical arrangement of two squares, each divided into four quarters, enclosed within a rigid framework of rails and hedges. (It is worth noting that, despite the particular layout depicted here, the term 'quarter' simply referred to a division within the garden: it was not necessarily square and there were not necessarily four of them.) A plan of the town of Hull from 1539 (fig. 17), drawn to show the state of coastal defences at the time, also indicates a series of formal gardens laid out around the inside of the city walls, most of which are set out in four or more quarters.

At Lyveden New Bield in Northamptonshire, this most important and undisturbed example of an extant Elizabethan garden in England was laid out by its owner, Sir Thomas Tresham, in a series of terraces and quarters. Famous for its impressive garden lodge, the building of which came to an abrupt halt on the death of Sir Thomas in 1605, it is nevertheless still possible to see the layout of the rest of the garden. Reached via a series of six terraces that rise up from the manor house at the north of the site, the most striking elements that can still be seen today are the 'lower orchard', likely to have been divided, as now, into four quarters, and the 'moated orchard', an ordered geometric arrangement of circular beds set within another square formed by the canals around it (fig. 18).[3] Although, like the lodge, and for the same reason, the fourth side of this moat was never completed, it is still easy to see the effect of the intended arrangement.

16 A symmetrical and ordered garden from Thomas Hyll's *The Gardeners Labyrinth*, 1577
17 View of Hull showing formal gardens around the city wall, 1539

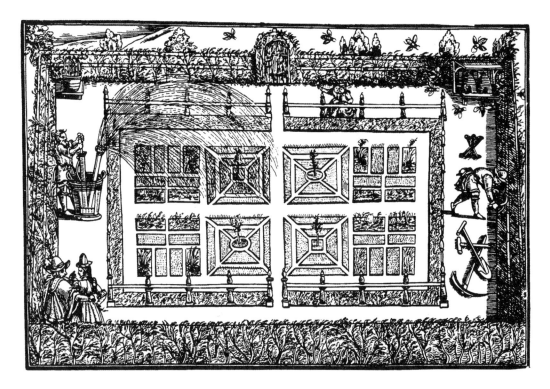

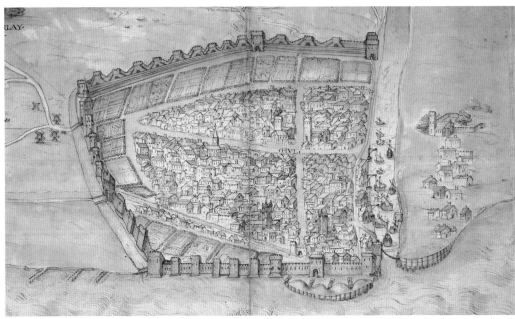

Contemporary authors also agreed on this ordered and geometrical layout. Markham advised the English husbandman: 'After you have chosen out and fenced your garden-plot…you shall then beginne to fashion and proportion out the same, sith in the conveyance remaineth a great part of the gardiners art'.[4] He then goes on to describe in detail how to lay out alleys and quarters and suggests ways of ornamenting them that will 'breed infinite delight to the beholders' (fig. 19). However, he concedes that from the model he offers, 'any industrious braine may with little difficulty derive and fashion to himself divers other shapes and proportions, according to the nature and site of the earth'.[5]

Parkinson realises too that 'To prescribe one forme for every man to follow, were too great presumption and folly: for every man will please his owne fancie'. Nevertheless, like Markham, he goes on to set out the basic ground rules for the layout of a garden, observing that the 'foure square forme is most usually accepted with all', describing alleys, squares and a variety of ways of ornamenting them. But then, 'let every man chuse which him liketh best, or may most fitly agree to that proportion of ground hee hath set out for that purpose'.[6] Lawson also agrees that the 'form that men like in generall, is a square', but nevertheless adds: 'wherewith every particular man is delighted, we leave it to himself'.[7]

These examples reveal some important contemporary assumptions about late six-teenth-century gardens. Firstly, it is clear that there was a basic, accepted framework of how a garden should be laid out, which Parkinson neatly sums up as a 'four square forme', divided by alleys or walks and enclosed with walls, fences, hedges or ditches.[8] Lawson, who had been gardening for forty-eight years by the time he published his book, went so far as to provide a simple illustration, 'rough hewn' as he modestly describes it, of the 'generall' form of a garden, containing six quarters, which shows all these basic features (see fig. 47).[9]

Secondly, the design chosen for the garden was inevitably dictated by the limitations or otherwise of the site. As Parkinson puts it, 'all men doe well know, that some situations are more excellent then others', but advises that if the plot is the wrong shape, 'longer than the breadth, or broader than the length', it can soon be brought to the square form.[10]

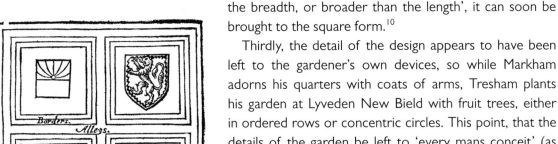

Thirdly, the detail of the design appears to have been left to the gardener's own devices, so while Markham adorns his quarters with coats of arms, Tresham plants his garden at Lyveden New Bield with fruit trees, either in ordered rows or concentric circles. This point, that the details of the garden be left to 'every mans conceit' (as Parkinson puts it),[11] is reinforced by the observation that of the few descriptions we have of Elizabethan gardens, they tend, as previously discussed, not only to be very grand and probably untypical, but also to bear little resemblance to each other.[12] This may of course simply be due to variations in reporting by contemporary observers but it does support the idea that within the basic framework, the detailed design of the garden was not prescribed but left to the individual. Despite this, one common feature of all these gardens remains the square or rectangular geometric layout.

What then were the origins of this basic garden design and how was it developed by the gardeners of early modern England? From where did they get their inspiration, what outside influences affected their choices and how did they put these ideas into practice? Was there a discernible 'style' of gardening and did this change over the period in question? What, in fact, did the late sixteenth-century garden look like?

These questions will be explored by examining both prescriptive designs and actual garden practice to trace how various new influences were being adopted and adapted, if at all, by English gardeners. We need to begin by stepping back even further in time to con-

sider briefly the medieval garden in England and Europe, in order to understand the inherited legacy on which early modern gardeners were building. It then becomes possible to
see how future generations of gardeners took up new ideas, rejected others and continued
to create and develop gardens that not only reflected the society in which they lived and
their place within that society, but also their individual tastes and preferences.

It is well established that the great gardens of royalty and the aristocracy were heavily
influenced by designs and ideas from Renaissance Italy, either first hand or via classical
literature.[13] However, taking a wider view that encompasses all gardens, it seems that many
features of early modern gardens in England simply evolved from medieval and monastic traditions and that at a practical level most gardeners, rather than creating something
from scratch, were starting with an existing plot which would already have had some kind
of form and structure. During the reign of Elizabeth, many familiar features of medieval
gardens remained much in evidence: enclosed by walls or hedges, they contained walks,
arbours, mounts, grassy banks, roses and fountains, all features that were 'destined to linger
on, relabelled or transmuted, as part of the Renaissance garden'.[14]

Three types of medieval garden have been identified from contemporary sources which
relate directly to different levels – albeit only the higher orders – of the social hierarchy: the
herber garden, the orchard garden and the pleasure park. While those at the very top would
have embraced all three types of garden alongside their properties, owners of more modest
means are more likely to have restricted their garden layout to just the herber garden.[15]

Herbers were small ornamental gardens, generally characterised by a turfed area or
lawn with herbaceous borders and square beds, enclosed within walls, trellis or hedges. In
the thirteenth century, a well-travelled German Dominican churchman, Albertus Magnus,
wrote that such a garden would contain 'a great diversity of medicinal and scented herbs'
and that it would be square. It might also contain fruit trees for their 'perfumed flowers and
agreeable shade'.[16] His detailed description of the pleasure garden is recognisable in contemporary paintings from around Europe spanning the next three hundred years – paintings
which have probably done more than anything else to inform our view of what a medieval
garden looked like. Although these imagined gardens are often full of allegory and symbolism, the basic features portrayed by the artist must surely draw on familiar contemporary
ideas and images.

As such, they show enclosed, grassy areas with flowers and fruit trees set out in an
orderly geometric fashion, often with a central fountain. These gardens as depicted in paintings are peopled by gentlewomen sewing or reading, reclining lovers and musicians: clearly,

these are areas for contemplation, leisure and pleasure and, by being enclosed, are literally and metaphorically cut off from the 'real' world outside the gates and walls (fig. 20). It is also clear that these gardens were only for members of the social elite – noble men or women – or they were monastic gardens, another estate that was 'set apart'.

What these paintings do not show, however, is what was probably the most important part of the garden, that is the productive, utilitarian vegetable garden which would have supplied a significant proportion of the dietary needs of the household, whatever its size,

and which must surely be the type of garden to which the majority of people were limited. Unlike elite pleasure gardens depicted in art, most gardens were part of peasant holdings which generally consisted of a small dwelling house, possibly some outbuildings and an adjoining plot of land on which to grow garden produce.[17] Unfortunately, images for these types of garden are almost non-existent. The best we can do is study maps and surveys, some of which contain sufficient detail to indicate the essentially geometric layout of a garden, which was to remain the basis of garden design throughout this period.

A rare sixteenth-century map of the village of Wilton in Wiltshire (fig. 21), for instance, reveals that most of the houses have an adjoining plot of land that is either arranged in

21   Map of Wilton, Wiltshire, showing houses and their gardens, c.1565

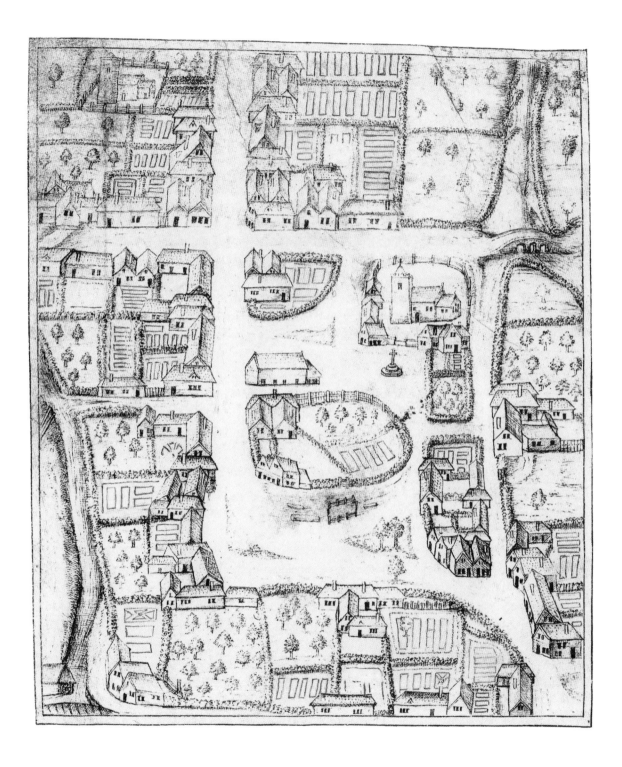

orderly beds, the most useful form for growing vegetables and medicinal herbs, or planted with fruit trees. In only one quarter of one single garden is there any suggestion of an ornamental bed. It is also worth noting in passing that there was nothing particularly 'English' about these garden features: they formed part of a common European tradition which can be traced throughout the medieval period. An extant ninth-century plan from the St Gall Monastery in Switzerland shows a regular layout of a garden that looks remarkably similar to the artisans' gardens depicted in the Wilton map, and a number of studies that have examined the various components of early Tudor gardens confirm their place within a European tradition.[18]

At the same time, however, changes were afoot in the gardens of Renaissance Europe which had yet to reach England. In Italy in particular, the design of the garden was becoming the domain of the architect and it was planned as part of an overall design that was seen as an extension of the house. Renaissance ideals of harmony and proportion were reflected in these designs – straight alleys, walks, arbours, hedges and walls dividing the garden into regular sections and ornamented, for instance, by the symmetrical planting of trees, placing of pots or positioning of painted stanchions.[19] An example of this layout, albeit a somewhat extravagant one, is clear in an engraving made in 1573 of the gardens of the Villa d'Este at Tivoli in Italy (fig. 22).

While this idea of architectural harmony is an extremely important concept to be taken into consideration, it is nevertheless of limited use in explaining the form of most gardens. It necessarily implies a whole new house and garden being designed and built from scratch, which was very much the exception rather than the rule.[20] So what then, apart from the concept of architect as garden designer, was new about European Renaissance design that could be more readily emulated?

The garden historian Sir Roy Strong has argued that the late fifteenth-century garden in Italy could in many ways be seen as the multiplication of the single medieval garden into many gardens. While retaining and nurturing many of their characteristic features such as walks, mounts and arbours, they were rearranged to reflect the new ideals of the Renaissance.[21] This idea has since been examined in more detail and in more practical terms by David Jacques, who has identified the developments in Italian and French garden design during the early sixteenth century as characterised by the division of the garden into a series of square compartments, or *compartimenti*. Each of these compartments functioned as a single design unit but, taken together, they could also be appreciated as a symmetrical and harmonious whole.[22] This can be seen in the engraving of Villa d'Este, but perhaps even more clearly in the detailed drawings of the French architect Jacques Androuet du Cerceau, published in his *Le premier volume des plus excellents bastiments de France* (figs 23, 24; also

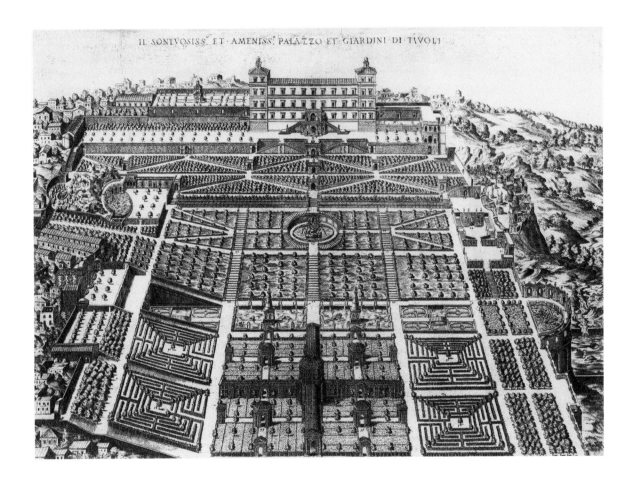

IL SONTVOSISS. ET AMENISS. PALAZZO ET GIARDINI DI TIVOLI

fig. 25). Here we can see the ordered symmetry of the compartments creating a unified whole, but also that the actual design and purpose of each bed is subject to almost infinite variety: from the intricate swirling patterns, circles, oblongs and squares in the *compartiments* of the gardens at the Château de Vallery, to the slightly less extravagant labyrinths and varied layouts of what appear to be more utilitarian garden areas depicted at the nearby Château de Montargis in the Loire Valley.[23]

The appearance of few Elizabethan gardens was ever recorded in detail by artists or surveyors, unlike their Italian and French counterparts, and even fewer gardens remain extant. We have therefore to rely mainly on maps, such as the so-called 'Agas' map of London, a few outline plans for gardens, such as those by the Elizabethan mason and architect Robert Smythson, a couple of sketches of London palaces by the artist Anthonis van den Wyngaerde and that which can be gleaned from the backgrounds of contemporary portrait

23　Jacques Androuet du Cerceau, gardens at the Château de Montargis, France, 1576
24　Jacques Androuet du Cerceau, gardens at the Château de Vallery, France, 1576

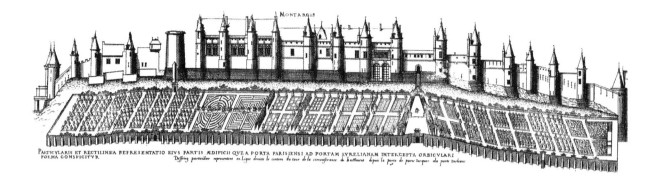

paintings (such as figs 66, 94). The extant garden at Lyveden New Bield, as already mentioned, represents a rare example of a garden that has remained relatively undisturbed since its creation and as such provides valuable evidence to add a little flesh to the bones of the scant information at our disposal. But what becomes immediately obvious from looking at any of these examples is that the sophisticated geometrical designs seen in Italian and French gardens had yet to cross the Channel: there is no evidence, for instance, of anything like the intricate patterns depicted in du Cerceau's drawings.

There is, however, some indication that the idea of arranging gardens into compartments was beginning to be adopted. While the 'Agas' map of London (c.1561) reveals that most gardens simply had a somewhat haphazard arrangement of regular beds dictated by the size and shape of the plot available – similar in fact, to those depicted on the map of the

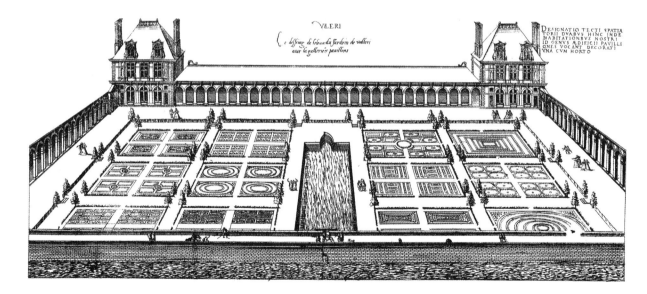

village of Wilton (see fig. 21) – several of the more sophisticated London residences, such as Arundel Place and Paget Place, along the bank of the River Thames between the City and Whitehall, already had their gardens divided into *compartimenti* or quarters, as they were known in England (fig. 26). The map also clearly shows a compartmented garden at Ely Place, in contrast, say, to the garden of Gray's Inn, which is not (fig. 27).[24] In another part of London, just outside Bishopsgate and shown in detail on the Copperplate map of London (*c*.1557; fig. 28), the Giardin di Piero, in common with most other London gardens, also has a random arrangement of oblong beds, while the grounds at St Mary's Spitel show areas clearly divided into compartments or quarters.

Later in the century, a survey of Toddington Manor, Bedfordshire, dated 1581 (fig. 29), shows the 'great garden' divided into nine quarters and the 'little garden' into four, but there is still no indication of any intricate design within the compartments. And at Lyveden New Bield, although Sir Thomas Tresham designed a series of rectangular gardens and terraces to rise up to the lodge at the top of the garden, these also reveal little evidence of elaborate or symmetrically arranged compartments. The only exception was the 'moated orchard',

26   Elite London gardens divided into *compartimenti*, detail from the 'Agas' map, *c*.1561
27   Compartmented garden at Ely Place, detail from the 'Agas', *c*.1561

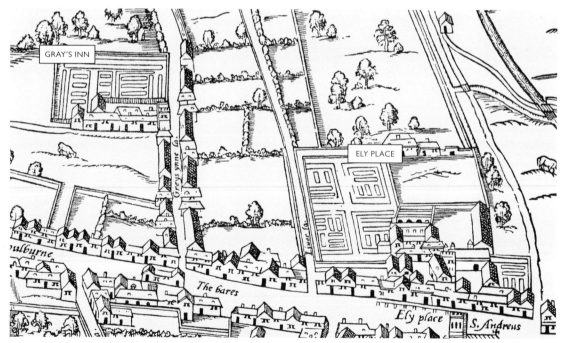

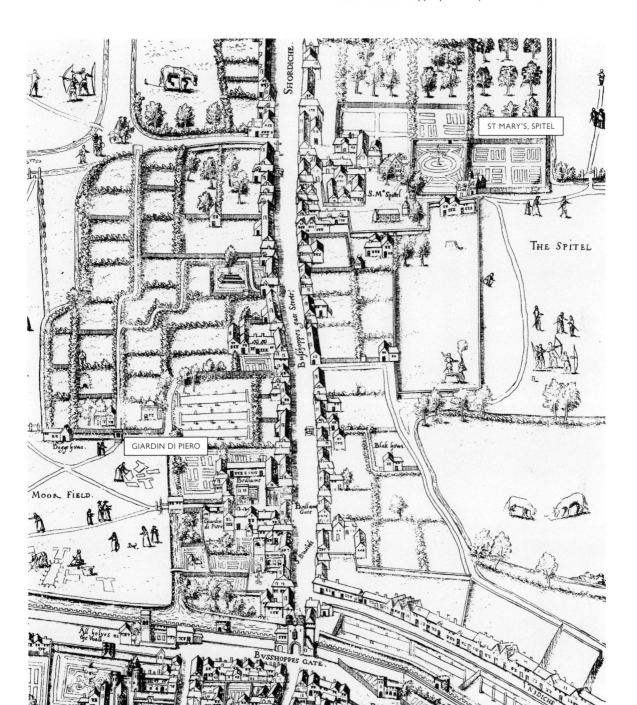

28 Giardin di Piero and compartmented gardens at St Mary's Spitel, detail from the Copperplate map of London, *c*.1559

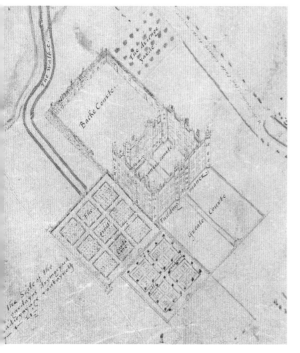

which comprised a series of concentric circles which Tresham intended to be planted with fruit trees on the outside perimeters and a regular arrangement of raspberries and roses in the inside beds (fig. 30).[25] The whole was set within a square, bordered by canals and with spiral mounts at each corner (see fig. 18). However, the mounts at the northern end of the garden were considerably smaller and less imposing than those to the south and from any of these vantage points, the circular pattern of the trees, once planted and established, would have been difficult to discern. Even at the close of the century then, Sir Thomas Tresham was laying out his new gardens in a relatively simple geometric design, apparently dictated as much by the utilitarian desire for productivity and the limitations imposed by the lie of the land as by any other aesthetic considerations.[26]

That this concept was also being taken up more generally in the gardens of England is evidenced in the garden literature referred to at the beginning of this chapter. Although these books were not published until the early years of the seventeenth century, they were written by authors who had lived and gardened throughout the latter years of the previous century and must therefore have been reflecting accepted practice at that time. Markham, Lawson and Parkinson all seem to take for granted the general layout of the garden, not suggesting anything new or radically different, but describing what appeared to be the norm.

Having said that, earlier writers such as the Elizabethan garden author Thomas Hyll do not discuss the form of the garden in the same way as their successors.[27] Although Hyll describes the layout of a garden bed, it is in functional terms: 'The beds also ought…to be trodden out narrow…and the pathes of these of a seemly breadth, for the easier reaching into the middle of the beds, or at the least freelier, to the furtherance and speed of the weeders.'[28] This is a reminder of the practical nature of gardening, a factor which must never be forgotten in the creation of any garden. Narrow garden beds, such as those shown in the maps of London and Wilton, were designed to be reached easily from paths on either side which, as Hyll points out, would speed up the tending of the garden, particularly important with the rapid turnover of vegetable crops, many of which would have been planted and harvested within a matter of weeks. The form here is dictated by the purpose.

What appears to have changed by the end of the century, however, and is reflected by later writers, is the introduction of a consideration of aesthetics. Lawson, ever the practical northern gardener, simply notes that 'the eye must be pleased with the form',[29] but Markham and Parkinson take this idea further: for them it appears that the orderly structure of the garden is an inherent aspect of its beauty.

Markham devotes two chapters of *The English Husbandman* on how to 'beautifie the garden', in which he explains in minute detail how to lay out the squares, alleys, walks and quarters. He advocates the use of gravel and sand for the alleys, walks and for in-filling the knots in the quarters because it is easier to keep them neat and tidy, without the inconvenience of 'any grasse or greene thing to grow within them, which is disgraceful'. The idea of green things destroying the beauty of a garden may seem a little odd to the modern gardener, but we can only agree when Markham points out that walking on wet grass both requires 'bootes of extraordinary goodness' and will eventually lead to the path becoming 'uglie to the eye'. For Markham, beauty is found in the symmetrically ordered formality of straight lines and geometric shapes; plants and flowers are barely mentioned. He briefly reviews plants which are suitable for bordering knots – slow-growing evergreen shrubs such as privet (he calls it 'Primpe'), box, lavender or rosemary which can be kept clipped to a precise neatness, and then in a final short paragraph at the end of this section he mentions the 'most quaint, rare' practice of planting flowers in the garden. Even then, they should be planted in blocks of 'one kinde and colour'.[30] The disadvantage of this method of filling the garden with colour is that it will not last the whole year: flowers by their very nature have a habit of blooming, fading and dying, flopping over, spreading and generally behaving in an unruly and disorderly fashion. Although for Markham the emphasis seems to be on creating a permanent structural garden which can be kept in order without these inconveniences, this is not a view reflected by all garden writers and, presumably, not one necessarily adhered to by all gardeners.

Parkinson in *Paradisi in Sole* agrees that the beauty is in the form 'as the beauty thereof may be no lesse than the foure square proportion', suggesting a symmetrical arrangement of the placing of arbours at the corners, a fountain in the middle and 'convenient roome for allies and walkes'. However, unlike Markham, he does not see flowers as quite such an untidy inconvenience, noting rather that the alleys between the squares should be wide enough to prevent harm to herbs and flowers that might be growing by the sides of the paths and therefore be knocked by passers-by. He also notes that wider paths will make life easier for the weeders to 'cleanse both the beds and the allies'.[31] By contrast, Francis Bacon, while agreeing with his contemporaries that a garden is best when square, with fair alleys and stately hedges, makes the radical suggestion that the alleys, far from being kept clear of any encroaching plants, should instead be planted with them: 'But those [plants] which Perfume the Aire most delightfully, not passed by as the rest, but being trodden on and crushed are Three: That is Burnet, Wilde-Time, and Water-mints. Therefore you are to set whole Allies of them, to have the Pleasure, when you walke or tread'[32]. While it is unlikely that Bacon was the only early modern gardener who seemed to flout the rules and appreciate plants in this way, enough has been said here to show that the 'four square form' was generally accepted as being the ideal for a sixteenth- or early seventeenth-century garden layout. The idea of the basic form of the Italian and French Renaissance *compartiment* appears to have been accepted and adopted, if not yet the detail.

The idea was adopted, that is, by those who had the resources to overcome the limitations of site and situation and create exactly the garden they wanted. Of course, most people had to make do with what they had, 'because a more large or convenient cannot be had', although Parkinson points out that even if the ground on which the garden is to be laid out is not of the correct proportions, it can soon be brought to square form by the judicious positioning of walks, alleys, squares and knots.[33] An example of this could be the garden of the Clothworkers' Hall in London, where the irregularly shaped piece of ground is 'squared up' with the careful placing of two knots (fig. 31).

This plan, by Ralph Treswell, comes from a collection of his surveys of London properties carried out in the early years of the seventeenth century, collated and published in a single volume by John Schofield in 1987.[34] There are fifty-three plans in all, of which seventeen show gardens, but there is little evidence here of their conforming to the 'ideal' form. One of the larger properties, belonging to Sir Edward Darcy on Billiter Street, has two gardens (fig. 32). In one at least, an attempt has been made to lay out the garden in a regular form – it is square and set regularly with trees and a central fountain – but the other is an irregular-shaped piece of land which simply takes up the remaining available space between neighbouring properties.

In a city in which space was at a premium, it is hardly surprising to find that this is a common feature of London gardens. Whereas some elite properties had large compartmented gardens with knots, fountains, walks and alleys conforming to the ideal, other garden owners, such as Mr Beastney or Robert Wood, had to be content with small irregular plots, limited by their surroundings – the City Wall in the case of the former and the ditches of East Smithfield in the latter (figs 33, 34). With the best will in the world, there is little scope here for the 'foure square forme'.

Despite such limitations and exceptions, it is still possible to maintain that the general aspiration among Elizabethan gardeners was for a regular, ordered, four-square layout of gardens. Having established this, and remembering the views of contemporary authors at the beginning of this chapter that the details of the garden can be left to the gardener's own devices, it now remains to discover something of what this actually meant. What were the uses of the gardens? What did they contain and how were the contents arranged? What new practices were being carried out in order to create and maintain them?

Given the paucity of information on 'ordinary' Elizabethan gardens and the tendency of later studies to concentrate on the ornamental and aesthetic aspects of gardens, it is easy to overlook the fact that the main purpose of any garden was to produce food to maintain the household. And this applied right across the social strata. A small plot of land round a peasant cottage would supply vegetables for the family, thereby providing a valuable addition to their limited diet. A slightly larger garden area would mean that fruit could

31   Garden of the Clothworkers' Hall, Mincing Lane,
detail from Ralph Treswell's *Survaye*, 1612

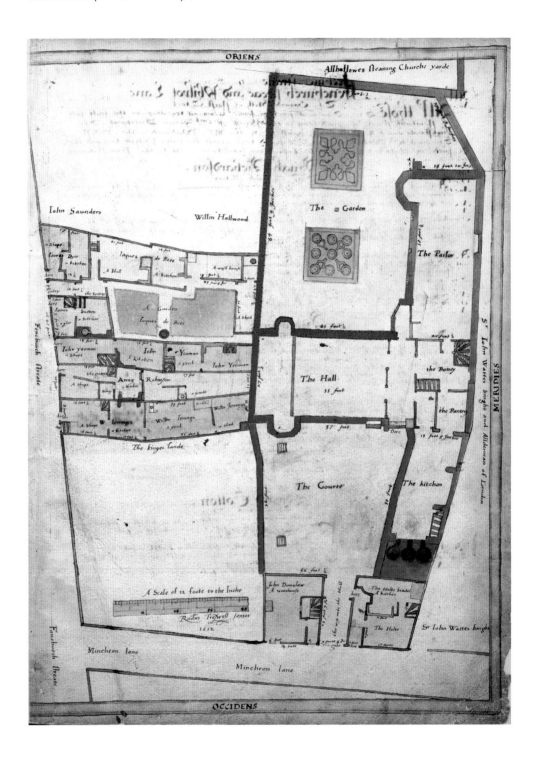

32 Sir Edward Darcy's garden, detail from Treswell's *Survaye*
33 Mr Beastney's garden, detail from Treswell's *Survaye*
34 Robert Wood's garden, detail from Treswell's *Survaye*

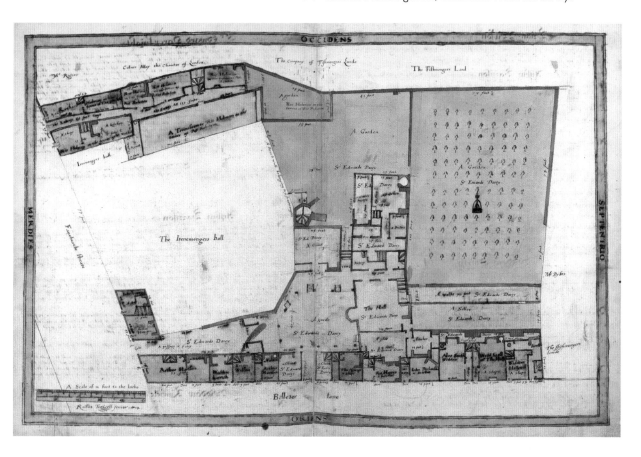

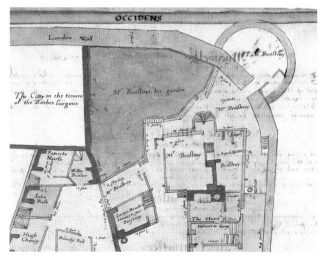

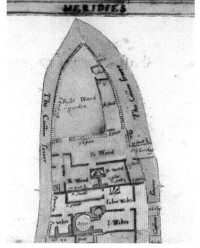

also be grown. Apples, for instance, mainly dried or made into cider, provided an important dietary supplement and, again, this is well illustrated in the c.1565 map of the artisans' cottages in Wilton, Wiltshire (see fig. 21). The more extensive gardens of the gentry and aristocracy, in addition to vegetable gardens and orchards, were likely to include fish ponds, rabbit warrens and dovecotes, and the grandest would have incorporated a deer park, all, as the contemporary observer William Harrison noted, to supply the household with the 'daily provision of…flesh'.[35] At his Nunwell estate on the Isle of Wight, Sir John Oglander recommends 'a small warren for some rabbits when thy friends come. Build a pigeon house and fit up a fishpond or two that at all times thou mayest have provisions at hand.'[36] In addition to feeding the household, provisions such as these from the garden and the wider estate, as Oglander indicates, also had a valuable role in demonstrating the owner's social standing in the community through his gifts and hospitality. As Ralph Austen later observed:

> One way to gaine, and keep a good name is by Gifts and Benefits: the worst temper of minds are wonne, and held by Gifts and good turns, it's naturall to all creatures to love those that do them good. Now who can so easily give so great, so many, and so acceptable gifts as the husbandman that yearly nurseth up multitudes of Fruit-trees, and hath store of pleasant fruits, wines and delicates made of them.[37]

It has already been seen that in medieval times it was only the elite who could afford the luxury of a purely ornamental garden, and even then it would have been in addition to a productive garden. This situation must have continued into the Elizabethan era and the reason, for example, why only ornamental gardens are depicted in portraits and other paintings is because they were indicative of the owner's social standing and because, not to put too fine a point on it, they were more aesthetically pleasing than the cabbage patch. Most of the extant evidence for gardens relates almost exclusively to the houses of royalty and aristocracy, where the ornamental and privy gardens were clearly of great importance, but even where household accounts exist, they yield little information about vegetable production and consumption since no transactions would have taken place, except perhaps the occasional buying of seeds or paying of a gardener or other labourer to dig, sow and plant. Most such work would have been carried out by estate workers and included in their regular wages, so little detail emerges. Evidence of the utilitarian nature of gardens, however, is implicit in a number of other documentary sources.

Thomas Hyll's *The Gardeners Labyrinth* (1577) is a practical guide on how and what to plant in a garden, and is concerned with the cultivation of what he calls 'hearbs and roots of the Kitchin'. (At this time, we remember, the word 'herb' had a much broader definition than now, encompassing all herbaceous plants – that is, any flowering plant that was not a shrub or a tree – rather than the narrower definition used today which is limited to specific plants used for their scent or flavour.) Hyll includes vegetables such as cabbage, leeks, onions, spinach, beets; what we might call flavouring herbs such as rocket, parsley, chervil, dill and mint, as well as 'divers Physick herbs' such as gentian, harts-tongue, self-heal and lungwort used 'in curing sundry griefes'.[38] In the second part of his book, which reads more like a herbal than a practical gardening text, he also mentions the cultivation of cucumbers, gourds, melons and 'pompons'. Although Hyll mentions some 'delectable' and 'pleasaunte floures' such as marigolds, columbine, lavender, gilliflowers, pinks and carnations, these are all grown along with the other herbs already mentioned and even they have their uses 'to beautifie and refresh the house'.[39] The petals of flowers, for instance, were distilled to make scented waters, their essential role in overcoming ever-present and less pleasant odours being easily overlooked in our sanitised times, while lavender and marigolds were used in medicinal preparations (fig. 35). Indeed, the utilitarian garden would always have flowers, because most plants, whether herbs, medicinal plants, salads, vegetables or fruit trees, produce flowers as part of their natural life-cycle: the presence of colourful blooms in a garden is not only synonymous with the pleasure garden.

Further, albeit scanty, information on the gardens of ordinary Elizabethans can be gleaned from a collection of inventories relating to Stratford-upon-Avon from the late sixteenth century. As the birthplace of William Shakespeare, records from this small town and from this period have been the subject of intense scrutiny, providing valuable insight into the experiences and concerns of the Stratford townspeople. However, even though we know that many properties were attached to significant strips of land the width of the house and extending behind it some two hundred feet, reading through these extant inventories reveals only a few references to gardens.[40] Outside spaces are referred to variously as 'the yeard' or 'the bakside' and presumably must have been where the hens, geese, pigs and 'stalles of bees' mentioned in almost every case were kept. Implements such as spades, shovels, rakes and 'dungpyks' appear reasonably frequently, but there is no mention at all of anything which one would associate specifically with gardening, such as watering pots or the wide range of tools for grafting and weeding described and illustrated in Mascall's 1572 gardening manual (fig. 36). Why this should be so is open to speculation – perhaps only those who gardened by trade owned gardening tools, or perhaps they were so common that they were simply included in the inventories along with 'all other things forgotten' – but the fact remains that the only Stratford gardens specifically mentioned are those belonging to the larger houses. Even then,

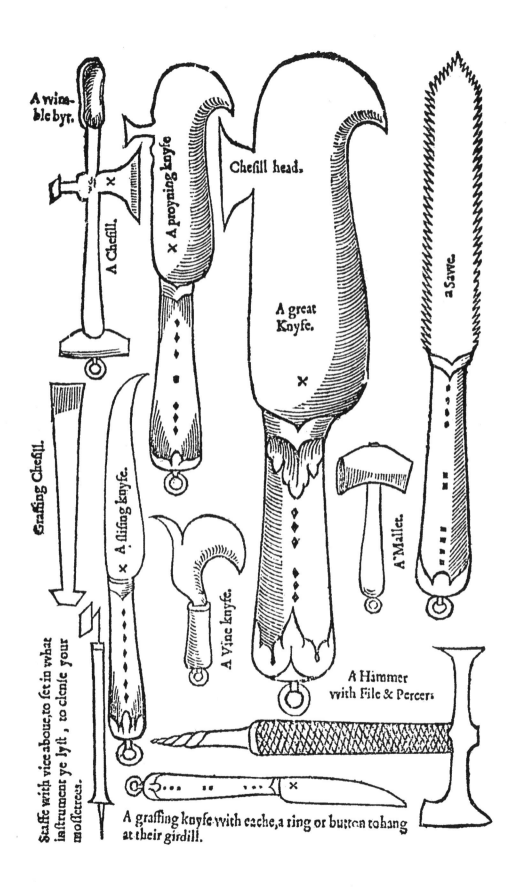

A wimble byr.

A Chefill.

A proyning knyfe.

Chefill head.

A great Knyfe.

a Sawe.

Graffing Chefill.

A flifing knyfe.

A Vine knyfe.

A'Mallet.

A Hammer with File & Percers

Staffe with vice aboue, to fet in what inftrument ye lyft, to cleaue your moffettees.

A graffing knyfe with eache, a ring or button to hang at their girdill.

although Alderman Whately's long and detailed inventory of 1593 refers to his garden, it emphasises the importance of its produce by including in the list 'ynons, garlicke, hempe, flex and the frute on the treese'.[41] From this, it seems that for the majority of ordinary Stratford townsfolk, the spaces around their houses were much more likely to be given over to practical purposes than to the luxury of ornamental use. The case for the ubiquity of the utilitarian garden still stands.

Further evidence can be found in a contemporary account of Elizabethan life: William Harrison's *Description of England*, first published in 1577. As a rural clergyman, Harrison speaks as an ordinary Elizabethan about the everyday things of life or, as an editor of his works puts it, he comes 'exceptionally close to that elusive aspect in the study of the past, what common people thought about common things'.[42] In it, Harrison describes every aspect of the society in which he lived, including a section on gardens and orchards, which raises a number of interesting points. He reaffirms that in the gardens of the 'poor commons', you will find growing 'melons, pompions, gourds, cucumbers, radishes, skirrets, parsnips, carrots, cabbages, navews, turnips and all kinds of salad herbs'– much the same, in fact, as the contents of Hyll's garden.[43] At first glance this may seem like an unusually exotic range of produce to be growing in ordinary gardens, but it seems that the cultivation of melons, cucumbers, pompions and gourds was commonplace. Indeed, there is evidence that cucumbers had been grown in England since medieval times. The purchase of seeds appears in the accounts of the Archbishop of Canterbury's gardener at Lambeth for 1322, and notes on cultivation appear in an instruction manual on planting a kitchen garden written 'for the helpe and comfort of poore people' by Richard Gardner of Shrewsbury in 1599.[44] In his *Herball* of 1597, Gerard describes and illustrates seven kinds of cucumber, four kinds of melon, seven kinds of pompion and two types of gourd. These fruits all belong to the same botanical family and grow on a similar-looking plant but produce a wide variety of fruits 'differing very notablie in shape and proportion, as also in taste'[45].

These plants are referred to by contemporary authors almost interchangeably, Gerard for instance noting that 'doubtless the Muske Melon is a kinde of Cucumber'. Pompions, or pompons as Hyll calls them, were probably what we now call pumpkins and may also have included marrow and courgette varieties, although these terms are never used. The only perceived difference between melons and pompions was that melons were preferable because they were sweeter, giving 'a most pleasant taste, like Sugar' (fig. 37).[46] It is clear that, despite the different terms used to describe them, an extensive range of varieties of this plant was being cultivated in early modern gardens.

Harrison also observes that as well as being grown in the gardens of the poor, this same produce is being 'fed upon as dainty dishes at the tables of delicate merchants, gentle-

1 *Melo.*
The Muske Melon.

2 *Melo Saccharinus.*
Sugar Melon.

3 *Pyromelo.*
Peare fashion Melons.

4 *Melo Hispanicus.*
Spanish Melons.

men and the nobility', implying that the same kind of garden produce is being grown and consumed right across the social strata.[47] Peas, beans, cabbage, carrots and turnips were staples of the national diet from medieval times, providing the whole population with some proportion at least of their diet, and there is no reason to believe that this situation would have changed much by Harrison's time.[48] Indeed, study of household accounts show that this was still the case well into the seventeenth century (see Chapter 4).

Of course, what was different as we move through the social ranks, and as identified by Harrison, was that some gardens contained more than vegetables and herbs:

> If you look into our gardens annexed to our houses, how wonderfully is their beauty increased, not only with flowers…and variety of curious and costly workmanship, but also with rare and medicinal herbs sought up in the land within these forty years; so that in comparison of this present the ancient gardens were but dunghills and laystows to such as did possess them.[49]

And later he writes:

> And even as it fareth with our gardens, so doth it with our orchards, which were never furnished with so good fruit nor with such variety as at this present. For besides that we have most delicate apples, plums, pears, walnuts, filberts, etc., and those of sundry sorts, planted within forty years past, in comparison of which most of the old trees are nothing worth, so have we no less store of strange fruit, as apricots, almonds, peaches, figs, corn [cherry] trees in noblemen's orchards.[50]

These words highlight two features in particular. Firstly, Harrison is observing a change in contemporary gardens, noting the increased range of plants that are now growing in them (a theme to be extensively explored in later chapters). Secondly, he emphasises the orchard as an essential part of any garden that was more than just a basic plot. There is abundant evidence to support this view: many of the illustrations in this chapter indicate the presence of fruit trees or at least an orderly arrangement of trees set out as an orchard. The setting up and maintenance of an orchard is the major subject of Lawson's *New Orchard and Garden*, and the earlier work by Mascall, *A Booke of the Arte and maner, howe to plant and graffe all sortes of trees*, is also, as the title suggests, concerned almost exclusively with the cultivation of fruit trees.

Like vegetables, fruit formed a major part of the foodstuffs produced by the household but, unlike vegetables, it was not essential. What it offered was variety, sweetness, seasonality and even colour to what was otherwise a fairly monotonous diet. However, to be able to grow fruit implied a degree of wealth above subsistence level: at the very least, fruit

38   Cherry, from *Tradescant's Orchard*, c.1620

trees take up more space, so more land would be required. Fruit trees take a number of years to nurture to maturity and they produce only one crop a year. They are more vulnerable to frosts and bad weather and require more skill and care to look after them. All this requires a degree of time, effort and money: to be able to place a bowl of fruit on the table, as well as offering diversity and ornament, was to display the wealth, status and hospitality of the host. As Ralph Austen noted (see p. 74), the esteem in which fruit was held is indicated by its role as a gift. For instance, in 1599 John Wynn of Gwydir sent a basket of plums to Sir Richard Bulkley of Beaumaris, apparently in return for the 'hogshead of Graves wine' sent by Sir Richard the week before.[51] Clearly, gifts of food from the garden or estate were recognised as tokens of regard between social peers and fruit, it seems, was always acceptable.[52] But even among fruit-growers and gift-givers, there was still a degree of hierarchy involved. As indicated by Harrison's *Description*, there were several categories of fruit trees: those native to this land, which could be found in any orchard in England, such as apples, pears, plums and several varieties of nuts. These required the degree of cultivation just referred to but did not need any special conditions – anyone with the space and time could grow them. However, by Harrison's time, new and exotic, or 'strange', fruits were being introduced from abroad – he mentions apricots, almonds, peaches and figs being cultivated in the orchards of noblemen. These required considerably more resources than native varieties to be grown successfully, although there is little information regarding how this was actually achieved. Lawson, while more or less ruling out the possibility of even trying to grow such fruits in the north of England where he lived and gardened, nevertheless describes how apricots, peaches and cherries were grown against walls 'to have the benefit of the immoderate reflex of the Sun, which is commendable, for the having of fair, good, and soone ripe fruit'.[53]

This was clearly also the practice of a near neighbour of Lawson's, Richard Cholmeley of Brandsby, who during the twenty-one years (1602–23) that he ran this estate took delivery of apricot trees, cherry trees from London, grape vines and peach trees for his garden. Where details are given, these are planted against the protective walls of buildings, described variously as the 'Westend', the 'Southende on the East side of the window', the 'stable end'. The apricot trees were planted against the 'haule chymbney' and on the 'Southsyde of Brandesby kylne', presumably walls which would have had the additional benefit of being warmed by fires on the other side.[54] Whether this proved a successful measure is unfortunately not recorded, but it is interesting to note such attempts to overcome the adverse cold northern climate in order to cultivate these more tender fruits.

In 1595, Robert Sidney wrote to his wife at their home in the warmer climate of the south of England in Kent: 'Sweetheart. I pray you remember to send to Jacques, the gardener, to come to Penshurst against Alhalowtyde, and to bring yellow peaches, apricots, cherry and plum trees to set along the wall towards the church'. In this case, there is evidence that this was a successful enterprise. Over the following years there are many mentions in Sidney's letters to his wife of the fruit thereby produced: 'I thanck you for your peaches, of which the King and Queen, my Lord of Suffolk and my Lord of Worcester had the most part'; 'the apricots and also the cherries are very fayre and I will divide them according to your desire'; 'the King had the cherries you sent and hee had not had then any so fayre as they were'.[55] The prestige gained from being able to please no less a person than the king with such a gift cannot be underestimated.

Building a walled garden, which created a micro-climate conducive to the growing of such fruits, appears to have been the main method by which their successful cultivation was achieved at this time. Indeed, Sidney's estate manager, Thomas Golding, reports in May 1611 that 'the long easterly wyndes and the late straunge frosts have taken all [the fruit] awaye againe, especially all suche as are generall in orchardes and stand abroad from the walls.' However, in the walled garden at Penshurst 'there were never more Appricockes, Mellicotoones and peaches'.[56]

That people were able to grow such fruits as these, only rarely seen in our gardens today, is the subject of much debate, especially as evidence indicates that the climate was in fact cooler during this period than now.[57] However, the circumstances were very different. It has already been noted that considerable time, effort and expense needed to be invested in the cultivation of these fruits, but those who had the means to do so did just that, because this was the only way to obtain them. Nowadays, it is more economic to import such fruits from sunnier climes. Our Elizabethan predecessors had no such alternative available to them.

Finally, Harrison also mentions 'capers, oranges and lemons...beside other strange trees brought from far whose names I know not'.[58] Such tender trees would have required special protection indeed to thrive in this country, so it is fascinating to try to discover how they might have succeeded. Sir Robert Sidney's father, Sir Henry, paid out £1 6s 8d in 1574 'for making the hotehous'.[59] Frustratingly, there is no further information, apart from the fact that this was clearly part of a major rebuilding programme of the house and gardens at Penshurst. Much is made too of a famous orange-house at Beddington in Surrey, the home of Sir Francis Carew, who acquired the property in 1554. It appears that Carew purchased the trees in 1562 but there is no mention of the orange-house until 1608, despite the existence of records for much of the intervening period.[60] The assumption has been that the orange-house must have been built soon after the arrival of the trees, because otherwise the trees would not have survived, but the evidence indicates other plausible explanations.

More than a hundred years later, following a visit to Beddington in 1658, John Evelyn refers in his *Diary* to 'the first Orange garden of England', noting that the trees were now sadly overgrown, but describing how they were 'planted in the ground & secured in winter with a wooden tabernacle and stoves'.[61] Where he got this information from is unclear, but it offers the suggestion of an earlier, albeit less permanent, method of protecting the trees. Markham also refers to the building of 'pentisses', a kind of sloping roof placed against a wall to provide shelter from the weather, giving further credence to this idea.[62] Another possibility is that the trees may not have survived at all and that new ones were purchased for the orange-house. Whatever the case, the fact remains that Elizabethans were at least experimenting with these new and exotic plants.

It was not just unusual fruit varieties that were being introduced into gardens up and down the country – an increasing range of 'out-landish' flowers and plants was also becoming available to gardeners in England. The wave of new plant introductions into Europe had begun with the great voyages of discovery by the Spanish and Portuguese towards the end of the previous century and by the Elizabethan era these plants were making their way to England. John Gerard, herbalist, surgeon, enthusiastic plantsman and gardener, is credited with compiling the first catalogue of garden plants in 1596, listing more than a thousand varieties growing in his own garden.[63] The following year, he published his famous *Herball*, which comprised almost 1400 folio pages containing 1800 illustrations (fig. 39). Among other information, he gives the provenance of each plant, many of which had been brought from 'forren places', although at this point in time, even if they originated in the New World, they were all brought to England from Europe. For instance, Gerard writes of 'Indian Cresses': 'The seedes of this rare and faire plant came first from the Indies into Spain…and from thence into France and Flanders, from whence I have received seede that hath borne with me both flowers and seede',[64] or of the Marvel of Peru: 'The seed of this strange plant was brought first into Spaine, from Peru…and since dispersed into all the parts of Europe: from which myself have planted many yeeres'.[65] It was not until the early years of the following century that exotic plants and seeds from beyond Europe were brought directly to England by adventurers from these shores.

Apart from Gerard's catalogue and *Herball*, however, we have little evidence of which exotic plants and flowers were growing in the generality of gardens in England at this time and it has to be acknowledged that Gerard represented the exception rather than the rule – he was both an avid plant collector and an avid gardener. He frequently refers to his garden in London in the *Herball*, often written with a detectable note of pride at his achievements: 'Of Oleander: These grow in Italy, and other hot regions by rivers, and the seaside; *I* have them growing in *my garden*' (my emphases).[66] And his reputation as a plants-

THE
HERBALL
OR GENERALL
Historie of
Plantes.

Gathered by John Gerarde
of London Master in
CHIRVRGERIE.

Imprinted at London by
Iohn Norton
1597

man was widespread: he was employed by the great Elizabethan statesman Lord Burghley to superintend the planting
of his new garden at Theobalds, Hertfordshire, in the 1570s
and 80s and it appears that he also worked in the garden of
Cecil's house in the Strand.[67]

Despite this, we know almost nothing about what was
actually planted in these gardens. Of the various contemporary descriptions of Theobalds, it is its enormous size,
the geometrically patterned layout and the artificial devices
that are commented on, although one description refers to
'Tulipps, Lillies, Piannies and divers other sorts of flowers'
and another to a knot garden being 'planted with choice
flowers'.[68] It is of course possible that the dearth of information regarding flowers is due to the reporter, who may not
have appreciated what exactly he was looking at and only
named plants that he recognised; or he may not have been
particularly interested, preferring to relate the more obviously ostentatious features of the gardens. Even the earliest
and longest description we have of an Elizabethan garden,
that written in a contemporary letter by Robert Langham
describing the entertainment provided by the Earl of Leicester for the queen in 1575 at Kenilworth Castle, although
highly detailed, has almost nothing to say about the flowers.
He describes some planted round the obelisks (fig. 40): 'allso
by great...cost the sweetnes of savour on all sidez...from the redolent plants and fragrant earbs and floourz, in foorm, cooler and quantitee so deliciously variaunt'.[69]

Again, there is no further detail, although there clearly was an abundance of flowers in
the garden. Whatever the reason, the result is that we have little information to go on to try
to re-create a picture of the place of flowers in the Elizabethan garden. Both Burghley and
Gerard were renowned for their enthusiastic interest in exotic flowers, so they hardly represent the norm. As already discussed, Hyll devotes little space in his book to ornamental
flowers, and those he mentions are common: gilliflowers, violets, lilies and so on. Harrison
mentions flowers which increase the beauty of gardens 'sought up in this land within these
forty years' but gives no examples. He 'boast[s] a little' that his own garden contains more
than three hundred varieties of herbs, 'no one of them being common or usually to be
had', but then says that this is not comparable to the gardens of Hampton Court, Nonsuch

and Theobalds, reinforcing the idea that these gardens were exceptional.[70] Robert Sidney has nothing to say about flowers in his garden at Penshurst, although Tresham apparently planned to plant roses among the raspberries in the new circular beds at Lyveden New Bield and again among the fruit trees planned for a 'new gardening quarter'.[71] Nevertheless, it is difficult to escape the conclusion that flowers were not the primary preoccupation of most Elizabethan gardeners. Where the luxury of beauty and ornamentation was present in a garden, this was to be found in the ordered form and structure. It was only in the next century that the creation of the purely ornamental flower garden came to the fore.

Having said all this, what is known of what was added to Elizabethan gardens by way of ornament? What 'devices', to use contemporary parlance, were incorporated in garden spaces? After discussing the beauty to be found in the order of the trees themselves, Lawson briefly lists other artificial ornaments for the garden, including mounts, seats, the 'shape of men and beasts' (here he is talking about topiary rather than statuary), mazes, conduits or fountains, rivers and moats, although some of these features would clearly have been limited to the gardens of the elite.

The four spiral mounts, one at each corner of the moated orchard at Lyveden New Bield, have already been mentioned and Roy Strong draws particular attention to heraldic beasts mounted atop painted wooden poles which featured in the gardens of royalty and the nobility. These can be detected in two sketches by Wyngaerde of the gardens at Hampton Court and at Whitehall Palace (see fig. 42), as well as in the background of a painting of *The Family of Henry VIII*, with its two views into the Whitehall gardens.[72] Langham also refers to the 'obelisks, sphearz, and white bearz all of stone upon their curious basez' at Kenilworth (fig. 41).[73]

Such costly displays were unlikely to have appeared in ordinary gardens, but there were other elements that were included in gardens from those of the elite to those of the lesser gentry: for example, water features including conduits or fountains, rivers, moats and ponds. For fountains in particular there is a reasonable amount of evidence. Wyngaerde's drawing of Whitehall Palace depicts a large central fountain in the garden which has been identified as the first

42   Anthonis van den Wyngaerde, *View of Whitehall Palace and the Great Garden* (detail), 1540–50
43   Detail from the 'Agas' map of London showing the Whitehall fountain, *c*.1561
44   Detail from the 'Agas' map of London showing the St Augustine's Friary fountain, *c*.1561

42   Anthonis van den Wyngaerde, *View of Whitehall Palace and the Great Garden* (detail), 1540–50
43   Detail from the 'Agas' map of London showing the Whitehall fountain, *c*.1561
44   Detail from the 'Agas' map of London showing the St Augustine's Friary fountain, *c*.1561

source of evidence for the introduction of the fountain into the English Renaissance garden (fig. 42).[74] The contemporaneous 'Agas' map also shows this fountain at Whitehall (fig. 43), as well as an elaborate fountain in the gardens of St Augustine's Friary by All Hallows under London Wall (fig. 44). This fountain is also shown on the Copperplate map along

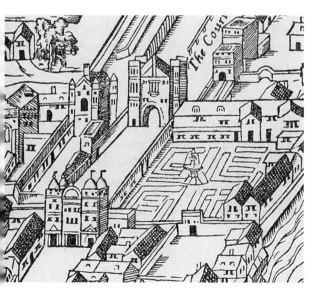

with another fountain at St Mary's Spitel (see fig. 28), and Treswell's survey of Sir Edward Darcy's orchard shows a fountain at its centre (see fig. 32).

However, although such features were undeniably ornamental, their primary purpose was utilitarian, to provide, among other things, a source of running water to irrigate the garden. Lawson enumerates further advantages: 'moattes, fish ponds, and especially at one side, a River…will afford you fish, fence, and moisture to your trees; and pleasure also'. The pleasure seems to be added as a secondary concern. Lawson also includes an ornate conduit in the centre of his garden plan, further on noting that 'If there were two or more, it would not be amiss' (see fig. 47).[75] It is interesting, and perhaps not insignificant, that this ever-practical northern gardener chose to refer to this as a conduit rather than a fountain, emphasising its functional rather than ornamental aspects, and he clearly views this as an essential part of any garden.

Seats in gardens, which appear in a variety of forms in a wide range of gardens of the time, are another notable feature. Turf seats appeared frequently in medieval gardens and can be seen in many contemporary paintings (see, for example, fig. 20). There is evidence too that the tradition of the turf seat continued long into the Elizabethan era. For instance, at an entertainment provided for the queen in 1585, it is reported that Elizabeth sat 'in a fine Bower made of purpose covered with Greene Ivie, and seats made of earthe and sweete smelling hearbes'.[76] Later, there is evidence that elaborate, more permanent garden seats in the Italian Renaissance style were being built and incorporated into the gardens of the elite, such as that which can be seen in the gardens at Llannerch (see fig. 122). And there is evidence that seats were also a feature of lesser gardens. Hyll describes the growing of climbing plants over wooden frames in order to protect the 'sitters thereunder' from the heat and the sun.[77] In another illustration, which appears in a number of contemporary texts (apparently the garden of a London brothel), two figures can be seen sitting under an arbour in the corner of the garden (fig. 45).

Lawson recommends 'seats and banks of Cammomile' along the walks in his garden and new seats were built and painted for the gardens at Penshurst in Kent.[78] That seats should be a feature of lesser gardens is perhaps not surprising, because in the larger gardens there were more permanent architectural structures such as banqueting houses and galleries in which garden owners and visitors could sit and view the gardens.[79] Less wealthy owners perhaps substituted these with sheltered seats in which they too could rest and enjoy their gardens.

Finally, attention must be turned to what is ubiquitously considered to be the defining element of Elizabethan gardens, the knot garden or maze, apparently a central feature of all gardens of pleasure in the sixteenth century. There is evidence that knots existed through-

out the sixteenth century, the earliest use of the word in relation to gardens occurring around 1500. The *OED* cites the following reference from 1502: 'For diligence in making knottes in the Duke's garden. Clypping of knottes, and sweeping the said garden'; and in 1531 the accounts for the Bridge House garden in London show payments made to William Tryme and John Davy for 'ij days cutting of knottes in the garden'.[80] Cardinal Wolsey's garden at Hampton Court was apparently 'so enknotted, it cannot be exprest'.[81] Despite such references, however, in the absence of any explicit descriptions or visual images, it

is difficult to ascertain what exactly was meant by 'knot'.[82] In fact, the word seems not to have meant anything particularly specific and early knots may have been little more than the geometric arrangement of beds into the compartments discussed earlier and as seen, for instance, in the woodcut illustration in Hyll's *Gardeners Labyrinth*, in the gardens shown on the 'Agas' map of London and the map of Conwy (see figs 16, 26, 27 and p. x) or in the simple geometric arrangements depicted in Wyngaerde's view of the garden at Richmond Palace, *c.*1550 (fig. 46).[83] In the last case, one of the compartments appears to contain a maze as well as these simple knots. Like knots, mazes had long been components of gardens but, unlike knots, their form was much more precise. However, although always differentiated from knots, it appears that during this period a maze was simply another way of infilling a bordered square within an ornamental design.

It is evident from this that knot gardens were clearly extant in sixteenth-century England; what they actually looked like, however, remains as yet unproven. The 'knotty problem of knots' – what they were, what they looked like, how they were made – is the subject of Chapter 7.

This chapter set out to discover what a late sixteenth-century garden might have looked like. It has been established that the productive elements of the garden were of utmost importance and were the major feature of most gardens right across the social strata; ornamental flowers appear to have been of relatively little importance. Where resources allowed for more than the most basic of gardens, considerations of the form of the garden were evident in the geometric layout, whether of raised vegetable beds, orchards or ornamental compartments. Italian and French Renaissance elements were clearly beginning to be introduced into elite gardens and the arrival of new plants and flowers from abroad heralded a new era of experimentation with these exotic varieties. Perhaps the most significant feature, however, was that this was the beginning of a time of change. Medieval gardens had remained much the same for centuries, but the Elizabethan era saw the introduction of new ideas and practices, evidenced in many areas of life, but also in its gardens. As Harrison noted with approval, within forty years past, gardens 'were never furnished with so good fruit nor with such variety as at present'; their beauty was wonderfully increased with flowers, costly workmanship and new plants from abroad; and gardeners were 'so curious and cunning... now in these days that they presume to do in manner what they list with Nature'.[84] So, how were these ideas taken up and developed by the gardeners of the early seventeenth century? This will be the subject of the chapters that follow.

4
CONTINUITIES

Early Seventeenth-century Gardens

New ideas and influences take time to disseminate. Although the Elizabethan era has been identified as a time in which signs of change were beginning to appear, the latest fashions – due to a host of diverse factors – were taken up only gradually and with varying degrees of enthusiasm among the gentry of the land. How such changes were received and implemented will be explored in later chapters but, from the opening decades of the new century, there is plenty of evidence to suggest that in many aspects, the preoccupations of gardeners and garden owners in fact remained remarkably similar to those of their predecessors. They were still influenced by the same practical considerations: local conditions, climate, topography, existing garden layout and costs. The balance between utilitarian and ornamental aspects were all as relevant as they had ever been, just as were the more subjective considerations of individual tastes and preferences. Although change was in the air, it is the continuities in garden design, practice and activities in the early years of the seventeenth century that will be the focus of this chapter.

The general acceptance of a geometric arrangement of quarters as the ideal layout for a garden continued well into the seventeenth century. For instance, a series of architectural plans of elite houses and gardens drawn by Robert Smythson during a visit to London in 1609, such as one of Wimbledon House, reveal designs still adhering to the regular lines and shapes of the 'four square form'.[1] That garden layouts remained little altered is also evidenced by contemporary gardening authors such as Markham, Lawson and Parkinson. These writers and gardeners all lived and worked during the last decades of the sixteenth century and their books, despite being published in the seventeenth century, must have reflected, to some extent at least, late Elizabethan gardening practice. It is almost certain that if major changes had occurred during the intervening years, these new gardening books would have reflected those changes. That they did not reinforces the point that garden layouts remained much the same throughout the period and that Jacobean gardens were still being laid out according to late sixteenth-century ideals.[2]

Such a layout is depicted in detail by Lawson in the garden plan included in his *New Orchard and Garden*, published in 1618, which shows a simple geometric arrangement of square plots, divided by alleys and bounded by fences and wooded walks (fig. 47). Of the six squares he depicts, three of them are set with fruit trees, two of them are given over to the kitchen garden and one contains garden knots. While Lawson concedes that this ideal will not be within every man's means – 'the better sort may use better formes, and more costly worke' – it nevertheless reinforces the idea of the ordered layout which was well established in the Elizabethan era. At the same time, the uses of the various compartments conform to the accepted notions of orchard and garden. The utilitarian aspects continue to be an overriding concern, with five of the six quarters given over to productive use, with

47   Plan of a garden, from William Lawson's *A New Orchard and Garden*, 1618

A. All thefe fquares muſt bee fet with trees, the Gardens and other orna‑ments muſt ſtand in ſpaces betwixt the trees, and in t.ie borders and fences.

B. Trees 20. yaid‹ a ſunder.

C. Garden Knots.

D. Kitchin Garden.

E. Bridge.

F. Condüit.

G. Staires.

H. Walkes fet wich great wood thick.

I. VValkes fet with great wood round about your Orchard

K. The Out fence.

L. The Out fence fet with ſtone fruit.

M. Mount. To force earth for a Mount of ſuch like, ſet it round with quick and lay boughes of trees ſtrangely in‑tetmingled, the tops inward, w th the earth in the midd'e.

N. Still-houfe.

O. Good ſtanding for Bees, if you have an houfe.

P. If the river run by your doore, and under your Mount it will be pleaſant.

just one – the garden knot – being purely ornamental. Lawson himself notes on his plan that ornaments should be confined to 'the spaces betwixt the trees, and in the borders and fences'. Elsewhere, he briefly describes what he means by 'ornament', and includes flowers, mounts, walks and seats, as well as water features such as a conduit (fountain), a river and moats, but it is clear from his description that for Lawson the real beauty and delight of his garden lies in the blossoms, fruits and 'comely order' of the trees in the orchard.[3]

Examination of other seventeenth-century sources also confirms that gardens were still being laid out along these lines. For instance, a detailed description in Sir John Oglander's memorandum book shows that his garden at Nunwell on the Isle of Wight contained two orchards, as well as an upper garden containing more fruit trees, a courtyard with vines and apricots, a bowling green with vines and raspberries, and a hop garden. The household accounts indicate the presence of a kitchen garden and the purchase of cabbage plants and other seeds.[4] Whether the bowling green was also used for its intended purpose is unclear, but the various elements of the garden are overwhelmingly weighted in favour of the utilitarian aspects and in fact most were already in place when, following the death of his father, Sir William Oglander, in 1609, Sir John inherited the family estate at Nunwell at the age of twenty-three. At this time, it consisted of 'the Howse on Eastnunwell, together with Bruhowse, Barne, Stables, Warren, gardens, Orchardes, Hoppegardens, Boowlingegreene, and all other thinges thereunto adjacent'. Sir John embarked on a programme of rebuilding because, as his father had been absent from the estate for many years, 'all the Ancient howsinges weare rotten'.[5]

Sir John Oglander is well known as a diarist and commentator on the society in which he lived and his commonplace books contain copious notes on any manner of subjects from the tumultuous political events of the time to practical advice on how to run the estate. They contain – to name but a few – household accounts, family history notes, recipes for medicine, advice to his children and grandchildren, marriage guidance, comments on current events and the weather. Of particular interest here are his references to the garden. By far the most detailed description of the garden, of which there is now little trace, occurs in the fourth commonplace book, covering the period from December 1631 to December 1633. Sir John writes:

> I have with my owne handes planted 2 younge Orchardes at Nunwell, the lower with Pippin, Pearmaynes, Puttes, [?Harnyes] and other good aples, and all sortes of good pears[,] in the other Cherryes, Damsons and Plumes, in the upor garden Apricockes, Melecatoons and figges. An[d] in the Parlour garden, in one knott all sortes of Gilliflowers in the other knott all sortes of ffrench fflowers, and Tulippes of all sortes[.] Some

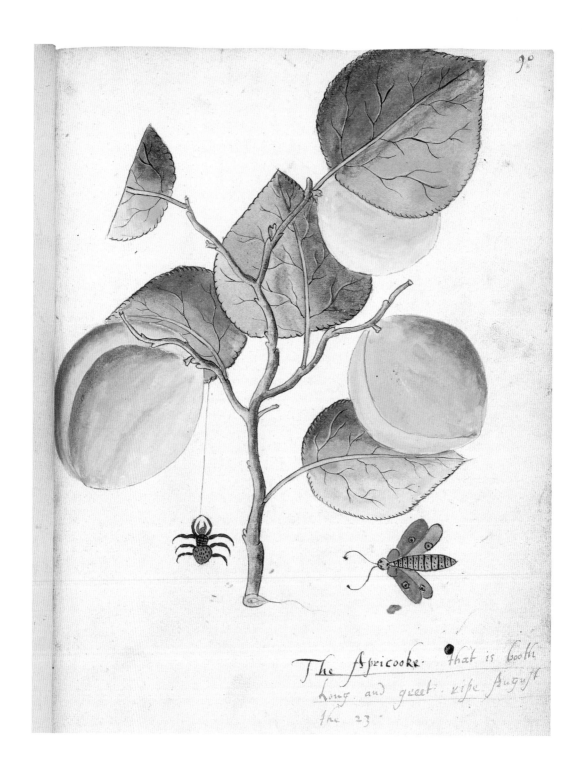

rootes cost me 10s a Roote. An[d] in the Courte, Vines and Apricockes, in the Bowling Greene the vine and frame with infinito of Raspases, Insomuch as of a rude Chaos I have now made it a ffitt place for any Gentleman and had hopes that my sonn George would have succeded me and have Injoyed the fruites of my Labours.[6]

This description provides a wealth of information, crucial to the further understanding of the layout and contents of Sir John's garden, as well as to his hopes and aspirations concerning the future of the estate. He begins by describing two orchards that he has recently planted, one with varieties of apples and pears, the other with cherry, damson and plum trees. In the upper garden, he has planted apricots, melacotons and figs. The planting and maintaining of orchards was common practice in the sixteenth century and continued into the seventeenth, contributing to both the productive and the ornamental aspects of the garden. Although not all the fruit trees planted in Sir John's two orchards can, strictly speaking, be called native species, they had all been cultivated in England for so long that they might as well have been and their inclusion in this part of the garden is neither surprising nor unusual. In contrast, the cultivation of more exotic fruits not naturally suited to the English climate, such as the apricots, melacotons and figs he goes on to mention, required an element of expense and effort indicative to a degree of the prosperity of the owner. A number of elaborate methods of cultivating such fruits had been experimented with since Elizabethan times but Oglander makes no mention of anything like this. The garden at Nunwell's southerly location on the Isle of Wight meant that it would have enjoyed one of the most favourable climates in the country and the tender fruit trees referred to here would only have required the benefit of being grown in a walled garden or against a south-facing wall in order to be protected and productive.

There is an extant map of Nunwell dated 1748 which, even allowing for changes that would have been made over the intervening century, appears to show the basic layout of Sir John's garden as he describes it (fig. 49). On this map, a clearly annotated wall is marked running directly east–west, with the south side looking over what is likely to be – by virtue of its physical location on the upward slopes of the hill – the 'upper garden', just where Sir John describes the growing of his apricots, melacotons and figs. Beyond this lies one of the two orchards mentioned by Sir John. Again, it is marked as such, although on this section of the map only the northern part of the orchard is seen: it actually extends up the hill and to the south, covering an area at least three times as large as the second, smaller orchard shown lying beyond the ornamental garden to the east.

The map section also indicates that 'the Courte' to which he refers was adjoining the south side of the house, so this would have provided another suitable location – enclosed,

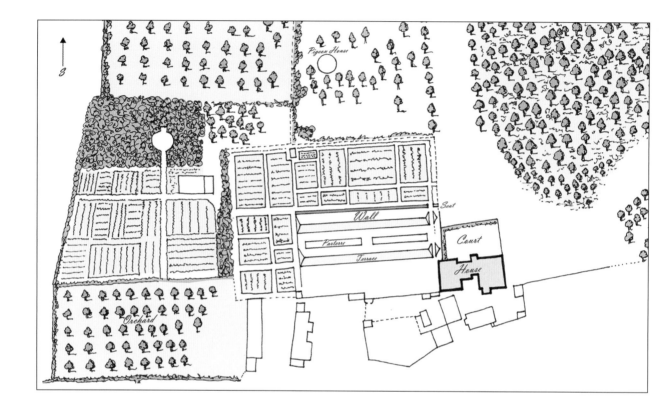

and with a south-facing wall – for the growing of apricots and vines, again, just as Sir John mentions in his description. Unfortunately, the bowling green given over to the growing of raspberries is not shown: it may have occupied the large open space immediately to the east of the house or, more likely, the rectangular area at the western end of the lower orchard. Less specifically, this map also indicates a garden made up of the conventional geometric arrangement of square and rectangular beds, divided by walks, alleys, walls and hedges.

Sir John's description indicates that, like Lawson's plan, most of these divisions were given over to productive use but his words and the map also clearly indicate the presence of an ornamental garden, shown north of the dividing wall and in front of the house and court. This area is marked as containing both a parterre and a terrace – ornamental features which by the time the map was drawn in the eighteenth century are highly likely to have replaced the seventeenth-century knot gardens described by Sir John. The details of this flower garden, or 'parlour garden' as Sir John refers to it, will be discussed later. Suffice to say here that it appears to be the only purely ornamental area of the garden at Nunwell. The basic Jacobean house built by Oglander still stands today, facing east and situated at the foot of a hill which slopes up to the south, as indicated earlier. The brick facade and frontage were added at the end of the eighteenth century and until recently Nunwell House remained the family home of the Oglanders.[7]

Despite the prescriptive advice offered on the ideal layout of a garden by authors such as Lawson and Parkinson, they also recognise that many must 'bee content with such as the place will afford them'.[8] In practice, few gardens begin as a flat canvas and few people could afford the extensive and expensive earthworks required to make them so. The positioning of the various elements of the garden therefore had to be adapted to suit the local terrain. Nunwell's gardens are an excellent case in point: the house is set at the base of a ridge with much of the land to the south of the house stretching up the hill so, while this was suitable for the planting of orchards and trees, as shown on the map and as can still be seen today, the formal gardens were all laid out in the relatively flat land to the east of the house (fig. 50). It seems that the basic layout of Sir John's gardens was dictated primarily by practical considerations regarding the lie of the land. Similarly, the garden notes of Sir John Reresby, writing in Yorkshire at the same time, describe an 'irregular, slightly organic arrangement' of walled gardens and forecourts, again suggesting a layout suited 'for convenience…rather than for aesthetics'.[9]

Although there is nothing as helpful as a plan or map to guide us, the detailed correspondence and memoranda of Sir Thomas Temple reveal, among a great deal of other information, something of the planning and layout of a new garden to be created at his home in Burton Dassett in Warwickshire. This previously unexplored evidence includes a remarkably comprehensive body of letters, written over a little more than three years between 1630 and 1634, from Sir Thomas to his estate steward, Harry Rose, who managed the house and land at Burton Dassett in Sir Thomas's absence.[10] Although he had handed over the running of the family estate at Stow to his son a number of years previously, Temple retired to live with his daughter and son-in-law at their home in Wolverton in north Buckinghamshire and it was from here that he re-established his links with the nearby house at Burton Dassett, where he was born and where, it appears, he spent much of his declining years.[11] These letters offer exceptional insight into the activities of an amateur gentleman gardener of the period and, furthermore, are backed up by notes in a detailed memorandum book kept by Sir Thomas and a letter of instruction written to 'Richard the Gardiner of Weston', who was to carry out the work on the new garden.

It is clear that, in line with what has been established as general practice, much of the garden was given over to orchards, areas for vegetable growing and to hops, but the new garden was to be a small, enclosed, ornamental garden which Sir Thomas variously refers to as his 'Parlour gardine', 'that smale gardine which will yeild to me some sweette ffloweers', 'my l[itt]le gardine at Dassett paled' (fenced), 'the paled Gardine...before the Parlour wyndow'. In his written instructions to Richard the gardener, dated 1 February 1631, Sir Thomas gives detailed information about how he wishes his new garden to be laid out.[12] The detail given here is reiterated in another letter to his steward Harry Rose, 'whereby eyther of us may have knowledge and remembrance of what I [illegible] in my Gardine', as well as by notes of his plans made in his memorandum book earlier the previous year. These documents tell us that the new garden is to be enclosed, first with an upright hedge and then 'paled' with a wooden fence, although the wall of the house and some other buildings – 'Rose his chamber', the 'woole house' and the 'milke house' are all mentioned – also appear to form part of the enclosure. In November 1631, Rose is instructed to get some good labourer to cut down a tree to provide timbers 'to finishe the dore first & pales of the Parlour gardine'. This work is to be done before the gardener, Richard, arrives. His time is clearly limited and Sir Thomas apparently intends to use his expertise to set out and plant the garden. He instructs that the garden should be divided into three parts: the first part, next to the pales, 'I would have made in a bed, wherein a single table I would have damaske roses plantted, in the second table of red roses, in the third table clove gillyflowers in the fourth table violetes in the fifth table primeroses'. The next third of the ground is to be made into an 'Alley for passage' and the last third is to be 'plantted as before' – presumably, in the same way as the first bed he describes. Vines and a variety of other fruit trees are to be planted along the various walls. Other features he mentions are the 'paled gardine dore' and 'the Quarter next to the window'.[13] From these somewhat scanty details, it is nevertheless possible to speculate on what this garden may have looked like: five 'tables', a word used a number of times by Sir Thomas, apparently simply meaning a plot of ground for planting, are arranged symmetrically in two areas of the garden, referred to at least once as 'quarters', separated by an alley, enclosed within a hotchpotch of walls, hedges and pales (fig. 51).

We have no idea of the size of this garden, although Sir Thomas refers to it as 'small' and 'little', and there is no clue to the location of the garden door or whether, in fact, it is a door out of the house into the garden or simply a door out of the garden. There is nothing about the arrangement of buildings around the perimeters of the garden, although

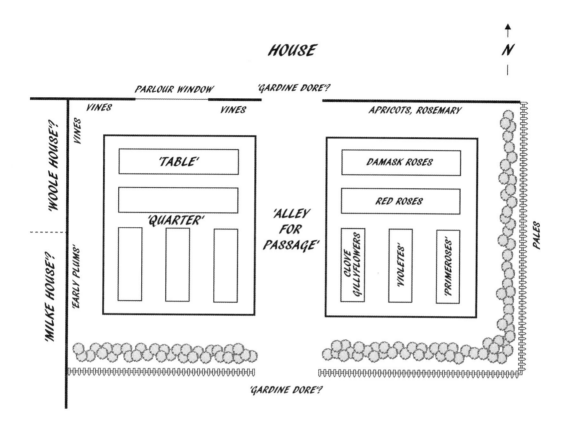

it is likely that the woolhouse and milkhouse opened out onto the kitchen yard and it is the back walls of these buildings that formed part of the garden – the east-facing walls referred to by Temple against which the early plum trees should be planted. It is likely too that Rose's chamber was situated above these two buildings, looking out over the garden or the kitchen yard. The five tables could, of course, have been laid out in any number of ways within the quarters, although there seems to have been room for only two quarters, rather than the ideal 'four square form' described in gardening literature. A quarter, as has been noted before, simply referred to a section of the garden, usually a square, but did not necessarily imply a specific number.

This garden plan provides another excellent example of how garden designs had to be adapted to suit specific local conditions. What also becomes quickly apparent is the remarkable similarity between this garden layout and that depicted, for instance, in the maps of London showing the compartmented gardens at Ely Place and St Mary's Spitel dating from the mid-sixteenth century or those used to illustrate Hyll's *Gardeners Labyrinth* from the same period (see figs 27, 28, 16), indicating once again that basic garden layouts

52 Grapevine, from *Tradescant's Orchard*, c.1620.

had changed little since then. Also, the plants Sir Thomas chose to grow in his new garden could have been found in any Elizabethan or even medieval flower garden: there is no sign here of any of the exotic new varieties being imported into England by this time; no sign even of tulips which had been a popular addition to fashionable English gardens for nigh on thirty years. So, although changes were undeniably taking place in the opening decades of the seventeenth century, examples such as this indicate that they were not necessarily being taken up by all and sundry in the gardens of rural England. The 'paled Gardine' planned by Sir Thomas Temple and laid out by Richard the Gardiner in 1631 had its roots firmly planted in the previous century.

It is worth lingering at Burton Dassett in the company of Sir Thomas a little longer in order to see what more is revealed about the horticultural techniques employed in his garden. While contemporary literature has plenty to say about gardening skills and practices, and while much of it claims to be written from experience, what Sir Thomas's cor-

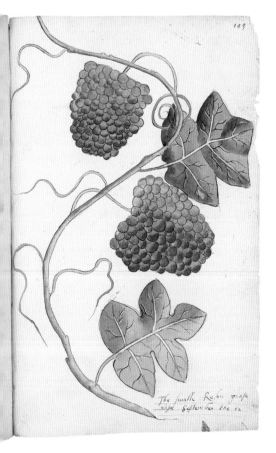

respondence offers here is a rare insight into activity that was actually being carried out in an early modern garden.

Detailed correspondence and advice between Temple, Rose and Richard the gardener in January 1631 regarding the gathering and setting of vine cuttings provide a fascinating case in point.[14] Sir Thomas had instructed Rose to ride to Stratford-upon-Avon, some fifteen or so miles to the west of Burton Dassett, to gather some buds, or cuttings, from vines (or 'grape plants', as Temple refers to them elsewhere) growing in the garden of one Mr Hall, the physician. These had been recommended to Temple by his sister-in-law, the wife of his brother Sir Peter Temple, who lived in Stratford in a house close to Mr Hall, and he had asked her 'to request the same Mr Hall...to gratifie me with some such shutes of his vine'. That news of them should have travelled so far is interesting in itself and what was special about these particular vines we have no idea – unless, perhaps, few people were growing vines in the Midlands at this time – but Sir Thomas clearly thought it was worth arranging to collect them over this not inconsiderable distance. It is pleasing to realise in passing that this Mr Hall must be none other than John Hall, the son-in-law of William Shakespeare, who inherited the house and garden at New Place after the playwright's death in 1616. It is therefore possible to speculate that Shakespeare himself planted these vines!

This interesting diversion aside, once the cuttings had been gathered, Sir Thomas issued precise instructions as to what should be done with them so they did not die, as seems to have been the fate of the previous year's cuttings. Firstly, he instructed that they should be dealt with as quickly as possible: 'the sooner after these are planted the more hope there is that they will grow'. Secondly, they were less likely to be affected by the frost if they were planted in the ground. They should be planted in a mixture of sand, enriched with 'beastes blood, if it may be gotton'. Some of the cuttings were to be set in clay and sent to his daughter's house at Wolverton for planting there. Richard the gardener had recommended taking longer cuttings, with nine or ten joints or buds, as opposed to the usual six or seven. This allows for more of the joints to be planted in the ground, presumably increasing the chances of the cuttings taking root. Nevertheless, Sir Thomas hedged his bets, and instructed Rose to plant some longer cuttings and some shorter, as before. The cuttings should be set in the planting hole 'slope wise' and, he added, the right way up, although he was confident that no one he knew would 'commit such an absurditye' as to plant them upside down. Finally, they should be planted in a number of different locations – in the same place as they were set the previous year, by the side of the woolhouse door, by the Hall door and some in the paled garden, round the Parlour window – in case this might have any effect on their growth. Unfortunately, we do not learn the fate of these new cuttings but it is interesting that, thirty years later (in the late 1650s), this method of taking cuttings was more or less reiterated by the keen gardener and writer Sir Thomas Hanmer, who from 'My owne observation of Vines' agrees that the best time to take cuttings is February, that they should be planted at an angle and that the buds should face upwards. However, he recommends shorter cuttings of just four buds in length.[15]

Temple showed equal concern for some 'bayslips', which presumably were cuttings from a bay or laurel tree.[16] Again, they should be planted as soon as possible 'lest thei should be killed' and he instructed that they should be set in a variety of locations, such as against the kitchen window, on the contraryside of the pales and some next to the door, but always in a shaded position, for they 'will prosper best in the shade, it is thought'.[17] Again, there is no record of whether these experiments were successful or not but, as most of the information from Temple was based on sound horticultural practice, there is no reason why they should not have been.

Further insight from Burton Dassett into gardening techniques includes advice from Richard who recommends the planting of flax on open ground in order to keep the weeds down, and the sowing of french beans, again to combat weeds, but also to improve the soil for future planting. He particularly recommends this for ground which has just been ploughed for the new Orchard, as it will be better for the 'prosperitye of the trees' but with less work and therefore less cost.[18] The purchase of large quantities of beans and peas for sowing is a regular feature in many sets of household accounts: for instance, at Brandsby in Yorkshire, records indicate that peas were grown as part of a pattern of crop rotation.[19] It is now known to modern gardeners that the planting of legumes such as peas and beans does indeed improve the growing conditions by 'fixing' nitrogen, an important plant nutrient, in the soil, rather than depleting it. This fact was clearly observed, if not necessarily understood, by early gardeners and farmers.

It is, in fact, highly likely that many horticultural techniques used in the garden would have been borrowed from established agricultural practice. As just mentioned, one major concern was soil fertility. At a time when artificial fertilisers were not an option, a great deal of thought had to go into how best to fertilise the soil with animal manure, compost and other nutrient-rich additives such as rotted straw, potash and sludge from the bottom of rivers and ponds.[20] Sir Thomas Temple frequently refers to cleansing his ponds and 'scowring' his ditches – presumably this is why.[21] The bailiff at Warwick Priory was paid 4s in 1620 for 'scowring' the ditch, with the added detail that this would clear the water which ran through the ditch and into the house to be used for brewing.[22] Sir Ralph Verney experimented with the use of potash on his meadows at Claydon in Buckinghamshire, regularly seeking highly prized potash-makers as tenants. As well as supplying London soap-boilers with this vital ingredient, the by-product of this process could be used as a fertiliser and it is likely that these tenants were able to negotiate lower rents in return for this valuable commodity. At the same time, the Verney estate records also reveal that Sir Ralph gave gifts of potash, dung and pigeon dung to his tenant farmers – not, it seems, from altruistic motives but in order to keep up the quality of the grassland and therefore the level of the rent.[23]

Additives such as clay, sand and lime were also applied to soil to improve its structure, drainage and nutrient-holding ability, and crop-rotation systems were implemented to ensure that the soil did not become exhausted. Nowadays, as issues such as recycling of waste materials and organic farming methods are once more coming to the fore, we have much to learn from our gardening predecessors. One early book to be published in English on agricultural practices was Fitzherbert's *Boke of Husbandry* (1534) in which he discusses the 'dongeing and mucking' of fields, suggesting a two-field rotation system for the sowing of barley followed by a crop of wheat or rye, and manuring the field before the barley is sown. He notes that cattle produce better dung than horses, but that best of all is pigeon or dove dung: indeed, he cautions that it should be applied thinly as it is so rich.[24] More than a hundred years later, Sir John Oglander was still recommending that 'piginsdoonge' is best to enrich 'Base and Barren' land, along with lime, marl (clay), sea sand and ashes, 'if you will play the good Howsband and Phisition to your grownde'.[25] In 1618, Richard Cholmeley of Brandsby in north Yorkshire records the planting of 'liquorice setts bought at Pontefract' in the middle of the dovecote garden, his description making it clear that these plants require a continual dressing of good fertiliser.[26]

That a pigeon house was a major feature of the garden at Nunwell House is seen by looking again at the map of the estate (see fig. 49); Temple noted in his memorandum book in 1629 that a mason was to be commissioned to make a pigeon house at Court Place; the household accounts for Trentham Hall in Staffordshire reveal that, in May 1635, Raphe Sutton the carpenter built two turrets for the garden, to which were added 2 windows, 200 yards of plasterwork and 300 pigeon-holes, while at Warwick Priory, Sir Thomas Puckering's steward apparently lived in a chamber above the dove house.[27] These were substantial structures (fig. 53) but, although such pigeon or dove houses could be fairly elaborate, their primary function was still a utilitarian one: pigeons and doves were raised as a source of food but also the dung was not to be wasted, instead being put to good use on the ground.

As well as pigeon dung, waste products of all kinds were used for manuring. For instance, Sir Thomas's instructions for building a new stable include the fact that it must have a 'hole to flinge the horse dung forth to the banke on the north side of the said woolhouse', while ground for plants in his new paled garden should be 'stoared with gardine stuffe' for their better prosperity.[28] The vine cuttings already discussed were to be planted in a mixture of sand and beasts' blood, and it cannot be a coincidence that Sir Thomas instructed Wattes the carpenter to provide 'a peece of Oake to make the pryve house neare the Muckhill' on the south side of the kitchen garden.[29]

In the more densely populated areas of London, where animal dung was not in such ready supply as in the country, methods of manuring and rotation used to cultivate intensively grown crops in early market gardens were held up as an exemplar in seventeenth- and eighteenth-century literature and advice. In this case, it is likely that the carts and boats bringing produce into the city's food markets (fig. 54) would never return empty but would

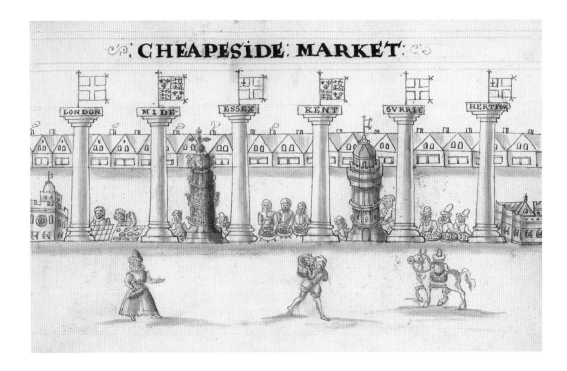

carry away with them the refuse and dung from leystalls, where the 'soyle of the hole paryshe' was collected.[30]

One of the reasons given in support of the petition for the formation of the Company of Gardeners presented to the Lord Mayor of London in 1606 was the vital role that gardeners played in taking 'awaie the dung and noysomenes of the cittie' to fertilise their garden plots.[31] Even Verney's potash-makers were known to return from selling their wares in London carrying night soil to fertilise their fields.[32]

Later in the century, John Evelyn's plan for his new garden at Sayes Court (c.1653) included a dung pit located close to the hog yard, the stable and the kitchen garden (fig. 55). The 'new house of office' (or privy) was also conveniently situated here and technology included a pump and cistern 'removed to the nursery for infusion of Dungs and watering the Garden'. It would be hard to find the cycle of waste, fertilisation and vegetable growth more graphically illustrated than here.

Another aspect of estate management from which techniques may well have been transferred to the garden is that of hedging. Along with ditching, mowing and 'work in the garden', this appears as a regular activity in household accounts. The gardeners at Warwick Priory and at Trentham Hall buy plants by the hundred for setting as hedges; labourers are

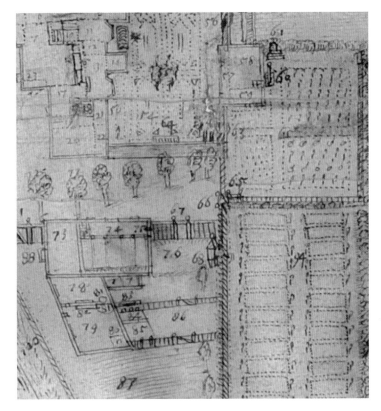

From Evelyn's key:

60   The Pumpe and Cisterne

65   The Nursery

67   The Pale, and doore to the Dunghil

68   The New House of Office over the Dunghill

73   The Coachhouse

74   The Stables

75   The hole to throw the Dung into the Dungpitt

76   The Dungpitt, lying to the Stable, Kitching garden, privy and hog-pen

77   The Hog-sties

78   The washouse

79   Brewhouse

83   The Hogg-pen

84   The Henhouse

85   The Calfe and Cowhouse

86   The Close common for the Cowes & hens

94   The Kitchin Garden

paid by the day for hedging and ditching at Halland House in Sussex; Sir John Oglander advises that a hedge should replace the timber fencing which is now rotten – 'a good white thorne hedge will doo as well as ever the pales did'.[33] It is clear that this was an important task that occupied estate labourers for much of their time.

Sir Thomas Temple devotes pages of his almost indecipherable writing to the planting, stocking and cutting of hedges with details of varieties to be used, how far they should be set apart, at what depth and so on. From the context, hedges were important for marking boundaries, for keeping livestock in and people out. For instance, he instructs Rose to mend 'the hedge by the Gateside with thornes, that Straglers may not pass hereby'. However, and arguably of greater importance, hedgerows and trees were also established and managed as a valuable economic resource. It seems that they were planted, grown and cut in a cycle of about three years to produce wood: for use in the house as fuel, floorboards, doors and repairs; for use on the estate as posts and rails for fencing; and also to provide rootstock for replanting. The surplus was sold: one of Harry Rose's responsibilities was to keep the

'wood booke', recording such transactions.[34] By the seventeenth century, woodland was becoming scarce in south Warwickshire, so being able to raise planting stock 'in house' had obvious advantages and it is clear from other sources that this kind of self-sufficiency was common practice on rural estates.[35] There are, for instance, numerous references in Richard Cholmeley of Brandsby's memorandum book to the planting, felling and selling of 'heaps' of ash trees for timber, as well as to the sale of brushwood, or 'garcel' for making fences and 'dead' hedges – that is, a hedge made of dead wood rather than living plants. At Warwick Priory, a dead hedge was used to protect the newly planted quicksets.[36] Although hedges in gardens would have served different purposes – for making divisions, for protection against the elements or, as Sir Thomas reveals, 'to drie cloathes'[37] – the techniques of raising stock, planting and maintenance would have been the same as those practised on the wider estate.

Sir John Oglander too was particularly concerned that his Nunwell estate should be as productive and self-sufficient as possible: 'Live not in Countery withoute Corne and Cattell aboute thee, for he that putteth his hande to the purse for every expence of householde is like him that thinketh to keep water in a sive', he warns his son in 1612. He adds that for provisions laid by and stored rather than being bought 'there is one peny in fower [four] spared'.[38] As well as the garden areas already noted, and aside from the purely agricultural land used for raising livestock and food crops, Sir John also variously refers to the rabbit warren, the fish ponds, the dove house and the kitchen garden – all of course essential sources of food for the household and for entertaining friends and, as discussed earlier, potential waste products for future use. He also mentions keeping bees to make mead, which he appears to be suggesting as a cheaper alternative to French wine.[39]

Contemporary illustrations of utilitarian gardens often show beehives – that in Hyll's *Gardeners Labyrinth*, for instance, depicts two beehives in the far right-hand corner standing on a covered wooden bench (fig. 56); Lawson's garden plan (see fig. 47) reserves two places as 'good standing for bees' and the plan of Sayes Court also reveals that Evelyn had a beehive in his private garden. There is evidence of beekeeping in England as far back as Roman times, the bees of course providing honey for sweetening, for making into mead and metheglin – a medicinal version of mead – and for beeswax, used in making medicinal salves and sweet-smelling candles. These were far superior to the normal tallow candles, their correspondingly high cost restricting their use to the wealthy and to the Church. In medieval times, monasteries kept beehives to provide wax for the candles and honey for use in the infirmary. Oglander suggests that candles could be made at home to save money.[40]

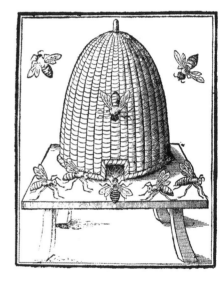

He who by Bees doth ever thinke to thrive,
Must order them, and neatly trim his Hive.

A number of instructional manuals were available for the would-be beekeeper. Some were complete books in their own right, such as Charles Butler's extremely detailed book on the management of bees, *The feminine monarchie* (1609), or John Levett's equally detailed dialogue, *The Ordering of Bees* (1634; fig. 57). Others were bound together with works on husbandry or gardening, such as Hyll's 'A profitable instruction of the perfite ordering of Bees' (1574), which appeared as an appendix to his *Profitable Arte of Gardening*, because, as he says 'most men do joyne them both together, as when they place theyr Bees in their Gardens'. And some were simply chapters included in other works such as Markham's *Cheape and Good Husbandry* (1614) or Lawson's *Country Housewifes Garden* (1618). Much of this contemporary literature drew its inspiration, as has been seen, from classical works and it appears that bees were held in great respect. 'In their labour and order at home and abroad they are so admirable, that they may be a patterne unto men both of the one and of the other...their labour never ceaseth', wrote Charles Butler in 1609.[41] Much else was written about their order of government, providing a 'lively image of a perfite commonwealth...to be ruled by one'.[42] The ever pragmatic Lawson, however, points out that 'Much descanting there is...about the Master Bee, and their degrees, order, and Government: but the truth in this point is rather imagined, than demonstrated'. He will set down only what he knows to be true through his own experience and observation, 'being a Bee-Master myself'.[43] Yet, as indicated here, there was much mystery and misinformation surrounding the lives of bees, illustrated for instance by two sixteenth-century works which both refer to the 'ruler' of the hive as the king.[44] By the following century, though, the sex of the 'master' bee had been correctly determined: Butler, Markham and Lawson all refer to her as the queen bee.

Aside from analogies relating the government of bees and men, which the authors dwell on to varying degrees, they also all focus on the practical aspects of managing bees. Various methods of housing and managing the bees are discussed, but essentially it was agreed that they must be kept warm and dry, in a sheltered area, off the ground, in a small contained hive or 'skep' as they were sometimes known.[45] These were usually made of straw or wicker and Lawson recommends standing them within a wooden frame. He comments that his friend, the honourable Lady Margaret Hoby, a near neighbour at Hackness, makes seats in the stone walls of her orchard for her bee skeps (such, perhaps, as those seen in fig. 58), but Lawson maintains that wood is better.[46] Markham recommends that the best hives are made of wood, daubed with a mortar made of lime and cow dung.[47] Lawson, referring directly to 'Mr Markham's' advice, does not 'discommend' this method, but he still maintains that straw hives are better and more commonly used 'I think, with all the world'.[48] It is interesting that such matters are discussed and debated between friends and neighbours, as well as in contemporary literature.

Although the benefits of beekeeping seem obvious, evidence – or more to the point, lack of evidence – suggests that it was not necessarily a common practice. Sir Thomas Temple refers on a number of occasions to an old beehive garden and also requests that his vine cuttings are planted 'near the bees' at Burton Dassett: whether these are two different gardens, one obsolete and being replaced by a new one, or whether they are one and the same, is difficult to ascertain but clearly bees were kept there. However, there are few details of bees, beehives or beekeeping in contemporary household accounts, except occasional passing references such as Temple's or Oglander's, or a note in Richard Cholmeley's memorandum book that mentions honey stolen from his beehives. Lady Hoby, whose beekeeping habits have been noted by Lawson, recorded in her diary in September 1599 that first she went 'to take my Beesse' and then spent the rest of the day seeing 'my Honnie ordered'.[49] The Essex

clergyman Ralph Josselyn noted in his diary in June 1645 that he had been stung by 'one of our bees'. Yet in, say, the detailed Puckering accounts, there is no reference at all to bees or beekeeping, although honey does occasionally appear in other records as a household purchase: Joyce Jeffreys, a spinster of Hereford, paid 4s for two quarts of honey in 1647, but this is the only purchase of honey noted in more than ten years of account-keeping.[50] Examination of documentary records for Stratford-upon-Avon reveal that just six out of 172 inventories dated between 1538 and 1625 itemise hives of bees among the owners' possessions and, even from this tiny sample, it can be seen that only the wealthier residents kept bees. Alderman Whateley's long and detailed inventory of 1593, for instance, lists '19 stalles of bees with hyves as they stand', valued at the not inconsiderable sum of £4.[51]

Why this should have been so is open to speculation. It is possible that beekeeping was simply so common that few people thought it worth mentioning, but perhaps there are other conclusions to be drawn if we pause to consider some of the practicalities involved in keeping bees. There was an initial expense in setting up and stocking the beehives, which then required a suitable location, presumably at least a little distance from the house. Even

this implies a degree of prosperity not available to everyone. In addition, and judging by the number of instructional books available on the subject, a reasonable degree of skill was required to keep and manage the bees (fig. 59).

Before the development in later centuries of hives with removable combs, the only ways to harvest the honey were either by driving the bees from one hive to another (an almost impossible task) or by killing the bees by smoking or drowning, requiring a continual need to maintain and replenish the stock of bees. All the manuals suggest a variety of methods of doing this but none were especially successful, so until new methods were found, perhaps the practice was by this time beginning to diminish. Hyll notes that the practice of bee-keeping goes back to classical times although we now know from archaeological evidence that honey had been collected from beehives at least as far back as ancient Egypt and beyond.[52] However, by the sixteenth century, sugar was becoming increasingly available, so perhaps home production of honey was not seen as such a necessity. As noted earlier,

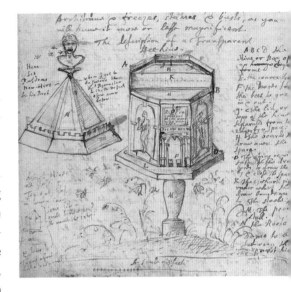

Oglander recommends keeping bees for making mead but at the same time advises always keeping in a good store of sugar, so in this case the honey was not necessarily intended for sweetening food. Hyll includes his treatise on beekeeping with his earlier publications but it is not included in his later book, *The Gardeners Labyrinth*. And, although Lawson includes provision for beehives on his garden plan, it is only as an optional extra: 'good standing for bees, if you have a house'. He begins his chapter on the 'Husbandry of Bees' by suggesting that the keeping of hives is as much for ornament in the garden as 'flowers, or forme, or cleanness'. Well-ordered bees, Lawson writes, 'make a pleasant noyse and sight', although he also notes that if they thrive, they will yield a great profit.[53] Furthermore, although beehives were placed in orchards and flower gardens because it was recognised that they fed off the flowers to produce the honey, what no one realised at the time was the vital role that bees play in pollination. As noted by Lawson, bees will thrive in a productive orchard, but we now know that this is a symbiotic relationship in which the bees play an essential part in ensuring the flowering and fruiting of the orchard.

By the 1650s, new forms of beehive were being experimented with: in 1655, Samuel Hartlib produced *The Reformed Commonwealth of Bees*, a genuine, if ultimately unsuccessful, attempt to promote the potential profits to be made from properly managed beekeeping, as a practical way of contributing to the improvement of the English economy, a national obsession in post-Civil War Britain.[54] Hartlib's book contained illustrations and descriptions of three radically new kinds of hives, which attempted to address the problem of how to harvest honey without having to destroy the stock of bees. However, they proved expensive to build and were not generally adopted, ultimately becoming an extravagant novelty item: Evelyn had a transparent apiary in his garden at Sayes Court. It was a gift from Dr John Wilkins, the Warden of Wadham College, Oxford, who had set up a number of these experimental hives, designed by Christopher Wren, in the gardens at the college.[55] Evelyn notes in his diary that some years later (on 30 April 1663) 'his Majesty [Charles II] came on purpose to see and contemplate [this hive] with much satisfaction'. Samuel Pepys also notes in his diary that he visited Evelyn's garden on 5 May 1665 and saw, 'among other rarities', the transparent beehive in which 'you may see the bees making their honey and combs mighty pleasantly' (fig. 60).[56]

So, although the utilitarian nature of beekeeping for producing honey and wax was still relevant, it could be argued that throughout this period the function of beehives in the garden was becoming more of an ornamental one. There are other examples of this conflation of utilitarian and ornamental: dovecotes and pigeon houses have already been discussed, but also included in this area could be fish ponds and ornamental water features, herb and flower gardens and the keeping of waterfowl, including swans. These elements will be discussed in detail in Chapter 8.

The supplying of the gardener with tools is an expense noted in most account books and one which adds a little more detail to our picture of the work being carried out in these gardens (fig. 61 and see figs 36, 74). As might be expected, there are payments for items such as spades, hatchets, rakes, shovels, scythes and scythe stones, a variety of hooks, cutting knives, wheelbarrows and a garden roller.[57] However, such purchases are few and far between: either the tools lasted a long time as a result of meticulous maintenance and repair, or perhaps in some cases they belonged to the gardener himself and therefore would not appear in the household accounts. More unusually, there are also payments for 'powder and shot' for the gardener. Presumably this was as some kind of pest control: crops of all kinds would need to be protected from birds and rabbits.[58] Elsewhere, there are records of payments for 'nayles', 'skinnes' and 'lether' and it is likely that these would have been nails and leather ties made from horse-hide used, as mentioned in the accounts of the Reynalls of Forde in Devon, 'to nail up the boughs of the trees in the garden' or similarly at Warwick Priory to nail 'my fruit trees to the walles'.[59] Other gardening equipment mentioned includes baskets, truggs, canvases and nets, either for gathering or protecting flowers, vegetables and fruits. The household accounts of Sir Thomas Pelham are particularly interesting for their mention of specific gardening equipment such as watering pots, a grafting saw and 'two earthen pots for the nursery'.[60] Two tin watering pots were also bought for the gardens at Warwick Priory.[61]

Purchases of garden seeds and vegetable plants are recorded in all the sets of accounts, giving an indication of the kind of produce that was being grown in gardens. Peas and beans, as already noted, seem to be ubiquitous and are purchased in large quantities variously measured in bushels, pecks and gallons. It has been established that they were grown as part of a crop rotation system to help maintain the fertility of the soil and in this case it is probable that they were used as fodder for horses, sheep, pigeons and pigs.[62] However, there is no doubt that these legumes were also grown in a garden context and for human consumption. Gerard,[63] Richard Gardner of Shrewsbury[64] and Parkinson all refer to them

as garden vegetables, although Parkinson observes that they are planted in fields as well, not for animals, but as food for the 'poorer sort'. At the same time, he also notes that peas are 'a dish of meate for the table of the rich as well as the poore', although he adds that the youngest and sweetest peas, in other words, fresh green peas, are reserved for the 'better sort'. The rest have to make do with the 'later and meaner kindes', which are more than likely to have been dried peas by the time they reached the cooking pot.[65] The accounts of John Willoughby of Leyhill in Devon show a payment to four women for planting beans, while his near neighbours, the Reynalls of Forde, make a similar payment to four 'pea-setters'.[66] Household accounts right across the country list regular payments for carrot seed, onion seed, cucumber seed, turnip seed and cabbage plants.[67] As has been discussed elsewhere, peas and beans, along with other staple vegetables such as carrots, cabbage and turnips, had formed the basic diet right across the social strata from medieval times and, particularly in the more remote rural locations, there is no reason to presume that this would have changed much.

There is also no reason to assume that the range of seeds grown was limited to the varieties mentioned, because in many cases normal practice would have been to collect seeds from plants and herbs to sow the following year; because they were not being purchased, they did not appear in the household accounts. Richard Gardner of Shrewsbury devotes the first chapters of his 1599 book on kitchen gardening to the growing of plants specifically for seed production, which were sown and cultivated separately from the crops grown for harvesting and eating.[68] This method, however, was not suited to all plants: as Hyll notes, 'Peas and Beanes for the Garden must have their seed changed every yeare, if not, the increase will be very smal, and grow lesse and lesse'.[69] As has been seen, early seventeenth-century accounts certainly bear out this practice.

Some records do indicate the purchase of an extended range of vegetable seeds for the garden. The Pelham accounts, for instance, record payments for parsnip, radish, lettuce and 'colliflower'.[70] Parkinson notes that cauliflower, or 'Cole flower' as he calls it, was seldom grown in this country because good seed was hard to find and it was difficult to germinate, although he adds that it has a much more pleasant taste than cabbages of any kind and 'is therefore of the more regard and respect at good mens tables'.[71] Perhaps this is why the gardener at Halland House persevered with its cultivation: from Parkinson's comments regarding peas and cauliflowers, it seems that there was a degree of hierarchy and demonstration of wealth and status even in the growing and eating of vegetables, and the Pelham family was one of the richest in Sussex.[72]

In addition to seeds, several garden vegetables were regularly purchased as plants. Cabbages and coleworts were grown ubiquitously and plants for setting in the ground were purchased by the hundred (fig. 62). Coleworts were grown as a 'cut and come again' crop – that is, regularly cutting the young leaves and letting them re-grow, rather than waiting, as was the case with cabbage, for it to grow larger and form a heart. Presumably, one reason coleworts were popular was because they yielded a crop quickly.

There are also occasional references to the purchase of artichoke plants: Jo. Grover is paid 2s for 'hartichoke plants' for the garden at Halland House in Sussex; at Gorhambury in Hertfordshire, there is a payment of 4s 6d for '120 hartichoke plants from London' and in Herefordshire, Joyce Jeffreys pays a gardener for '2 daies dressing hartichoks'.[73] Purchase of these plants seems quite expensive compared to, say, cabbages which could be bought for 4d the hundred.

The artichoke was in fact a relatively recent re-introduction into England; its history is complicated and unclear, but it seems that it was originally introduced by the Romans but

then departed with them back to warmer climes.[74] It next emerges gracing the tables at the court of Henry VIII and from then on it gradually appears in the gardens of early modern England.[75] William Harrison makes no mention of it in his list of vegetables growing in Elizabethan gardens, but there is a reference and illustration in Gerard's *Herball* of 1597, where he says it can be eaten raw or boiled, being 'accounted a dainty dish',[76] and by Parkinson's time he could claim that 'the manner of preparing them for the table is well known to the youngest housewife'.[77] The artichoke is a member of the thistle family and contemporary illustrations reveal various forms, some of which look like the familiar globe artichoke, others of which look far more like a common or garden thistle – apparently, both types were eaten (fig. 63).[78]

64 'The perfecte form of an Apple tree',
from William Lawson's *A New Orchard and Garden*, 1618

To add to the confusion, there is mention of artichokes being set in a garden in north Yorkshire, but these are recorded as being Jerusalem artichokes, a new introduction from North America. Richard Cholmeley notes their delivery from the gardener of a fellow Yorkshireman, Sir Thomas Fairfax. They appear to be a gift: 'His ladye sent me 31 setts', although Cholmeley had to pay the carrier for his time, his dinner and his horse.[79] However, as Parkinson is at pains to point out, these were not artichokes at all, but a root vegetable, thought, he believed, to be a variety of potato because of their similarity in looks and taste to that other recently introduced vegetable from the Americas. They had been mistakenly named artichokes 'from some ignorant and idle head', says Parkinson, because the boiled roots tasted like artichoke hearts.[80]

Aside from growing vegetables and herbs, the cultivation of fruit trees, and more particularly the cultivation of exotic fruits, continued to be of crucial importance into the seventeenth century. As well as the obvious benefits, the role of fruit as a gift and in hospitality remained a prestigious indicator of social standing within the community: Parkinson notes for instance that 'figges are served to the table...as a dainty banquet to entertain a friend, which seldom passeth without a cup of wine to wash them downe'.[81] At the same time, new techniques for its successful cultivation were instigated and developed as more exotic fruits and plants were introduced from abroad.

Evidence of such gifts from household accounts is scarce because, of course, no money changed hands. There were payments, however, which it has to be assumed were tips, given to the bearers of the various gifts between households. Sixpence was given to 'baylief Jenkins messenger that sent me olives' and a shilling to 'my cozen Nicolas Kemis his servant that sent me apples' by the Aubrey household in Llantrithyd in south Wales. Similarly, 'Lord Careys gardener bringing peaches', 'Lady Jenings gardener with plums' and 'Lady Winwoods footman with grap[e]s' were all paid at the kitchen door of the home of the Earl and Countess of Sussex at Gorhambury.[82] Gentry correspondence offers a little more information. For instance, gifts of fruit and other produce are regularly given and received by the Wynn family of Gwydir in the Conwy valley. John Wynn of Gwydir's gift of plums to Sir Richard Bulkley of Beaumaris in return for 'the hogshead of Graves wine' has already been mentioned, but other gifts from Beaumaris include, in December 1618, 'claret, pickled quinces, six lemons, a dozen small oranges and 100 chestnuts and walnuts for my Lady'. Another entry in 1620 mentions that although a buck is to be sent to the Bishop of Bangor, the promised lemons cannot be sent because they are under lock and key in my lady's closet.[83] Oranges and lemons appear frequently in the context of gifts, but it is not clear whether they have been 'bought in' (there are references elsewhere to the costs of oranges and lemons) or whether they have been grown in the gardens of north Wales. This, however, seems extremely unlikely, particularly in view of a letter sent from Sir John Wynn to his father in January 1613, who writes from Moulins in central France that there are 'orangers, citrioners and meurtriers' growing in the garden, but which, he says, have to be removed in winter to a house made purposely for them and which would therefore bring no profit but much pain to growers in England.[84] Boxes and baskets for 'orinnges and lemons' also appear in the Gorhambury accounts but, again, it is not at all clear where these fruits have come from.[85]

Other fruits we know were cultivated with great success. Robert Sidney's gifts of fruit to the king and queen and to his friends at court have already been mentioned, although at times his garden seems overly prolific: 'I thank you for the letter and peaches', he writes to his wife in September 1609, 'but you send me such store as I have not friends enow to bestow them on'. Sir Thomas Temple receives various fruit trees from friends and family and there is no reason to believe that the arrangement was not reciprocated.[86] Because of the degree of knowledge and resources required to grow fruit trees successfully, their cultivation remained an important indicator of the wealth and status of the garden owner, whether manifested by the sight of an extensive and flourishing orchard or through the production of exotic fruit for gifts or for the table.

The Graundd Cornation
peach Ripe September 4

An early seventeenth-century portrait of the family of Sir Thomas Lucy hanging over the fireplace in the Great Hall at Charlecote Park in Warwickshire confirms this view (fig. 66). Portraits such as this played a crucial role in the assertion of status, including as they did details that reflected the wealth and preoccupations of the family. The Lucy portrait shows the family arranged in a richly carpeted room and includes two dogs, a falcon on a perch, books on the table and a view of the garden in the background. The importance of the role of produce from the garden is emphasised by the prominent position in the picture of a bowl of cherries being held out by the eldest daughter to her mother, who is depicted taking some of the fruit out of the bowl. The eldest son and heir is climbing a flight of stairs from the garden and into the room, bearing a bowl of peaches – a fruit which Parkinson describes as 'well accepted with all the Gentry of the Kingdome'.[87] Furthermore, the fruit is not simply depicted in the portrait: it is shown being offered by the eldest children as a gift to their parents. The fact that Sir Thomas Lucy has chosen to display these particular aspects of his household in this portrait reveals their significance as symbols of his family's status.

While the importance of growing fruit may have remained constant, experiments with new methods of cultivation began during the seventeenth century, although not always with much success. The tried and trusted method of growing fruit trees within the protected micro-climate of a walled garden continued – as remarked earlier, Oglander grew 'Apricockes, Melecatoons and figges' in his walled garden on the Isle of Wight and Temple planted apricots and grapes in his parlour garden along the south wall of the house. He intended to allow the grape vines to climb up onto the roof tiles to 'be there the better ripened'. And in cooler northern climes, Richard Cholmeley was additionally taking advantage of walls warmed by fires to bring on his apricot trees.[88]

As more exotic and tender fruits began to be brought into England from the Continent, gardeners realised the critical importance of protecting these plants from the cold and of trying to emulate the conditions in which they grew naturally. A variety of ingenious methods for doing this were explored and Markham in particular offers a number of suggestions. In *The English Husbandman* (1613), he talks of 'divers Noblemen, Gentlemen' who have expended time, labour and cost in trying to preserve their fruit trees from inclement weather, but to no avail. However, the one method he has seen 'in one of the greatest Noblemens gardens in the kingdome' which is 'certaine and unfallible' was to build a large 'pentisse'[89] at the top of the wall and over the tops of the trees which are planted against it, which will protect the trees from damaging storms, frosts and winds.[90] In his next chapter, on the cultivation of vines, Markham describes in explicit detail an elaborate construction of bricks, wood and glass, which sounds remarkably like a greenhouse, in which to grow the grapes. Once the structure is built, the vines are planted outside it, but next to suitable square holes left in the brickwork at the bottom, so that 'as your Vine groweth, you shall draw it through those holes, and as you use to plash the Vine against a wall, so you shall plash this against the glasse window, on the in-side'. Thus the sun will hasten the ripening and increase the size of the grapes; the house will protect the fruit from inclement weather and they will hang 'unrotted or withered' until Christmas.[91] Regrettably, evidence of such a house ever being built has yet to be found, although the wooden pentisses Markham mentions appear similar to those described by Evelyn when he visited Beddington in Surrey – it is even possible that Sir Francis Carew is the nobleman to whom Markham refers.

In Markham's other great work on gardening and husbandry, his edited edition of Charles Estienne's *Maison Rustique*, published as *The Countrey Farme* in 1616, he addresses at length the problems of growing citrus, particularly orange trees. He begins by acknowledging 'their great tendernesse and incredible daintinesse' and actually admits that they will do much better if left where they are in their native soil. Nevertheless, 'if it please the Lord of the Farme to procure them', here is his advice.[92] As was discussed in Chapter 1, however, given that this book is a translation from French and that Markham simply augmented the text where he saw fit in order to include information specifically suited to conditions in England, it is not always easy to work out where he is referring to Continental practice and where to English. We know, for instance, from John Wynn's letter to his father, referred to earlier, that even in central France, the citrus trees were removed in the winter to a house made purposely for them.[93] Markham mentions twice the practice of removing the trees 'into vaults under the earth, carried thither upon little Wheelebarrowes'. However, his own advice is that orange trees will do better planted in the ground, so it is obvious that removing them to a warmer place in the winter is not an option. Instead he describes how the trees should be covered 'with a good store of boughes, held up with props, or else to make for everie one of them a lodging of Mats, with a door in it open to the South'. Great care must be taken to ensure that the plants are completely covered, although the tops and sides should be given plenty of room and not be 'pinched'. He cautiously advises that if the weather is 'gentle, meeke, and faire' the covers may be opened so the tree 'may enjoy the present heat of the Sunne'. He also recommends the lighting of fires around the trees in periods of extreme cold. Whether any of these measures was successful or not is unrecorded, and doubtful.[94] Parkinson noted in *Paradisi in Sole* that as orange trees are 'so hardly preserved in this our cold climate' he will not trouble to give 'any further relation of their ordering'.[95] Elsewhere however, like Markham, he passes on advice to those who insist on keeping them, observing that some plant them in 'great square boxes' so that they can be moved into a house or 'close-gallerie' for the winter, others cover them with boards or cloths, while others protect them with the warmth of a 'stove' (a kind of heated winter-house).[96] Nevertheless, he concludes that 'no tent or meane provision will preserve them'. Elsewhere Parkinson dismisses the practice of forcing plants in hot stoves because, in his experience, they will perish.[97]

What is fascinating to note here is that while early modern gardeners appreciated the need for good soil, water and warmth if tender plants were to thrive, they had not yet identified the last factor that is essential to plant life, which is, as we now know, light. They realised the importance of the sun but only because it gave warmth; it was only at the end of the eighteenth century that scientists observed the link between sunlight and plant life and the essential process of photosynthesis was discovered. It is no wonder that these plants, being brought from the long, bright, sunny days of more southerly climes, could not thrive: not only were they having to adapt to the short, gloomy, overcast days of the English winter (and sometimes summer), they were also, by being wrapped up or brought into closed galleries to protect them from the cold, being unwittingly deprived of essential light. More by luck than judgement, the practice of removing the covers on mild days, as advised by Markham, was probably the only thing that saved them. Thirty years later, although still none of this was understood, the practice of moving tender plants into a winter-house – with large south-facing windows to trap the warmth of the sun – was well established, the advantages being positively advocated by innovative gardeners such as Sir Thomas Hanmer and John Evelyn (discussed in detail in Chapter 9).

One other area in which a change in the growing of fruit can be traced over this period is in the cultivation of vines, but what is noticeable in this case is a *decline* in the practice. It is well known that in Roman and medieval times, the growing of vines in England was common but, by the end of the seventeenth century, viticulture was no longer being embraced with much enthusiasm. Although garden writers all included a section in their books on vines, they issued their advice with caution. Parkinson observes that it is 'a fruit-lesse labour for any man to strive these days to make a good Vineyard in England', noting that as the weather is no longer warm enough to ripen the grapes, it is not possible to make any good wine. He suggests instead that vines be grown for grapes to eat as fruit.[98] As we have seen, Markham recommends growing grapes, if one must, within the shelter of a house in the garden, because they will not 'by any meanes prosper in many parts of our kingdome'.[99] Lawson dismisses vines as something which only thrive in other countries.[100] Household accounts and other records which refer to vines are all located in the south of England: at Forde in Devon there is a payment for pruning the vines; Oglander and Temple both refer to the growing of vines, but in neither case do we have any idea whether or not this was a successful enterprise, and Christopher Browne writes from Sayes Court in Kent in 1642 to his daughter in Paris that 'the season hath continued so cold that our grapes which were wont to now be rype, are altogether [?greene] and skarse [scarce]'.[101] From this kind of evidence, that is, from contemporary observers 'on the ground', it certainly seems that by this time the climate in England was noticeably cooler than it had been in previous centuries and the conditions were simply no longer suitable for the cultivation of vines.[102] Having said that, Parkinson offers an interesting alternative explanation for this decline, putting it down to Henry VIII's dissolution of the monasteries in the sixteenth century: 'I have read, that manie Monastries in this Kingdome, having Vineyards, had as much wine made therefrom, as sufficed their covents [sic] yeare by yeare: but long since they have been destroyed, and the knowledge how to order a Vineyard is also utterly perished with them'.[103]

Contemporary evidence, therefore, indicates that, despite the possibilities and aspirations of the Jacobean reign, in many aspects, established gardening practices continued into the new age. Garden layouts remained essentially the same, although experimentation with new plants and techniques for cultivating them continued to be explored, many practices simply continued and, for the time being at least, the utilitarian aspects of the garden remained of primary importance.

And in many aspects, the work of the gardener also remained much the same during the early years of the seventeenth century as it had been during the Elizabethan era (fig. 67). But who was working in these gardens? Who were these gardeners? Who was directing and paying for the work? And what, exactly, was the nature of that work? The following chapter will consider these questions and attempt to put some flesh on the bones of the early modern gardener.

5

THE GARDENERS

Attempting to define the early modern gardener is not as straightforward as it might at first appear. He, and even more markedly, she, is a frustratingly elusive character, clearly vital in the creating and maintaining of sixteenth- and seventeenth-century gardens but, due to the essentially ephemeral nature of their work, maintaining a somewhat crepuscular presence. Despite this, careful study of references in household accounts, correspondence and memorandum books, as well as in contemporary literature, makes it possible to piece together a picture of the early modern gardener at work (fig. 68). While in many ways the role of the working gardener continued to be much the same throughout the period, some changes are discernible. At a practical level, for instance, gardeners were now required to keep up with the changing times and learn new skills such as how to deal with unfamiliar plants arriving from overseas, but at another level, there is evidence that the status of the working gardener, like the activity of gardening itself, became more elevated during this period. The continuities and changes in the role of the gardener in his garden are the subject of this chapter.

Who exactly, then, was working in the early modern garden? Available evidence identifies a wide range of workers employed in gardens, from unskilled labourers hired to undertake tasks such as hedging, ditching and digging, paid by the job, the hour or the day, or 'weeding women' employed by the hour during the summer months, to highly skilled gardeners who were hired seasonally by the hour or day. Others were employed as permanent members of the household. In that case, they seem to have come relatively high in the hierarchy of servants: at Quickswood in Hertfordshire, for example, the gardener, Cadwallider Morgan, was paid the same rate of £5 a year as the clerk for the kitchen, the yeoman of the wine cellar, the gentleman of the chamber and the chaplain. At Hatfield House, the 'Master gardener', Thomas Tudor, commanded a salary of £25 per year and was apparently the highest paid member of the household.[1] The vast gardens at Hatfield House were renowned throughout the country at this time, so perhaps we should expect their gardener to be exceptionally highly skilled and therefore suitably rewarded. Elsewhere, a portrait of Thomas Wentworth and his family (c.1575), includes a portrayal of his gardener, who is shown dressed in the household livery, again indicating his important position within the household (see fig. 76). Although it is difficult to make generalisations on such scant information, from these examples it is fair to assume that in some cases at least, the gardener was a valued member of the household, well-recompensed for his knowledge and skill and recognised as having served his apprenticeship and learned his trade from a master.[2]

The qualities of the ideal gardener are discussed by the contemporary gardening authors already cited: Hyll states that a 'fruitfull and pleasant Garden can not be had without the good skyl and diligent minde of the Gardener'.[3] According to Markham, the gardener is required to possess 'three especiall vertues, that is to say, Diligence, Industry, and Art', but noted that while the art can be taught, the first two virtues must be 'reaped from Nature', for without this love and labour in his blood 'it is impossible he should ever prove an absolute gardiner'.[4] Lawson cites the qualities of the ideal gardener as 'religious, honest, skilfull'. He also stresses the importance of rewarding the good gardener well for his work: not only will he have received his wages, but also these should be augmented with surplus produce from the garden after the house has been served.[5] It seems that, however expressed, the gardener was expected to possess certain skills and qualities above those of the ordinary labourer or estate worker. Clearly, good gardeners were to be sought and retained and, from the available evidence, it is possible to discern this difference between the work of 'the gardiner' and the work of the various labourers employed 'in the garden'.

The work of weeding women, for instance, appears regularly in household accounts from all over the country. This task was often undertaken by the wives of other labourers employed on the estate. At Halland House in 1636, Goodwife Rolfe, who becomes Widow Rolfe, continues to be paid for weeding even after her husband has died. Goodwife Upfold and Goodwife Starre are paid 2*d* a day for seventeen weeks' weeding in 1638, a rate which by 1641 appears to have increased to 3*d* a day.[6] By contrast, in the same period 'five poore women' are each paid 6*d* a day for weeding at Gorhambury, and at the Llantrithyd estate of Sir Thomas Aubrey, £3 is agreed for weeders from May to November. However, we do not know how many workers there were or for how many days a week they were employed.[7] Valuable as they are, examples such as these illustrate well the difficulties of interpreting this kind of evidence: as there was no consistency in the way such records were kept, it is not always easy to make direct comparisons, and generalised conclusions should therefore be drawn with caution. For example, just as it seems safe to make the assumption that weeding was a regular task undertaken by women, we find that during the summer of 1640, four men were paid 3*d* a day for weeding at Holme Lacy in Herefordshire.[8] Nevertheless, regular weeding clearly was one important role that women were paid to carry out in the garden. Other such tasks for women included gathering herbs and flowers for the still-house, planting and setting violets and in one case, planting beans at Leyhill in Devon. Housemaids were also known to help out in the kitchen garden.[9]

The heavier, menial, outdoor work – such as mowing, hedging and ditching – was done by male labourers who were also paid by the day but generally at a higher rate, presumably because the work, although still unskilled, was harder. At Gorhambury in 1638, Goodman Mason receives 10*d* a day for 'digging and hedging the kitchen garden'; at Trentham Hall in 1635, Hugh Lovatt is paid 'for 5 dayes labour at 8d per day filling the Cort with soyle'; at Stow in Buckinghamshire in 1625, Michaell Kempsall is paid 4*s* for four days 'gravelling the passage in the South Court levelling it & picking out the greate stones etc.', while Robert Clark the elder, John Shyrley, John Hostler and Robert Clark are each paid 6*d* for 'digginge up the foundacions of the orchard wall'.[10] As Lawson points out, the ground can be 'digged by some unskillfull servant: for the Gardner cannot doe all himself'.[11] The evidence certainly bears this out.

Sometimes labourers were paid on a piece-work basis: at Trentham Hall in Staffordshire, Richard Moare is paid 2*s* 8*d* per perch for 'the making of the south ends of the garden wall', while Timothy Addams receives 8*d* per foot for 'hewing 213 foote of Rayle for the Court'. The ubiquitous mole-catchers were paid by the dozen.[12] On other occasions they were paid

a fixed rate for a particular job – by 'the greate'. This appears to be an arrangement more favourable to the employer than the labourer: Sir Thomas Temple often urges his steward to find some good labourer whom he can pay 'by the greate', for instance to cut down an elm tree, but if that is not possible, then by the day.

In most cases, however, the more skilled work in the garden was left, not surprisingly, to the gardener. As noted earlier, sometimes he was a member of the household, paid a regular salary as with the gardener to the Cecil household at Quickswood in Hertfordshire, or Thomas Tudor, the master gardener at Hatfield House. In 1636, Owen Morgan, who worked for Sir Thomas Aubrey at Llantrithyd Place, was paid a half-yearly wage of 17s 6d.[13] More often, and no doubt because of the seasonal nature of gardening work, gardeners were employed on a daily rate. Their rates of pay were on a par with other skilled craftsmen: the Warden's accounts for the Worshipful Company of Carpenters for 1573 record carpenters, tilers and gardeners all being paid at the same rate of 1s 4d per day; at Trentham Hall in 1633 this same daily rate was still being paid to the stonemasons, carpenters and gardeners working on the rebuilding of the house and gardens.[14] At Halland House in Sussex, in addition to many days of unspecified work in the garden, 'Grove the gardner' was paid 1s a day for such specific tasks such as 'pruning and dressing of the trees in the garden'. However, in 1640 at Holme Lacy in Herefordshire, Brake the gardener was paid just 7d a day for the same task, but even this low rate was more than Richard Jauncy received for work done in the gardens of Joyce Jeffreys, also in Herefordshire at the same time. He was paid just 6d a day for sowing seeds and 4d for grafting plum trees.[15] Although these records span more than half a century, the variations are more likely to reflect differences between individual employers and geographical location than any discernible change over time, suggesting that, in terms of pay at least, little had altered for the working gardener over this period.

These occasional references give glimpses of the kind of work that a gardener was employed to do, but one particularly well-documented example gives a more comprehensive insight, that of Henry Broughton, the gardener to Sir Peter Temple at Stow in Buckinghamshire. Peter Temple was the son of Sir Thomas Temple and was running the family estate at Stow after his father's retirement to Wolverton.[16] Employed on and off throughout most of the year, Broughton was paid a relatively low daily rate of 6d. The areas in which he worked included the old kitchen garden, the new kitchen garden, the vineyard, the orchard, the South Court and the parlour garden, as well as around the fish pools. He made borders and quarters for the setting of vegetables, herbs, flowers and trees. He planted artichokes, cabbages and peas in the kitchen garden, he set trees in the orchard and sowed grass seed in the South Court. He pruned and nailed up the vines in the vineyard and clipped the hedges, knots and arbours, as well as the bushes 'in the old kitchen court to hang clothes on'. He tended the fruit trees and the roses, took up and re-set the maze in the parlour garden and gravelled the walks. His not so glamorous tasks included the carrying and spreading of muck and weeding – it seems that this is another example of a garden where weeding women were not employed. In the main, these were tasks that required the knowledge of a skilful gardener to carry them out successfully. As Sir Thomas Hanmer observed in his *Garden Book* in 1659, 'The pruning of vines well is of greatest difficulty...there needs an experienced pruner to doe it'.[17] It is notable that most of the gardener's tasks were still concerned with the utilitarian rather than the ornamental aspects of the garden.

More on the role of gardeners and garden workers can be gleaned from the correspondence of Sir Thomas Temple. After he had moved from Stow with his wife to live at the home of his daughter and son-in-law, Margaret and Sir Edward Longeville at Wolverton, Sir Thomas corresponded frequently, as has been seen, with his estate manager Harry Rose, who was responsible for maintaining the house and land at Burton Dassett in his absence. Of especial interest here are the letters of Sir Thomas to Rose regarding the hiring of labourers to start working on his new parlour garden at Dassett, particularly the hiring of Richard of Weston, 'Gardyner to my Grandson in law Mr Francis Norrice', who had recommended his services. First, Rose was instructed to get a good labourer to cut down the elm tree to provide timber for the pales of the new garden. Then he was to hire 'labourers of the better sorte' to help the gardener by carrying out the initial preparation of the ground – if they could provide their own spades, all the better! Only then would Richard of Weston be employed for a short while: 'longe I have hearde the said Gardiner cannot stay at Dassett', wrote Sir Thomas. It was agreed that Richard would come for six days in February 1631 and on two further occasions during the year. Because his time was limited, Sir Thomas was anxious to employ his skills specifically to make the parlour garden, with its flower beds, fruit trees and vines.[18] This delineation of roles is interesting: a labourer was hired to cut down a tree, better labourers were required for digging the ground for the garden and only then did the gardener arrive to design the layout and carry out the planting.

There are several other references to Richard the gardener in the correspondence and it is clear that Sir Thomas acknowledged his expertise and valued his advice. Regarding the planting up of a newly dug area, he advised Rose to ask 'what Richard the Gardiner of Weston should thinke fit'. Elsewhere, Temple wrote: 'I would have Richard sett or sow what he thincketh best', clearly content to trust his judgement. As cited in the last chapter, he also offered his opinion on the best way to take vine cuttings and his advice is repeated in minute detail by Sir Thomas in a subsequent letter to Rose.[19]

Furthermore, it seems that this gardener was literate. Not only did he receive written instructions from Sir Thomas but he also on occasion replied to him by letter. Temple notes that 'Richard wrighteth to me he wilbe at Dassett as soone as he can', and again that 'Richard wrighteth to me that his Abricot trees are dead & so cannot serve my turne'. While it is always possible that letters were being read to him and written for him by others, it nevertheless seems reasonable to conclude that Richard could both read and write.[20] As mentioned before, it is likely that most children, including those of husbandmen and labourers, attended petty school until the age of six, long enough to master the basics of reading, but writing was not taught until later, when some children may have moved on to grammar school.[21] That Richard the gardener was able to read is therefore not surprising; the fact that he could also write is perhaps more so.

More evidence of his standing is revealed in this correspondence. Richard, who came recommended by a relative, appears to have been able to lay down his own terms: he could come to Burton Dassett for a few days only – when he was available. Sir Thomas asked Rose to let him know when Richard arrived and when he had left – clearly, he was his own man. His advice was sought and followed: 'the Gardiner I thincke will approve this course', Sir Thomas wrote anxiously to Rose.[22] Examples such as this indicate that gardeners could earn a good reputation, locally at least, and that their superior skills and knowledge were respected by those who hired them. The fact that there are frequent references in many household accounts simply to 'work in the garden' or for payments 'to the gardener', where individual tasks are rarely specified, further indicates the degree of autonomy that was accorded this area of expertise.

Evidence of a growing recognition of the specialist skills of the gardener comes early in the seventeenth century when the Worshipful Company of Gardeners received its first Royal Charter in 1605 (fig. 70). In this context, the term 'gardener' embraced a wide range of occupations engaged in 'the trade, crafte, or misterie of Gardening', including botanists, florists, fruit-growers, herbalists, horticulturalists, market gardeners, nurserymen, plant merchants, seedsmen and sowers, as well as those we would call simply 'gardeners'.[23] The main motivation in setting up the Company, according to the preamble, was to regulate practice and prevent 'ignorant and unskilful persons', who had not been apprenticed to the trade, selling 'dead and corrupt plants, seeds, stockes and trees', thereby damaging the reputations of genuine gardeners and undermining the 'misterie' of gardening.[24] At the

same time, aligning themselves alongside other trade guilds and livery companies must also be seen as an attempt to elevate the status of the gardener and the activity of gardening to be on a par with other skilled crafts such as joinery, masonry or carpentry.

Having said this, in the early years at least, the influence of the Gardeners' Company was limited. It appears that its major concern was to protect the trade of those in the business of producing and selling foodstuffs, plants and seeds, and its jurisdiction was restricted to those working within a six-mile radius of the City of London. However, in 1629, Parkinson complained that most nurserymen he knows are not to be trusted – not 'one in twentie... do sell the right, but give one for another' – perhaps indicating the limited effectiveness of these measures.[25] Although there is no specific mention in the ordinances of the Company to apprenticeships, the preamble, as mentioned earlier, refers to unskilled people who have taken upon themselves 'to practise the said trade, not having been apprenticed thereto', which implies that it was established practice for gardeners to serve an apprenticeship. How these apprenticeships might have been regulated is a moot point: there is little extant information regarding gardening apprenticeships in rural areas, which would of course have included the majority of them, as statutory regulations were never systematically enforced in smaller towns and villages.[26] It is therefore unlikely that the setting up of the Gardeners' Company had much impact on gardeners working on rural country estates and, once again, there is little evidence of any great change in their working conditions over the period.

The example of Richard of Weston revealed that good gardeners could earn local recognition of their expertise but, of course, there were others whose reputations extended considerably further than this. Into this discussion can now enter such well-known individuals as John Gerard, John Parkinson and the John Tradescants. These men have already been encountered as renowned gardeners of their time, and further discussion of their work and influence can be found in the chapters that follow. Here, consideration will be given to how their role as gardeners fits into the general picture just described. Of course, one reason that these men are so well known is because they left behind them written records of their work, but the fact still remains that these were no ordinary gardeners. They were all men at the top of their tree: Gerard superintended the creation of William Cecil's garden at Theobalds, Parkinson was appointed Royal Botanist to Charles I and

71   Portrait of John Gerard, from his *Herball*, 1597
72   Attributed to Thomas de Critz, *John Tradescant the Younger as a Gardener*, 1648–53

Tradescant the elder worked on the creation of Robert Cecil's gardens at Hatfield House and was Keeper of the Royal Gardens at Oatlands Palace. On Tradescant the elder's death, his son took over this royal appointment which he held until the palace was demolished in 1650. In addition, they all had renowned gardens of their own which, by all accounts, they cultivated themselves.

Their reputations, then, were built on real skills and knowledge as gardeners and this important aspect of their lives is clearly reflected in their portraits. John Parkinson is depicted holding a Sweet William flower – also known at the time as Sweet John, the obvious reference to his own name perhaps influencing this choice (see fig. 1) – and John Gerard is holding the newly introduced potato plant (fig. 71). John Tradescant's posthumous portrait is encircled with flowers, fruit and vegetables (see fig. 165), and his son, John Tradescant the younger, is depicted holding a garden spade (fig. 72). Nevertheless, in no case was gardening their only occupation and none professed gardening as their trade. Gerard's portrait announces him as a surgeon and a member of the Company of Barber Surgeons; Parkinson was a member of the Worshipful Society of Apothecaries. The elder John Tradescant was employed in many and varied roles throughout his life, while the younger Tradescant, as well as his role as royal gardener, worked for a period at least as a merchant. He was described by a contemporary as having 'virtually given up these studies [botany] and now maintains trade with the Canary Islands'.[27] Admittedly, Parkinson, as far as we know, never actually earned his living from gardening, apart from writing about it, but Gerard and the Tradescants certainly did. What then are we to make of these facts and do they contribute in any way to the possibility of an elevated status for the gardener and gardening? Are we at any point able to talk about 'professional' gardeners or the 'profession' of gardening?[28]

Further investigation into the career paths of these eminent gardeners reveals a number of points relevant to this discussion. All these men came from relatively lowly backgrounds. In the case of Gerard, nothing is known about his family background or parentage. The only clues as to where he was born are from an entry in the *Herball* in which, when describing the bramble 'Rapis' (raspberry), Gerard relates that as a child he found it growing wild near 'where I went to school, two miles from Nantwich in Cheshire', and from the coat of arms used in his portrait, which might possibly link him to the Gerards of Ince in Cheshire.[29] The next we hear of him is in London where he had been apprenticed to the Barber-Surgeons' Company, of which he was made a freeman in 1569.[30] By 1577, he must have begun working for William Cecil: in his dedication to Lord Burghley at the beginning of his *Herball*, Gerard writes: 'under your Lordship I have served...now by the space of twenty years'.[31] How he made Burghley's acquaintance is unknown, but in order to be employed by so illustrious a person, who held one of the highest offices of state in the land, Gerard must have already earned his reputation as a gardener of note. At the same time, he was also establishing himself as a herbalist and a surgeon: in 1586, he was appointed as the curator of a physic garden to be set up by the College of Physicians and in 1595, the Barber-Surgeons elected him to the Court of Assistants. In 1607, he was chosen as its Master. There are obvious connections between the work of the surgeon and a knowledge of plants: indeed, Hyll in *The Profitable Art of Gardening* (1579) attempts to elevate the 'arte' of gardening by linking it to 'noble Artes, both Phisicke and Surgerie', neither of which can be performed without the third 'arte' of gardening to produce the necessary herbs and medicines.[32] In the same way, John Evelyn observed a few decades later that with a competent knowledge of medicine, 'a Gardiner becomes one of the most useful members of Humane Societie'.[33] Nevertheless, Gerard's apprenticeship and 'profession' was as a surgeon, not as a gardener.

One obvious reason for this is that the Company of Gardeners was not established until 1605, so apprenticeship to or membership of this Company was not even an option for Gerard, or indeed Parkinson after him. There is evidence to indicate that one way of attaining 'professional' status was through membership of a company and that to be admitted as a member was a sign that one had achieved gentry status.[34] For a man in Gerard's position who began life, at best, on the margins of gentility, apprenticeship and membership of a company would have been one assured route to a rise in status. Additionally, there was an order of civic precedence for livery companies, mainly based on wealth, which determined both prestige and potential income for apprentices and members: the Company of Barber-Surgeons and even more so the Company of Grocers, to whom Parkinson was apprenticed, were among the most important.[35] Allying themselves as they did to one of the major livery companies would also have enhanced these men's position in society.[36]

Similarly, Parkinson was an apothecary by trade, earning his living preparing and selling plant-based medicines. As with Gerard, little is known of his background and early life, but a recent biography has shown that it is likely that he came from a Lancashire farming family: the coat of arms displayed in his portrait has been traced to a farmhouse near Whalley, probably purchased in the time of Henry VIII.[37] Again, how he came to London is unknown, but by 1584 he was signed up as an apprentice to Francis Slater, a freeman of the Company of Grocers. Parkinson gained his freedom in 1593 and by 1594 had established his own apothecary shop just outside Ludgate. He was instrumental in the setting up of the Society of Apothecaries in 1617 and was elected a warden of the new society. The next few years were not easy, as many problems arose as a result of the split from the powerful Grocers' Company. Legal wranglings eventually reached the Star Chamber but the session, presided over by Sir Francis Bacon, found heavily in favour of the Apothecaries, reiterating the ruling that only members of the Society were now allowed to make and sell medicines, the Grocers' losing their right to do so. This judgement gave the Apothecaries a legitimacy to build their trade, becoming respected by doctors, physicians and botanists alike. It also had the personal backing of the king and reflected the spirit of the times, representing an essential step forward in the foundation of a scientific medical system, since the mixing and dispensing of medicines was now regulated by the Society. Parkinson's reputation grew over the years – he was, for instance, a major contributor to the 'Schedule of Medycines' commissioned by the Society in 1618 – and by 1640 his expertise had been officially recognised in his appointment as Botanicus Regius, Herbalist to the King.[38] Although gardening remained a passion throughout his life, forming the basis of his work as an apothecary and of his two published works (the first dedicated to Queen Henrietta Maria and the second to King Charles), like Gerard, Parkinson's professional status was defined by his occupation as an apothecary, not as a gardener.

John Tradescant's background is similarly obscure but we know that by 1610, at the age of forty, he was working as a gardener at Hatfield House, having clearly established his reputation as a plantsman by this time. By 1615, he was working for Lord Wotton as his gardener at St Augustine's in Canterbury, where Tradescant's son attended the King's School for four years (see fig. 102). He then moved into the employ of the Duke of Buckingham in 1624 and thence to establish his famous garden and museum in Lambeth. As far as we know, he was never apprenticed to any particular trade, but evidence such as his purchase of Bills of Adventure in the Virginia Company indicates that he may have been a man of independent means: although he clearly still needed to earn a living, perhaps he was more free to pursue his own interests without necessarily allying himself to a particular occupation. Tradescant the younger's reputation as a gardener appears to rest on his father's career, although he was admitted as a member of the Worshipful Company of Gardeners in 1634, probably becoming a freeman by redemption, that is by buying his admittance rather than earning his place through servitude or patrimony.[39]

What is remarkable is how the lives of these men followed similar paths, rising from apparently humble backgrounds to royal or near-royal appointment. They all gained their reputations at the time through their work and service, and in perpetuity through their publications. They all adopted the use of a coat of arms, a visible sign of gentlemanly status (fig. 73) and they were all, apart from Tradescant the elder, freemen of a livery company.[40] And they achieved this not, as in earlier times, through blood, patronage and inherited wealth, but through a reputation and status earned through skill and hard work, the changing times allowing them to rise through the social hierarchy and take their place as professional gentlemen, although apparently not yet as professional gardeners.

It has been argued that it was only at the end of the century that landscape gardeners, along with others from similar nascent professions such as surveyors, architects and artists, emerged to serve the needs of aspiring gentlemen who wished to buy advice in order to furnish their houses and lay out their gardens in line with the latest fashions.[41] With the benefit of hindsight, however, it could perhaps be said that in their advisory roles to the great and the good, men such as Gerard, Parkinson and Tradescant were in fact the precursors to these professionals. Whatever the case, they undoubtedly played their part in

(following pages) 74   John Evelyn's illustrations of garden tools, 1650

Elysium Britannicum.

The Instruments presented to
the Eye by the Sculptor, and
referring to the numbers as
they are described.

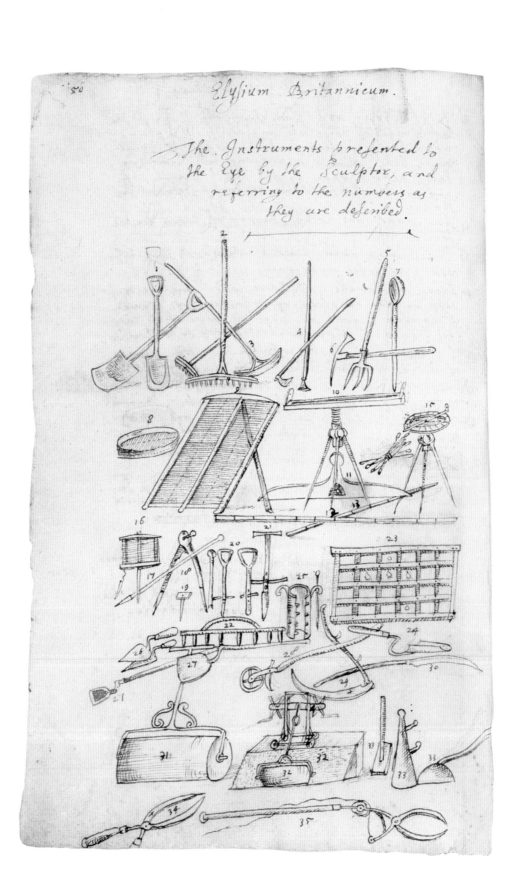

raising the status of the gardener in the earlier years of the century. It was to be left to John Evelyn, however, to make explicit this elevation in status of both the activity and the occupation of gardening and who was, as far as can be ascertained, the first person to refer to the art of gardening as a profession.

In the second chapter of his *Elysium Britannicum*, Evelyn attempts, like Lawson, Hyll and Markham before him, to define the gardener and 'how he is to be qualified'.[42] His definition of the gardener, as 'a person skillfull in the Arte of Gardening', is not particularly ground-breaking, but his discussion of the necessary qualifications is certainly more interesting. As well as being ingenious, diligent and patient (the kind of qualities already noted by other authors), for Evelyn, the gardener must also be skilful in drawing, designing, geometrics, optics, astrology and medicine, all technical skills that require a degree of 'bookish' learning and have been identified as one of the factors which distinguished a profession from a trade or craft.[43] Later in the book, Evelyn discusses and illustrates in detail more than seventy implements and other paraphernalia, 'Since Gardining...hath, as all other Arts and Professions certain instruments and tooles properly belonging to it' (fig. 74). As well as the spades, rakes, shears, wheelbarrows and so on that we would expect, he also includes levels, rulers, compasses, 'a Drawing-poynt to trace and design' and a table for plotting and setting out patterns.[44] This is a far more comprehensive range of tools than that depicted, for instance, in Mascall's much earlier garden manual (see fig. 36).

By suggesting the necessity for such an array of specialist equipment, Evelyn is at the same time implying the education to know how to use them and the means with which to purchase them. What he is doing is making a distinction between the professional gentleman gardener and the working gardener, and he does this explicitly. He goes on to list three further prerequisites to define his gardener, which may well reside in at least two if not three different persons: 'First, a good purse; Secondly, a judicious Eye; and thirdly, a skillful hand'. The first is the person at whose charge and for whom the garden is made; the second (who may well be the same person) is the 'surveyor' under whose directions the garden is contrived: 'yet is he in truth, properly, The Gardiner, by way of excellency, as in whome all the fore mentioned accomplishments concurr and center'. The third is the labourer or workman who brings the work to 'its final perfection'. By establishing the status of what he refers to as 'properly, The Gardiner' on a par with professionals such as architects and surveyors, Evelyn is seeking to elevate gardening as an elite activity: 'the Gentlemen of our Nation may not thinke it any diminution to the rest of their education, if to be dignified with the Title of Good-Gardiner'.[45]

This chapter began by identifying a hierarchy of people who worked in gardens, from labourers to esteemed members of the household, but within this new intellectual framework, Evelyn is drawing distinctions which establish a new hierarchy of gardeners: from the learned gentleman who is equipped with the education and knowledge to pursue gardening alongside other higher intellectual pursuits to the middling practitioners (such as Gerard, Parkinson and Tradescant) who approach it as a skill specific to itself. At the same time, he still acknowledges the importance of the labourers who actually do the work. But here he is dignifying gardening, 'that glorious name and Profession', as a liberal rather than a mechanical art, establishing it as a fitting occupation for a gentleman.

There is just one problem with all this and that is, despite all Evelyn's lofty aspirations, there is evidence that gentlemen had been engaged in gardening, to a certain degree at least, for a long time.

Having considered those who earned their living as gardeners, we now need to explore the role of the garden owners themselves in the maintenance of their gardens. These gardeners tend to be less well-documented than paid servants or workers, as their activities are not recorded in household accounts or on wage bills, so we must rely on other sources for evidence. In the first instance, as ever, contemporary literature offers a number of clues.

As already noted, William Lawson begins his book with advice on the importance of choosing the right gardener, but having extolled the virtues of the perfect example, we realise that this is, in fact, not the gardener for whom Lawson is writing his book. He ends the chapter by offering an alternative: 'If you be not able, nor willing to hire a gardner, keep your profits to your self, but then you must take all the pains: and for that purpose (if you want this faculty) to instruct you, have I undertaken these labours, and gathered these rules'. He appears to be drawing a clear distinction between 'the gardner' who knows his art well enough not to need further instruction, and the garden owner who may want to learn to do some of this work himself – always of course with 'good help...for no one man is sufficient for these things'.[46] Lawson's book appears to have been aimed at people like himself – that is, country gentry of some learning but who are involved at a practical level in the husbanding of their land. The fact that it was being written at this particular time (it was printed in 1618) suggests a new need for such a book, because gardening was becoming an acceptable activity for the seventeenth-century gentleman and, like other contemporary advice books such as Henry Peacham's *The Compleat Gentleman*, it perhaps offered another facet on how to live such a life.[47] Lawson's book proved popular, numerous editions being published to the end of the century, and it has to be assumed that some of its readers

A. The Iron Inſtrument with cheſſels at each end, the one bigger and the other leſſer, to keepe the cleft of the Tree open vntill the graft bee placed in the ſtocke, which with a knock vpwards will be eaſily taken away.

B. The ſmall Penne-knife with a broad and thinne ended hafte, to raiſe the ſides both of the bud and the down-right ſlit in the body or arme of a Tree to be grafted in the bud.

C. A pen or quil cut halfe round to take off a bud from the branch.

D. An Iuory Inſtrument made to the ſame faſhion.

E. A ſhielde of braſſe made hollow before to be put into the ſlit, to keepe it open vntill the bud be put into its place.

F. The manner of grafting called inciſing or ſplicing.

G. A Ladder made with a ſtoole at the toppe, to ſerue both to graft higher or lower, and alſo to gather fruit without ſpoyling or hurting any buddes or branches of Trees.

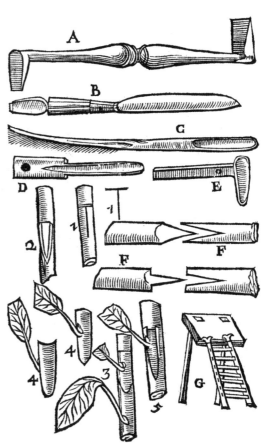

at least were putting what they read into practice. Garden owners clearly were involving themselves to some extent in the cultivation of their gardens.

Evidence in John Parkinson's book is much more specific. In his chapter on grafting in the orchard he states: 'yet because many Gentlemen and others are much delighted to bestowe their paines in grafting themselves, and esteeme their owne labours and handie work farr above other mens: for their incouragement and satisfaction, I will here set down some convenient directions'.[48] Grafting is an ancient horticultural technique (still used today), which involves joining two plants together so they continue to grow as one, thereby harnessing the best characteristics of each variety. It is a technique used particularly for fruit trees, usually combining a hardy rootstock with a less vigorous but better fruiting variety. It is a skilled task and one which Parkinson clearly sees as a suitable activity for gentleman gardeners (fig. 75).

This seems unequivocal and, like Lawson, Parkinson was seeking to offer advice not to gardeners by trade but to those gentlemen who liked to work in their own gardens. Despite the fact that gardeners were employed on most country estates, there were nevertheless gentlemen owners who clearly engaged in hands-on gardening. Sometimes this was because it was a more economical option, as implied by Lawson; sometimes because they felt that they had the greater skill, as Parkinson seems to be saying; and sometimes, as will be shown, for their own pleasure. Examination of a range of other contemporary sources helps to give substance to this notion of the gentleman gardener.

A portrait dating from about 1575 shows Thomas Wentworth (grandfather to the infamous Earl of Strafford) seated in his garden, holding in one hand a tree stock into which grafts have been inserted and, in the other hand, a grafting saw and a chisel or knife (fig. 76). There is another tree stock by his left foot into which grafts have also been inserted. Behind him stands the gardener, who is holding a bundle of grafts in one hand and some kind of garden tool in the other. Wentworth's wife, daughter and dog are standing to his left, in front of the family house and gardens at Wentworth Woodhouse, south Yorkshire. The significance of this is not just its visual evidence of a gentleman actively engaged in gardening, but perhaps even more telling is that it is this aspect of his life that Wentworth has chosen to be depicted in this family portrait. It clearly was of great importance to him, a skill of which he was particularly proud and an activity which he considered to befit his status. Furthermore, this portrait is dated considerably earlier than the garden manuals quoted earlier (and well before Evelyn attempted to define his gentleman gardener), which indicates that this was not a new phenomenon, but that these were skills and abilities with a long and respectable pedigree. Of course, of all the work in the garden, grafting is not only a skilled task but also does not involve much physical effort or getting your hands dirty. Wentworth is seated on a chair and the gardener is at his shoulder to provide the necessary equipment and, presumably, advice if required. While grafting could just about be described as manual labour, it is hardly as arduous as digging and muck-spreading!

It is with this in mind that we may approach the next piece of evidence. In 1631, Sir John Oglander wrote in his memorandum book: 'I have with my owne handes planted 2 younge Orchardes at Nunwell, the lower with Pippen, Pearmaynes, Puttes [?Harnyes] and other good aples, and all sortes of good pears[. I]n the other Cherryes, Damsons and Plumes, in the upor garden Apricockes, Melecatoons and figges.' Elsewhere he wrote: 'When I came to Nunwell I fownd not one Quince Tree, wherefor I sett at leaste 100 trees, being all Portingale quinces. There was neither any good Aple, Cherrye, Plum, Peare, Apricocke, Melicatoone, Figge or Vine. I planted them all, most with my own hands.'[49] Whether these are the same trees as those he had already mentioned is difficult to tell but, more significantly, he mentions on both occasions that he has planted them himself: this is not, therefore, an activity which he regards as beneath him. And it has to be said that planting this many trees, even as saplings, is no mean feat. A man in Sir John's position must have had many calls on his time, but he chose to do this work of planting trees himself rather than having it done for him, presumably because this was what he wanted.[50] Sir John's actual role in this tree-planting is unclear, and it is likely that the hard work of digging the holes, filling them with muck and so on was done by the labourers who appear in the account books as being employed year round at Nunwell on the usual tasks of walling, hedging, ditching, digging and weeding. Oglander's contribution may simply have been limited to inserting the sapling into the prepared hole and leaving someone else to finish the job. However, as there does not appear to have been a gardener as such employed at Nunwell, it is more than possible that Sir John himself had the necessary knowledge, skill and interest both to oversee and actively participate in the creation and maintenance of his own garden. This idea is reiterated in Sir John's writings, where he continues to display both a practical interest and knowledge of gardening and good husbandry. He gives specific advice about the planting of an orchard, for instance, including which varieties to choose, how best to manure the ground, how long to leave the rootstocks before using them for grafting and so on: 'If you desyre to have a good orchard plant him first with Crabstockes as you woold have then stand for good: after 2 yeares then graff them: placing good earth about the rootes.'[51]

Unlike garden writers such as Lawson and Parkinson who offer similar advice, Sir John is not writing a book for publication to a wider audience. He is giving specific advice to his descendants about how to make the best of this specific place, the family estate at Nunwell. He writes a long treatise entitled 'Observations in Howsbanderie' of which he says 'if thou beest not sckilled thie selve [,] make use of them and be sure to follow them t[i]ll experience hath taught thee better'.[52] We can only assume that this is how Sir John acquired his knowledge, through his own experience, which he is now passing on to his descendants. While good estate management would necessarily have been the concern of many rural gentlemen, in Sir John Oglander his intensely practical advice indicates direct involvement on his part and, as noticed in the case of Thomas Wentworth, it is possible to discern a degree of pride in his horticultural achievements. In the same way, Sir John Reresby in his 'Garden Notebook' lists 'The Names of the severall Trees planted by my selfe in my Orchards & Gardens at Thrybergh: Begunne 1633'.[53] Like Oglander, Reresby too considers it worthy of note that he planted the trees himself.

Sir Thomas Temple's memorandum books and correspondence also reveal a close involvement in the management of the estate lands and orchards at Burton Dassett, his many letters to his estate steward Harry Rose indicating his knowledge and expertise. As is extensively discussed elsewhere, he was particularly heavily involved in his latter years in the creation and planning of the new paled garden at Dassett. He issued precise instructions about how exactly he wanted the garden to look and what should be planted in it, as well as equally precise instruction regarding the preparation of the ground: 'the workemen are to caste one spitt of the uppermost earth upon or toward the said South wall', or again, the earth should be cast up towards the Privy hedges and 'if the ground on which the plantes are sett, were stoared with gardine stuffe also, the plantes would prosper the better', and so on.[54] Again, this indicates a degree of 'hands-on' knowledge and expertise on such matters and it is almost certain that Sir Thomas maintained an active interest in his garden throughout the remainder of his life. The gardening activities of Sir Thomas Hanmer and John Evelyn are yet to be discussed, but suffice it to note here that in both cases their extensive plans, notebooks and correspondence all point to active participation in the creation and maintenance of their gardens.

Having said all this, of course not all garden owners showed such an active interest. From the evidence that is available, gentlemen such as Sir Richard Leveson, Sir Thomas Puckering or Sir Thomas Pelham reveal no particular interest in gardening but were happy to leave everything to the gardener, their role being limited to paying the bills. As long as the end result met their expectation in terms of looking good and creating the right impression, they were content (their gardens will be discussed in Chapter 8). By Evelyn's definitions, these are the people 'at whose charge and for whose divertissement the Garden is made' but are not necessarily 'properly, the Gardiner'.[55] However, this was a matter of choice, and does nothing to detract from the notion that gentlemen gardeners were alive and well and gardening in early modern England.

What, then, about women in the garden? Although there is some evidence to suggest that women had an important role to play in the maintenance of gardens, this seems to have been assumed rather than specifically articulated and their actual presence remains largely silent and invisible. Where are they? Apart from the weeding women already mentioned, what other glimpses do we have of women in the garden?

Authors of contemporary household and gardening literature, such as Googe, Markham and Hyll, appear to have assumed that the growing of vegetables, flowers and herbs for household use was the responsibility of the housewife, but when it comes to detail and advice, little is forthcoming. For instance, in *The English Housewife* (1615), which addresses many areas of housewifery including medicine, cookery, dairying, brewing, clothmaking and so on, Markham has almost nothing to say about gardening, although he clearly sees it as an important duty: 'Let her diet be wholesome and cleanly...let it proceed more from the provision of her own yard, than the furniture of the markets'. However, considering the detail he goes into in other areas, when it comes to the kitchen garden, he simply suggests that she gain her knowledge through her own labour and experience and 'not by my relation, which would be much too tedious'.[56] His detailed advice on gardening appears in a section in *The English Husbandman*, published two years previously. In his translation of 1577 of Heresbach's *Foure Bookes of Husbandry*, Barnabe Googe reiterates that it is up to the housewife to keep the garden in order, 'for unto her belonged the charge thereof'.[57] Hyll admits, somewhat confusingly in the first chapter of *The Gardeners Labyrinth*, that in the past the 'charge and chiefest care' of the garden 'was committed unto the wife', but implies that this is no longer necessarily the case and goes on specifically to address the rest of this book to the 'husbandman or Gardener'.[58] No further mention of the wife is made in its considerable number of chapters covering every aspect of how to prepare, sow, plant and reap the products of the garden. The role of the housewife in the garden as presented in these texts is unclear and contradictory: although references to the preparation of medicines, food, preserving and the dyeing of cloth all indicate the obvious fact that women needed a good working knowledge of the garden, the importance of also cultivating the plants and maintaining the garden is somewhat overlooked or dismissed.

William Lawson was the first person to address a book on gardening specifically to women: his *Country Housewifes Garden* was published (and bound) together with *A New Orchard and Garden* in 1618, but the two books were completely different in content and approach. Unlike the detailed and specific advice based on his own experience that he gives in the *New Orchard*, the text of the *Housewifes Garden* is both straightforward and short. Much of it reads as no more than a plant list, annotated with a few tips on how and where best to grow the plants, based, it appears, on older manuals, with little that is new added by the author. It has been suggested that Lawson kept his information brief and basic because he was anxious not to overload his female readers with too much detail.[59] However, this argument is somewhat difficult to maintain when we realise that in the second section of this little book, 'The Husbandry of Bees', Lawson goes into immense detail about beekeeping, passing on what he has learned – based on his own experience of being a 'Bee-master' – specifically to the housewife. He seems quite happy that she can cope with the detail offered here. The book also includes a number of designs for knot gardens which Lawson mentions briefly but gives no instruction on how they can be achieved, instead leaving the housewife to work out how to devise and set out these complicated designs for herself. From this, we can perhaps conclude that, rather than underestimating the intelligence and abilities of his female readers, this is simply an area of gardening in which Lawson himself has no particular expertise or interest and he therefore turns instead to received wisdom from older sources for his information (for more on Lawson and knot gardens, see Chapter 7). In fact, why he should have decided to write this book at all is open to speculation – perhaps the recent success of Markham's *English Housewife* had encouraged Lawson's publisher to suggest this addition to the main text, in order to increase its marketability?

John Parkinson's *Paradisi in Sole* is dedicated to Queen Henrietta Maria and makes occasional references to 'Gentlewomen', generally in the context of their desire to have fine flowers in their gardens. However, at no point is there any suggestion that these women might be working in their gardens and perhaps, in fact, his dedication has more to do with status than gender. While Lawson's book is clearly addressed to the country housewife, who will necessarily be involved in her garden, Parkinson, as has been discussed previously, had a 'better sort' of reader in mind – the wealthy, leisured gentleman or gentlewoman with gardeners, labourers, weeding women and maids to actually carry out the work.

As recourse to contemporary literature is, then, unfortunately somewhat inconclusive on this question, what other evidence is there of women's activities in the garden? The wives of estate workers have already been mentioned as engaged in a number of menial and unskilled tasks that attracted far lower wages than their menfolk. There appears to be no evidence in household accounts and other documents that women were ever employed as gardeners – such records are far from complete but it seems reasonable to conclude that at this time there was little place for the professional or skilled female gardener in the early modern garden.

There is evidence, however, that some women, often left to manage estates in the absence of their men, were actively engaged in the garden. One of the best recorded examples is Lady Margaret Hoby, who kept a diary of her daily activities for six years between 1599 and 1605. Her husband was a Justice of the Peace and a Member of Parliament and was often away in London or on other business. Although the entries in her diary are frustratingly scant in detail, there are many references to time spent in the garden, gathering apples, sowing seeds, setting wheat and even setting trees. She also deals, as would be expected, with the produce from the garden, preserving quinces, making sweetmeats and collecting honey from her hives.

Lady Hoby also dyes cloth and wool, presumably using plants from the garden to prepare dyes. There is evidence, for instance, that saffron was grown in gardens for use as a dye: the Puckering accounts record its purchase, while the household accounts of Joyce Jeffreys in Herefordshire record the sale of saffron from her garden. She receives 10s for 'an ounce quarter', although on other occasions she records receiving just pennies for presumably much smaller quantities.[60] Lady Hoby also prepares medicines to ease pain, cure sores and so on, which she administers to members of her household, and these too would have been concocted using plants from the garden. There are references to her reading 'the Herball' to help her do this.[61] In 1599, this could well have been the recently published herbal by Gerard which, as its inclusion in a portrait of Susan Hanmer (wife of Sir Thomas Hanmer; fig. 77) demonstrates, remained an important volume for consultation by the lady of the house.

Margaret Hoby must have communicated with her neighbours about gardening matters too, as she and the beehives she keeps in the stone walls of her orchard are specifically mentioned in Lawson's book. He refers to her as 'that honourable Lady at Hackness, whose name doth much grace my Orchard', implying that she had, on occasion, been received as a visitor.[62] Lady Sidney's contribution to the supervision of the orchards at Penshurst has

also been mentioned, her role in providing gifts for her husband, the Earl of Leicester, and his friends at court clearly an important one.

The difficulty here is that, although women had a vital role to play in the early modern garden, with these few exceptions, they have left little record of their activities. Women have appeared and will continue to appear throughout this book but, rather than trying to make generalised assumptions based on a lack of evidence, we must be content with these occasional glimpses to add another dimension to our view of the early modern gardener.

6

NEW ASPIRATIONS

'A Garden of Pleasant Flowers'

11

The pitfalls in making arbitrary chronological divisions to describe the history of gardening have already been discussed but it is inevitable that as the long reign of Elizabeth came to a close, the new century and then the reign of a new monarch would bring with it new aspirations and opportunities for the future. Horizons were being continually widened by the spread and increasing accessibility of printed material, by expanding opportunities for foreign travel and by the availability of new luxury goods as London thrived and developed as a centre of global trade. Rare and exotic plants were arriving on English shores from all over the world. In 1597, Gerard described many plants in his *Herball* that he had obtained from 'forren places' including ginger from 'the Barbary', tulips from the Middle East, crocuses from Spain and Italy and potatoes and tobacco from the Americas.[1] Three decades later, in 1629, Parkinson says of Gerard that 'since his dates we have had many more varieties, then he ever heard of, as may be perceived by the store I have here produced'.[2] Already, the choice of plants available to the gardener or garden owner was far greater than it had been at the end of the previous century. Plant collectors were commissioned to travel abroad to seek 'curious' and 'outlandish' plants to stock the gardens of the nobility, and a lively nursery trade was developing in England and across the Continent (to be discussed in Chapter 10) which allowed these plants to be propagated, sold, exchanged and cultivated by avid plantsmen and gentleman gardeners across the land. At the same time, the ornamental garden was developing as a place in which rare and costly plants could be displayed.

Alongside these tangible factors, there were other agents of change at work. These included, as has been seen in Chapter 1, an acceptance of the emerging concept of science and experiment which slowly displaced the unchallenged wisdom of ancient authorities, as well as the magic, witchcraft and 'idle fables', as Parkinson dismissed them, which were popularly employed to explain the inexplicable in everyday life. Ideas of and attitudes to notions such as the commonwealth, the public good, civility, individual prosperity and social mobility were also shifting, as were moral attitudes to such previously frowned upon notions as leisure, pleasure and luxury (as seen in Chapter 2). The possibilities of the new age made the pursuit of these goals both acceptable and desirable, as discernible in gardens as anywhere else. It is this change in emphasis from the utilitarian, productive gardens that we have looked at so far, to the rise of the ornamental flower garden in the Jacobean era that will be the focus of this chapter.

Perhaps the best evidence that alerts us to these changes in the seventeenth-century garden comes, in the first instance, from contemporary gardening literature. A fundamental change already identified and discussed was the shift from the heavy reliance on classical and Renaissance texts for their authority, to a new approach based on empirical knowledge and experience. The works of Markham and particularly those of Lawson and Parkinson were based on the authors' own experience and their concern was to pass on practical advice, relevant to local conditions, to their readers.

Such literature represented a new approach to writing and publishing gardening advice. As discussed, many practices from the sixteenth century continued well into the seventeenth century – Lawson, for one, was writing about his forty-eight years of gardening experience, going back at least as far as 1570 (fig. 78). However, what appears to have happened is that, as the intellectual respectability of the new scientific methods began to be accepted, the literature in turn reflected this change in attitudes, by responding to a growing demand for books based on empirical knowledge and methods. Garden writers now had a new audience for their books: those who wanted real, proven advice that they could put into practice in their own gardens. One happy result for historians is that at last we have a literature that was beginning to reflect what was actually happening in the gardens of early modern England.

Markham and Lawson were clearly making moves in this direction but it was for Parkinson to make this new departure complete. He played a pivotal role in revolutionising both garden writing and gardening practices, advocating for the first time that 'beautiful flower plants' might be included in a garden for no other reason than their ornamental value. His two major works, *Paradisi in Sole* (1629) and *Theatrum Botanicum* (1640) form the main source of information about Parkinson, presenting a lively picture of his gardening activity in early modern London, as well as offering some insight into the life and mind of the man who wrote them. *Theatrum Botanicum* was a conventional medicinal herbal, but *Paradisi in Sole* did not fit so neatly into any recognised genre. At first glance, it looked like a traditional herbal, set out in a similar way with descriptions of the place, the time (or season), the names and so on of hundreds of plants, but in fact it was much more than this. As well as plant descriptions, Parkinson included a number of closely written chapters containing not just intensely practical gardening advice but also his own views on contemporary gardening trends, as well as a real attempt to understand the true nature of plants. A closer examination of Parkinson's life and work, then, as evidenced in his two publications, will provide valuable insight into the kind of changes that were occurring in the early seventeenth-century garden.

It is worth reiterating that, in tune with the times, and the ideas of Francis Bacon and his new scientific method, Parkinson was absolutely confident that experience, experiment and observation were the key to knowledge and he was highly critical of those who simply reproduced information about plants from earlier texts, without testing the validity of what

A NEW ORCHARD

and Garden.

OR

The beſt way for planting, grafting, and to make
any ground good, fora rich Orchard : Particularly in the North
parts of England : generally for the whole kingdome, as in nature,
reaſon, ſcituation, and all probability, may and doth appeare.

WITH

The Country Houſewiſes Garden for hearbes of common vſe, their vertues, ſeaſons, profites, ornaments, variety of knots, models for trees, and
plots for the beſt ordering of Grounds and Walkes.

AS ALSO,

The Husbandry of Bees, with their ſeuerall vſes and annoyances, all grounded
on the Principles of Art, and precepts of Experience, being the
Labours of forty eight yeares of William Lawſon.

Skill add paines brings fruitfull gaines.

Nemo ſibi naſcitur.

Printed at London by Bar: Alſop for Roger Jackſon, and are to be Gold at his ſhop
neere Fleet-ſtreet Conduit. 1 6 1 8

they were committing to print. In contrast to his predecessors, Parkinson passionately believed in the crucial importance of observing and understanding the plants that he grew in his garden and which were the essential tools of his trade. He increased his understanding and skill in growing new plant introductions by sowing, often unidentified, seeds brought from abroad, and then watching them grow and develop into mature plants. This of course took time, but Parkinson would not write about a plant until he had observed its properties for himself. He notes in *Theatrum Botanicum*, for instance, a German variety of spignel that 'when it is better grown up with me...I shall be the better judge'.[3] He does not feel at the time of writing that he is in a position to make authoritative comment on this new plant.

Underlining the same point, later in the book Parkinson complains bitterly that 'while I with care and cost sowed them yearely hoping first to publish them, another that never saw them unless in my Garden' already had descriptions ready for the press.[4] 'Another' must refer to Thomas Johnson, a fellow apothecary and alleged friend of Parkinson, who brought out his corrected and enlarged edition of *Gerard's Herball* in 1633, in which he makes many references to plants that he has seen growing in Parkinson's garden. However, at this time, Parkinson was putting the finishing touches to his own monumental tome, *Theatrum Botanicum*, and as a result, the publication of this book was delayed until 1640. Parkinson was therefore unlikely to feel kindly towards Johnson, but the real point here is the emphasis that Parkinson lays on the importance of observing the plants carefully and meticulously before rushing into print. Unlike Johnson's *Herball*, his *Theatrum Botanicum* was apparently more than fifty years in preparation and completion.[5] It was nothing less than the result of a lifetime's work and Parkinson was as scathing of those who did not devote the same time and attention to their work as he was of those who were apparently 'stealing' knowledge from his garden.

Little is known about Parkinson's garden, although we know from Parkinson himself that it was located in Long Acre, near Covent Garden.[6] It is likely to have been established around the beginning of the seventeenth century, since the renowned Flemish botanist and acquaintance of Parkinson, Matthias de l'Obel, refers to it in a publication of 1605, but Gerard, who was also known to Parkinson, does not mention it in his *Herball* published a few years earlier in 1597.[7] If the garden had been in existence at that time, he surely would have done so. Nevertheless, it was well known enough for various records of the plants growing in it to have been compiled by visitors to the garden, including a comprehensive list made in 1617 by another English herbalist and friend of Parkinson, John Goodyer. All in all, a total of 484 plants are recorded as growing in Parkinson's Long Acre garden and this number apparently continued to be added to until at least 1640.[8] His comment about the new variety of spignel indicates that at the time of writing, he was still acquiring new plants.

Parkinson also notes his regret that he had not thought to record the details of the many rare plants that he tried to grow in his garden without success. As well as the plants we know about, then, there were considerably more that we do not.[9] The actual number of varieties that Parkinson was attempting to cultivate was clearly greater than that indicated here and, of course, what made this collection even more remarkable was that a high proportion of the plants he was cultivating were new introductions from abroad (fig. 79). Although the garden fell into decline after Parkinson's death in 1650, these facts, together with the evidence of his lifetime's work in his written works, suggest that at the time, his garden in Long Acre must have been among the largest and best-known in London.

Parkinson's role as an apothecary gave him the motivation to grow and study plants in order to increase his knowledge and expertise, but it is clear too that he was a keen and skilful gardener and he applied the same careful, scientific method which established his reputation as an apothecary to his gardening practice. In *Paradisi in Sole*, Parkinson comments many times that men should no longer believe in ancient 'reports', 'tales and fables', for 'when they come to the triall, they all vanish away like smoake'.[10] He graphically illustrates his point by taking as an example the various practices advised in older manuals to change the colour or scent of plants. This included soaking seeds or watering plants with coloured dyes to make the blooms a particular colour, or applying spices or 's[c]ents' such as cinnamon or cloves under the bark of trees in order to make the fruits take on those smells and flavours, and we know that such practices were still being carried out by gardeners well into the seventeenth century. In 1620, the household accounts of Sir Thomas Puckering of Warwick record a payment of 6*d* for 'muscadine and sugar to steepe melon-seedes in before they bee pricked [planted] in the ground', in order, presumably, to enhance the sweetness of the fruit.[11] Today, ideas such as this seem nonsensical – and so they did to John Parkinson. If anyone had actually tried these techniques and put them to the test, as he had done, they would have seen that they did not work. Parkinson again emphasises the importance of practical experiment and observation as a basis for knowledge. 'I will shew you mine owne

experience in the matter', he writes: 'I have been as inquisitive as any man might be' and he can assert that 'there is not any art whereby any flower may be made to grow double, that was naturally single, nor of any other s[c]ent or colour that it first had by nature'.[12]

This is in stark contrast to the view of William Harrison, who was marvelling more than fifty years earlier in 1577, that gardeners were so 'curious and cunning' that they do 'what they list with Nature',[13] and in the final chapter of 'The Ordering of the Garden of Pleasure', Parkinson grapples at length with this problem.[14] He introduces the Baconian notion of reason by which he hopes to 'perswade many in the truth' and the truth that he is so anxious to convey is that nothing exists that has not been found in nature first. If men say they have created 'by art' plants that are not as they are found in nature, then they are liars, 'feigning and boasting often of what they would have, as if they had it'.[15] He employs a number of arguments to prove his point but the most persuasive is that he has made trials with many different types of plants of the various methods that are reported to change the nature of plants – their colour, their scent, whether they are single or double-flowered varieties – but when put to the test 'I could never see the effect desired, but rather in many of them the losse of my plants'. Once again, he asserts that all these 'rules and directions set down in bookes, so confidently, as if the matters were without doubt or question:

whenas without all doubt and question I will assure you, that they are all but meere idle tales and fancies'.[16] He is absolutely confident of his own observations and experience and equally confident, if modest, in his conclusions: 'although they have not been amplified with such Philosophical arguments and reasons, as one of greater learning might have done, yet they are truely and sincerely set down'.[17]

It may seem that for the times Parkinson was advocating somewhat radical notions, but in fact it appears that he was simply reflecting changing times and attitudes. New ideas about the advancement and dissemination of knowledge could be applied to gardening as well as anything else and this gave him the confidence to communicate his own experiences in this way.[18] He offers an alternative explanation of the curiosity and cunning of gardeners referred to by Harrison. Parkinson maintains that plants and flowers cannot be changed or altered: 'we onely have them as nature hath produced them, and so they remaine'. But, according to Parkinson, what the gardener can do, by careful selection of the better flowers, nurturing, 'good ordering and looking unto', is to *improve* what can be found in nature. By employing good horticultural practice, such as enriching the soil with compost, spacing plants correctly, pruning, working with the vagaries of the weather and so on, it is possible, for instance, that flowers can be made 'somewhat fairer or larger' by the intervention of man.[19] In the same way, while Parkinson argues that no man can make flowers 'to spring at what time of the yeare he will', he demonstrates throughout his book that it is perfectly viable, by careful choice of the right plants, to have flowers in the garden every month of the year.[20]

At the same time, it was also possible, as Parkinson well knew, to 'trick' nature into performing supposed miracles. A well-documented example is the story of Sir Francis Carew who, in preparation for a visit by Queen Elizabeth to his house at Beddington in Surrey in August 1599, managed to delay the ripening of the cherries on a tree in his garden for a full month by covering it with a canvas in order that they would come to maturity precisely in time for Her Majesty's arrival.[21] But as far as Parkinson was concerned, the role of the gardener was not to try to control nature in this way but to use his knowledge and skill to work in harmony with nature in order to bring to perfection the plants and flowers in the garden (fig. 81).

It was not just Parkinson's extensive knowledge of plants and the innovative way that he chose to disseminate it that make his book such an important source of information about early seventeenth-century gardening. As well as the hundreds of pages of plant description, in *Paradisi in Sole*, Parkinson also offers gardening advice to his readers: which plants to choose, how to plant them, how to look after them and how to maintain and propagate them, advice on garden design, composting, hard landscaping, how to make windbreaks to

81 Jacques le Moyne, *Madonna Lily*, 1585

82 Jacques le Moyne, *Clove Pink*, 1585

protect plants, how to create 'hot beds' to force young plants in the spring and so on. As ever, his advice is entirely practical, based on either his own experience or, interestingly, on what he sees going on in gardens around him. Fascinating to the modern gardener, parts of this book read like a review of contemporary practice, with Parkinson's own experience and opinions added.

He discusses, for instance, various methods of propagating gilliflowers, which he describes as 'the chiefest flowers of account in all our English Gardens' (fig. 82). There are two ways to increase these fair flowers successfully, he says: 'The one is by slipping which is the old and ready usual way, best known in this Kingdome; the other is more sure, perfect, ready, and of later invention, *videlicet*, by laying downe the branches'.[22] Both methods, using cuttings or by layering, were 'frequently used' and, according to Parkinson, both gave good results. He adds meticulously detailed instructions on the correct technique, at the same time offering a number of explanations as to why such propagating methods sometimes failed. Not only is he advising his readers what to do but he is also advising them on what not to do – advice which would make perfect sense to any gardener today.[23] This indicates once again the stress on observation and experience, as well as giving us an idea of the kind of practices that people were carrying out in their gardens.

Other small details that add to the picture of the garden here are his suggestion that the rooted cuttings can be transplanted either into the ground in beds or into pots; they should be kept watered either using a watering pot or by setting the pots into containers half full of water. As to pest control, there seem to be as many methods tried then as now – with apparently the same degree of success. He describes many 'waies and inventions' to destroy earwigs, enthusiastic nibblers of gilliflowers, but offers his own verdict as to the 'best and most usual things now used', which is animal hooves, upturned on long canes stuck into the ground, which draw the pests up and away from the plant. These can then be easily knocked out by the gardener and 'with ones foot may be trode to peeces'.[24] This method (although using small flower pots rather than horses' hooves) is once again being recommended by organic gardeners today. Further on, he describes making windbreaks to protect young seedlings from cold northerly and easterly winds: 'set great high and large mattes made of reedes, tyed together, and fastened unto strong stakes, thrust into the ground to keepe them from falling'.[25] This is better than a brick wall, he claims, and although he does not explain why, this again is sound thinking. Windbreaks such as the mats described here, or hedges, allow some air to pass through them, thus avoiding the damaging turbulence that can be caused by a solid, impenetrable barrier such as a wall.

Many other examples abound and, when reading Parkinson's detailed instructions and explanation, it is not difficult to conjure up a picture of the early seventeenth-century gardener tending his plot, gathering and sowing seeds, nurturing and watering cuttings, protecting his tender young plants and fighting the never-ending battle against 'infestuous vermine'.[26]

As well as such down-to-earth advice, Parkinson also offers his opinion on current fashions in gardening, a notable example being his description of the various methods and materials that can be employed to set out the form of 'knots, trayles and other compartiments' in the garden. These can be living materials and he goes through the pros and cons of a variety of different plants commonly used in this way, including germander, hyssop, thyme and lavender, but eventually recommends a relatively new plant introduction, dwarf French or Dutch box.[27] This is interesting in itself as, although box has been used commonly ever since as an edging plant, Parkinson appears to have been the first person to recommend its use as such in English gardens. He considers it a 'marvailous fine ornament',[28] perfect for

bordering knots, because it is low-growing, slow-growing, evergreen and can be 'cut and formed into any fashion one will' (fig. 83).[29] Similarly, knots can equally be formed of dead materials such as lead, wooden boards or tiles. Here he is even more forthright in offering his opinions. He clearly does not approve of the idea of using lead borders, 'cut out like the battlements of a Church', although this fashion has obviously 'delighted some, who have accounted it stately (at the least costly) and fit for their degree', but in his opinion, lead is too hot in the summer and too cold in the winter.[30] It is not easy to decide which he disapproves of more: the use of the material itself, or its use for no other reason than that it is expensive and therefore showy. He also describes the surprising practice of using sheep bones to mark out the patterns of the knots – set side by side, over time they will become white and 'prettily grace out the ground'. The fashion of using jaw-bones on the other hand, a practice he attributes to 'the Low Countries and other places beyond the seas', is so gross and base that he will make no further mention of it. The best of dead materials, in his opinion, are pebbles, which he describes as the most recent trend: 'And lastly (for it is the latest invention) round whitish or blewish pebble stones, of some reasonable proportion and bignesse, neither too great nor too small, have been used by some' (fig. 84).[31]

From the way Parkinson is writing, it seems that he did not necessarily have direct experience of laying out a garden in this way himself, but it is clear that he must have seen other gardens, talked to other gardeners, taken into account their views and formed his own

impressions. In passing on all these opinions, prejudices, likes and dislikes, John Parkinson
gives a wonderful picture of just one aspect of gardening (the bordering of beds and knots)
in early seventeenth-century London. As he concludes himself: 'thus, Gentlemen, I have
shewed you all the varieties that I know are used by any in our Countrey, that are worth
the reciting'.[32]

There are many other examples but the point is that Parkinson shows himself to be
aware of changes in practice and changes in fashion, even if he does not always approve
of them. His is not just prescriptive advice, but a report of practice that is actually going on
around him and this is one further aspect of this book that makes it a valuable documenta-
tion of contemporary gardening practice.

First and foremost, however, this publication is about plants and flowers. Parkinson places
them firmly at the centre of his book and at the centre of the garden, and his enthusiasm
for the beauty of the plants shines through. The opening decades of the century had seen
a huge increase in the number of plants available. For the previous thirty years, what he

delightfully refers to as 'outlandish' plants had been arriving in London from all over the world, many from the Mediterranean region – in particular Spain, Portugal, Italy and North Africa ('Barbary') – but also from the New World (North and South America, the Bermudas and the West Indies). Although no plant-hunter himself – there is no evidence that Parkinson ever left London once he had established his business there – his interest, both as an apothecary and as a gardener, and as evidenced by the huge collection in his garden at Long Acre, made him a passionate collector and cultivator of these exotic plants. Whether obtained through his wide circle of friends, contacts and commissioned agents or purchased in the London markets, Parkinson had a whole host of new plants and flowers with which to furnish his garden and about which to write. As he points out in his 'Epistle to the Reader', there are now so many 'beautifull flower plants' available and people are faced with such an overwhelming choice that they do not even know what they want: 'whereby many that have desired to have faire flowers, have not known either what to choose, or what to desire'.

Although Parkinson includes a discussion of English flowers, in which he takes account of all the usual suspects – primroses, violets, columbines, pansies, poppies, roses and 'the Queene of delight and of flowers, Carnations and gilliflowers' – because these are so well known to all, he intends to pass over them briefly.[33] He devotes far more time to his descriptions and instructions regarding outlandish flowers, many of which are plants that grow from bulbs such as crocuses, tulips, irises, anemones and so on. He admires these fine flowers for many reasons but, for him, their outstanding quality is that they help to provide colour and interest in the garden throughout the year: they 'shew forth their beauty and colours so early in the yeare, that they seeme to make a Garden of delight even in the Winter time…the more to entice us to their delight'.[34] Of native plants, although primroses and violets showed their faces in the spring, most of the flowers that traditionally adorned the English garden only had a brief flowering season in the summer, leaving the garden bereft of colour for much of the year.[35] In fact, this short summer flowering season offers one explanation as to why flowers appear not to have been a major feature of sixteenth-century gardens: what these exotic introductions were providing were not just new varieties of flowers but a whole new way of furnishing a garden. Plants could now be selected – and Parkinson supplies appropriate guidance on choice – in order to provide flowers in the garden for every month of the year. The importance of this cannot be underestimated, and he is to be commended for moving so quickly in response to this new phenomenon.

Parkinson's admiration for these new plant introductions did not end there. He describes many of them as 'orderly' and 'stately' because by their very nature they grow upright and 'rise almost to an equall height, which causeth the greater grace'. They can be planted in

20

an orderly fashion, in rows or blocks, and be trusted to stay there – unlike many English plants that have a tendency to spread and ramble in a very disordered way: compare, for instance, tulips and lilies to scrambling roses or honeysuckles. In a manner reminiscent of a modern television gardening programme in its quest to appeal to an ever wider audience, he advises that this quality makes the new plants useful for small gardens, because they take up less space. Tulips in particular, by virtue of their many colours, can be planted in such a way that they resemble 'a peece of curious needle-worke, or peece of painting' and, by choosing a succession of varieties that flower at slightly different times, it is possible to keep a border or bed in flower for more than three months.[36] He even manages to invest these plants with attributes of gentility: 'they carry so stately and delightfull a forme...that there is no Lady or Gentlewoman of any worth that is...not delighted with these flowers'.[37] These are all qualities that inform a new approach to gardening and, although Parkinson cannot be credited with the introduction of new plants into England, he can certainly claim some credit for seizing the moment and showing people how best to display them in their gardens.

Of course, new plants also require new techniques to be learned in order to grow them successfully, and 'because our English Gardiners are all or the most of them utterly ignorant in the ordering of these Out-landish flowers', Parkinson himself will 'take upon mee the forme of a new Gardiner, to give instructions to those that will take pleasure in them'.[38] At first sight this seems a somewhat arrogant stance on Parkinson's part but, if people – gardeners in particular – had never seen these plants before, why would they know what to do with them? He begins with the basics – which way up to plant the bulb, for instance – before moving on to more detailed instructions on how to nurture tender plants grown from seeds, how to protect them from the cold with straw and advising only to water them with water that has been standing in the sun and not drawn straight from the well.

Even more fundamental than this, however, gardeners were now required to rethink their traditional cycle of planting. It was 'the usuall custom' for English flowering plants to be planted in the spring and removed at the end of the summer but many of the new varieties, particularly the bulbs, needed to be planted in the previous year, during July, August or September, and then left in the ground over the winter in order for them to be ready to produce their spring display of colour. These plants would therefore have to be grown in separate beds from the English flowers, otherwise they would be disturbed when the latter were dug up at the end of the season. Again we are reminded that the introduction of these new plants did far more than simply provide a wider variety of flowers for the garden. New methods, techniques and ways of thinking also had to be adopted in order to accommodate them. It introduced a whole new way to garden.

What probably remains the most remarkable feature of *Paradisi in Sole*, however, is that it is the first book to consider that the ornamental value of the plants within it can be the primary purpose of a garden, being included for no other reason than that they are 'very beautifull, delightfull and pleasant'. Not only are they a worthy subject for a book but they are also worthy of their own garden.[39] It recommends that, where possible, they be separated into a new garden: the garden of pleasant flowers, or the garden of pleasure.

Parkinson of course was not the first person to advocate a separate garden for flowers: woodcuts and paintings of medieval gardens, for instance, indicate small, enclosed areas with grass, flowery meads, fruit trees and flower beds, peopled by such figures as gentlewomen sewing or reading, reclining lovers or musicians (see fig. 20). Clearly, these gardens were for contemplation, leisure and pleasure, but equally clearly they were the sole preserve of the elite, attached as they were to castles, palaces and also monasteries. Privy gardens, too, such as those maintained or created during the reign of Henry VIII at Whitehall, Hampton Court and the Tower of London, were simply that – private areas, reserved exclusively for one person or group of people, usually, as in these cases, a king or queen.[40] Although these may well have been separate ornamental areas filled with flowers and set aside for pleasure, this is not the issue here: the point is that they were separated not because they were flower gardens but to keep them private. Richard Surflet's translation of *Maison Rustique* (1600) also indicates a separate garden for flowers but, as has been observed on many occasions by now, this representation of French practice did not necessarily reflect contemporary English practice, nor did it intend to. Yet even in this case, the author is at pains to justify the place of the pleasure or flower garden within the country farm. While claiming that one of its main purposes was to provide, as suggested earlier, a place of recreation and solace for 'the chiefe Lord', he also recommends, on a more practical note, that this is the place 'to set Bee-hives in'.[41] The essential role of bees in the utilitarian garden has already been discussed, and to place the hives close to flowering plants makes obvious sense (fig. 86).

Surflet goes on to describe the flowers which should be planted in this garden. There should be two beds, one containing flowers to make nosegays and garlands – again, the provision of flowers for scent having a more important purpose than we might invest it with today – and a second for other 'herbes of good smell', not necessarily suitable for nosegays but which instead may be used for cutting, strewing on the floor or scenting rooms. There is no mention at all of the ornamental or decorative beauty of the flowers and, interestingly, it is recommended that this garden be set right next to the kitchen garden.[42] Similarly, Lawson makes no mention of this in his main work *A New Orchard and Garden*,

where he includes a single (short) paragraph recommending the planting of flowers in the orchard. However, in the companion volume, *The Country Housewifes Garden*, he refers to two gardens, a kitchen garden and a 'summer' garden of flowering herbs. Again, Lawson appears to be recommending this separation for practical purposes only, suggesting that although they are all ultimately destined for use in the house, it is sensible to keep the vegetables separate from the herbs as the kitchen garden 'must yeeld daily roots' and will therefore 'suffer deformity'. In contrast, the plants in the permanent bed of herbs can be left undisturbed or simply cut for use.[43] Once again, what Lawson is definitely not talking about is a separate area just for pleasure.

Parkinson, however, specifically states that in an ideal world the flower garden would be separated from the kitchen garden and would be positioned with the house to its north side, providing the garden with both shelter and the full benefit of the sun. The fairest rooms of the house would look out into the garden, so that 'besides the benefit of shelter it shall have from them, the buildings and rooms...shall have both sight and sent of whatsoever is excellent...which is one of the greatest pleasures a garden can yeeld his Master'.[44] And this, Parkinson appears to be endorsing, is reason enough to fill this garden with beautiful flowers.

Ideally, the kitchen, or herb garden as he calls it, should be positioned on the other side of the house, not least because the scents arising from cabbages and onions are 'scarce well pleasing to perfume the lodgings of any house'. However, Parkinson, ever practical and perhaps with an eye to broadening the appeal of his book to a wider audience, recognises that not everyone will be in a position to do this and instead 'must make a vertue of necessity...by making their profit their chiefest pleasure, and making one place serve for all uses'.[45] This bluntly reminds us once again of the utilitarian nature of most people's gardens, a fact fully acknowledged by Parkinson. He does not for one moment suggest replacing kitchen herbs and vegetables with ornamental flowers; he is merely recommending them as a desirable addition for those who are in a position to indulge in this luxury – for luxury it is: ornamental flowers produce no tangible 'profit'.

Although the 'Ordering of the Garden of Pleasure' makes up by far the greatest part of this book – 460 pages out of 612 – it is only one part. Parkinson includes sections on the kitchen garden and the orchard because, in his view, these were still essential elements of the garden.[46] His reason for not going into great detail about the kitchen garden is that: 'I thinke there are but few but eyther know it already, or conceive it sufficiently in their minds'. Furthermore, it is not the purpose of his book: 'this worke permitteth not that libertie'.[47]

The purpose of Parkinson's book was to offer new information about a new kind of gardening, and his target audience appears to have been those who were in a position to indulge in this, 'the better sort of Gentry of the Land'. Although he constantly and consistently qualifies much of his advice to include 'all men', he also makes many references to Gentlemen, Gentlewomen and to gentry tastes and, of course, his book is dedicated to Queen Henrietta Maria, whom it is reasonable to assume he knew personally. His appointment as Royal Botanist certainly allows for this possibility. At the same time, his book is intensely practical and is perhaps also aimed at gardeners such as himself – for instance, as seen in Chapter 1, Tradescant, Evelyn, Hanmer and Reresby all possessed their own annotated copies. However, it is unlikely that 'all men' would have been able to afford to buy this large and lavishly illustrated volume: if for no other reason, its readership would necessarily have been restricted to those who could afford to buy it. So although this was a new book for a new kind of gardener, it and the kind of garden it describes were only within the reach of the privileged few rather than the many.

To sum up, Parkinson brought a new approach to both garden writing and to gardening. In the same way that attitudes towards the new science made possible this new and radical approach, so too did changing attitudes towards luxury and conspicuous consumption. As has been seen, in the sixteenth century, ideas of pleasure, luxury and recreation were strongly associated with idleness and self-indulgence, traits condemned first by Christian humanists and then by Puritans because they were non-productive and contributed nothing to the common good. However, by the early decades of the new century, times and attitudes were changing: for instance, the pursuit of individual profit and prosperity was recognised as a factor in maintaining social stability, the opening up of international markets made trade in luxury goods both possible and desirable and the rise in conspicuous consumption had become largely unstoppable. Shopping and the acquiring of goods that were not strictly necessary – satisfying wants rather than needs – became acceptable, and the seventeenth century saw a 'gradual emergence of a new idealogy, accepting the pursuit of consumer goods as a valid object of human endeavour'.[48] It is in this context and as a response to the changing times that we have to place John Parkinson and his *Paradisi in Sole*. He recommends plants and flowers as objects of beauty and delight for no other reason than that they are pleasurable and he is the first garden writer to advocate English gardens as places to display beautiful flowers. He offers this advice without apology – he sees no need, as his predecessors had done, to justify gardens and plants with uses and virtues. In the same way that the consumption of luxury goods was becoming accepted, so too was the display of rare and costly plants in the garden. It has been discussed earlier and at length that the cultivation of exotic fruits in the garden was an outward and visible sign of the wealth and status of the owner. But even this could still be viewed as 'profit' – either as foodstuffs for the household or as gifts which would have been reciprocated in kind or favour. It seems that by the time Parkinson published this book in 1629, ornamental flowers, arguably even more of a luxury than exotic fruit as they have no use or profit at all, were becoming a new status symbol of the rising gentry class.

What other contemporary evidence then is there to back up these ideas? Before looking at evidence of actual gardens, let us spend a moment or two in the company of Sir Francis Bacon. As well as his vast intellectual output and important influence on the new empirical scientific method of enquiry, Bacon's probably most frequently quoted words come from his famous essay 'Of Gardens', published in 1625, a year before his death: 'God Almighty first planted a Garden. And indeed, it is the purest of human pleasures'.[49] These opening lines still appear to this day on posters, garden plaques and tee-shirts, in titles for garden books, chapters in garden books, as well as the whole essay still being published and republished in its own right. It is now even available as an e-book, such is its long-lasting appeal to the garden enthusiast and writer.

'Of Gardens' was part of a series of fifty-eight essays covering a huge range of topics and it describes, as Bacon puts it, 'a Princely garden' in which he has 'spared for no cost'. It is not a model, he says, but the 'generall Lines of it' and it is frequently held up as an example of an idealised early seventeenth-century garden. However, although this is not a description of an actual garden, it has been argued that it is based on Bacon's observations of some of the finest gardens that he knew, as well as reflecting features of his own garden at Gorhambury in Hertfordshire.[50] And, aside from recommending that it should cover at least 'thirty acres of ground' (an extremely large garden plot!), much of what he says falls in line with what we know of contemporary gardens. It 'is best to be square' and each section of the formal arrangement should be symmetrical, lined with alleys and walks and including 'arbours with seats, set in some decent order'. The garden he describes is also, as was often the way, a curious mixture of distinctly old-fashioned features with new, forward-thinking ideas. Perhaps most interestingly, it also reflects Bacon's own individual likes and dislikes. For instance, he describes two garden mounts, features which had been around since medieval times, for this garden. One is a grand affair, somewhat reminiscent of that described by Markham in *The English Husbandman*,[51] 'to be Thirty Foot high' with 'three Ascents and Alleys, enough for foure to walk abreast', which should be set in the middle of the main garden, topped perhaps with a fine banqueting house – a place from which to see and be seen. At the same time, Bacon also recommends a '*Mount* of some Pretty Height', clearly a much less elaborate construction, to be set in the 'side-grounds' further away from the house and looking out into the fields beyond the boundaries.[52] He includes Italianate features such as ornamental fountains, although he does not like pools because they are 'full of Flies, and Frogs' and dismisses decorative knots and topiary as 'toys' and 'for children'.

Of particular relevance here is the first third of his essay, which is devoted to planting. Like Parkinson, Bacon sees gardening as a pleasure although, unlike Parkinson, he does not even mention the utilitarian aspects of the garden – and his list of flowers evocatively describes their colours, fragrances and rambling beauty in a way which is perhaps due more to his attributes as a writer than as a gardener. While it must be remembered that this is an essay, not a book of gardening advice, Bacon does nevertheless display a degree of horticultural knowledge. He suggests, for instance, as Parkinson does, flowering plants for every month of the year in order to create a 'perpetual spring' in the garden, including old English favourites such as roses, gilliflowers, honeysuckle, violets and so on, as well as new foreign varieties such as iris, tulips, hyacinths and lilies (fig. 87). As well as visual pleasure, he is also

87   Varieties of hyacinths, from John Parkinson's *Paradisi in Sole*, 1629

88   Jacques le Moyne, *Strawberry Plant*, 1585

delighted with fragrance, 'the Breath of Flowers, is farre Sweeter in the Aire' and he recommends that fragrant herbs such as thyme and mint should be planted in the walks and alleys so that they will be trodden on and crushed, thereby releasing their perfume into the air. He also mentions the 'most Excellent Cordial smell' of dying strawberry leaves, which indicates as clearly as anything else that here is a man who really gets out into his garden and absorbs these sensory experiences for himself. Whether the garden Bacon describes in this essay is real or imagined, it does not detract from the fact that this is a vision of an ideal garden and, for Bacon, that is a garden full of flowers.

It has already been noted that documentary sources relating to Elizabethan gardens show a particular paucity of information about flowers in the garden. Available evidence for the early seventeenth century continued with only occasional specific references to flowers but, although rare, they do offer insight into the growing interest in ornamental flowers for the garden. There are, for example, a number of references to the gardens at the home of Sir Henry Fanshawe at Ware Park in Hertfordshire. The much-travelled diplomat and writer Sir Henry Wotton observes in his 'Elements of Architecture' (1624) that despite the many delightful gardens he has seen on the Continent, which 'have much more benefite of Sunne than wee',

> yet have I seene in our *owne*, a delicate and diligent *curiositie*, surely without *parallel* among foreign *Nations*: Namely, in the Garden of Sir *Henry Fanshaw*, at his seat in *Ware-Parke*, where I wel remember, he did so precisely examine the *tinctures*, and *seasons* of his *flowers*, that in their *setting*...should be...like a piece not of *Nature*, but of *Arte*.[53]

This description is reminiscent of Parkinson's reference to planting differently coloured tulips so that they resemble a tapestry or painting, and the letter-writer and court commentator John Chamberlain agrees that at Ware Park you shall 'see as fresh and flourishing a garden (I thincke) as England affoordes'.[54] In her memoirs, addressed to her only son and written in 1676, Lady Ann Fanshawe (Sir Henry's daughter-in-law) writes of the praise bestowed on

10

his grandfather's garden at Ware Park, 'none excelling it in flowers, physic-herbs, and fruit, in which things he did greatly delight'.[55] As this garden was worthy of so much comment, it is likely that it represented the exception rather than the rule. Nevertheless, these various sources indicate without a doubt the existence in the early seventeenth century of a much admired flower garden at the home of Sir Henry Fanshawe at Ware Park.

Similarly, there is a painting of Newburgh Priory in Yorkshire which has been identified as depicting examples of 'two pre-Civil War flower gardens'.[56] It shows the south front of the house, with two gardens laid out in widely different styles, and the colours used in the painting indeed suggest that they are flower gardens. Although the painting has been dated to about the end of the seventeenth century, the two gardens have been identified as a Jacobean garden (nearest to the house) and a later Caroline garden in front of it.[57] However, given that this is an apparently unique record of this latter type of garden, with no further corroborating evidence the certainty of this assertion must be brought into question. In the end, maybe this painting does little more than present the possibility that there were ornamental flower gardens laid out at Newburgh Priory in the early seventeenth century.

More useful perhaps are extant plant lists from two other Yorkshire gardens of this time, one compiled by the Reverend Walter Stonehouse relating to his garden at Darfield, south Yorkshire, in 1640 and the other, a more recently discovered list contained in the garden notebook of Sir John Reresby of Thrybergh, covering the years from 1633 to 1644.[58] Stonehouse's list consists of a catalogue of 450 plants made up in 1640, to which a further 416 were added over the next four years. There is also a remarkably detailed scale plan of his 'best garden', which is made up of five geometrically patterned beds marked with numbers corresponding to the plant lists.[59] Unlike the slightly conjectural evidence for Newburgh, this appears to be an example of a real ornamental flower garden and, more critically, a garden that can be more precisely dated. From Stonehouse's notes and plans, together with the fact that until at least the beginning of the twentieth century, parts of the garden remained extant, it is possible to piece together a reasonable picture of how this garden may have looked (figs 89, 90). The garden shown in the plan was just one of three sections, the other two being the 'saffron garth' and the orchard, although fruit trees appear to have been grown on the walls of all three gardens. Stonehouse's 'best garden', shown in the plan, was about thirty yards square, but although not particularly large, it contained, as noted earlier, several hundred varieties of plants. The ornamental beds may well have been laid out at an earlier date but Stonehouse's list refers specifically to the plants growing in it around 1640 and, from the evidence, we can be almost certain that these plants were actually planted, as opposed to just being planned. In 1648, during the years of Civil War unrest, the Reverend Stonehouse was stripped of his ecclesiastical living and imprisoned

89   The Rev. Walter Stonehouse, 'A Modell of my Garden at Darfield, 1640'
90   Re-creation of a knot garden, based on Stonehouse's plan,
at Moseley Old Hall, Staffordshire

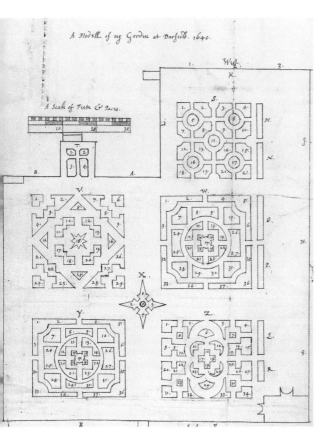

by the Parliamentary Commissioners. On his release a few years later, he returned to his garden and noted sadly on his list that most of the plants had not survived in his absence and that he now had 'no hope of a new colony'.[60] Clearly, he was mourning the loss of what by all accounts had once been a delightful garden.

Sir John Reresby was a near neighbour of the Reverend Stonehouse and had inherited the estate at Thrybergh Hall in Yorkshire on the death of his father in 1628. In common with other gentry gardens of this period, much of Reresby's interest was in fruit-growing – he lists many varieties of pears, plums, apples and cherries as well as the more exotic peaches, nectarines, apricots, quinces and figs – but he also includes an extensive list of tulip varieties and more than four hundred herbaceous plants that were growing in his garden. Evidence of his enthusiasm for gardening begins with the enclosing of orchards and gardens around the Hall with dry-stone walls and the commencement of his garden notebook in 1633.[61] This document was continued until 1644, when the outbreak of Civil War led to

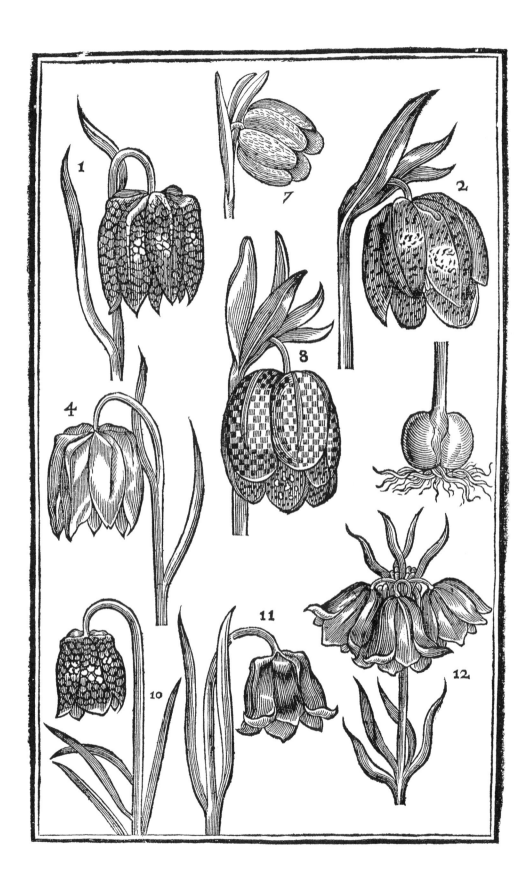

Sir John's imprisonment and eventual death from fever in 1646. The notebook consists of about seventy-five leaves (although nearly half are blank) and is invaluable as a record of the full range of plants and trees that were grown at Thrybergh during this relatively short period. A list of 'the seuerall Trees planted by my selfe in my Orchards & Gardens at Thrybergh: Begunne 1633' is followed by twelve pages of fruit tree varieties growing or planted there. Most of the rest of the notebook is filled with the names of flowering plants including 'My best Tulipas 1641', 'My Choyce flowers & plantes with a mem. what month they beare' and so on. On folio 22, he begins a systematic alphabetical list, dated 11 April 1642, of all the plants in his garden, which continues to folio 54. Many of the entries are indexed in a way that suggests that there was, or was intended to be, a plan of the garden indicating where the plants were situated but, unfortunately, there is no trace of this now. Reresby's list reveals an enthusiasm for 'outlandish' plants – as well as many varieties of tulips already referred to, flowers such as anemones, colchicum, fritillaria and lychnis, to name but a few, are also mentioned (fig. 91). There are many native plants too, of course, including roses, lavenders, peonies and gilliflowers. It is a list of plants comparable to Tradescant's plant list of 1634, Stonehouse's list and those recorded as growing in Parkinson's garden at Long Acre.[62] Many of these plants were, as noted before, cross-referenced to pages in Parkinson's *Paradisi in Sole*. Should we conclude, therefore, that Sir John Reresby was another contemporary plant enthusiast and his garden somewhat exceptional?

It is difficult to know since Reresby's notebook gives little else away, but what we have is a comment written by his son in his memoirs some twenty years or so after his father's death, which sheds some light on the question:

> My father was exactly curious in his garden, and was of the first that acquainted that part of England (so far north) with the exactness and nicety of those things – not only as to the form or contrivance of the ground, but as to excellency and variety of fruits, flowers, greens, in which he was rather extravagant than curious, for he placed his pleasure not only innocently but pleasantly in it.[63]

As his son would only have been ten years old when Reresby was imprisoned, it seems unlikely that what he wrote came from personal recollection but, rather, that his father's garden had a reputation for introducing innovative ideas to this part of England. The son comments on both the layout of the garden (its 'form or contrivance'), about which we know little, but emphasises more his father's extravagant choice and range of plants, as just described. He was clearly both knowledgeable and skilful ('exactly curious') but also took great pleasure in his garden. There is an implication that whereas he exercised a careful control over the wider estate, when it came to the ornamental flower garden, he was prepared to be more lavish. We have no way of quantifying his extravagance, but the fact that it was noteworthy must be of significance. It is known that when the elder Sir John took over the estate from his father in 1628 he was forced to run it on somewhat limited means. Alterations to the garden, like those to the Hall, were made on a piecemeal basis, for instance enclosing courtyards that were already flanked by buildings in order perhaps to save on the expense of new walling.[64] However, it seems that once he had planted his orchards (still a primary concern), Sir John then turned his attention to his passion for flowers and he remained, we are told, 'ever constant to his garden'.[65] After his death, the family moved away to London and his son and heir spent much time travelling on the Continent, returning to Thrybergh Hall only in 1659. By this time, of course, the flower collection would have been long gone through neglect and, as the younger Sir John puts it, 'the form of gardening was so different to what was used at this day, that it was almost as chargeable to me to put the ground into that method and form as to replant it as if it had never been enclosed'. Instead of reviving his father's reputation and passion for plants by replanting the flower beds, he installed a fountain, a parterre and a grotto in the summer-house.[66] This is a good example of how quickly garden layouts can be transformed. Within a generation the garden was completely altered, highlighting again the need for caution and precision in the dating of gardens.

From these examples it is possible to discern an increase among enthusiasts for the growing of flowers in the garden, and further examination of the commonplace books of Sir John Oglander add to this picture. Unlike his northern compatriots, Sir John does not actually provide much horticultural information about flower varieties and so on – from the extant manuscripts, at least, it seems that he did not keep detailed plant lists – but what his writing offers are other clues about his gardening interests which allow us to understand some of this evidence within a wider context. Sir John's interest in fruit-growing has already been discussed at length and that he was equally prepared to spend time and money on other parts of his garden is evident from his description of the garden at Nunwell, quoted in full in Chapter 4 (see pp. 95, 97). In it, he includes a description of what is obviously his flower garden: 'An[d] in the Parlour garden, in one knott all sortes of Gilliflowers[,] in the other knott all sortes of ffrench fflowers, and Tulippes of all sortes[.] Some rootes costs me 10s a Roote'. The map of Nunwell (see fig. 49) indicates an ornamental garden in front of the house, marked as containing both a terrace and a parterre, and it is highly probable that this was the location of Sir John's 'Parlour garden'. It is difficult to find any precise definition for what exactly is meant by a 'parlour' garden, but in this case we can see that it is an area of the garden close to the house, which can be easily reached or at least viewed from the parlour windows – just, in fact, as described by Parkinson when he recommended that the garden of flowers 'be in the sight and full prospect of all the chief and choicest rooms of the house'.[67]

The account books of Sir Peter Temple at Stow for 1625–26 mention a 'parler garden' a number of times, which contains gilliflowers and other herbs, as well as four knots that appear to require frequent clipping. Again, it is located under the 'parler windowe'.[68] His father, Sir Thomas Temple, also refers to his new garden at Burton Dassett as the 'Parlour gardine'. This too is to be planted with flowers and is situated immediately outside the parlour windows – there are instructions to plant over and around the 'South chamber window of the Parler'. The probate inventory of Sir Thomas Puckering of Warwick Priory refers to the 'great paved Parlour next the garden' and Evelyn mentions the new window in his parlour which looks out into his 'private garden of choice flowers'.[69] Sir Thomas Hanmer describes what he considers to be an essential part of any flower enthusiast's garden as 'a little private Seminary', in which to raise flowers and plants and to 'keepe such treasures as are not to bee exposed to everyone's view'.[70] The defining features of the parlour garden therefore seem to be its location (adjacent to the parlour) and the fact that it is an area separated from the rest of the garden, filled with ornamental flowers and generally set aside for private use. These features are reminiscent of those identified as appertaining to the earlier privy gardens of royalty and aristocracy and perhaps could be seen as a seventeenth-century manifestation of the same idea in the gardens of the gentry.

According to Sir John Oglander's description, the parlour garden at Nunwell was divided into two areas, or knots as he refers to them: one knot was for gilliflowers (traditional English flowers) and the other reserved for more exotic species, specifically all sorts of French flowers and tulips. Again, this arrangement is just as recommended by Parkinson, who suggests that because their horticultural requirements are different, the two types of plants should be kept in separate beds for ease of maintenance. Whether Oglander ever met Parkinson, or even read his book, is unknown but it is interesting that they were apparently advocating and carrying out similar gardening practices in different parts of the country at the same time. Sir John's parlour garden seems to match up to Parkinson's ideal of the garden of pleasure – a garden of flowers in full view of the main rooms of the house – and the flowers with which Sir John chooses to stock his garden follow the current fashion for exotic, foreign and unusual plants.

Such plants were of course costly items: Oglander mentions that some cost him ten shillings a root, a considerable sum of money to spend on a single plant, where other references in his account books note that 200 cabbage plants could be had for 1s, an estate labourer was paid 4s a week and a barrel of figs was purchased for 8s.[71] Elsewhere, we learn from John Chamberlain that in 1609 Sir Henry Fanshawe had 'fowre or five flowers from Sir

Rafe Winwood that cost twelve pound'.[72] To spend large sums of money on flowers was not unheard of, it seems, and Sir John Oglander himself writes that he has been 'so foolish as to bestowe more moneyes then a wise man would have in fflowers for the Garden'.[73] It is, as was noted in the case of Reresby, difficult to quantify such remarks, but throughout his writing Oglander displays a careful, if not parsimonious, attitude to his financial affairs: 'If I spend as mutch this year as I did the last, I shall be like a man in a storm not well knowinge what course to take', he notes in his account book on 4 September 1623. Things do not appear to have improved much by 1632 when he notes again, if more succinctly: 'I must spend lesse otherwayes I shall be undone'.[74] Even so, despite these obvious concerns over expenditure, Sir John was not averse to spending money on other extravagances. On 4 August 1624, a ship from North Africa came into port on the Isle of Wight and Sir John went aboard to buy tobacco, sugar, silk stockings and dates, for which he paid the princely sum of £3 13s.[75] Clearly, Sir John was taken by all sorts of exotic goods from abroad, not just flowers, and that he considers he has spent more than he should on garden plants may be an indication of not simply his love of flowers but also the degree of importance he attaches to such displays of luxury and wealth.

It is significant too that even though Sir John does not name the varieties of flowers in his garden, he wants to record that they were 'french flowers'. Unusual and therefore more desirable plants were being imported from all over the world, but particularly from the near Continent – Holland, Flanders and France. We know that in 1610 John Tradescant was dispatched to the Continent to buy plants to stock the newly laid-out gardens at Hatfield House: in the company of the French king's head gardeners, Jean and Vespasien Robin, he visited, among other places, Paris and Rouen. There he purchased, along with a large number of fruit trees, 'flowers called anemones', 'On[e] bundall of genista hispanica' and 'on[e] great hamper of flowers and Seeds'.[76] Later in the century, Sir Thomas Hanmer's extensive lists of plants and prices include tulips, ranunculus, irises and anemones all obtained from the leading Paris nurseryman Pierre Morin, as well as anemones and tulips from another French nurseryman, Monsieur Picot. Hanmer also notes that roots and bulbs were more expensive in France than in England – many of the prices are measured in pounds rather than shillings – but this does not stop him buying them from there.[77] It may be that there was an implied prestige in buying plants from France: by the early seventeenth century, the Continent, particularly France, was seen as a primary source of everything that was luxurious, stylish and fashionable.[78] This could explain why, although he gives no further details about his plant purchases, Sir John mentions that they were French. Clearly for him, and as would have been recognised by his compatriots, this was a noteworthy attribute.

Similar prestige applied to tulips imported from Holland, and the Englishman's passion for tulips in ever more varieties has been well documented.[79] Since Gerard had described only fourteen varieties of tulip in his *Herball* published in 1597, the market for tulips had grown stupendously. Because of the enormously wide variety of these bulbs that could be horticulturally reproduced and exported with ease, it was possible to both supply the ordinary gardener with the more common varieties and satisfy the demand of the wealthy connoisseur for rare and highly sought after specimens. In 1629, Parkinson wrote at length on well over a hundred varieties of tulip, claiming that they were 'greatly desired and accepted as any other the most choisest' by the 'better sort of the Gentry of the land'.[80] That Sir John Oglander had 'Tulippes of all sortes' as well as French flowers in his garden suggests that he too considered himself among the better sort of the gentry and that displaying these flowers in his garden was an outward and visible sign of this.

In contrast, the garden created by Sir Thomas Temple and Richard the Gardiner at Sir Thomas's Warwickshire home in Burton Dassett – his 'little gardine at Dassett paled' – tells another story. Despite the intense 'hands-on' interest in the maintenance of his estates and orchards revealed in his correspondence, it was not until Sir Thomas retired from his active public life and was well into his sixties that he turned his attention to creating this garden. It is clear from the correspondence and his memorandum book that there already was an orchard and garden at the house at Burton Dassett, but that around this time (1631) there was some minor renovation going on – there are references to the new orchard, the old bee garden, the old garden and so on – but the paled garden appears to be a completely new addition. There is, however, nothing ostentatious about this little garden although it is, notably, a flower garden. It is laid out conventionally and in a number of ways is quite old-fashioned. It is planted with roses, violets, gilliflowers, primroses and honeysuckles, all native plants described by Parkinson as 'English flowers', and which, as has been noted before, would not have been out of place in any sixteenth-century garden. There is no sign here of Oglander's passion for exotic or costly plants from France or elsewhere. Even the fact that the garden is paled with a wooden fence is somewhat out-dated, the move to the use of unsupported hedges having begun in the previous century.[81]

It is probably significant that by this time, Sir Thomas was an old man – he was seventy-one when he died in 1636 – and that he was feeling his age comes through strongly in his letters. He writes of his age as 'a sickness of itself' and he complains more than once about a fall which has left him lame. A number of his letters to Harry Rose begin with words to the effect that he is writing this down before he forgets, and on one occasion he asks for a copy of the letter back so that he can remember what he has told him. He writes to his daughter that he is thankful 'of so many children & grandchildren, that can supplie our wantes

of legges, eyes, etc.' Somewhat poignantly, one of his last letters to Rose is to ask him to order a new pair of boots, but they need to be a little longer and wider than previously, 'for that I am continues troubled with cornes & weare alwaies or for the most parte 2 paires of wollen stockinges in regard of cramps & my hip bone put out of joynte'.[82] Despite these ailments, what advancing age and retirement from public life brought him was the time and leisure to indulge in his enthusiasm for his little garden at Dassett. And although Sir Thomas was clearly interested in experimenting with different horticultural techniques such as how to establish vine-cuttings or bay-slips, it is difficult to detect in him any particular aspirations for the fashionable or new, and there is little evidence that he was concerned with showing off his garden. Rather, it seems that he was simply displaying a desire for a fragrant and pleasant place, filled with flowers and plants that he liked – and knew – in which he could while away the remainder of his days.

The evidence presented here offers a few glimpses into the seventeenth-century 'garden of pleasant flowers'. Gardeners and garden owners such as Walter Stonehouse and Sir John Reresby give us detailed information about the planting of the garden, while others, such as Sir John Oglander and Sir Thomas Temple, because of the more personalised nature of the evidence, offer deeper insight into the creation and maintenance of these contemporaneous gardens of pleasure. Together, all these aspects make a significant contribution to enhancing our picture of the early seventeenth-century garden.

Evidence such as this, valuable as it is, however, remains sparse and rooted in particularity. We have noted before, and examined evidence for, the huge number of variable factors involved in creating a garden – space, cost, purpose, local conditions, as well as questions of taste and personal likes and dislikes. In addition, those who left records of their gardens did not necessarily concentrate on the same aspects of it, so records are at best subjective and incomplete: attempting to form a general picture of the place of flowers in the English garden based on rare and specific examples remains problematic and inconclusive. Similar difficulties arise in attempting to trace the history and place of another apparently central element of the early modern garden, the knot garden. The lack of visual evidence and problems in defining exactly what was meant by a 'knot' were mentioned in Chapter 3. These complexities continued into the seventeenth century and are the subject of the next chapter.

7

THE KNOTTY PROBLEM OF KNOTS

An image of the knot garden seems firmly fixed in our modern minds as the defining element of the early modern garden, but the fact is that we know very little about them at all. Roy Strong has acknowledged that the history of the knot garden has thus far been 'wrapped in total obscurity' and C. Paul Christianson, writing on the gardens of sixteenth-century London, agrees that, as no unmistakable images survive, the actual design of early garden knots remains a 'matter of recurring speculation among garden historians'.[1] Regardless of this, however, such gardens continue to be confidently reproduced at such historic sites as Hatfield House, Kenilworth Castle or Shakespeare's garden at New Place in Stratford-upon-Avon, thereby perpetuating and giving substance to our possibly misplaced perceptions. That knot gardens were being laid out in English gardens throughout the sixteenth and seventeenth centuries is not in question: the many contemporary references to 'knots' indicate that they were a feature of gardens at this time. What is in question, given the lack of specific descriptions or visual images to help us, is what exactly was understood by this term and what, therefore, these gardens might actually have looked like.

This chapter attempts to unravel some of the complexities surrounding the history of the knot garden and to define its place more convincingly within the early modern English garden. To this end, extant evidence in painting, maps, plans and contemporary literature will be re-examined and reassessed in order to try to establish, not what we would like it to tell us, but what, if anything, it is really telling us about knot gardens of the period.

Documentary evidence for knots in sixteenth-century gardens has already been mentioned, including the ubiquitously quoted reference to Cardinal Wolsey's 'Knotts so enknotted, it cannot be exprest', and indeed there is a tendency nowadays to associate knots with Tudor gardens. In 1613, Markham wrote of knot gardens that they were 'ancient and at this day of most use amongst the vulgar though least respected with great ones',[2] implying perhaps that by the early seventeenth century knot gardens may have been becoming unfashionable, at least in the grandest gardens.[3] However, other contemporary sources indicate a different story and there is plenty of evidence to suggest that knot gardens continued to be laid out in the gardens of the gentry long into the seventeenth century.

For instance, in June 1625, Henry the Gardener at Stow spent three days 'Clypping the quarter hedge of the Parler Garden' and a further three days 'cutting out of the knottes' there. He then passed another day 'clipping the 2 knottes in the Parler garden'. For these seven days' work he received 3s 6d. In 1641, on the other side of the country in Herefordshire, Joyce Jeffreys paid her gardener '18d and diet' for three days' work 'making a knott', although there is no further detail. Parkinson's lengthy discourse on the various contemporary fashions in materials used to border knots has already been discussed in detail, but he offered no advice on how actually to lay out a knot. This is curious given the precise detail he entered into on many other practical gardening matters. Sir John Oglander wrote in 1633 of two knots in his garden at Nunwell, as remarked earlier, one filled with 'all sortes of Gilliflowers', the other with 'all sortes of ffrench fflowers, and Tulips of all sortes'. Sir Arthur Ingram and Lionel Cranfield, first Earl of Middlesex, both maintained knot gardens at their respective properties in Yorkshire and Hertfordshire and, although he does not refer to them as such, the new garden laid out by Sir Thomas Temple at Burton Dassett in the 1630s contained two simple knots, or quarters, reminiscent of the simple geometric compartments already identified as a feature of sixteenth-century gardens (see fig. 51).[4] In the late 1650s, Sir Thomas Hanmer, writing from his home at Bettisfield in north Wales, noted a change in the layout of 'knotts or quarters' which, he says, were now 'much different' from his father's time. They were no longer hedged with privet, rosemary or other tall herbs, but instead were laid open, the borders only upheld with low, coloured board, stone or tile.[5] Although suggesting a change in style over the years, Sir Thomas still refers to these as knot gardens. Also, the border materials he mentions here are the same as those described by Parkinson in 1629, perhaps indicating the length of time it took for new fashions to reach the Welsh borders from London. From evidence such as this, it seems that although the idea of the knot may well have developed over time, far from passing out of fashion, knots, in whatever form, remained an important element of rural gentry gardens throughout the period.

But all this still gives us little idea of how these gardens might have looked. There are other clues, including illustrations printed in contemporary literature or the occasional depictions of gardens in paintings and on maps and plans, but, unfortunately, these can often be misleading, because they are not necessarily, for reasons to be explored, representative of the reality on the ground. Difficulties arise because the evidence, such as it is, is open to a variety of interpretations and is often found wanting. This is a problem that particularly manifests itself in the increasing number of re-creations and restorations of historic gardens, because the fact remains, as already stated, that despite this lack of evidence, an image of what we think these gardens looked like persists. Theoretical studies and practical re-creations apparently start from the premise that we do know how these gardens looked, even though we have yet to find the proof.

An initial problem arises in defining what exactly was meant by a 'knot'. As has been seen, although references to knots appear throughout the period, the term does not seem to apply to anything specific and in the absence of visual images or descriptions, there are few clues as to what was actually being referred to. On the one hand, it could describe the kind of intricate interlacing designs such as those found in contemporary gardening manuals (fig. 93), although as will be shown and contrary to the assumptions of modern

authors and garden designers, there is little evidence to support the idea that this type of complex knot garden was ever made in England. On the other hand, it seems that any simple arrangement of beds within borders, as discussed in Chapter 3 and as illustrated in the extant sketch of *c*.1550 of the garden at Richmond Palace by Wyngaerde (see fig. 46) or in the ubiquitous image of an Elizabethan garden from Hyll's *The Gardeners Labyrinth* of 1577 (see fig. 16) could also be referred to as a knot.[6]

Such problems with terminology continue into the seventeenth century. Contemporary garden writers such as Markham appear to use the words 'knot' and 'quarter' interchangeably and Lawson refers simply to 'borders and squares' when describing areas in which to plant flowers. Later in the century, the French garden designer André Mollet in his *Jardin de Plaisir* illustrated in detail some extremely intricate designs for knot gardens, which he described variously and interchangeably as knots, parterres and compartments throughout the work (see figs 114, 115). His English contemporary, John Evelyn, similarly conflated the terms knot, parterre and compartment.[7]

In addition to these difficulties, if we bear in mind that many English gardening books were originally derived from French sources, there also arises the possibility of confusion resulting from poor translation. For instance, in the text of Estienne's frequently reprinted *Maison Rustique* (1564), eventually translated into English at the beginning of the following century, the French word *compartiment* is translated as 'proportion' or occasionally 'quarter'. In the titles for the designs, it is possible that *compartiment* could mean knot, but proportion is more likely. For example, *Compartiment Simple* is translated as 'A simple proportion, or draught of a knot', or for a more complex design, *Bordure avec son compartiment due milieu* appears in translation as 'A border with his severall proportion in the midst'. There seems to be no direct translation from French into 'knot'.[8]

Further room for confusion arises when we remember that in English the word 'knot' refers to both the garden design and the process of tying the lines in order to make them:

> Upon this line you shall make knots…and then another knot for the second or inward circle of the round…to every knot of the said line for to make your rounds withall, you shall make fast, right over against the knot…by the means of these knots shorter or longer…[9]

Unfortunately, none of this helps to clarify what was actually understood by the word 'knot', except that it was apparently a wide-ranging term used to describe any kind of design set in a geometrical border within the garden.

So where else can we look in order to advance our knowledge of the early modern knot garden? One extremely useful source of images of the early modern garden and the knot is in the background of contemporary portraits. There are not many of them, but those that are extant have been comprehensively collated and examined by Roy Strong and the results of his deliberations are set out in *The Artist and the Garden* (2000).[10] This seems a good place to pick up the story and see what more these paintings can reveal about the development of the knot through the late sixteenth and early seventeenth centuries.

One of the earliest portraits to depict an English garden in the background is Rowland Lockey's *Sir Thomas More and Family*, dated 1594 (fig. 94). It is an updated version after Holbein's original from the 1520s, which depicted the seven figures shown left and centre in this painting: Sir Thomas More, his father, his son, his three daughters and his daughter-in-law. In this updated version, a new generation, More's grandson, his wife and their two sons, have been added to the portrait. The garden shown through the window only appears in this later painting, behind the new family group. Obviously, as these two groups of people were not contemporaneous, there is no sense in which this portrait is a depiction of reality.

The garden in this painting has been dated to between 1520 when More bought the land for his new house in Chelsea, and his execution in 1535.[11] However, as the garden in the background of this later painting does not appear in the original portrait, this does leave its dating open to question. While it is always possible that this image represents a garden as it was in the 1520s, Lockey's positioning of the garden within his new composition, framing and giving prominence to the new family group, clearly associates the garden with the later generation. Also, by this time the More family no longer lived at the Chelsea residence, so there is no sense in which this can be a 'real' view, and it is extremely unlikely that Lockey would have had any idea what the garden had looked like more than half a century earlier. It seems more probable that the artist depicted a garden which was contemporaneous with Sir Thomas's descendants and one which would be familiar to him: that is, a garden of the late Elizabethan era.

That being the case, we can see that this is a simple garden layout, comprising one hedged compartment, set within a larger area, with walls on at least two sides (fig. 95). The compartment contains five squares, or quarters, and an L-shaped border, each edged with low hedging and surrounded by wide paths. The relative size of the garden can be ascertained by the depiction of the two figures walking side by side along the outer path. There are three trees and, although they are not planted symmetrically, the overall impression is

of a geometric and ordered pattern within the garden. There is, however, no sign of anything more intricate: it seems that this is an example of exactly the kind of garden described earlier – a simple arrangement of bordered squares, set within an enclosed compartment, which may well have been referred to as knots. The More family portrait is unarguably a valuable source of visual evidence depicting an early modern garden, and what it is showing us is a garden of the late sixteenth century.

Another family portrait, that of Thomas Wentworth and his family in front of their home and gardens at Wentworth Woodhouse in Yorkshire, dating from *c*.1575 (see fig. 76) also

reveals a garden, just visible in the background, made up of a similar, if somewhat irregular, arrangement of beds and borders. Again, there is no indication of intricate knot designs.

The gardens illustrated in these portraits differ little from the one shown in Wyngaerde's mid-sixteenth-century sketch of Richmond Palace (see fig. 46) or those depicted in the map of London from *c*.1561 (see fig. 27), or in a painting of Conwy Castle from *c*.1600 (fig. 96 and see p. x). These all indicate the prevalence of these simple knot designs up to the end of the century.

And as we move into the seventeenth century, a series of portraits continues to depict this kind of garden layout. For instance, a detail from the portrait of *Sir Thomas and Lady Lucy with Seven of their Children* of *c.*1622–4 shows, somewhat opaquely in the background, a formal garden at Charlecote Park, set out in geometric hedged compartments (fig. 97; see fig. 66).

There are other examples, all dating from the early decades of the 1600s, which show, equally obscurely, variations on the arrangement of geometric patterns within the garden, but while these later gardens are more formal and sophisticated in their execution, they seem little different in essence from the Elizabethan gardens already discussed. What they do reveal, however, are early signs of a more open, cut-turf style of knot design that became fashionable later in the century. As mentioned, Sir Thomas Hanmer observed and noted this change in the style of knot gardens. An example of such a design, albeit on a grand scale, may also be seen in the magnificent garden depicted in a portrait of Lord Capel of Hadham and his family from *c.*1640 (fig. 98).

From the paintings examined here then, it is possible to discern a development of the knot garden from the simple compartment as seen in the More portrait, through its more sophisticated execution as seen at Charlecote, to the grand open layout depicted at

Hadham Hall. Nevertheless, none of these portraits depicts the kind of interlacing knot gardens which appear in gardening manuals and which are often assumed to be the essence of the Elizabethan garden. Evidence for this in any of the portraits is less forthcoming and less persuasive.

In fact, there is only one such painting. A portrait from 1606 of the young Lettice Newdigate is identified as a 'unique view of an Elizabethan knot garden' and clearly shows a view of the garden with two interlacing knots in all their complexity (fig. 99).[12] A third knot, made up of a more simple arrangement with a fountain in the centre, is also depicted. Although the dating of this painting places it outside the Elizabethan era, it is perfectly possible that the garden itself could date from then. However, the fact that it is apparently a unique view of this type of knot is hardly compelling evidence of the prevalence of this style during the late Elizabethan period. There is one other portrait that depicts something more like an interlacing knot garden, but it is shown in a painting dated c.1625–30, putting it well outside the Elizabethan era and possibly even beyond the reign of James I (fig. 100).

AN. DNI
1606

ÆTATIS
SVÆ 2

Lettice Daughter of Sᴿ Inᵒ Newdigate Kᵗ Wife to Bolton

While it is possible to take the view that this garden is simply old-fashioned, at the same time, there is no reason to assume that it is not in keeping with its given date. Perhaps we should consider instead that, by the 1620s, geometrically arranged compartments, interlacing knots and formal cut-turf gardens were contemporaneous, being created in the broad sweep of gentry gardens across the land according to taste, wealth and fashion. As has been seen in other contexts, garden styles cannot be easily pigeon-holed into a series of chronological phases.

There are of course other problems with using such portraits as sources of evidence. An obvious limitation is that they represent only the tiny proportion of the population who would have been in a position to commission them – the elite – and as such they tell us nothing about what was going on in the generality of gardens. Additionally, even among these, there are few contemporary portraits that depict gardens at all in the background. The overview here is not exhaustive but even Strong's comprehensive examination of what

appears to be all the relevant material amounts to no more than a dozen or so paintings from the period. On a more pragmatic note, most of the garden images are extremely indistinct, which obviously diminishes their usefulness in adding definition and precision to our somewhat hazy picture.

More fundamentally, however, using paintings as evidence of actual practice is inherently problematic in itself because, in the absence of corroborating data, it is impossible to know whether or not the images bear any resemblance to reality, as this was not necessarily their purpose. Family portraits of this period played a crucial role in the assertion of status and, as such, include details which reflect the wealth and preoccupations of the family. The portrait of the Lucy Family at Charlecote Park is an excellent case in point (see figs 66, 97). As noted, the family is portrayed in a richly decorated room, with the patterned carpet, the falcon, the books on the table and so on, all prominently displayed. The importance of the garden is emphasised by the prominent position within the composition of some of its produce – a bowl of cherries involves three members of the family, and a bowl of peaches is carried into the room directly from the garden by Sir Thomas's young heir. This suggests that the garden, as depicted here, was an essential part of the assertion of this family's status and was included for this reason. Unfortunately, while it is possible that this was a faithful reproduction of the garden at Charlecote Park, for the purposes of the painting that was not the most important consideration: the artist added the garden as part of the overall message and not, regrettably, to record the history of garden design for future generations. This does not mean that there is nothing to learn from such paintings, but it must be borne in mind that the images within them are just as likely to be reflecting the intentions, aspirations and contemporary ideals of their sitters as they are to represent reality.

There are other pictorial representations which occur in maps and plans, such as that of All Souls College, Oxford, dating from the late sixteenth century, or two knot designs depicted in a survey of the garden at the Clothworkers' Hall in London, drawn by Ralph Treswell in 1612 (fig. 101; see fig. 31). Both clearly show intricate interlacing knots and, as with the paintings, it is always possible that they are accurate representations of the gardens. However, in the absence of any supporting evidence, and given that the originators of these images would not have had the privileged aerial view required to reproduce something so precise, there is little reason to assume that they were. As will be discussed, these designs are so similar to those depicted in contemporary gardening manuals that it is plausible that the map-maker simply copied them from there, rather than from real life.

One further example of this type of depiction of knot gardens comes from a plan drawn around 1642 of the gardens at the home of Lord and Lady Wotton at St Augustine's in Canterbury (fig. 102). Unusually, in this case there is a corresponding contemporary description of the garden, written by a 'Lieutenant of the Military Company in Norwich', who visited the garden in 1635. Although he describes the long walks, the woody mazes, the high mount and the 'neete and curiously contriv'd fountain', not only is it impossible to discern any of these features on the plan, there is also no mention whatsoever of what appear from the image to be prominent knot gardens.[13] We are again left to conclude that the plan of the garden shown on this survey is simply a general representation of a garden rather than an accurate rendition. The depiction of the patterned knots, which are only crudely represented, lends further weight to the idea that they may well have been copied from another source.

A final piece of extant visual evidence for the possible layout of a knot garden is the plan, already discussed, drawn by the Reverend Walter Stonehouse in 1640 of his garden at Darfield in Yorkshire. This shows five different knots of complex geometric, but not interlacing, design (see fig. 89). However, unlike the other pictorial representations we have, this one contained flowers. By 1640, as described earlier, ornamental flowers for the garden were becoming more available and therefore more popular, so perhaps we should not be

Catte Streete

Highe

Streete

Weste North Este

surprised to see their place in this later garden. Unfortunately, it is unclear from the plan how the borders of the knots are formed, whether they are hedges or paths. The twentieth-century recreation of a knot garden at Moseley Old Hall in Staffordshire (see fig. 90), based on this plan, has interpreted them as hedges, but then in-filled with gravel rather than flowers. But whatever the case, this plan does not match any of the images we have looked at so far and the fact is that our knowledge of the early modern knot garden remains sparse and inconclusive.

Given this paucity of evidence, from where can we get our picture of how these gardens looked? What are the sources of the images which allow sixteenth- and seventeenth-century gardens to be confidently reconstructed? Responses from those actually involved in such projects have proved instructive. For instance, it seems that the design for

the famous knot garden at Shakespeare's New Place in Stratford-upon-Avon was taken, reasonably enough, from a contemporary gardening book.[14] The original design for this garden was executed by Ernest Law in 1920 and Law's own notes confirm that the 'whole is closely modelled on the designs and views shown in the contemporary books on gardening', specifically mentioning *The Gardeners Labyrinth*, Markham's *Country Housewive's Garden* (sic) and Lawson's *New Orchard and Garden*. Setting aside for the moment the fact that there are no patterns for knots in Lawson's *New Orchard* and that Markham did not write any book called the *Country Housewive's Garden*, Law nevertheless claims that they were followed with 'fidelity and completeness'.[15] This knot garden was renovated in 2016 as part of the major overhaul of the New Place garden, recreating Law's twentieth-century design.[16]

As another example, the reconstruction of the Elizabethan garden at Kenilworth Castle carried out in 2009 by English Heritage is based on a valuable contemporary description of the garden and meticulous archaeological evidence (fig. 103). Robert Langham's account of the Earl of Leicester's spectacular entertainment laid on for Queen Elizabeth at Kenilworth

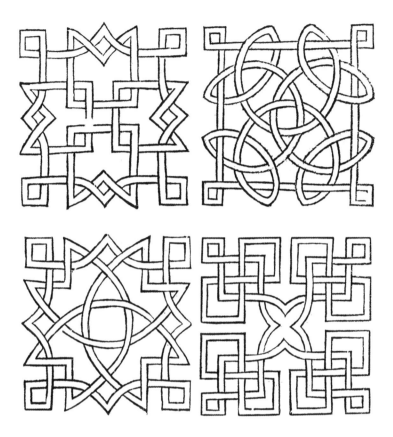

in 1575 contains much lavish detail, including a short section on the 'beautifull Garden'.[17] He mentions the terrace, the obelisks, the spheres and the statues of white bears standing on their intricate bases (see figs 40, 41, 127). He also talks about the symmetry and the graceful proportion of the four even quarters that make up the garden. Unfortunately, he has little to say about the flowers and nothing to say about how they are arranged within the quarters. But, again, for the purposes of re-imagining this garden and in the absence of any other evidence, the designs for the Elizabethan garden at Kenilworth were taken, like those for the New Place garden, from a contemporary book of garden designs. In this case, they are based on a highly influential book of Italian Renaissance designs, Sebastiano Serlio's *Tutte l'opere d'architettura et prospetiva* (1537–51).[18] Herein, it appears, may lie the source of our misplaced assumptions and confidence.

Many designs for knot gardens appear ubiquitously in almost all contemporary gardening literature, from Hyll's 1578 edition of *The Gardeners Labyrinth* (fig. 104) through to Parkinson's *Paradisi in Sole* of 1629 (see fig. 108) and beyond, and a cursory glance lends weight

105   Detail of Hovenden's map of All Souls, Oxford (see fig. 101)
106   Detail of *Lettice Newdigate, aged Two* (see fig. 99)
107   Detail of the garden at the Clothworkers' Hall (see fig. 31)

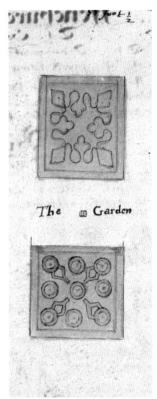

to the idea of an Elizabethan and early Stuart obsession with intricate knot gardens. When looking at these, however, it becomes immediately obvious that the designs are very similar to those depicted in the maps, plans and paintings just considered and it is hardly surprising that they have been taken as evidence that such designs were a feature of late Elizabethan gardens (figs 105–7).

However, there is another possibility that needs to be considered. Whereas such images from contemporary books may have been inspiring gardeners to execute these designs in their gardens, it is equally likely that they were similarly providing inspiration for the artists and map-makers commissioned to include images of gardens in their work. This idea requires further investigation, and a more careful study of these books reveals a number of interesting points.

As with much of the material found in contemporary garden manuals, most of the designs for knot gardens presented within their pages are derivative, and the original source appears to have been the immensely popular gardening book *Maison Rustique*, first published in France in 1564 by Charles Estienne and reprinted numerous times over the rest of the century. This book was also translated into English in 1600 by Richard Surflet and published as *The Countrie Farme*; reprinted in 1606, then revised, augmented and republished by Markham in 1616.[19] All three of these English editions reproduce sixteen knot designs exactly as they appeared in the original French publication of 1564. According to the authors, the knot designs that appear in the many manifestations of *Maison Rustique* are attributed to 'Mounsier Porcher, Prior of Crecy in Brie, the most excellent man in this arte, not only in Fraunce, but also in all Europe'.[20] It is a pity that Mounsier Porcher was not able to copyright his designs, because they appear again and again in numerous works: they are faithfully reproduced in all six editions of the anonymous *Orchard and the Garden* published between 1594 and 1654 and most of them appear in *Certaine excellent and new invented knots and mazes* of 1623, which were, based on this evidence, anything but 'new' or 'invented'. Copies of these designs, although not absolutely identical, are printed in the 1635 edition of Markham's *The English Husbandman*, although they do not appear in the original 1613 edition. It is also interesting that all these images were being printed in publications produced by different printing houses. At this time it was common practice for printers to add images to texts from their supply of stock printing blocks, which could be used repeatedly. When they wore out, new ones were cut and sometimes – as appears to have been the case here – they were passed, or copied, from printer to printer.[21] The images that appeared in these books therefore had far more to do with the printer than with the author. By way of illustration, the compilation of *Certaine excellent...knots and mazes* is in fact highly likely to have been put together entirely by the printer, made up from his supply of printing blocks. It was published anonymously but there is a note 'To the Reader' that appears in an unlikely position at the end of the book, signed by 'I.M.'. Given that the letters J and I were used interchangeably at this time, these initials must refer to the printer, John Marriott, who was responsible for the production of this book.

Parkinson's *Paradisi in Sole* contains what at first sight appear to be six original designs for knots, all different in style from those just mentioned. However, it transpires that four out of six of these designs (fig. 108) were also direct copies: this time they are of Italian origin, from a plan of the botanical garden at Padua University by Girolamo Porro, dated 1591 (fig. 109).

What is curious is that despite the appearance of such illustrations, few authors of contemporary gardening manuals refer in any detail to the making of knots in their texts. Hyll's *Gardeners Labyrinth*, for instance, contains no mention other than the title page's 'wherein are set forth divers Herbers, Knotts and Mazes'. He explains in great detail the treading out of paths and alleys so that weeders and gardeners can reach the beds easily – 'The quar-

108   Four knot designs, from John Parkinson's *Paradisi in Sole*, 1629
109   Detail of a plan of the botanical garden at Padua University, 1591

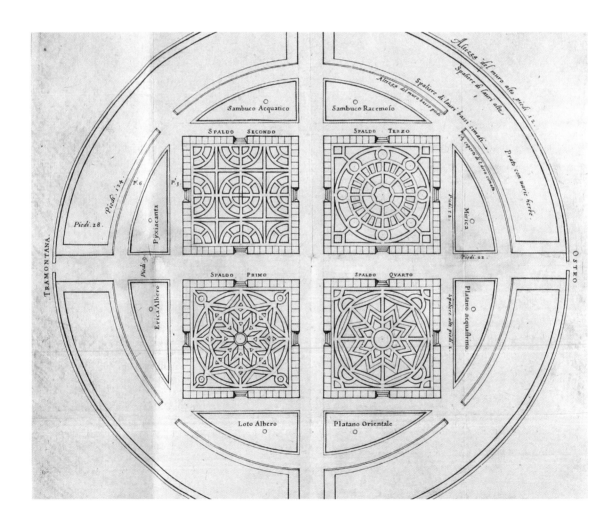

ters...shall in handsome manner by a line set downe in the earth, be trodden out into beds, and seemly borders'[22] – but Hyll's considerations in laying out these quarters are wholly practical, not ornamental.

Having said this, there is a somewhat puzzling illustration in this same book of the first complex interlacing knot pattern to appear in an English gardening book and it is unique in that this design (or indeed anything remotely like it) is not reproduced in any other gardening manuals (fig. 110). It has frequently been observed that this design is so complex that it could never have been successfully executed as a garden knot – with which it is difficult to disagree – and the suggestion is that it is more likely to be an embroidery pattern. Furthermore, there is no reference to this illustration in Hyll's text and, as it appears on a page between the end of Part 1 and the beginning of Part 2, the likelihood is that this illustration was simply added by the printer to separate the two parts and therefore had little relevance to the text. In a later edition, published in 1608, the complex knot pattern has been replaced by one of the more intricate designs from *Maison Rustique*, which would by then have become available, but again there is no reference to it in the text and again it appears between the two parts of the book.

Hyll's earlier gardening book, *The Proffitable Arte of Gardening* (1568), contains no illustrations of knots but has two examples of mazes, which are referred to in the text: 'Here by the waye (gentle Reader) I doe place two proper Mazes'. However, he only recommends them to those who have a space in their garden that can be spared – such is the implication – for such frivolities. He offers no further advice, 'But lette them be ordered as lyketh best the Gardyner, and so an ende'.[23] Hyll is clearly neither interested nor knowledgeable regarding their creation and upkeep. Copies of these illustrations reappear in the third edition of *The Gardener's Labyrinth*, without the accompanying text. Again, it is difficult not to conclude that they have simply been added by the printer rather than included by the author, and when looking at the illustrations of mazes in Androuet du Cerceau's *Premier volume des plus excellents bastiments de France* of 1576 (see fig. 23), it is possible to speculate that they may have been copied from there.

Markham's *English Husbandman* of 1613 also contains instructions on how to lay out a knot or quarter but, like Hyll, his concern is with the practicalities of the groundwork – laying out lines, marking alleys and measuring borders – not with the intricacies of laying

out complex designs.[24] In fact, although the later edition of this work (1635) contains illustrations of such knots, once again copied from *Maison Rustique*, Markham makes no reference to these in the text but specifically refers his readers back to 'not onely the Country-farme, but also divers other translated bookes' if they want instruction on how to make more complicated knots.[25] After saying he will leave the detail to the gardener to make 'what sort or kind soever you please' within the quarters, Markham nevertheless adds some detailed suggestions, including using coloured gravels and sands to draw a nobleman's coat of arms in the quarters, or the 'quaint' practice of using flowers with the quarter to make it appear like 'a knot made of divers coloured ribans'.[26] This is perhaps the closest description we have of an interlacing knot, but it is highly reminiscent of a description in Surflet's *Countrie Farme*, a translation of a French book with which we know Markham was familiar. It may well be that he is simply repeating what he has read there but, as noted before, information derived from French books does not necessarily reflect English practice.

These observations, particularly the apparent use of an embroidery pattern in Hyll's book, raise yet another interesting possibility, that several of these designs were sourced not from gardening books at all but from contemporary pattern books, such as Walter Gedde's *Book of Sundry Draughtes, principaly serving for glasiers and not impertinent for plasters, and gardiners: be sides sundry other professions* (1615). This book contains a collection of intricate designs, similar to those considered here, but while it is feasible that they could have been followed by a glazier as a pattern for a window – which seems to be the author's intention – it would be extremely difficult for them to be executed on the ground by a gardener. In this case, it is possible, perhaps, that the 'gardiners' and 'other professions' mentioned on the title page were included by the printer with a view to broadening the market for his book.

The *Trevelyon Miscellany of 1608* is another contemporary collection, as implied by the title, of images from the everyday to the divine and everything in between. Among its 600-plus pages, Thomas Trevelyon includes the by now familiar images of labyrinths, mazes and interlacing motifs for knot gardens, although he neither identifies them as such nor names his sources. There is no indication of the context within which these designs might be used. The editor of a facsimile edition of this book (2007) has noted that 'while Trevelyon gathered his material from print sources, transforming black-and-white woodcuts, engravings, and texts into a colorful oversized hand-illustrated manuscript, his devout contemporaries were converting these same sources into embroidered and printed works of art…these images were part of a common vocabulary'.[27] There is, then, much evidence to indicate that these woodcut images were being reassembled and recycled for use in many different areas – including gardening – being reused by the same printer, being shared between printers for use in books on the same subject or being shared between different creative art forms. A modern example of such practice can be seen in the knot garden at Sudeley Castle in Gloucestershire (fig. 111), where the design is based on a pattern seen on a dress worn by Elizabeth I in a portrait that hangs in the castle (fig. 112). It is precisely this practice of reuse of patterns and images that are seen in the early modern gardening manuals.

The constant recycling of these woodcuts, coupled with the fact that they are rarely referred to in the texts with which they appear, confirms the conclusion that the images in these books were the responsibility of the printer rather than the author. Then, as now, pictures were likely to make any publication more saleable and the additional cost to the printer of making the woodcut blocks (whether new or reused) would mean that he could charge more for the book. From 1598, the price of books had been regulated by a Stationers' Company Ordinance, but illustrated books were exempt from these regulations, because the number of illustrations, the quality of the images and so on could vary enormously from one publication to another.[28] A highly illustrated book containing original woodcuts, such as Parkinson's *Paradisi in Sole*, would command a much higher price than a gardening manual with only a few recycled woodblock images within its pages.[29] But even a small number of illustrations would increase the value to some extent, so it was in the printer's interests to include images where possible and if he did not have suitable ones to hand, new ones could be commissioned, or copies made. If the printer was commissioning an artist to draw these images or an engraver to cut them, it is likely that they would have looked not to real gardens but to other printed sources, such as *Maison Rustique* or, more likely, the English *Orchard, and the Garden*, for their inspiration.

Accepting this scenario, it therefore follows that the creators of the map of All Souls College or the plans of the Clothworkers' Hall in London or the garden at St Augustine's in Canterbury may have similarly referred to such sources for their depiction of the gardens. The artist who painted Lettice Newdigate's portrait could also have employed this method in his depiction of the knot garden, hence its similarity to designs in the books and on the maps and plans. It seems possible to conclude, therefore, that artists were simply utilising these designs to represent an ornamental garden, which may or may not have borne much resemblance to its actual form. We should therefore be cautious of accepting them as proof of how an early modern knot garden must have looked.

Finally on this point, the idea that the illustrations had little connection with the authors of the books is given added weight by comments made about the images by the authors themselves. Parkinson writes that 'because many are desirous to see the forme of trayles, knots and other compartiments…I have here caused some to be drawne, to satisfie their desires'.[30] As has been seen, his book contains just six designs derived from Italian sources but, other than this, he makes no reference to them in his text. Lawson likewise writes in his preface to the reader that 'The Stationer hath…bestowed much cost and care in having the Knots and Models by the best Artizan cut in great variety', but, again, he provides no details of how to make the knots or execute the designs.[31]

The woodcuts to which Lawson refers are simpler than those discussed earlier but are equally derivative and appear in the second part of his publication, *The Country Housewifes Garden* (fig. 113). However, he glosses quickly over how these can actually be achieved: 'I leave every house-wife to herself', he offers not particularly helpfully.[32] This is despite the

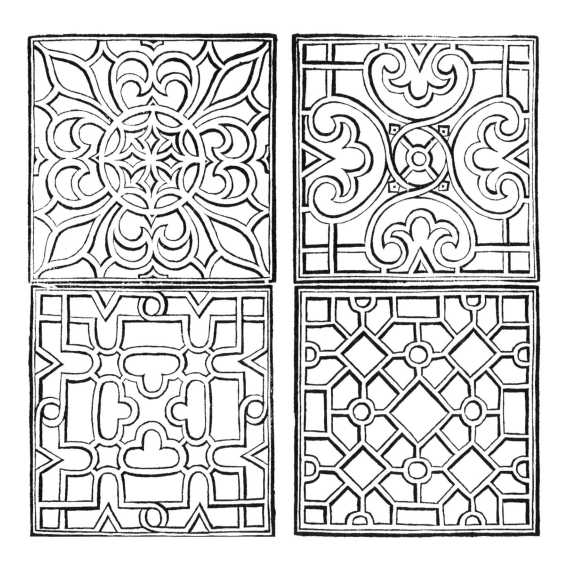

detailed and specific advice on other gardening matters that he gives in the first part of the book, *A New Orchard and Garden* (in which, incidentally, there is no mention at all of knot gardens) and has been explained away by the fact that Lawson does not want to burden the simple housewife with too much information. As yet no one has addressed the contradiction that he leaves this most complicated of aspects to her own devices.

What makes this all more interesting is that, unlike the manuals referred to earlier, Parkinson and Lawson's books were not derived from other sources but were original works based on their own practical experience of gardening. It is, therefore, even more puzzling that neither of them gives any instruction on the making of the kind of knots illustrated in their books, and it is difficult to avoid the conclusion that this was an area of gardening in which they had little interest or expertise. In the case of Lawson at least, he appears to have simply resorted, as his predecessors had done, to passing on received wisdom from older French sources without further input from himself – it has already been noted that Markham referred his readers to other translated sources for such advice. But this still leaves the question of why these authors, who were wholly engaged in the practicalities of contemporary gardening, should have no interest whatsoever in the making of intricate knot gardens. Perhaps we should consider that, in fact, this was not an activity in which either they or their English gardening contemporaries were engaged.

Some final clues that may help define the form of knot gardens in the seventeenth-century English garden are offered in a much later publication by the French garden designer André Mollet. *Le Jardin de Plaisir* was first published in 1651 but translated by Mollet himself and published in English in 1670. After working for Charles I in the 1620s and again for Queen Henrietta Maria in 1642, Mollet returned to England soon after the Restoration to work on the garden at St James's Palace. His English translation is dedicated to the king so it is likely to have been written somewhere between 1660 and 1665, the year of Mollet's death. The book consists of a number of ideal garden layouts, albeit on a suitable scale for royal palaces, and some extremely intricate designs for knots, parterres and 'ground-works'. As noted earlier, Mollet uses the words interchangeably. He also provides detailed descriptions on how to realise these designs, giving precise measurements down to one twelfth of an inch. Of relevance to this discussion, he talks of two different kinds of knots: the 'Knot in Embroidery' and the 'Compartment of Turff' (figs 114, 115). These, as is immediately clear, are considerably more intricate than anything we have seen illustrated thus far. Of the latter design, Mollet writes:

> they are more proper for this Country [England] then any other Country in the world by reason that the Gardeners are more expert and skilful in laying and keeping of Turff then any other Country Gardiners. Nevertheless, since it may be this Books fate to cross the Sea, we shall give some short directions to the Out-landish Gardiners, how to chuse the fittest Turff for this use, as also how to keep and order it after the English manner.[33]

This reveals a number of things. It seems to be generally acknowledged that turf knots are suited to the English climate and conditions: cooler temperatures and rain provide green and verdant grass and lawns. A French visitor to Hampton Court in 1663 described a 'hand-some *parterre* made in grass in the English manner.[34] Mollet also implies that the method of making turf knots is so well known in England that he does not need to describe it, only

doing so for the benefit of 'Outlandish' gardeners. The method he describes is surprising: the turf is cut, lifted and 'plac't with Art according to the Traces of our Ground-works'.[35] This technique could explain how it was possible for the more intricate designs to be executed, and may have been what Hanmer had in mind when he described the 'Parterre as the french call them, are often of fine turfe, kept low as any greene to bowle on, cut out curiously into Embroidery of flowers, beasts, birds or feuillages'.[36] This method apparently proved less popular in England than the *parterre à l'anglaise* in which the pattern was cut out of the grass, as opposed to the other way round.[37] This idea of cut-turf work, however, fits with the few visual depictions we have of earlier examples, such as the garden at Hadham Hall (see fig. 98), as well as making some sense of references in manuscript sources to cutting turfs and cutting knots.

The more elaborate cut-turf knots referred to by Mollet and Hanmer apparently look forward to the more intricate designs associated with the end of the century, such as the gardens of William and Mary at Hampton Court beautifully illustrated in a plan dated *c.*1702–14, now partially reconstructed at Hampton Court (fig. 116).[38]

So what does all this tell us? From a re-examination of the evidence, it seems that, contrary to popular opinion, there is little to show that the interlacing knot was ever a predominant feature of sixteenth- or early seventeenth-century English gardens, or indeed, that it existed at all. The introduction of the compartment system into England appears to have

continued to be the fashion into the seventeenth century, while all the evidence for interlacing knots appears, ultimately, to relate back to Continental gardens, books and influences. This gives rise to the possibility that patterns in books were just as likely, if not more so, to be a direct source of inspiration for the artist of a portrait as for the designer of a garden and, as observed *ad infinitum*, the images of gardens and garden designs which appear in these sources were not necessarily a reflection of what people were actually doing in their gardens. Telling too is the fact that most contemporary garden writers show a distinct lack of interest in the making of complex knots, which is surprising given the detail they go into about almost every other aspect of gardening. It indicates that knots were not something with which they were particularly engaged or, at the very least, not something with which the ordinary gardener was engaged.[39]

Be that as it may, there is no doubt that knot gardens existed in some form or another throughout the period and there is plenty of evidence to support the fact that what contemporaries referred to as a knot was an ornamental garden feature that extended from the early sixteenth century through the Elizabethan era and well into the seventeenth century. They were clearly still being made and maintained in the gardens of the rural gentry during the 1640s, 50s and beyond. However, from the available evidence 'on the ground', they were more likely to take the form of geometric bordered compartments, sometimes filled with flowers, which in some cases became more complex and sophisticated throughout the period, eventually giving way to the open cut-turf designs as described by Hanmer and Mollet and observed by the latter as being a peculiarly English tradition. It is likely that more elaborate knots did not reach England until later in the seventeenth century when French and Dutch-inspired designs began to appear in royal gardens, such as those illustrated in the garden of Hampton Court Palace. As ever, the particular form of a knot within any garden would have depended variously on the wealth, status, location, age, fashion-consciousness and preferences of their owners.[40]

8

ARTIFICIAL ORNAMENT IN THE GARDEN

For John Parkinson, the garden of pleasure was, quite simply 'a garden of pleasant flowers', filled with rare delights. For William Lawson, the greatest joys of the garden and orchard were found in the trees and flowers and, in 1659, Sir Thomas Hanmer still agreed that flowers, trees and plants were the chief ornaments in a beautiful garden.[1]

However, it was not just about plants and flowers. Many other ornamental features were beginning to appear more frequently in gardens at this time, features such as terraces, steps and walkways – the kind of ornamentation that we might nowadays describe as 'hard land-scaping' – as well as artificial embellishments such as statues, ornate fountains, summer-houses and banqueting houses. Ornament in the Elizabethan gentleman's garden, as we have seen, tended to be functional: fountains conveyed vital water to the garden, seats and arbours provided rest and shade, pigeon houses and fish ponds supplied food for the house-hold. Entering the seventeenth century, although these considerations remained, there is evidence that, like the planting of beautiful flowers, other ornamental components were becoming an increasingly notable feature of gentry gardens – ones that moved beyond the functional to being designed for ostentation and show. It is this development, of gardens as suitable sites for the conspicuous display of wealth and status, that will be the main focus of this chapter.

Many of the structural elements just mentioned had their roots in the high Renaissance style of early sixteenth-century Italy, these gardens being characterised by a reshaping and levelling of the terrain with terraces, retaining walls, steps and balustrades, and featuring statues set into niches or made into fountains.[2] By the beginning of the seventeenth century, this ornate architectural style was beginning to influence the creation of elite English gardens, such as those at Hatfield House in Hertfordshire, the home of Robert Cecil, or Wilton House in Wiltshire, the ancestral seat of the Earls of Pembroke. These gardens are well documented and, as befits the high rank of their owners, were showcases of extravagance and ingenuity.[3] The antiquary and writer John Aubrey, a contemporary visitor to Wilton House, remarked on 'the magnificent garden and grotto', picking out for particular mention the fountains, with 'two columnes in the middle, casting water all their height; which causeth the moving and turning of two crowns at the top of the same', the brass statue of a glad-iator and a 'portico of stone, cutt and adorned with pyllaster and nyckes, within which are figures of white marble, of five foot high'. In the grotto was 'a contrivance, by turning of a cock, to shew three rainbowes'.[4] And so on. This garden, along with others of its ilk such as those created at the beginning of the century at the London palaces of the new queen, Anne of Denmark, was executed by Isaac de Caus, a French Huguenot landscape designer, working with and influenced by his brother Salomon, a hydraulic engineer respon-sible for many of the automata that were notable features of these gardens. No longer

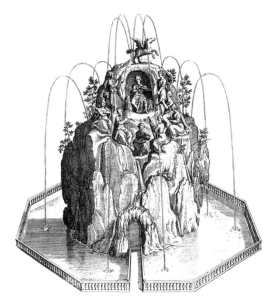

relying on gravity to feed fountains, de Caus devised many ingenious devices to lift water by pump, air or steam to produce an amazing variety of flamboyant effects in the garden (fig. 117). Heavily influenced by Italian architecture and design, these Frenchmen were already demonstrating how an amalgam of various styles from around the Continent, together with new technology, were being brought together in the gardens of the English aristocracy.[5]

Fascinating as they are, however, these gardens are not the subject of this book. What is of interest here is to what extent, if at all, elements of elite gardens were being incorporated into the gardens of the lesser gentry. Just as today when fashions from the catwalk eventually reach the high street, watered down, simplified and cheaper, so it appears to have been the case with fashions in garden design which took not years but decades to filter through the social strata. The kinds of features mentioned here as being characteristic of the sixteenth-century Italian Renaissance style were still being incorporated into gardens in England as late as the 1660s, more than 150 years after their first inception in Europe. In the next chapter we will see how John Evelyn was influenced by his first-hand knowledge of Italian styles when designing gardens at Wotton House and Sayes Court.

Another example is provided by a contemporary painting of the house at Llannerch, Denbighshire, which depicts a spectacular garden created by its owner, Mutton Davies, who was similarly inspired on his return from the Grand Tour in 1658 to create this impressive Italianate terraced layout, complete with 'formal walks, clipt trees and hydraulic statues' (fig. 118). It has been suggested that this garden was so grand that, were it not for corroborating evidence of its existence, it could well be dismissed as fictitious. But evidence there is. As well as contemporary references to 'costly devices' such as a sundial that squirted water into one's face or streams that were diverted into the grounds, the remains of the garden were still extant in the early nineteenth century.[6] That a garden was built at Llannerch in the mid-seventeenth century is therefore not in doubt, but whether the garden ever looked as grand as it does in this image is a moot point. The painting's lack of perspective combined with the bird's-eye view gives an 'endearingly naive' impression of an Italianate garden, which possibly owes more to the owner's aspirations and ambitions than to reality.[7] The fact that Sir Thomas Hanmer, a gardening aficionado, who lived in nearby Flintshire, claimed that he knew of no noble gardens in Wales reinforces this point (see p. 264). What the

(facing page) 117   Design for a Mount Parnassus, similar to the one installed at
Somerset House for Queen Anne of Denmark, c.1606
118   The house and gardens at Llannerch, Denbighshire, c.1667

painting does well, however, is to illustrate the kinds of features that the aspiring gentleman might have wished to add to his fashionable garden.

Where else, then, can we look for evidence of the introduction of ornament and artifice into the generality of seventeenth-century gardens? Reference to household and building accounts suggests that, at best, it was piecemeal – a new fountain here, a statue there and, for the better off, perhaps a banqueting house. People incorporated these various elements into their gardens as the fancy took them and as resources allowed. As ever, wealth and social standing were significant factors in the dissemination of current trends – not just through affordability and a desire to display their status but, for some at least, the opportunity to view these new developments for themselves, whether through travelling abroad,

connections at court or access to elite gardens through social networks. In other cases, the ideas may have come second- or third-hand, via fellow-gardeners, friends and neighbours. As has been discussed at length, few people were in a position to build a new garden from scratch, so most would have been content to incorporate a mixture of new features along-side the old, as well, of course, as simply displaying their personal preferences.

One particularly illuminating source of evidence in this regard is found within a set of accounts relating to the rebuilding and remodelling of Trentham Hall in Staffordshire during the 1630s under the direction of Sir Richard Leveson. Although Leveson had inherited the title to Trentham Hall from his father's cousin and namesake, Vice-Admiral Sir Richard Leveson, following his death in 1605, he did not actually take up residence there until 1627 and it was only after this time that the rebuilding work on the family's Staffordshire seat began.[8] The main documentary evidence comprises a single account book, entitled 'Moneyes dysbersed about the building at Trentham, 1633–38', which details the weekly expenditure for the entire five-year period. Although most of the entries refer to work on the house, information is also provided regarding the immense amount of work involved in creating the structural elements of a fashionable gentry garden.[9]

This unusually detailed account makes it possible to trace the development over three years from what was essentially a building site, with much hewing of stone and digging of foundations, to the creation of an established garden maintained by gardeners and a bevy of weeding women. Closer examination of these accounts, together with information relating to other contemporaneous gardens, have proved them invaluable in offering some insight into the styles of garden that were being created at Trentham and elsewhere.

Supporting the evidence from the Trentham building accounts are two contemporary engravings from Robert Plot's *Natural History of Staffordshire* which show the house after its facelift in the 1630s (fig. 119 and see fig. 121).[10] Although this book was not published until 1686, we can be quite sure that these show the newly renovated house and garden as it was in the 1630s, because in the first engraving the names of both Richard Leveson (RICHARDUS) as well as that of King Charles (CAROLO BRITANIAE REGE) are clearly depicted along the top of the stone wall lining the court that leads to the main entrance of the house (fig. 120) and, in the second, it is possible to make out the rest of his name (LEVESON) along the front wall. As well as supporting the dating of this engraving, this coupling of a Latinised version of his name with that of the reigning monarch is surely indicative of the high aspirations with which Leveson has imbued his newly refurbished house and garden. He is literally stamping his identity – and his ambitions – on his front gate for all to see. It is satisfying to note that the

building accounts record two payments made on 12 October 1633, one to Thomas Griswell and his son and another to John Parson, for 'hewing letters for the cort wall' at 1s 6d per day.

These accounts make it clear that most of the initial work on the garden was structural. It is also clear that there was already a garden on this site and that the work done at this time was a remodelling of an existing structure. For example, on 30 March 1633, Richard Moreton and Thomas Greatbatch were digging the foundations for a new garden wall, while at the same time Richard Moare was pulling down an existing garden wall in order to remove '2 doores and put them up in the south side of the garden'; John Parson spent four days 'taking downe a window into the garden' and Goodyeare Holt took up part of the wall to make a seat. There are many such examples of this judicious reuse of materials.

Mention of windows and doors in gardens may at first sight seem somewhat surprising, but there are other similar references in contemporary household records. For instance, the accounts of Sir Thomas Aubrey at his home in south Wales list a payment 'unto the glayser for mending the orchard windows' and elsewhere in the Trentham accounts there are payments recorded for 'making an arch of Iron for the garden window' and another for 'maintayning the windows at Trentham and Lilleshall & glazing 12 foote in your garden with old glasse & mortering there'.[11] Windows can also be seen in the painting of the garden at Llannerch in the wall that faces the lower fountain. The 'paled gardine dore' in Thomas Temple's garden has already been mentioned; a painter at Penshurst in Kent colours 'all the dores about the gardens' and two painters working at Warwick Priory prime the door between the great garden and the orchard.[12] And there are further references to garden doors at Trentham: 'for a doore way in the south side of the garden', 'for making a portall door into the kitchen garden' and 'work over the garden doore in the Cort wall next the garden'. Although it is not always clear whether the garden door is a way out from the house into the garden, or whether it allows for passage from one part of the garden to the next, its general purpose is obvious. Reasons for the presence of windows in garden walls are slightly more difficult to define. In the case of Llannerch they may simply have been added for decorative effect and indeed this may well have been their purpose in the other examples cited here. However, the fact that the windows were glazed suggests that they may have been positioned in order to provide a view out of the garden, as the walls, certainly as shown in the painting, were quite high. If the latter was the case, then a simple 'viewing' hole in the wall would have negated any protection against the weather that would have been afforded by the enclosed garden walls so, presumably, they were glazed in order to maintain this benefit.

The use of high walls and hedges both to enclose the outer boundaries of gardens and to subdivide gardens into various compartments was a characteristic practice of large gardens in the sixteenth century and it is clear that this continued well into the seventeenth century. Contemporary drawings, descriptions and paintings – such as the one of Llannerch – indicate walls and hedges enclosing the various compartments, with doors and windows connecting, either literally or visually, one part of the garden to the next. There was evidence of these divisions in the gardens at Nunwell House (see fig. 49), and at Holme Lacy, the home of Viscount Scudamore in Herefordshire, there were at least three garden enclosures: the Great Garden, 'my Lady's garden' and the kitchen garden are all mentioned in the accounts. Furthermore, each enclosure had a door, all of which were, again according to the accounts, in constant need of repair and for which new keys were regularly purchased.[13] Locks were mended and keys made for the kitchen garden door at the Cecil household in Hertfordshire as well as at another of Richard Leveson's properties at nearby Lilleshall – the relevant bill from the blacksmith is still pinned into the account book.[14]

In line with these observations, it seems that the new garden being built at Trentham Hall also retained this same basic layout. The account books indicate a number of compartments with references to 'Sir Richard's garden', 'my ladies garden', a kitchen garden and an orchard, as well as a magnificent fountain and a high mount, all of which are likely to have been enclosed in their own separate areas. Between the compartments would have been wide gravel walks, and again 'the walke in the south range of the house' is mentioned in the account books. It is not particularly detailed, but this division of the garden into compartments with dividing walls and walks is clearly depicted in the second engraving of Trentham Hall (fig. 121). It is also possible to discern steps, gates and doors into and out of the various compartments of the garden.[15] As well as adhering to a traditional layout for this garden, the 'high mount', a feature readily identifiable with both medieval and Tudor gardens, is also retained. William Hunt was paid 'for getting 195 foote of flagge and Steppes' for the mount and it is likely that it was already a part of the garden and that it was simply being renovated. But whatever the case, it is interesting to see that these distinctly old-fashioned features were still being incorporated into new gardens as late as the 1630s.

Steps, as well as being installed as here for the mount, were a significant feature of larger gardens. Rather than working with a sloping garden, each compartment was levelled, with connecting steps in between, to create terraces much in the Italianate style. This time-consuming and costly operation is once again illustrated in the painting of Llannerch, the shape of the walls in particular indicating the degree of slope on which this garden was built, although each compartment appears flat and level. At Trentham, the account book indicates that in October 1633, William Gervace was paid for six days' work 'hewing stone for the to[e]rrice in the garden'; the following February, another worker was similarly paid for 'hewing 52 steps for the coming out of the garden into the house' and a further payment

121   View of Trentham Hall showing the extent of the gardens,
from Robert Plot's *The Natural History of Staffordshire*, 1686

was made to William Hunt for 'getting 52 foote of steppes for the stayres out of the house and into the garden'. This was evidently a major operation involving a number of different workers in a great deal of hard work. The resulting steps can be seen in the engraving of Trentham Hall, coming from the house into the garden containing the fountain.

Contemporaneous records indicate that similar alterations were being carried out in other gardens around the country. Sir Arthur Ingram, for instance, had terraces built at his homes in Yorkshire: a new terrace was constructed at his house in Sheriff Hutton in 1621 and two years later, in 1623, another was built at his house in York. These both appear to have been renovated some fifteen years later, when one William Butler was contracted to rebuild the terrace at Sheriff Hutton in the same manner as 'the new terris in the garden at Yorke'.[16] At the same time, away in Sussex, Sir Thomas Pelham paid a total of 15s 6d to 'Merick for laying 46 foot of stone & a halfe foot for stares in the great garden at 4d per foot'. Although there is not much detail here, it is clear that both Ingram and Pelham,

218

of whom it has been said that 'ostentation came easily',[17] were similarly engaged in the construction of new, fashionable gardens, and that steps and terraces were important features.

Other structural features mentioned in the Trentham Hall accounts include a number of garden seats. Two workers are paid 'for fynishing the seate in the garden wall' and later for making an arch and a seat in 'my ladies garden', with 8½ feet of skew (specially shaped stones for creating curves) for the inside of the seat. Two further seats were made in the wall of Sir Richard's garden. These could well have been quite elaborate affairs, such as the one depicted in the painting of Llannerch (fig. 122), or possibly resembling an extant stone seat at Edington Priory in Wiltshire, dating from about 1600,

which comprises two wide, high arches, finished with classical pediments, with the seat behind, deeply recessed into the garden wall.[18] Household accounts and correspondence also indicate that there were garden seats at Holme Lacy in Herefordshire, Penshurst Place in Kent, Halland House in Sussex and in Sir Thomas Puckering's new garden at Warwick Priory.[19] Seats in the garden would have gone hand-in-hand with the activity of walking in the garden, providing places of rest and refreshment, as well as a point from which simply to sit and view the garden.

By the summer of 1634, it seems that the basic structure of the new garden at Trentham Hall had been laid – walls were built, doors and windows in the garden installed, arches and seats completed, steps and terraces constructed. On 7 November that year, construction began on the waterworks which were clearly a major part of the overall project: the final entry in the account book is a summary of 'the whole charge of all the worke for the building of the mannor house at Trentham' and it includes a reference to the conveyance of water to all the 'houses of office', which presumably were added as part of the rebuilding programme. At the same time, work also began on the construction of a fountain in the garden, which continued for almost a year. The completion of the fountain appears to mark the end of the structural work at Trentham, the final payment for 'paynting the fountaine' being made on 12 September 1635, ten months after the work had begun the previous November.

Water features in the form of pools, basins, moats, canals and fountains had been used in gardens since medieval times and fountains in particular had a place in even quite small gardens. As well as bringing vital water to the garden, they also added sensual pleasures. Sunlight playing on the constantly moving water and the sounds of bubbling, trickling and splashing around the fountain contributed to a sense of refreshment and relaxation. They also provided a visual focal point for the garden, adding an element of height, either through the construction of the actual fountain itself or by the jets of water being forced into the air. And fountains could be built on any scale, from the flamboyant extravagances of elite gardens such as Wilton House to a simple feature such as the one shown on Lawson's ideal plan of a garden (see fig. 47). Both Lawson and Parkinson considered a fountain, or conduit, to be necessary as a practical means of bringing water to the garden, but by the 1620s they were also being installed in fashionable gardens as an ornamental focus and this appears to have happened at Trentham Hall and elsewhere. For example, at the same time as this fountain was being built, another was being constructed a little further north at Rock Savage in Cheshire, the home of Sir Thomas Savage. The accounts record payments for work and labourers 'in and about the makinge and dressinge of the newe Fownetayne placed in the middle of Rocksavage garden'. It was completed in July 1624 in time for 'his Lordship's' arrival in August that year.[20]

In the absence of expensive pumping mechanisms which, it has already been noted, were only the preserve of the extremely wealthy, even to provide an apparently simple jet of water would have required a degree of hydraulic ingenuity. The woodcut from Hyll's *Gardeners Labyrinth* (see fig. 16) depicts a simple system of pumping water from a tub in order to irrigate the garden. Parkinson observes that water can be brought to the fountain either in pipes under the ground or carried by hand and emptied into 'large Cisternes or great Turkie Jarres'.[21] On a slightly larger scale, country houses would make use of the local topography to pipe water from ground higher than the house, in order to fill cisterns which would in turn convey water to the house and garden. For instance, water was piped from a nearby spring and through the fields to Claydon House in Buckinghamshire, the fountain at Rock Savage was fed through underground pipes and at Bolsover Castle water was similarly conveyed from the surrounding hills to feed a three-storey cistern house just outside the perimeter walls.[22] At Trentham Hall, the force of gravity was similarly harnessed and a series of pools, trenches, dams and pipes were constructed in order to transfer water to various parts of the estate including, of course, to the new fountain.

This whole project must have been a major feat of construction: specific entries in the account books such as 'to Thomas Greatbatch four days digging in the trench for water', 'to Rowley 6 days stopping water in the trenches and upper poole', 'to John Bradwell 4 dayes sawing a trough to bring water out of the pool' and many similar entries for other men 'at the same work' all bear witness to the scale of this undertaking. Following the initial construction of the watercourses to the house from the upper pool, work then continued on the fountain. Four men worked six days a week, every week for nine months, although the precise nature of their work is unrecorded. However, there are other more specific entries. On 25 April 1635, William Vaughan was dispatched to the quarry 'to get up some great white stone for the fountain'. In June, Goodyear Holt spent eight days laying stone foundations for the fountain and a plumber was brought in for '5 dayes casting pipes for the fountaine'. Finally, the painter arrived on 15 August to spend the next five weeks adding the finishing touches. As well as payments for his labour, he was also reimbursed for two payments for 'colors for the fountayne': on 12 September he received the substantial sum of 10s 2d and two weeks later, on 26 September, he received a further 8s. There are no details as to the colours used but the finished construction must have been an impressive sight.

It is quite difficult now to imagine the use of paint and colour on structures such as this because none now remains but we know, for instance, that the fountains and conduits along the processional route through London of the new Queen Elizabeth were freshly repainted for the occasion of her 'Royal Entry' in 1559, and the accounts of Sir Arthur Ingram at Temple Newsam in Yorkshire record a payment of £2 10s for 'the ffountayne coullerde twice in oyles'.[23] A painter was employed at Penshurst Place in Kent to colour 'all the doors about the garden' as well as the new garden seats, and a man was paid 10s for 'colloring all of the seates in the garden' at Halland House in Sussex.[24] The household accounts of Sir Thomas Puckering at Warwick Priory contain a number of payments to painters for work about the garden, including 9s to two painters for 4½ days' work, each priming the seat around the 'Ewe' tree, a garden door and 'the 3 stair-cases in the said garden ashcolour'.[25] It seems that the use of paint and colour was a common practice in fashionable early modern gardens.

The illustrations of Trentham do not, unfortunately, give much away about how the fountain looked, but a glance at the work of the contemporary architect Inigo Jones, though his designs were clearly at the pinnacle of such work, gives an idea at least of the kind of intricate and ornate fountains that were fashionable at this time (fig. 123). Other examples can be seen in the background of the painting of the Capel Family at Haddon Hall (see fig. 98), the portrait of the Countess of Arundel at Arundel House (fig. 124) or, once again, in the garden at Llannerch which depicts two fountains (see fig. 118).

It is clear that fountains such as these – including the elaborate one at Trentham which took ten months to construct or that built at Rock Savage at a cost of £35 – were clearly more than just functional objects in the garden: they were also about ornament, ostenta-

123   Inigo Jones's design for a fountain, *c*.1633
124   Detail of the fountain from Daniel Mytens, *Althea Talbot, Countess of Arundel*, 1618

tion and show. Having said this, there is no mention whatsoever of fountains in some of the other rural estate gardens we have looked at, such as Nunwell House, Burton Dassett, Holme Lacy, Halland House or Warwick Priory. Clearly, these gardens must still have had some kind of water supply but, according to the extant records at least, their owners were not moved to install impressive fountains.

This is not to say that they did not have water features of any kind – far from it: many gardens incorporated streams, rivers, pools and canals. Lawson highly recommends a 'River with silver streams', where 'you might sit in your Mount, and angle a [s]peckled trout or some other dainty fish'. If your estate did not have a handy river or stream running through it, then a moat could be dug and filled with water 'whereupon you might row with a Boat or fish with nets'. Sir Thomas Tresham's moated orchard at Lyveden provides an excellent example of the kind of feature that Lawson must have had in mind. It is not difficult to

imagine sitting at the base of this mount on the banks of the moat, whiling away an hour or two quietly fishing or simply taking in the 'fresh, sweet and pleasant aire' (fig. 125).[26]

Even something as seemingly simple as this would have required a great deal of hard labour: the canals had to be dug out (in fact only three sides of the square were ever completed at Lyveden) and the soil removed. In many cases the soil would have been used, again as at Lyveden, to build the mounts and perhaps a raised terrace on one or more sides of the moat, for walking and viewing the grounds. Nevertheless, the moated orchard and the more conventional lower orchard, a rectangular compartment set with rows of fruit trees, were clearly also part of the aesthetic design of the garden: in 1605, Robert Cecil described Lyveden as 'one of the fairest orchards that is in England' (see fig. 18).[27] The importance of the orchard in the seventeenth-century garden has already been discussed in detail, but this example serves as a reminder that as well as its obvious utilitarian purpose, orchards added to the beauty of a garden. Here, Tresham further enhances the ornamental aspect of his orchard by enclosing it with a moat.

Similarly, many estate accounts refer to pools, but they generally seem to have fulfilled a basically utilitarian function, supplying water to the house, irrigating fields, providing drinking water for animals or being stocked with fish for food or sport. They are usually referred to in the context of required repairs being carried out, as is the case, for instance, at Holme Lacy where the upper pool, the 'Duck' pool and the 'pool head' all on occasion needed the attention of the 'waterworks keeper', who was paid £6 13s 4d a year for his services. One of the pools conveyed water to the house.[28] By the eighteenth century it is possible that these pools had become part of a formal canal garden, but this is unlikely to have been in place in the seventeenth century, so exactly what these pools were for at this time is uncertain. Given the time and money spent on them, however, they were clearly important. Likewise, in 1623, Sir Thomas Aubrey at Llantrithyd in south Wales spent fifty shillings on the repair of the 'pond heads', mentioning both the upper mill pond and the great pond. It appears that as well as stocking them with fish, they were also part of an impressive system of canals and other water features in the gardens there.[29] Sir Thomas Temple makes many references to the pools at Burton Dassett, but his concern is mainly with cleansing and 'scowring', particularly of the 'pool heads', which presumably were the upper pools which fed the others. On some occasions at least, the scouring also involved the draining of the pools, one purpose of which appears to have been to provide a valuable fertile compost which would enrich the soil in the fields and the garden. At one stage Temple even contemplated devising some kind of 'pitt' or sump to collect the debris washed out of the pool.[30]

Temple's other concern was that the water should be made and kept clean for drinking – whether by animals or humans is not clear. His instruction that 'I would have a smale [small] trench to run directly with some fall only . . . perhaps to run into the kitchin' is a timely reminder that, away from elite houses and gardens, even having a running water supply for domestic purposes was not to be taken for granted. On just one occasion, Temple hints at a possible ornamental use for the water in his garden: 'I would have a short trench, whereby the water may fall into the Poole', he wrote in 1634. Given this essentially practical approach to the necessities of estate work, it is somewhat surprising, therefore, that on another occasion, Sir Thomas requests the local carpenter to make a 'bridge & a dore on the same, extending somewhat broader then the bridge, whereby the swans may be fed at the osyer lland'. Elsewhere, he ensures that 'foode for them' should not be forgotten.[31] It is known that in medieval times at least, swans were bred for food, but this is not necessarily the case here. After elucidating the practical reasons for moats and ponds (for 'fish, fence and moisture to your trees'), his contemporary Lawson adds that swans and other water birds will also provide pleasure, and this seems to have been the case with Sir Thomas Temple.[32] In 1632, he writes to his son, now head of the family home at Stow, who is having trouble with straying swans: 'I have hearde the Swannes I sent...do not abide so well in your Poole...but wander sometimes into Dadford Towne'. Temple remembers that forty years before, his own father had the same problem with some swans he had tried to keep on the 'Swans Iland in the Great Poole in the olde Parke', and he advises that the swans should be 'marked with a Crosse in their Beakes' so that they can be identified and kept 'from stragling'.[33] His letters seem to demonstrate a level of concern over and above that of simply maintaining a good food supply. Sir Arthur Ingram also kept swans on the ponds in his gardens at York and Temple Newsam, purchasing two cygnets in March 1625 and there are swans depicted on the river that borders the garden at Llannerch (see fig. 118).[34]

Perhaps the last word on water features should go to Sir Francis Bacon. His oft-quoted remark that pools make a garden unwholesome, being full of flies, frogs, slime and mud, as well as the water having a tendency to discolouration, 'Mossinesse' or 'Putrification', is essentially true.[35] But there he is talking about ornamental pools, full of standing water which become stagnant. The answer, he says, is to keep the water moving and this of course is what was happening with the pools, ponds and fountains described above: water was continually conveyed to wherever it was required through a series of pools, trenches, canals and conduits.

Other garden ornament which was beginning to make its mark in the gardens of the gentry around this time was statuary. Deriving once again from Italian Renaissance gardens, this relatively recent fashion can arguably be traced to that 'connoisseur, collector and promoter of all things Italian', Thomas Howard, Earl of Arundel, who, on his return from a tour of Italy in 1614, famously laid out his garden at Arundel House on the Strand with antique statuary.[36] A representation of this garden can be seen in the background of a portrait of Arundel from around 1627 (fig. 126), which, although it is unlikely to be an accurate depiction of the garden (as has often proved to be the case), nevertheless reflects the collection of antique sculpture imported from Italy for which Howard had become renowned.[37] Corroborating evidence is also found in a contemporary text, Henry Peacham's Compleat Gentleman (the 1634 edition), where the author attributes 'the first sight [in England] of Greeke and Romane Statues' to Thomas Howard, when he 'began to honour the Gardens and Galleries of Arundel-House about twentie yeeres agoe and hath ever since continued to transplant old Greece into England'.[38]

Statues such as these were a late arrival in England, although representations of heraldic animals and beasts had featured in aristocratic Elizabethan gardens, such as those seen in views of the garden at Whitehall Palace in The Family of Henry VIII (c.1545), depicting white

126   Detail from Daniel Mytens, *Thomas Howard, Earl of Arundel*, c.1627,
showing the collection of antique statues displayed in his garden at Arundel House

hounds sitting atop decorated wooden poles,[39] or the 'white bearz all of stone' referred to
by Robert Langham in his description of the gardens at Kenilworth Castle (fig. 127). Arundel's fascination with European cultures and the arts was reinforced by lengthy sojourns
abroad where he made personal connections with scholars and artists: he had his portrait
painted by Rubens on a visit to the Netherlands; he appears to have had a pivotal role
in introducing both the artist Sir Anthony van Dyck and the engraver Wenceslaus Hollar
to England, and the architect Inigo Jones was a frequent travelling companion. The Earl's
interest was intellectual as well as aesthetic and he gained a reputation as an expert in collecting and the arts. Arundel's collection was clearly exceptional, but it influenced the dissemination of new ideals of gentility through didactic courtesy manuals such as Peacham's
Compleat Gentleman. According to Peacham, on ascending the throne in 1625, King Charles
himself had taken up the fashion introduced by Arundel, demonstrating a 'Royall liking of
ancient statues'. Ten years later, Peacham defines this appreciation and knowledge of classical art as a desirable attribute in the aspiring Stuart gentleman.[40]

127   White bears reinstated in the Elizabethan garden
at Kenilworth Castle, Warwickshire

Given this, is there evidence that the fashion for statues was, in fact, being disseminated to the gardens of our rural gentry? Returning to Trentham Hall, there is one reference in the accounts to a statue in the new gardens being created there. We know little about it except that in July 1635, Mr Hall, his two sons and his man were each paid for five days' work polishing it. This does not tell us much, but we can assume that it must have been a fairly substantial feature to require so much work. Elsewhere, in March 1627, Sir Thomas Aubrey of Llantrithyd paid 30s to 'the workman that made the statues', and the Oglander papers reveal a single payment of £2 on 29 April 1642 to 'Crocker for the making of the statue' at Nunwell on the Isle of Wight.[41] This is the only ornament mentioned by Sir John Oglander in this detailed description of the garden but it seems that, by this time, even the most rural of gentry gardens were beginning to incorporate such decorative features. Unfortunately, we have no further detail at all about these statues – for instance, we have no idea what form they might have taken – but it is perhaps possible at least to gauge the quality of these statues by the prices paid for them. They are clearly a far cry from the original statues being imported into the country by the likes of Arundel, or even from new classical-style imitations being commissioned from the sculptor Nicholas Stone, master-mason to both James I and Charles I, who charged up to £50 a piece for making statues for the nobility.[42] Cheaper replicas were clearly good enough for Oglander and Aubrey in their remote estates on the Isle of Wight and in south Wales.

One other gentleman who displayed a penchant for statues in his gardens was Sir Arthur Ingram, who employed local stonemasons, Thomas Ventris and his son, to carve an impressive number of stone heraldic beasts to be placed in the grounds of his various houses in north Yorkshire. One of these limestone carvings – a lion atop a brick pedestal – can still been seen *in situ* in the grounds of Sheriff Hutton Hall, the site of one of Ingram's Yorkshire residences.[43] It is interesting that Ingram was still installing these old-fashioned heraldic devices (last seen in elite Elizabethan gardens) as late as the 1630s and that, in 1639, he even had some of them transported from Yorkshire to his house in London. What we seem to be seeing in Ingram is another instance of early seventeenth-century garden design being dictated not only by current fashions but also by personal preference: while the new gardens at Temple Newsam, York and Sheriff Hutton definitely involved innovative and fashionable Italianate features such as steps, terracing and fountains, it seems that, at the same time (as also seen in other gardens) Ingram was harking back to the previous century for at least some of the inspiration for his garden.

It was suggested at the beginning of this chapter that there was a move during this period for the gardens of the gentry to become places in which they could demonstrate their social aspirations, introducing elements which moved beyond the merely functional to a display of their often new-found wealth and status. Perhaps the ultimate addition to a gentleman's garden in this regard was the banqueting house. As with many garden features already discussed, garden buildings, banqueting houses and banqueting rooms were all elements found in Tudor palaces and houses of the aristocracy. The banqueting house or room was defined, in simple terms, as a place in which a banquet took place – that is, a meal of sweetmeats, dainties and wine, served either after dinner but in a different room, or as a separate entertainment. Lady Margaret Hoby made her own sweetmeats from garden produce such as fruits, nuts and root vegetables, chopped, cooked and preserved in honey and spices.[44] Thomas Puckering's wife also made sweetmeats, the household accounts recording the purchase of 'preserving glasses', 'a piece of glass to lay sweetmeats upon in preserving' and 'some silver plates for [serving] sweetmeats'.[45] Sometimes, the sweetmeats were bought: Joyce Jeffreys of Hereford paid 6d for a box of dried sweetmeats, somewhat curiously, from

Mr Paule the draper, although on another occasion she preserved her own apricots.[46] The banqueting house located in the garden, or the banqueting room located on the roof or top floor, offered delectation not just to the taste buds but also to the other senses as they provided a place from which to take in the sights and scents of the garden. And like the food that was served inside them, these buildings tended to be of a fanciful and frivolous nature.

Although their function is not always made clear, it seems that by the seventeenth century, many gentry households boasted some kind of summerhouse, garden house or banqueting house (or even houses) in their grounds. The household accounts for Sir Thomas Aubrey at Llantrithyd Place record payments in 1627 for 'leddinge', 'a vane' and wainscoting to the 'somer house in the upper garden'. There are also references to 'the hows in the orchard', plastering the 'garden house' and the 'oriell' which required the attention of two tilers, two joiners and a glazier. Whether these refer to one building or more is difficult to tell but the fact remains that, along with the other alterations he was making to the mid-Tudor house he had inherited, Aubrey was keen to update and improve his garden in line with recent, more fashionable, tastes and developments.[47]

Other passing references to banqueting houses in various household accounts indicate that by this time they were perhaps not particularly unusual: in 1624, a banqueting house at Rock Savage in Cheshire is mentioned, which in 1633 required re-plastering. In 1637, the banqueting house at Holme Lacy was in need of repair and in 1638 a new bolt was made for the banqueting house door at Halland House. References such as these are frustratingly short on detail but at least indicate their presence in some gentry gardens. Other sources offer a little more. Most dramatically perhaps, Sir Thomas Tresham's triangular lodge at Rushton and the unfinished garden lodge at Lyveden New Bield probably represent two of the most extraordinary garden buildings extant from this period. But as well as being resplendent buildings in their own right, they are also imbued with a religious symbolism that has made them the subject of much historical scrutiny, which is beyond the scope of this book.[48] In addition to being places of covert worship, however, it is clear that these buildings had a more conventional, secular purpose. The garden building at Rushton was used as a warrener's lodge, while the unfinished lodge at New Bield provided an endpoint to a walk up from the house, offering impressive views over the garden. Servants' quarters and a kitchen in the base of the building indicate the intention also to use the lodge as a place to entertain guests. However, these buildings were somewhat exceptional. Sir Arthur Ingram built a more modest banqueting house at his home in York in 1632, but details regarding the lead roof, the paved floor, colouring and gilding indicate that it was still an elaborate construction. Four years later, he built at least two more banqueting houses at Temple Newsam.[49] We can get an idea of how such banqueting houses might have looked

by glancing again at the painting of the house and garden at Llannerch, where two such houses face each other at either end of the raised terrace (see fig. 118), and an extant example of such an arrangement can be seen at the site of Campden Manor in Gloucestershire, the early seventeenth-century home of Sir Baptist Hicks. The house is no longer standing – it was destroyed by fire during the Civil War – but the archaeological remains of the garden reveal a raised terrace, at either end of which two elaborate, but not identical, banqueting houses still remain (fig. 128).[50]

This somewhat disparate picture is enhanced by a more detailed description of the construction of a new banqueting house at Warwick Priory, completed in 1620 for Sir Thomas Puckering, who actually visited Campden Manor to view the house and garden. While there, he would have seen the two banqueting houses in Hicks's garden which may well have inspired the final decoration of his own house, which was completed over the following months.[51] Most of the actual building work appears to have taken place before these accounts begin in 1620, but from March through to October there are payments for the finishing touches to the banqueting house, including steps, stairs and rails up to the house from the garden, the making of 'iron work' for the windows, as well as payment of numerous bills, first to carpenters, masons and joiners and then to plasterers and painters for labour and materials. These last two payments, together with the purchase of 630 tiles, 'half of them greene, and half of them yellowe, to pave my Banquetting-house with', more than hint at the extent of the elaborate and colourful decoration of the interior. And as a garden feature, the outside must have been equally impressive. Although it is not entirely clear from the accounts, it seems that the banqueting house was situated in the middle of the 'Great Garden'. What is clear, however, is that it was raised, presumably to give a better view over the garden from inside and to make a greater impression from the outside. At least three staircases, with posts, rails and balusters – all painted the same ash colour as the seat and door in the garden – were built from the garden up to the banqueting house. There is also a payment for 40 feet of 'Rowington stone' from a local quarry which was to be made into steps up to the banqueting house, but whether these steps are part of the three staircases already mentioned, or whether they formed a fourth, even more grand, ascent is open to speculation. At the same time, a 'newe garden' was made, perhaps to make up for the space lost to the banqueting house in the great garden.[52] All this work was done at the same time, using the same labourers, materials and colours, thereby creating a coherent and co-ordinated 'new look' to the gardens at Warwick Priory. It seems that, like Leveson at Trentham Hall, Puckering was intent on making his mark in the local community with this conspicuous display of wealth and status.

While we should be wary of the dangers of drawing conclusions from lack of evidence, it is difficult to escape the assumption that, although gentlemen such as Sir Richard Leveson, Sir Thomas Puckering and Sir Arthur Ingram invested much time and expense in the creation of their new gardens – and it is clear that these gardens incorporated many of the latest fashionable styles and features – they do not appear to share, say, Sir John Oglander's or Sir John Reresby's passion for exotic flowers and plants, or even Sir Thomas Temple's love of sweet-smelling flowers. Following the completion of the building work at Trentham Hall, for instance, the first payments for plants start to appear in the accounts but most of these are of an uninteresting nature: young hedging plants and oziers [willow] were purchased by the hundred, along with young fruit trees for the orchard. The Puckering accounts also indicate the routine purchase and planting of quicksets for hedging, but little more is known about the planting at Warwick Priory, and although Ingram buys large quantities of flowering plants, some of which he has shipped north by boat from London, the only varieties specified are traditional and easily available roses, honeysuckles, sweetbriar and eglantine. In fact, a visitor to Ingram's garden in York commented on the lack of flowers, noting that the garden was 'disposed into little beds, whereon placed statues, the beds all grass'. He also observed the lack of fruit trees, implying that Sir Arthur did not engage in the cultivation of fruit in his garden, something which, as has been seen, was a major preoccupation in many gentry gardens.[53] Ingram, it seems, was no plant connoisseur and his was apparently not a plantsman's garden.

Nevertheless, as seen in the gardens just mentioned and through glimpses of those owned by Sir Thomas Aubrey and Sir Thomas Pelham, it is clear that these gentlemen were anxious to create gardens that were 'fit and answerable to the degree they hold', complementing their newly renovated houses, displaying their wealth, reflecting their status and defining their standing in the community.[54] They did this not necessarily through the planting of their gardens but by incorporating, to one degree or another, the kind of structural and decorative elements that defined the high Renaissance style of the previous century. Their gardens at Trentham Hall, Warwick Priory, Temple Newsam and Halland House provide particularly good examples of such features being gradually incorporated into the gardens of the gentry a century and a half after they were first seen in Italy.

For one final example, it is only necessary to look over the proverbial garden wall from Leveson's garden into that of his near neighbour, Sir Walter Chetwynd at Ingestre Hall. This house and garden is also featured in Robert Plot's *Natural History of Staffordshire* in which we see a grand garden laid out before us, incorporating terraces, steps, balustrades, statues and fountains (fig. 129). There is no date for the Ingestre gardens but it is known that the house was rebuilt around 1613, so it is likely that the gardens would have been created around this time and would have predated, and therefore quite possibly inspired, the layout of the new garden at Trentham. Although these illustrations have their limitations, the gardens at Ingestre appear to be on a much grander scale than those at Trentham which, it could tentatively be suggested, are a somewhat low-grade imitation of both the Italian Renaissance style and Leveson's neighbour's interpretation of it.

This example also serves to remind us that, although it is possible to identify common features within these various gardens, there were also significant differences. As has been observed earlier, these differences could be due to any number of factors, including the

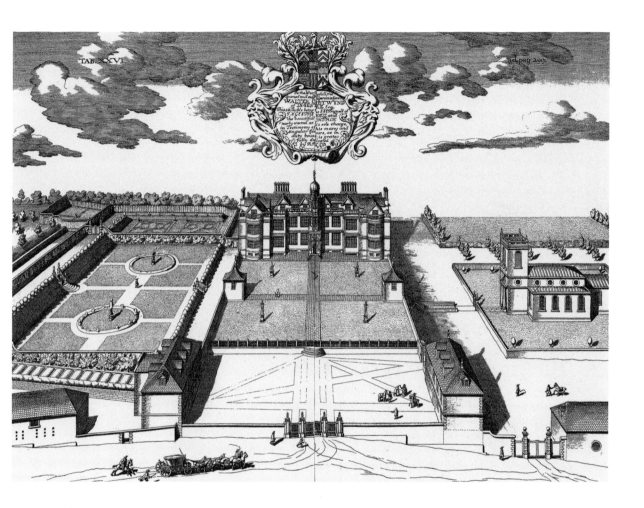

constraints imposed by the physical layout of the existing garden, the balance between utilitarian and ornamental purposes, as well as personal tastes and aspirations. But probably the most significant limitations on the realisation of those aspirations would have been, then as now, financial ones. Not to put too fine a point on it, whatever their ambitions, some gentlemen were simply more wealthy than others. Given both the disparity and paucity of evidence of such gardens, it is difficult to make direct comparisons but it seems that, for instance, Leveson's rebuilding project, which cost a total of £6,165 17s 4d, was financed by a 'windfall' of more than £8,000 raised by the sale of a large amount of property acquired through his marriage in 1629. It was with this money (rather than his limited annual income of about £300 a year) that he chose to renovate his house and gardens in order to make his mark and define his status in the local community – and perhaps at court. The lettering on his court wall indicates a hope at least that the king might visit, although there is no record of this ever having happened. However, financial disputes and debt were difficulties that accompanied Leveson throughout his life.[55] By way of comparison, Sir Thomas Puckering, whose annual income is estimated at about £2,000 (similar to that of Sir Walter Chetwynd at Ingestre), was apparently more financially secure.[56] The extent of the work undertaken at Warwick Priory (of which, of course, the garden was only a part) indicates perhaps a more stable financial footing on which Puckering was able to base this conspicuous display of wealth and status.

For some of the other gentlemen, meanwhile, such motivation does not appear to have been their major concern. Sir Thomas Temple, for example, who was creating his small pleasure garden at Burton Dassett in his retirement, had passed on such issues to his son and heir at Stow.[57] Even so, his gentlemanly status afforded him the luxury of being able to create a garden of sweet-smelling flowers for no other purpose than to enjoy them, or to produce fruits such as grapes and apricots for the table or to exchange with his friends and acquaintances. So, although there was nothing ostentatious about his garden, it was still an important assertion of his standing in society. In the same way, for other floral enthusiasts such as Sir John Oglander and Sir John Reresby, their gardens provided them with the opportunity to indulge their passion for exotic and beautiful flowers and plants which were by then becoming more and more available. Again, to have the means to display such objects of luxury in the garden was clearly an indication of their social standing but, from the available evidence, it seems reasonable to assume that in these cases the owners were not especially concerned with conspicuous display. These seem to be more modest gardens, eschewing – perhaps deliberately – the Italianate taste of the court.

From the evidence presented in this chapter, then, what more can be said about the use of artificial ornament to enhance the gardens of the rural gentry? Perhaps the most important point is that it is almost impossible to make generalisations. From the extant evidence available it is extremely difficult to ascertain how representative the gardens under discussion here actually were and, as has been amply demonstrated, there are many disparate factors that influenced the creation and maintenance of gardens during this period. For some people, their major concern was the overall impression of a structured and ornate layout to their gardens, which provided a suitable backdrop for hospitality, entertainment and conspicuous display. In such cases, incorporating new trends and fashions into their gardens was of utmost importance. (Having said this, even those who were clearly extremely wealthy still exercised personal choice, opting for what might be considered 'old-fashioned' elements in their new gardens, such as Ingram's carved beasts or

Leveson's high mount.) For others, trees and flowers were the thing and even where their status might allow them to include other embellishments, there is little mention of such features. But, whatever the case, whether filled with flowers or ornament, whether modest or showy and whether fashionable or not, it is clear that the ornamental pleasure garden was becoming a significant feature of early seventeenth-century gentry gardens.

9

WAR AND PEACE

Gardening in the Mid-seventeenth Century

'A Friend, a Booke, and a Garden shall for the future, perfectly circumscribe my utmost designes'.[1] Although to modern ears this may sound like the perfect antidote to our hectic lives, John Evelyn wrote these words in 1651 in a mood of quiet gloom, facing an uncertain future in the new world of the Cromwellian regime. Turning his back on political ambitions which had evaporated with the execution of Charles I, he devoted himself to study – it was during this period that he started to put together *Elysium Britannicum*, his monumental work on gardens and gardening – and to the creation of a garden in his new home at Sayes Court in Deptford to the east of London.

The literature, gardens and gardening activities discussed so far have taken us through the years of relative peace and prosperity prior to the upheaval of the Civil Wars, but what of the remaining years of our period? Looking ahead to 1660, is it possible to discern further changes in the practices of early modern gardeners? It has already been noted that little new gardening literature was published during this period, but was this because resources and concerns were being directed elsewhere, or was it simply that in uncertain times people preferred the familiarity of tried and trusted texts? Using extant records of gardening activity during this period, in particular those of John Evelyn and Sir Thomas Hanmer, this chapter will consider whether the gardeners of the 1640s and 50s were looking backwards to more settled times for their inspiration or forward to a new way of thinking which was only to come to fruition in the Restoration era.

In order to consider these questions, we need to understand the prevailing circumstances in which these people found themselves. On 22 August 1642, King Charles raised the Royal Standard at Nottingham, effectively marking the start of the Civil Wars, which continued until the end of the decade, culminating in what Evelyn referred to as 'the fatal Tragedy', the execution of Charles I in 1649.[2] This was followed by a further decade under the rule of Parliament, an untried and untested new regime. With the benefit of hindsight, we now know that this situation did not last for long and that the Restoration was only a matter of years away. But people at the time had no such knowledge and the response of many to 'England's Troubles', as they were referred to by contemporaries, was one of anxiety about what the future might hold. So, as we look at gardens and gardening practices during the 1640s and 50s, we need constantly to bear in mind that the figures we are meeting were facing an unknowable and possibly hostile future.

The Civil Wars had a devastating effect on the entire population, but the brunt of the financial costs fell on the land-owning gentry. Sir John Oglander was probably speaking for many of his peers when he wrote in 1643 of the 'tyrannical misery that the gentlemen of England did endure'.[3] Cripplingly high taxes to pay for the wars, often payable to both the Royalists and to Parliament, increased purchase taxes on many essential commodities, costs incurred in quartering soldiers and losses through pillaging and plunder all contributed to financial difficulties, debt and sometimes ruin. Incomes fell as tenant farmers, no longer able to afford the rents, either moved away or demanded lower rents. Fewer people to work the fields and lack of cultivation made the land less viable and trade in agricultural goods was severely disrupted. On top of this, crops, land and farm buildings were destroyed during sporadic skirmishes and properties were severely damaged by garrisoned troops. Campden Manor in Gloucestershire, where just a few years earlier Sir Thomas Puckering had been admiring the new banqueting houses, was burnt to the ground, and Lady Sussex at Gorhambury House described vividly the misery of living with the constant threat of imminent attack and plunder: 'I have made up some of the dors and pilede them up so with wode that I believe my House is able to keep out a good many now'.[4] Also, of course, the gentry were directly involved in the war effort. As members of the traditional governing elite, they had to take up new roles as military leaders or regional administrators, marshalling endless demands for supplies, conscripts and money from their local communities. All this gave them little time to devote to the efficient running of their country estates.[5]

Obviously, the parliamentary cause had its supporters among the gentry – Sir Thomas Fairfax and General John Lambert being two notable examples – but for the most part the land-owning classes remained loyal to the king and, after his execution, to the house of Stuart and to the traditional form of government.[6] Neutrality, the preferred position of many moderates, became less and less of an option with the result that many left the country either as voluntary or compulsory exiles. For instance, neither John Evelyn nor the Buckinghamshire landowner Sir Ralph Verney could bring themselves to swear the Covenant of loyalty to Parliament in 1643 and they left for the Continent – Evelyn before anyone caught up with him and Verney, despite his parliamentary sympathies, actively refusing to take the pledge.[7] Once the dust began to settle under the new regime in the early 1650s, many of the exiled gentry started to return to England, but many had lost land and property and were often hugely in debt. Not only this, but they had also lost their prominent positions in court, Parliament and society – in short, any of the roles in public life that they had previously enjoyed. 'I confess I love Old England very well, but as things are carried heere the gentry cannot joy much to be in it', wrote Verney on his return in 1653.[8] With a lack of anything else to occupy their time, many returned to their neglected country estates and some, quite simply, turned to cultivating their gardens.

Verney arrived home to debt and financial insecurity but, determined to rebuild the family estate at Claydon, he embarked on a programme of improvement which, combining a frugal lifestyle with the selling of all his other lands, he succeeded in doing – the family still live on the estate today.[9] He took a great interest in the garden, stocking it with fruit trees, 'ordinary usefull herbes' and vegetables. This was definitely a utilitarian garden and Verney's careful management of resources is obvious in his correspondence. He stocked his orchard with cherry trees but these were grown from cuttings gathered out of the woods because, although bigger and better ones could be had from elsewhere, they were more expensive – 3d to 1s for each tree as opposed to 2s per hundred. The seeds from the fruit trees in the orchard, which included apple, walnut and chestnut, were carefully saved, presumably so they could be planted and grown on without the expense of buying more new trees. Rather than building a new banqueting house, Verney issued instructions for the chicken house to be repaired, and there are mentions of pheasants, partridges, rabbits and deer all reared on the estate. Despite being delighted by the glorious gardens he saw in Italy while he was away, Verney, unlike some of the gentlemen met in the last chapter, was not in a position to imitate them on his return. His was not a garden for show: the only flowers mentioned are traditional varieties such as roses, violets, July flowers (gilliflowers) and sweetbriars which, as noted before, were neither unusual nor expensive. By 1658, it is apparent that the situation was starting to improve: new stone seats, some stairs and coping stones for a balcony were being ordered for the garden. Two years later, after the Restoration, Verney regained his county responsibilities as a magistrate and Lieutenant and in 1661 he accepted a baronetcy.[10] But during the preceding years, his garden clearly had offered him some solace and purpose.

At Holme Lacy in Herefordshire, the Royalist supporter Viscount Scudamore did not take up the option of exile and, despite the occupation of Hereford by the Parliamentarian forces in 1642, contrived to avoid involvement in any confrontation. However, this situation did not last and he became involved in a major struggle the following year, which ended with the surrender of the Royalist garrison and Scudamore being placed under arrest until 1647. His absence from his estate was hardly his choice but, once released from prison, he spent the remainder of the 1640s and the 1650s devoting himself to the gardens and particularly to the creation of new apple orchards at Holme Lacy. He discovered and developed a celebrated new variety of cider apple named the 'Scudamore crab', resulting in the production of a cider for which Holme Lacy became famous. Some years later, Evelyn described Herefordshire as 'but one entire orchard' and Scudamore can take much of the credit for the contemporary popularity of orchard planting in the county.[11]

The Yorkshire gardener Sir John Reresby did not fare so well in the war. He took up arms and fought for the king, resulting in him being imprisoned in 1644 and his estate being confiscated by Parliament. He was released in 1646 but died soon after of a fever. In 1659, his eldest son, John, after travelling extensively on the Continent, returned to take over the management of the estate at Thrybergh once more. Like Verney, he set about restoring the family finances, the house and the garden. Although Sir John was keen to preserve his father's reputation in the garden, he had different ideas, the 'form of gardening' nowadays being different from that of his father's time. Perhaps also, he had different tastes: where the father's passion had been for flowers and fruit trees, the son eventually installed a 'fountain in the middle of the parterre' and a 'grotto in the summerhouse'.[12] This hints perhaps, at changes that were to come.

Having glimpsed the effects of the Civil Wars on these few gardens in England, we have, fortuitously, two major sources of evidence that greatly enhance our picture of gardens and gardening during this time and they are the diaries, correspondence and drawings of John Evelyn and the notebooks and manuscripts of Sir Thomas Hanmer. The work of both these men during the mid-seventeenth century provides particular insight into the world of the gardening enthusiast during this time: as well as writing and reflecting on contemporary gardening practice, producing the literature for which they are well known, they were also both actively engaged in creating gardens during the 1640s and 50s. Hanmer's writings provide details of the garden he created at the family home at Bettisfield Hall in Flintshire, as well as evidence that he was also involved, a few years earlier, in the planting of two other gardens, one at his mother's dower house in nearby Haulton and one at his house in Lewisham near London. Likewise, from Evelyn's copious correspondence we have evidence of his involvement, in an advisory capacity at least, with the remodelling of the garden at the Evelyns' ancestral home at Wotton in Surrey and with the garden at the nearby house of his friend Henry Howard at Albury, as well as the major work he undertook in developing the garden at Sayes Court, his own home for more than forty years. In addition to his extensive writings, Evelyn also produced plans and drawings of all these gardens, allowing us to compare both the differences between the gardens and, in the case of Wotton House, the differences in the garden before and after the alterations were carried out.

Both Hanmer and Evelyn were Royalists and, like some of the gentlemen already mentioned, expediently removed themselves to the Continent during the Civil War years and this experience was reflected in their gardening practice once they returned home. In May 1644, Sir Thomas, a former cup-bearer to the king, obtained leave (on payment of a fine to Parliament) to take his family to live in France and for the next six years he lived variously in Paris, Nantes and Angers. There is also some evidence that Hanmer had previously spent several years travelling on the Continent with his brother, although few details are known.[13] He returned to England in 1651, settling back into his ancestral home at Bettisfield later in the decade.

Evelyn left England in 1643: 'the Covenant being pressed, I absented myselfe', he wrote in his diary, thereby avoiding, as noted earlier, swearing an oath of loyalty to Parliament.[14] He embarked on a Grand Tour of Europe, spending several years travelling in Holland, France and Italy, recording in his diary visits to ancient sites, including churches, colleges, monasteries and military installations as well as grand palaces and magnificent gardens, still finding some time too for study at the University of Padua. In July 1646, he reached Paris and met a number of Royalists, either compulsory or, like himself, voluntary exiles from England. It is possible that he may have met Verney and Hanmer, who were also in Paris around this time. Evelyn also made the acquaintance of the king's ambassador in France, Sir Richard Browne, and in 1647, married his daughter Mary, who was then just twelve years old (Evelyn was twenty-seven). In 1652, he returned with his wife to England for good to take possession of his father-in-law's somewhat rundown estate at Sayes Court in Deptford.

In several ways, then, there are identifiable similarities between Hanmer and Evelyn's experiences during these years: they both spent a significant amount of time living and working abroad, particularly in France, where it is possible that their life-long acquaintance began. It is known that Sir Thomas corresponded with Sir Richard Browne on a number of occasions while he was in France and, once Evelyn and Hanmer had returned to England, their respective homes in Deptford and Lewisham made them close neighbours.[15] In his diary, Evelyn records that on 1 April 1657 Hanmer visited him and a few weeks later, on 22 May, he visited Hanmer.[16] Their well-documented correspondence indicates a shared interest in horticultural matters that continued over many years. As will be demonstrated, they were both, to varying degrees, exposed to and influenced by the Continental gardening styles that they encountered in France and, once they returned home, both continued to purchase plants from the nurserymen they had come to know in Paris. Both returned to the uncertain world of the new Cromwellian regime and, with no role in the new order, devoted themselves instead to the renovation of their respective estates and, in particular, to their gardens.

Probably the most complete picture we have of a mid-seventeenth-century garden is the one created by Evelyn at Sayes Court in the early 1650s, beautifully depicted in an extant detailed plan drawn by Evelyn in c.1653 (fig. 130). This garden is mentioned in his diary and in his correspondence with his father-in-law, from whom Evelyn had taken over, as mentioned earlier, management of the family seat. Whether this plan was carried out exactly as shown is of course a moot point, but it is indicative of his intentions and parts of it at least are referred to elsewhere in Evelyn's papers.

Little is known about the garden at Sayes Court before Evelyn began work on it in the 1650s, although his first (of only two) diary entries referring to his new garden implies that

NOBILISSIMO VIRO Dᵒ Dᵒ RICH:

he was working from a fairly blank canvas. On 17 January 1653, he records: 'I began to set out the Ovall Garden at Says Court, which was before a rude ortchard & all the rest one intire fild of 100 Ackers, without any hedge: excepting the hither holly-hedge joyning to the bank of the mount walk: and this was the beginning of all the succeeding Gardens, Walkes, Groves, Enclosures and Plantations there'.[17]

The only other clues are a few references to the old garden in correspondence to Sir Richard in Paris from his father, Christopher Browne, who lived at Sayes Court until his death in the 1640s. It appears from his remarks that the war was taking its toll and this could explain the dilapidated state of the garden by the time Evelyn took it over. Browne deplores the difficulty of finding workmen to plash the 'Barbary' hedge, observing bitterly that 'to follow the drummer and to plunder' is 'a newe trade more easie and proffitable'.[18] Elsewhere, he refers to the digging and replanting of the old orchard a number of times: whether referring to national events or more specifically to the family's penurious state is difficult to know but he writes in November 1643 that 'my thoughts being now in these desparate tymes more fix't upon the meanes to preserve that wee have lost than to adventure any part thereof towards the improvement of that which is to come'.[19] Earlier the same year, he wrote that two men 'have alreadie diggd the Mount and planted it with beanes and pease'.[20] Whether this was the normal practice at Sayes Court or another sign of straitened times is impossible to tell, but planting an ornamental feature such as the mount with staple food crops such as peas and beans is certainly unusual. Elsewhere, Browne mentions gravel walks, borders with a variety of herbs and flowers, roses, strawberries and raspberries, so the garden, such as it was, clearly fulfilled the usual utilitarian and decorative functions. Presumably, the few years of neglect before Evelyn took over the garden would have been long enough for all trace of the flowers and soft fruit to have disappeared.

Evelyn set about renovating the garden with enthusiasm, creating, as the plan graphically reveals, a garden which consisted of a series of hedged, fenced and walled enclosures, representing a miscellany of styles that reflected Evelyn's various interests and influences. There is little attempt at any overall symmetry, which in any case is made virtually impossible by the irregular shape of the land available. As can be seen from the plan (which is orientated south–north), it was an elongated triangular plot, bordered to the north by the River Thames and to the east by a ditch which ran from the Thames to feed the carp pond at the southern corner of the garden. The likelihood is that the plan was drawn to be sent to his father-in-law in Paris, with whom Evelyn kept up a continual correspondence about the renovations of the house and garden. In February 1652, he writes to Browne promising that 'likewise you will receive a full and perfect Ichnography of all such alterations as I

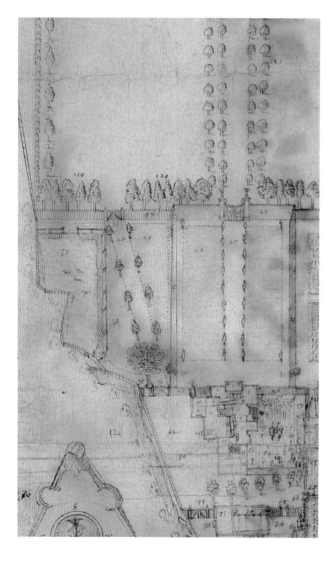

131 Detail of Evelyn's plan of Sayes Court (see fig. 130), showing the entrance leading to the house.

From Evelyn's key:

25 The Court, with faire gravel walkes planted with Cipresse and the walls with fruit

26 The Bowling Greenes betwixt.

29 Grasse plotts where the Cowes are milked

30 The carpe pond...likewise the watring place

31 The Garden dore out of the Court

132 Detail of Evelyn's plan of Sayes Court (see fig. 130), showing the oval garden.

From Evelyn's key:

36 The Garden, and walkes of Gravel about the oval Square

37 The evergreen thicket, for Birds, private walkes, shades and Cabinetts

38 The Grasse plotts sett about with a Border, in which flower Potts

39 The Round Parterre of Box with 12 Beds of flowers & passages betwixt each bed

40 The Mount, Center, and Dial

43 The Long Pourmenade from the Banquetting house to the Island

44 The Banquetting House

47 The Terras walke or mount

92 The Holley hedge, at the side of the mount or Terras

93 The Berbery hedge

have made in this ruind place, which if approved by you will add much to our satisfaction.'[21] Although no trace of this garden now exists, the plan is so detailed and its key so well annotated that it is possible to walk round it, albeit in our imaginations, in just the same way as the many visitors recorded in Evelyn's diaries would have done.

Presuming an arrival by road, the first obvious feature would have been the double row of lime trees lining the walk to the main gate (fig. 131). This is something with which Evelyn had been especially taken on his travels in Holland during the previous decade, where he

had admired the neat orderliness of the Dutch towns and in particular the Dutch practice of planting long regular rows of trees. Following a visit to Wilhelmstadt he comments in his diary on 'a stately row of Limes on the Ramparts' and in Amsterdam, he notes 'Streetes so exactly straite ... being so frequently planted and shaded with beautifull lime trees, which are set in rows before every mans house'.[22] Evelyn appears to have been innovative in adopting this method of planting in his own garden at Sayes Court and is credited with being the first person to use the term 'avenue' to describe such tree-lined routes.[23]

After entering the gates into the walled court in front of the house, the path continues between two bowling greens, a common feature of gardens since Elizabethan times. Beyond the wall to the right was a milking close planted with walnut trees and beyond that the carp pond, also used, according to Evelyn's detailed annotations, as a watering place.[24]

Turning to the left in front of the house led through a garden door out of the court and into what Evelyn describes in his diary as 'the Ovall garden' (fig. 132).[25] This was a purely ornamental garden, consisting of gravel walks set about an 'oval Square', with four evergreen thickets at the corners of the square and forming the oval, grass plots set with flowers in pots, a round parterre divided into twelve beds of flowers with paths between them and a dial set on a mount in the centre. Cypress trees, a popular choice for ornamental gardens because of their pleasing conical habit, punctuated the corners of the parterres and grass plots. The symmetry of this garden is somewhat compromised by its slightly offset placement within its boundaries, which are different on every side: a wooden pale to the south, a brick wall to the east, a hedge to the north and rows of fruit trees to the west. It recalls Parkinson's observation that despite the 'four square proportion' being ideal, 'many men must be content with any plat of ground', including, it seems, John Evelyn.[26]

What is particularly interesting about the oval garden is that it is almost identical to one belonging to the renowned nurseryman Pierre Morin in Paris that Evelyn was taken to visit by a friend in April 1644. He described it thus: '[It] is of an exact Oval figure planted with Cypresse, cutt flat & set as even as a Wall could have form'd it: The Tulips, Anemonies, Ranunculus's, Crocus's &c. being the most exquisite; were held to be the rarest in the World'.[27] It appears that as well as the exquisite planting, Evelyn was so impressed with its design that once he returned to England and Sayes Court, he set about making his own copy of the garden that he had admired in Paris. It must be emphasised that this was no subliminal influence at work here – it was Evelyn's declared intention. He refers on more than one occasion to 'my Morine Garden' and he writes to his father-in-law in September 1652 asking for clarification of the measurements 'for my better comparing of my plot with that of Mr Morines'.[28] It has been suggested that Richard Browne was in fact the 'friend' referred to in Evelyn's diary who first took him to view Morin's garden, and that his house was almost next door to Morin's garden, so maybe this was not as demanding as it sounds.[29]

There is a drawing of Morin's garden executed by Richard Symonds in 1649 which makes the similarities between this garden and Evelyn's recreation of it obvious (figs 133, 134). Although it is not known, apart from Evelyn's description of it, what was planted in Morin's garden, it seems clear that Evelyn was also anxious to obtain from Morin some of the same plants for his own garden. He requested Browne on a number of occasions to supply him with seeds and plants from Morin, in particular Alaternus (a kind of evergreen privet) and 'Cypresse' seeds. Morin had apparently made his fortune importing Alaternus bushes from the south of France and selling them on from his Paris nursery.[30] Evelyn seemed particularly keen on them for his garden: 'Of *Alaternus* I have thousands', he wrote to Browne, 'and yet I desire more seeds.'[31] He uses them, among other things, to plant up the evergreen thickets in the oval garden. That this venture was clearly a success is confirmed in a subsequent letter, of 1657, when Evelyn wrote that 'This moyst summer has made my Oval perfect, & the place most beautiful'.[32]

To the north of the oval garden was a terrace or mount, as Evelyn describes it, edged with the holly hedge which he noted in his diary as being already extant when he took over

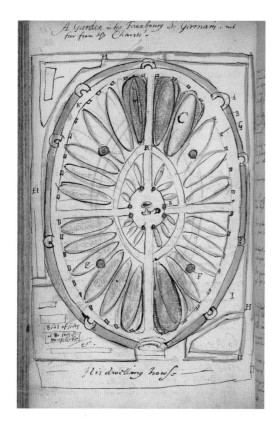

the garden and presumably the same mount referred to by Christopher Browne in his letter of 1643. North of the terrace and west of the house was Evelyn's second ornamental showpiece, the Grove, which more or less forms the central feature of the garden around which the other elements are arranged (fig. 135). This grove was filled with a mixture of oak, ash, elm, beech and chestnut trees: 'I planted this yeere in my grove 500 trees of good nature brought out of Essex & yet intend to plant therein 800 more', he reports to Richard Browne in a letter of January 1653.[33] In the centre was a mount planted with bays and a circular walk planted with laurel. Radiating out from here in a geometric pattern were six straight paths. In addition there were a number of what Evelyn calls 'Cabinetts', small enclosed gardens formed of clipped evergreen hedges – another use to which Evelyn put his supply of Alaternus plants – 'hidden' at the end of 'Spiders Clawes' or dog-legged paths. There were fourteen such cabinets in Evelyn's grove, little nooks that provided places for private contemplation. This kind of layout of green rooms or *cabinet de verdure*, set within a wood or *bosquet* cut through with paths and alleys radiating from a semicircle or other

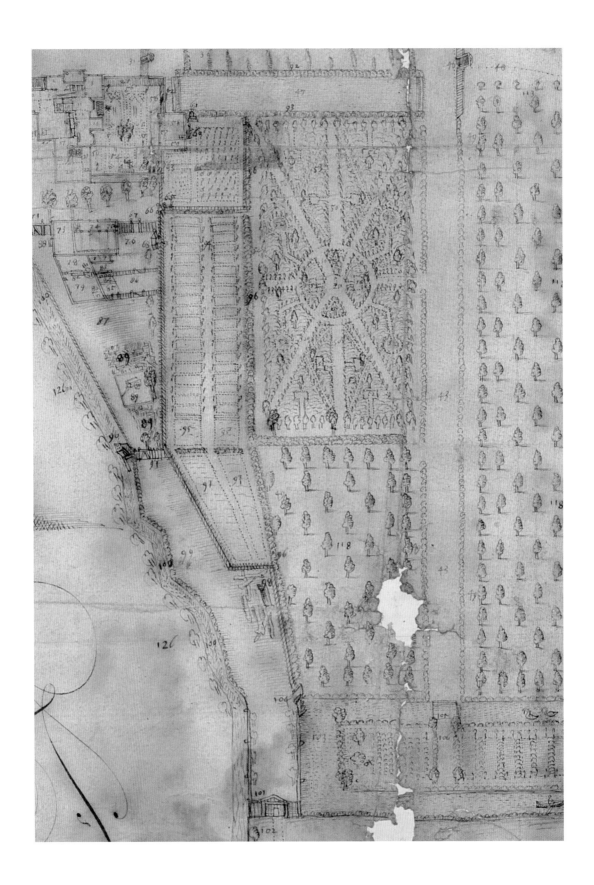

135   Detail of Evelyn's plan of Sayes Court (see fig. 130), showing the Grove, the Promenade and the Island.

From Evelyn's key:

50   The Grove with the several walkes

51   The mount or Center planted with Bayes, but the Circle walke with Laurel

52   14 Cabinetts of Aliternies, and a great French walnutt at every one

53   The Thicketts

43   The Long Pourmenade

103   The moate about the Island

105   The Drawbridge of the Island

106   The Island just as it is planted with an hedge of severall fruits twixt 8 bedds of Asperge &c: At the two ends are raspberries, and a Summer house at the marke * the mulberrie tree at the mark X

97   Plotts for pease and beanes &c.

95   A Plott for melons

94   The Kitchin Garden made into 38 bedds of Pottherbs besides borders &c.

central point, is reminiscent of the style emerging on a much larger scale in the designs of Mollet and André Le Nôtre in the royal gardens of France and around Europe.[34] Again, it is not unreasonable to assume that Evelyn's choice of design was influenced by gardens he had seen or heard of on the Continent.

Running alongside the west of the oval garden and the grove was a long promenade which stretched the entire length of the garden, from a banqueting house (see fig. 132) at the southern end to a bridge across to a small island at the northern end. As already noted, such banqueting houses and islands had been ornamental features of grand Elizabethan gardens and early seventeenth-century gardens, but it is interesting that, as well as the majority of the length of the promenade being hedged with apple trees, Evelyn's island was given over to the growing of raspberries and asparagus and the moat around the island was 'stored with Carpe, Swannes, Duckes &c', all of which were valuable sources of food.

This conflation of the ornamental with the utilitarian seems an appropriate transition point in the tour as it essentially marks the end of the ornamental aspects of the garden and from here on it can be seen that the rest of Evelyn's garden is still chiefly a utilitarian one. Even the trees in the grove, he informs his father-in-law, when they 'spring up too thick' can be transplanted elsewhere to provide necessary firewood.[35] A glance at the plan shows that the orchard takes up a large proportion of the entire garden area and an extant agreement dated 27 January 1652 between Evelyn and Matthew Blissett, a gardener from 'East Greenwich in the County of Kent', details the supply and purchase of more than four hundred cherry, pear and apple trees.[36] Moving back towards the house from the island are two large plots for peas and beans, then a large kitchen garden containing two plots for melons and thirty-eight further beds of vegetables, salads and herbs for culinary use.

The adjacent dung pit has been discussed in Chapter 4, but serves to remind us of the ever-present practicalities of gardening in the seventeenth century.

The remaining two small areas of the garden consist of a nursery and what Evelyn refers to as his 'Private garden'. The nursery, equipped with a 'Pump and Cistern for the infusion of Dungs', was an area for bringing on new plants and seeds before transplanting them into the garden. He writes excitedly to Browne in September 1652 that 'I am transplanting my Glorious Nursery of neere 800 plantes (two foote high & and as fayre as I ever saw any in France) about our Court, and as farr as they will reach in our Oval Garden'.[37] The private garden of 'choice flowers, and Simples' was located between the nursery and the house and was, as noted of many other examples, outside the parlour, which now had a new window to look out into the garden. This garden was enclosed within walls, with doors out into the nursery and into the oval garden, laid out in the usual four-square form with a fountain in the centre, an aviary outside the parlour window, a beehive against the northern wall and a gardeners' 'toolehouse' that was also used to store fruit – all fairly conventional. What was unusual was the presence of an 'Elaboratorie' in this garden, which Evelyn describes as having a 'Portico of 20 foot long upon Pillars open towards the Private Garden'. Ironically, this ultra-modern addition to the garden appears to incorporate the only reference at Sayes Court to Evelyn's well-documented interest in the classical past, although perhaps, as in his writing, it was an attempt to invest the activity of gardening with an intellectual status (see Chapter 5). The purpose of this laboratory is not made clear but, given Evelyn's association with the Hartlib circle and his interest in the new science, it is certainly a possibility that this was where he would have made trials of plants, particularly 'the ever greenes', continually arriving from France, secured by Browne, many of which he says were 'unknown to me', but for which he was nevertheless prepared to 'give any price'.[38] Comments such as these make it clear that Browne was introducing Evelyn to a range of plants seemingly not yet available in England.

So, what does this brief tour of the garden at Sayes Court reveal about gardens and gardening in mid-seventeenth-century England? Despite an eclectic selection of innovative features – the avenue of trees, the oval garden, the grove, the 'Elaboratorie' – in essence this garden is still quite conventional. It contains features that would not have been out of place in an Elizabethan setting and provides all the utilitarian functions required of a garden. At the same time, it allows space for Evelyn to indulge his passion for plants and trees; the prominent place of the ornamental garden, the development of which has been traced here over the preceding decades, now seems established and accepted. Influences from abroad, in terms of inspiration, ideas and plants, are all evident, particularly Evelyn's persistent seeking out of evergreens and new varieties of flowers with which he is unfamiliar – his interest in science and experiment is happily married to his interest in gardening.

Given the variety of styles and influences at work in the creation of Sayes Court, when the two other gardens with which Evelyn was involved are considered, the contrast in styles is even more marked. The first of these was the garden at the family home at Wotton in Surrey, inherited by Evelyn's elder brother George from his father in 1640, in which Evelyn aided his brother with its comprehensive redesign in the 1650s. The work on this garden is mentioned in his diary, in a series of letters from George to his brother written while Evelyn was still in France, and by a series of drawings executed by Evelyn which are extremely illuminating in that they show the garden both before and after its remodelling, as well as highlighting some of the features mentioned in other sources. Elements of this garden are still extant today (see fig. 138). The second garden is that of Evelyn's friend and neighbour, Henry Howard, who owned a house near Wotton, at Albury. There are at least four references to this garden in Evelyn's diary, suggesting that work on the garden was being carried out during the period from 1655 to 1670, together with a detailed plan drawn by Evelyn, of uncertain date but likely to be around 1680.[39] Obviously, this plan postdates the building of the garden, leaving Evelyn's part in the actual design somewhat ambiguous, but, whatever his involvement, there are similarities in layout and style between this garden and that at Wotton.

The earliest description of the garden at Wotton comes in Evelyn's diary where, in an entry dated 1620, he records: 'The house is large and antient, suitable to those hospitable times, and so sweetely environ'd with those delicious streames and venerable Woods, as in the judgement of strangers, as well as English-men, it may be compared to one of the most tempting and pleasant seates in the Nation...for it has risings, meadows, Woods & Water in aboundance'.[40] This is a somewhat nostalgic and idealised description of the house and garden at the time of his birth, obviously written with hindsight, the allusion to hospitality and abundance also harking back to a bygone age when all was well with the world.[41] Evelyn's most authoritative biographer and editor of his diaries, E. S. de Beer, dated the writing of the extant diary to the 1680s when Evelyn wrote it up from notes he had kept throughout his life, so all entries have to be read with caution and bearing this in mind; in this case, as Evelyn obviously was not keeping notes from the year of his birth, the description must either be a later childhood memory or hearsay.[42] By way of corroboration, however, there is a drawing executed by Evelyn that shows the house and garden as it was 'before my Bro: alterd it & as it was 1640' (fig. 136).[43] This drawing depicts a large rambling Tudor house with a fairly small walled garden in front of it, divided into three, with a hint of a geometric arrangement of knots or beds in one of them and some kind of garden structure, possibly a still-house or summerhouse. Outside the wall is a stream or 'moate', as Evelyn annotates it in his drawing, which in his diary he describes as being 'within 10 yards of the very house'.[44]

Still further from the house, and the vantage point of the picture, is an area roughly depicted as a mound of trees – presumably the 'venerable Woods' of his description.

A second drawing, which was apparently done at the same time, shows the view from the opposite side of the house (fig. 137).[45] From this it is possible to see that the 'moate' opens out into a large pond and that there is a large barn and a pigeon house. The mound of trees now forms the background of the drawing. All in all, the garden at that time comprised a fairly random arrangement of utilitarian and ornamental areas close about the house, with woods and meadows extending further afield, indicating that it was probably little changed from the previous century, which seems to concur with Evelyn's description of his childhood home before the garden was remodelled.

The next reference is in his diary for May 1643 when Evelyn notes that with his brother's permission he has embarked on some alterations to the garden at Wotton, mentioning specifically 'a study, a fishpond, Iland, and some other solitudes and retirements, which gave first occasion of improving those Water-Works and Gardens, which afterwards succeeded them'.[46] Another drawing by Evelyn, dated 1646, shows these additions to the garden, with a small garden pavilion and pond labelled 'this study & pond was made by me'.[47] As indi-

The prospect of the old house at Wotton 1640
from the Browewhile

cated in the diary entry, however, this minor work was merely a prelude to a much more comprehensive overhaul of the garden carried out by George Evelyn with his brother's help and advice a few years later (see figs 139, 140).

The nature of this renovation is best described in a series of letters written by George to John while the latter was still living in France.[48] Once again, the evidence in the letters is corroborated by more drawings done by Evelyn which illustrate the new garden once it was completed in 1653. The letters are not in particularly good condition – many are damaged, torn, incomplete and undated – but enough can be seen to infer if not George's complete reliance on advice from his brother, at least a wish for his approval of the plans. He informs John in a letter written in 1650 of 'work I have in hand which is levelling my hill behind the house and makinge a Bowlinge Green, some walkes and other devices...I intend to make upon my hill a very spatious Grotto'. In another letter he promises to send John a plan of the new garden and hopes that he will be pleased with it. It also appears that a Cousin Evelyn (also, confusingly, called George) was the 'Architector' of this plan and came up with the original design for the garden. Not that John Evelyn seems to have approved of it: he notes in his diary a visit in February 1649 from George Evelyn, 'my kinsman, the great Travellor, and one who believed himselfe a better architect than realy he was; witness the portico in the Garden at Wotton' – hardly a ringing endorsement.[49] Perhaps brother George had the same reservations, because although he makes several references in his 1650 letters to his cousin as the architect, at the same time he is asking John for his 'noble advice; which I shall endeavour in all particulars to observe'. And it is clear that John does offer advice, particularly on the waterworks and the decoration of the grotto. 'For the water I shall punctually observe your directions', writes George, but regarding the furnishing of the intended grotto, he remarks ruefully that 'I wish our country afforded me with such gallant materials as your letters dictate'. He assures his brother, however, that he will do his best to obtain the recommended materials, enlisting the help of friends and engaging the services of a 'Barbadoes Merchant to furnish me with the curious Rocks of that Iland & with Corall, Conching & other shells' for which he will spare no cost. The acquisition of such rarities seems not to be a great problem for those with sufficient means and the right contacts.

As well as advice about the design, George also frequently requested John to send him plants and seeds from France: he seems particularly anxious to obtain melon seeds, which he mentions on a number of occasions: 'if you cannot send us of the Spanish seed, be pleased to afford us of your French ones: they far exceed our English'. He also asks for cypress seeds and plants of another tree that 'you informed me you had frequently in your garden in France which … kept green all the year'. It is interesting, again, that seeds and plants from France – as well as rocks and shells for decorating grottoes – were apparently more desirable than English ones and that George shared his brother's enthusiasm for the wider variety of evergreen trees now available for the garden.

George Evelyn's ambitions for his garden need putting into a context. His brother's diaries covering the years he was travelling around Europe reveal that he was much taken with the Renaissance gardens of Italy and France. John describes with enthusiasm, for instance, the grottoes in the Tivoli gardens at the Villa d'Este which are richly decorated with shells and coral, or the gardens of the Grand Dukes at Pratoline which are 'delicious and full of fountains' and where the walls of the grotto are 'richly composed of Coralls, Shells, Coper & Marble figures; with the huntings of Severall beasts, moving by the force of the water'.[50] It seems that at this time in his life at least, Evelyn's interest in gardens was more concerned with the artificial, the ingenious and the mechanical rather than the plants, which he rarely mentions. Also, not only was this part of the diary written retrospectively but much of it has been shown to be taken from travel books of the time, and may therefore not represent what Evelyn actually saw.[51] Nevertheless, this does not detract from the essential point that he has chosen to describe these elements of the garden because these are the aspects that attracted his attention. What seems clear is that his descriptions of these wonderful gardens with their elaborate waterworks and richly decorated grottoes had inspired his brother to attempt to emulate them. The fact that cousin George Evelyn, the dubious architect, had also travelled much in Italy probably aided in the execution of these ideas.

By the following year, 1651, however, the original plan had been changed because, according to George, the ladies of the house had persuaded him that they would rather have a garden and a fountain instead of a bowling green. He obviously complied as he writes to John on 29 September 1651 'that I have almost levelled the hill behind the house & built my walls, the nexte worke wilbe to designe the ground for a garden and fountagne'. Again he resolves to send the plan to John in France 'to begg your advise & observations', but in fact John returned to England soon after this and was able to view the completed alterations for himself. It would be difficult for us to envisage the extent and form of these alterations were it not for the fact that a number of Evelyn's drawings and plans of the finished garden are extant (figs 139, 140).[52] These show precisely the classical Italianate layout of the garden: 'I have resolved the plott for a garden where in the middle I will have a [?piscine] with water running and in the middle...some device of waterworks', writes George. We can clearly see the portico with its classical pillars (still to be seen at Wotton today, fig. 138), as well as steps, arches and walls and the levelled terrace which offers an excellent vantage point over the whole garden to the house.

139   John Evelyn, 'Wotton in Surrey, The house of Geo: Evelyn Esq.', 1653
140   John Evelyn, view of Wotton with the garden, grotto and environs, c.1650s

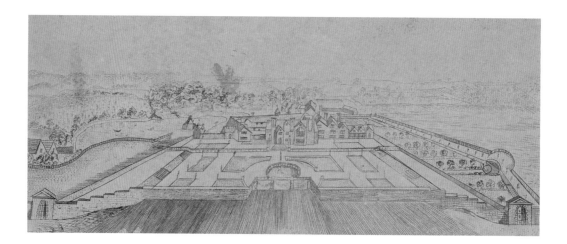

The vista is equally impressive from the viewpoint of the house looking up the terraces to the mount. Comparison with the earlier drawings of the house and surrounding area shows that this garden was a complete reworking of the original. It was a huge and expensive undertaking, literally moving mountains to redirect watercourses that were close to the house, to fill in the moat, to level the garden and to build the terraced mount at the southern end of the garden.[53] The mount was planted with rows of trees; the pools were filled with running water; steps, arches and the portico, complete with a statue of Venus,

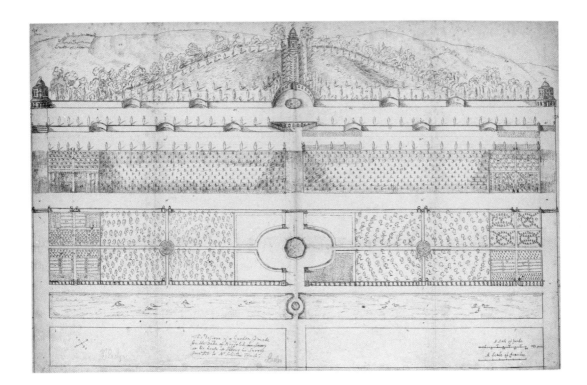

were built. The result was an unmistakably Italianate garden, of whose impact Evelyn was in no doubt:

> I should speake much of the Gardens, Fountaines and Groves that adorne it were they not as generally knowne to be amongst the most magnificent that England afforded ... and which indeede gave one of the first examples to that elegancy since so much in vogue and followd, for the managing of their Waters and other elegancies of that nature.[54]

A number of years later, Evelyn produced a similar plan, although on a grander scale, for his neighbours at Albury Park (fig. 141), the basic structure of which can still be seen today. A diary entry in August 1655 records a visit by Evelyn to Albury, in which he notes that Howard had already begun to build and alter the garden. Evelyn, though, records nothing indicating his own part in this project until twelve years later, when he visits Howard again, noting that 'I designed for him the plat of his canale and garden, with a crypta through the hill'.[55] Whether he designed it at this time, or had already done so at an earlier date is uncertain. However, we know that this ambitious plan was carried out, firstly because on a third recorded visit to Albury in 1670, Evelyn says that he found it 'exactly don to the

257

142   The 'crypta' at Albury Park today. The entrance to the tunnel can be seen in the centre of the semi-circular walls of the upper terrace, as in the plan (see fig. 141)

Designe and plot I had made, with the Crypta through the mountaine in the parke' and secondly because this 'crypta' (tunnel) can still be seen today (fig. 142).[56] Therefore, the plan must postdate the building of the garden, possibly bringing into question the extent of Evelyn's own involvement with the project. It could be that the plan was an updated version of a much earlier one, perhaps as alluded to in these diary entries, or it could simply have been a representation of the reality on the ground at that time.

Whenever it was made and whatever Evelyn's involvement, this is clearly another example of an Italianate garden being built in England. The fact that it was next door to the Evelyn garden at Wotton may simply be a coincidence, but it is more likely that other influences were at work. Howard himself had also travelled much in Europe, as had his grandfather, the Earl of Arundel, whom Evelyn had originally met in Padua, just before the Earl's death in 1646. As seen in the last chapter, the earl had created a classical setting in his garden at Arundel House in London to display the collection of ancient statues that he had brought back from his travels abroad, so it is perhaps not surprising that when his grandson

258

came to build a garden at one of the family's country houses, he chose to experiment with this kind of design. The fact that his friends the Evelyns were building something similar just next door may well have also influenced his thinking. It is perfectly plausible that Henry Howard looked to Wotton for inspiration and to John Evelyn for advice on how to go about realising his ambitions.

As was discussed in the last chapter, there is plenty of evidence to show that during the first half of the seventeenth century, various features of Italian Renaissance gardens were being gradually introduced into gentry gardens around England, but what appears to have been happening at Wotton, and then at Albury, is the wholesale remodelling of the garden into a completely new style, reminiscent once again of the garden depicted in the painting of Llannerch in Denbighshire (see fig. 118), created around 1660 and similarly inspired by the travels in Europe of its owner, Mutton Davies. Evelyn claims that the garden at Wotton was one of the first examples of such a garden to be seen in England: whether this somewhat immodest claim is true or not, the fact is that by this time, Italian and classical influences were simply one of a number of styles that were inspiring English garden design. As noted previously, fashions from Renaissance Italy took a long time to take hold in England and it seems that, by the time they had, newer ideas were also afoot. It could be argued that gardens such as those at Wotton, Albury and Llannerch were slightly anachronistic, as new influences from around the Continent, particularly France and Holland, were travelling much more quickly and taking their place in English garden design. This is amply demonstrated by Evelyn himself in the creation of his own garden at Sayes Court, a garden which presents a miscellany of different styles and influences, which was, as has been seen, how most gardens evolved. To be able to embark on a complete overhaul and produce a new garden in a single unified style such as at Wotton or Albury was in fact extremely unusual, because in most cases the resources to do this were simply not available.

For the likes of John Evelyn, left relatively unscathed by the ravages of the Civil Wars, what the years of the interregnum offered was time to devote to their gardens. Evelyn's various forays into practical gardening as described earlier are mainly confined to the 1650s when, not to put too fine a point on it and as indicated by the quotation at the beginning of this chapter, Evelyn had nothing better to do. His years of enforced retirement gave him an opportunity to indulge in one of his many and varied interests. When it came in 1660, the Restoration was for him an event 'without parallel'. Evelyn was at last able to take up public office, working on various commissions for the government including providing for the sick and wounded as a result of the Dutch wars, examining the work of the Royal Mint and drawing up plans for the rebuilding of London after the Great Fire in 1666. He was also a founder member of the Royal Society, reflecting his intellectual interest in the new science.

All this of course left little time for hands-on gardening, although the many horticultural publications which appeared throughout his long life as well as his work on the unpublished *Elysium Britannicum*, which he wrote and rewrote for more than forty years, all bear witness to a continued and life-long interest in gardens and gardening.

Shedding further light on our knowledge of gardening during this period are the papers of Sir Thomas Hanmer of Bettisfield in north Wales (fig. 143), which provide a wealth of information about how another gentleman gardener approached and carried out his gardening. In addition to the draft manuscripts of his *Garden Book* (discussed in Chapter 1), there are also two small notebooks kept by Hanmer, annotated in various places with dates which allow us to place them with some certainty to between 1654 and 1657. The first memorandum book (Bettisfield 1663) is randomly arranged and in two parts, each beginning from either end of the book.

The first part concerns accounts, bills, debts and various reminders to himself, while the second part is exclusively concerned with garden notes. There are many lists of plants, including planting plans for his gardens, plants that Hanmer has purchased from various nurserymen in both England and France and plants he has given to and received from various friends and relatives.[57] It also contains notes gathered from various people about plant care and maintenance which, together with the planting plans, are of particular relevance to this chapter (fig. 144 and see figs 146, 147). The second notebook (Bettisfield 1666), covering the same period and dedicated exclusively to garden notes, appears to be a tidied up version of the first, with neat headings and many blank pages in between, indicating perhaps an intention to fill these in at a later date as he gathered more information. It seems a reasonable assumption that this was an initial attempt to channel his notes and thoughts into some kind of order with a view to compiling his garden book.

In addition, among the bundle of unbound papers which includes one of the manuscript versions of his *Garden Book* is an essay written by Hanmer, possibly intended as a preface, which also repays close attention.[58] As well as setting out his reasons for writing his book at all and the contents therein, he gives an account of the current state of gardening, comparing it with how things have changed since his father's time – a period which, of course, was contemporaneous with the gardens examined so far from earlier in the century. He observes, for instance, that the wealthy nowadays are no longer satisfied with 'good houses, Parkes, handsome avenues and issues to and from their dwellings' and instead are turning their attention to 'very costly embellishments of their Gardens Orchards and Walkes', noting that 'the whole designe or laying out of our garden grounds are much

(following pages) 144 Two pages from Sir Thomas Hanmer's notebook, *c.*1654–7

Left wth Mr Rose . Apr . 1654 .
9 Rootes wch Tho. Thunder delivered
  to him last wynter viz —

Angelica small roote —
Laure. Bol. vas. roote .
Seville
Gen . Hand god roote wth ofsetts .
Mor . Crane . god roote
Pirrehot gold roote —
Pelican .
Susan .
Vesta . 1

Sigismunder . great roote crimson
  & white
fine braue d'Amors lite bol, sn roote,
yellith Rose dd . white agat all
  white edgd wth crimson .
Roses fancy pinke cold & white
  greene seedes .
white Diana of Maulart .
  Tuberas from Ld Colrani
Browne purple de Marais . died
Gen . Goydi, gddel io edyd of white

  to haue her hastillias frō her

On ye right hand of the walke
1 Blood pear. 2 great primitive 3 bon critin.
4 Bergamot 5 Anthony pears.
On the left hand
1 Binfield 2 Tradescants. 3 bon critin.
4 Bergamot. 5 Sr Nath. Bacons pear

More Tulips left with
Rose in August 1654.
1 Gen bol. 1 purple first, 1 land-
schap bol, 1 Argos, 1 Juncil.
1 St Nicaise

Mr Rose. 1655.
Rose had from mee this yeare
1 pelicon, 1 peruchot, 1 Dorillet,
1 ag. hanns. 1 gen. goyen.

I had from him a small ofset of
the dutchess of venis, 1 palse za-
bloou he calls it, but tis a bra-
bauson.

L. Lambert.   very
Iuni 1655. I sent him by Rose a great
mother roote of Ag. Hans:

different from what our fathers used'. Hanmer then goes on to give what appears to be a detailed description of how gardens looked, an account that has been much studied and quoted by garden historians as being a definitive (not to say almost unique) description of a mid-seventeenth-century garden. However, it soon becomes apparent that he is describing neither his own garden nor indeed any other gardens that he knows in Wales, so it begs the question as to where this description of fashionable gardens is coming from.

Closer examination reveals the likelihood that at times at least he is describing fashions he has seen in French gardens: he refers, for instance, to parterres 'as the French call them', and *Compartements* 'as they call them'. He describes 'great grounds', divided into three sections: the parterre next to the house, compartments filled with knots, flowers, grasswork, dwarf trees and topiary beyond this, with labyrinths, walks and tall trees furthest from the house, all embellished with fountains, grottoes, statues and so on. He also describes how the parterres are cut out into 'Embroidery of flowers, beasts, birds and feuillages...filled with severall coloured sands and dust with much art, [and completely unlike Hanmer's own garden] with but few flowers'. It becomes clear at this point that Hanmer is describing the layout of gardens that belong to someone else ('they') and, as just suggested, it is likely that this is the kind of garden he may have seen in France and elsewhere on the Continent.[59] Indeed, Hanmer makes a clear distinction between 'these large groundes' which 'cannot well be less than two or three hundred yards in length' and the smaller garden, presumably such as his own, which will suffice 'most gentlemen', comprising a square or oblong plot of only fifty or sixty yards, divided perhaps into two or four knots or compartments. This advice is reiterated by the author and gardener John Rea, who suggested that twenty yards square was a sufficient size for the flower garden of a gentleman and just thirty square yards for a nobleman; Parkinson's notion of a garden being 'fit and answerable to the degree they hold' still appears to appertain here.[60] Although there is little indication of the actual dimensions, Hanmer's description is reminiscent too of the modest garden laid out by Sir Thomas Temple at Burton Dassett.

That such gardens fall outside Hanmer's own practical experience becomes even more obvious when we consider a letter from him to Evelyn in 1668 in which he states: 'In answer to your desire of being enformed what gardens there are in Wales...I know not of any noble ones...Many gentlemen...have pretty handsome little groundes but nobody hath ventured upon large spacious ones with costly fountains...or great parterres.'[61] All this presents somewhat of a conundrum. On the one hand, Hanmer begins his essay from a thoroughly personal viewpoint, with specific references to, for instance, 'our late Warr', setting out precisely why he is writing this book and what it will and will not contain. On the other hand, he then moves on to this more general description of knots and parterres, as if they are nothing to do with him but complying with a general perception of what such gardens looked like, even though, as his letter to Eveyln indicates, he does not know of any. It is therefore difficult to escape the conclusion that the fashionable gardens Hanmer describes are those that he has seen in France or, possibly, read about in books which, as has already been discussed, were often French in origin. What is clear is that this is not a description of his own garden or gardens in his local area. In our search to uncover the reality of gentry gardens in rural England and Wales then, we must approach such evidence with caution.

More helpful are a number of descriptions of planting in Hanmer's own gardens, the most detailed of which is a manuscript headed 'Flowers in the Great Garden December 1660. Bettisf.', supplemented by a further description of 'Fruit Trees in the Great Garden at Bettisfield 1660'. Here he describes precisely what flowers were planted in how many rows in each bed within the garden.[62] The beds themselves are 'boarded', with paths in between, and his concern is to provide the best way for the flowers to be displayed. Rather than the quarters being surrounded by tall hedges, as in his father's time, they are now 'layd open and exposed to the view of the chambers and the knotts and borders upheld only with very low coloured boards, stone or tile'. There seem to be at least four central beds, each with thirteen rows, or 'ranks' as Hanmer calls them, each containing varieties of flowering bulbs including tulips, fritillaries, jonquils, hyacinths and so on. Besides these, there are further beds, 'full of anemones on the outsides and tulips and narcissuses in the midst, with some gilly flowers... and cyclamens at the four corners'. These vivid descriptions bring clearly to mind the various quarters that made up Hanmer's flower garden, but there is no reference at all to the intricate knots and parterres described in his essay. Another account details the planting of tender fruit trees, including apricot, peach, cherry and plum, around the walls of the Great Garden, noting varieties, provenance and the precise location of each tree. There are no apples or pears, but these presumably were grown in the adjacent orchard, which is also referred to here.

In addition to these two manuscripts, Hanmer also kept similar notes in his memorandum book on two other gardens with which he was involved, at his mother's home in Haulton, near Bettisfield, and at his home in 'Lewsham' (Lewisham), near London. The planting of these gardens has thus far passed without comment from garden historians, but there is a document which records an agreement, dated 24 January 1652, between Hanmer and Thomas Price, a carpenter, to 'pale about the new garden at Haulton in the new orchard where the house stands'[63] and the notebooks contain planting plans for both this garden and the one at Lewisham. On one page of the first memorandum book there is a list dated September 1654, entitled 'My flowers at Haulton' (fig. 146). There is not as much detail regarding the garden as there is for Bettisfield, but there appear to have been at least three

145   Anemones, from Crispin van den Passe's *Hortus Floridus*, c.1615
146   Page from Sir Thomas Hanmer's notebook, 'My flowers at Haulton', September 1654

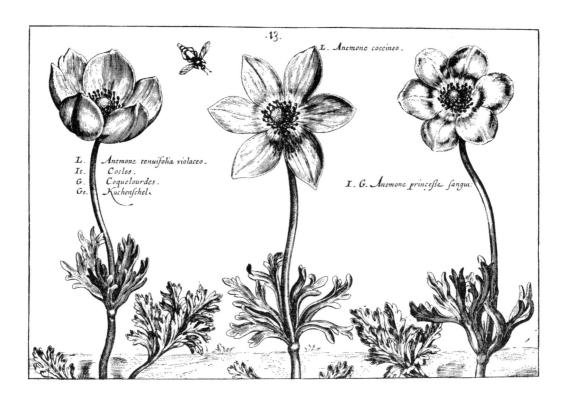

beds – Hanmer refers specifically to 'the best bed', 'the first bed on the left' and the 'far-thest bed on the left' – and he names more than fifty varieties of tulips planted there.[64]

Further into the notebook is another entry, dated 11 October 1656 and headed 'Lewsh.', followed by named varieties of plants set out in the form of a plan across the page (fig. 147). These have been annotated with comments such as 'excellent', 'very good' or 'bore not', clearly added at a later date.[65] Some of these entries are crossed out with a large 'X': perhaps these varieties failed and were removed?

These detailed notes reveal this as one way in which Hanmer accumulated his own knowledge: in his *Garden Book* he himself recommends 'writing downe in your Memoriall booke the name of every flower, and how it stands in each ranke, first, seconde, third, etc.'.[66] But, as well as plant lists, he also used his notebooks to record advice received from various people about the care of plants. He notes, for instance, the Paris nurseryman Monsieur Picot's advice on the best time to plant tulip bulbs, the results of his friend and fellow-gardener John Rose's experiments on how best to protect plants from the frosts and his advice on how to sow the seeds of 'beares ears' (as Hanmer calls them) or auriculas. This information eventually formed the basis of the advice on plant care and maintenance

Best Tulipes.
Best Bed.

1 Blindburg. maria. par. Clrmont. clari
   silla, palto de Leyde. Princesse.

2 Admirall Enchuson. the same, y samī
   pretty Betty, prruchot, the same.

3 six old Onions. 4 six lesser Onions samī
   5 faire Anne. Morell cramiosy. y samī
   Viceroy. the same. Peach Morillion.

6 florisantē. y samī, the samī, y samē
   best Onion Vinagriox.

7 Blind burg. the samē, y rest of the ranke
   is filled vp with offsetts of printaniers

8 all offsetts of printaniers.

9 Violetta, the samē, Louee Cedonalli
   belle holandē. passe Bilin, No. 1.

10 Venus. the samē. Delamore, Moul
   Diana, the samē, the samē

11 Marico, Odenard van bol bell brussel
   good susan, Adm of ffranc Luyman

12 Althozzi royal, old par. Jeron, para
   yon prassin, beau d'Armentiers,
   Althesse royal, the samē

13 Belli breve, the samē, my Nonpancils
   Carthago, the samē. Ag. rampart

14 Vesta of y orchard, par florison set
   for Vesta last yeare, from Carthago
   Moul. par Jeron, y samē, Belender

15 My Bembrigo the samē the same
   Louee Bembrigo, same, same.

16 Beau de Harlem, par florison
   with an offsett by it, my Deane
   same, Odenard Creme, par francois

Leuth 11 Oct 1656

1 prim. 2 mor cram 3 r. pas labr

4 Vesta 5 par. prieur 6 par prieur

2 bel. brieve 2 susan 3 mislaid

4 prudent 5 bol le port 6 od. charm

3 mor. cr. 1 mor lxe 3 Habilla

4 bist h. brab. 5 carth or flor 6 hron

4 ofsew carth. 2 cruo nat. 3 mislay

4 mislaid 5 whit. Dian. 6 Argus.

5 Juxtael. 2 Ohren. 3 bel. hosande

4 prin thalr. 5 sigism. 6 sigism.

6 brab: goyeu 2 Aohan. 3 butch. ven

4 h. eron. dol. 5 sanr 6 clains. bol

7 par ofkin 2 brabking. 3 carth.

4 carth. 5 mislaid. 6 mislaid

8 kerlah. 2 herueh 3 mislaid

4 pallas. 5 pallas. 6 distribte flor

which appeared in the *Garden Book*. There Hanmer offers conventional advice on soils and composts, watering, propagation, selecting and sowing seed, planting and so on – although it is clear from the way he writes that he is offering readers the benefit of his own experience. Other subjects on which he chooses to write demonstrate his own particular problems and concerns. For example, he offers advice on how to keep cats off newly dug soil, as 'they delight to scrape in it, and urine and dung upon it' (as anyone who lives next door to a cat-owner will testify!): he suggests pinning down nets over freshly sown or newly planted beds. As a definitive sign of the times, he adds a paragraph on 'How to Packe up Rootes and send them to Remote Places' – for a man who both sends and receives plants from as far afield as France, this is obviously a crucial concern.[67]

The section which demonstrates more clearly than any other the changes in techniques and practices which were taking place in the mid-seventeenth century is Hanmer's advice on the 'Houseing and Covering of Plants'.[68] Methods of protecting tender plants in the earlier part of the century have been discussed at length in Chapter 4, but Hanmer's comments repay further consideration. The first factor to note is that by this time, the choice of rare and exotic plants available to gardeners in England was continually becoming much greater. Hanmer, like Evelyn, was particularly taken with evergreen plants, or 'Greenes' as he calls them, because 'being never wholy unclothed of their sweet and beautifull leaves [they are] therefore much esteem'd by us'.[69] Many of these plants required protection over the winter: 'All such as come newly to us out of the Indyes or other Hot countreys, and many other flowers which wee have not had long here, must be brought into a house in November and continue there 'till March or Aprill.'[70]

It seems that the provision of such a 'house' was fairly common practice by this time: 'all that are curious in plants have a roome purposely for this use adjoyning to their garden', Hanmer notes, but he also offers detailed instruction on how this house should be constructed, 'otherwise it will kill more plants than it will preserve'.[71] Whereas it had long been understood that plants from foreign climates needed to be kept in a warm environment and protected from harsh elements such as violent rain, frost and snow, what was apparently now recognised was that plants 'will perish for want of ayre (without which nothing can live), as certainly as with cold'. This was something not appreciated earlier in the century, when Markham was recommending completely wrapping plants up to protect them and Parkinson was observing that this simply did not work, even though he did not know why (see Chapter 4). According to Hanmer, then, the room should be large and high, so that the plants do not become 'choked with being constantly there', and should be well provided with large, south-facing windows and doors which should be opened on mild days to allow the air in, but must be shut fast in the cold and frost. Hanmer's notebook indicates that he probably got this information initially from Rose, who advised him that 'oranges die most in England for want of aire in temperate wynter weather and that wyndowes doe not let in aire enough, but great doores'.[72] This replenishing of fresh air into the room would certainly have increased the plants' chances of survival because, although this was not properly understood at the time, we now know that plants do in a sense 'breathe' (absorbing carbon dioxide and releasing oxygen) and that keeping them in an enclosed environment will eventually exhaust their supply of essential carbon dioxide.[73] The additional advantage of large south-facing windows was that during the daytime they would trap whatever warmth was available from the winter sun and, of course, a still unrecognised but crucial benefit was that large south-facing windows also allowed in sunlight – essential to healthy plant life.[74]

On 'violent cold nights' additional methods for heating needed to be employed. In the published edition of Hanmer's book, he suggests 'a pan of coales, a stove or other devyce to keepe a moderate heate'. In one of the other manuscripts he is more explicit about other devices, suggesting that a pile of fresh horse dung will produce enough steam to warm the air. He concedes, however, that this is 'somewhat offensive and troublesome', which is presumably why he decided to leave it out of the other versions.[75]

So, albeit often through little more than trial and error, knowledge of and techniques for cultivating exotic plants had moved on since Parkinson had more or less dismissed the idea of hot stoves as a waste of time in the preservation of tender plants. This was now a worthwhile exercise in which to invest time and money, as it seemed to have at least some chance of success.

It is clear from these documents, nevertheless, that Hanmer's main interest was in flowers, especially rare and costly flowers, for the ornamental garden. Although the printed edition of his book has no title, the other two manuscript versions are entitled 'Of a Flower Garden' and 'Of Flowers' respectively, reflecting Hanmer's preoccupation with this aspect of gardening. He refers to flowers, trees and plants as the 'chiefest ornaments' of a beautiful garden and his manuscript letters, notes and book all bear witness that his is a plantsman's garden. His advice is firmly rooted in his own experience, and his love for and knowledge of the flowers and plants within it are clear. He plans to include advice on their 'preservation and increase' but is not interested in their medicinal qualities 'whereof so many volumes have been written' and, like Parkinson before him and for the same reasons, Hanmer purposely omits 'all fabulous secrets for altering colors and other strange improvements'. Only directions that are 'agreable to truth and good iterated experiments' are included. His book will contain descriptions of 'the best Flowers', the 'much-esteem'd' evergreens, ornamental trees and shrubs that 'may be admitted into Gardens', as well as some 'common ones' to ensure flowers in all seasons.[76] The intensely personalised and particular nature of these

·13·

L. *Cyclaminos Italica rotundifolia.*
I. *Pan porcino.*
G. *Pain de porceau.*
Ge. *Verckensbroot.*
        Erdapfel.

descriptions indicates that they reflected closely the flowers in Hanmer's own garden, such as tulips of infinite varieties (including one first grown at Bettisfield, *Tulipa* Agate Hanmer), narcissus, crown imperial, anemones, ranunculus, martagons and cyclamen to name but a few of the flowering bulbs, as well as gilliflowers, roses and another of his especial favourites, auriculas or 'beares eares'. He describes a particular variety of fritillary, noting that 'it came up with mee 1660 in the end of January', and again of a crimson-coloured flower that 'Wee have two wee value', indicating that he has personally cultivated these plants in his garden. In contrast, if a variety of plant is outside his experience, he says so. For instance, describing the dog-toothed violet, he notes that there are only two kinds that he has seen but 'in Gerard [*The Herball*] there are two other sorts mentioned which I have not seene'; elsewhere he tells us that his full list of varieties of iris is taken from the printed catalogue of 1651 of the Parisian florist 'Monsieur Moryn'.[77]

It is clear too that tulips were a particular passion – Hanmer refers to them as 'the Queene of Bulbous plants' – but he considers these plants, rare and exotic at the beginning of the century, to be 'now soe well knowne in England that [they need] no description'.[78] Having said this, new varieties of tulip were still being raised, particularly in France, and

149 Auriculas, or 'beares eares', from Crispin van den Passe's *Hortus Floridus*, *c*.1615

150 Jacques le Moyne, *Daffodil*, *c*.1585

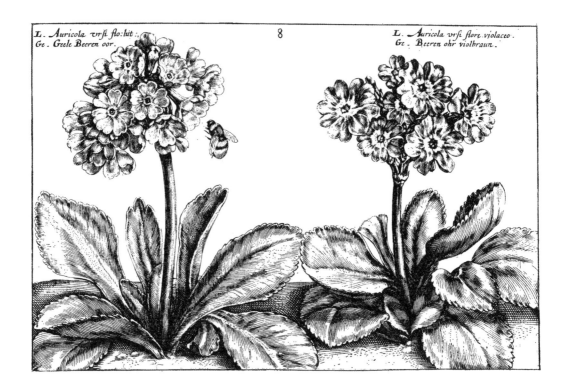

these were clearly of great interest to a connoisseur such as Sir Thomas Hanmer. He goes on to name many of these, categorising them by colour – purples, crimsons, 'scarletts' and so on, as well as a large number of 'new modish colors' – noting that these new varieties were becoming as esteemed in England as they were in France: 'wee did value in England only such as were well stript with purples and other redds, and pure white; but now, within a yeare or two, we esteeme (as the French doe) any mixture of odde colours, though there be no white with them...all which new colour'd Tulipes wee call Modes, being the fashion'.[79] As will be seen in the next chapter, Hanmer continued to purchase tulip bulbs and other plants from Paris long after he returned to England: it seems that France was considered to be an arbiter of good taste and fashion and therefore to be emulated.

Significantly, Hanmer is nevertheless happy to include all kinds of flowers in his garden, whether new, fashionable or otherwise, presumably once again reflecting his own preferences. Before leaving him in his garden of beautiful flowers, it should be said that, although Sir Thomas does not write about any other part of his garden, we know that there was an orchard at both Bettisfield and Haulton and it has to be assumed that there was also a kitchen garden.[80] It seems that these utilitarian aspects were simply not his concern.

3

Hanmer's particular interest was exactly as reflected in the heading of his manuscript, 'Of the Flower Garden', one he was clearly keen to share with his gentlemanly peers. The idea that Hanmer's manuscript may have been written for a small circle of garden enthusiasts has already been mooted and it seems, judging by the modest claim he makes in his letter to Evelyn, that many of his gentleman acquaintances indeed followed his advice and observations and, rather than building ostentatious fountains or parterres, took to planting flowers and trees in order to ornament their gardens.[81]

In Sir Thomas Hanmer, then, we have an example of a gentleman gardener who appears to have taken on board the radical notions being advocated thirty years earlier by John Parkinson, epitomising a legitimate and exclusive interest in the ornamental flower garden, while noting himself that this is a recent phenomenon. Hanmer observes that 'now...some spare no charge amongst other things in procuring the rarest flowers and plants'. He notes that while the Italians and Germans and then the French and Dutch have been 'diligent enquirers and collectors of...rarityes' for some years past, it is only recently that this habit has come to England. The novelty of these ideas is reiterated a number of times: 'this way of beautifying...comes apace into fashion', he writes, but few know how or what to choose, and their gardeners, unfamiliar with these plants, have not caught up with the new ways, 'being for the most part inexpert and dull'. Hanmer dates these changes specifically to the years since the war – that is, recently – and, as noted earlier, takes credit for having spread some of these new ideas among his fellow gardeners in north Wales. From our reading of Parkinson, this presents a slight contradiction, since he was saying much the same things thirty years earlier but, as has been seen, Hanmer's manuscripts are both practical and personal, and his experience of living in France and then in the remote Welsh borders must have differed greatly from Parkinson's experience of living throughout his working life in London, where such changes would have been much more immediate and obvious. Also, Parkinson was introducing his readers to new ideas, whereas by Hanmer's time, and as seen in the example of Evelyn's Sayes Court, the idea of an ornamental garden beautified with choice flowers had clearly taken hold and become accepted practice.

From this study of the gardens of Evelyn and Hanmer, what can be concluded about the state of gardening on the eve of the Restoration? In Evelyn's case we identified an eclectic mix of styles and influences, picked up from around Europe during the preceding decades, which resulted in the creation of two different but contemporaneous gardens at Wotton House and Sayes Court. Evelyn's drawings of Wotton in particular not only illustrate well the differences between the original Elizabethan garden and the new classically influenced design, but are also in complete contrast to the garden that Evelyn created at Sayes Court, which contained almost no Italianate elements at all. Hanmer's garden feels different again, with the emphasis on planting rather than the design, apparently still retaining the basic four-square form of the previous century, although the details of both the manner of the borders and in-filling have changed.

In terms of the innovations and trends from earlier in the century, it seems that there was a consolidation and normalisation of ideas and practices. Although nothing distinctively new had happened in the last thirty years (which, given the political upheavals, is hardly surprising), ideas that were new and innovative in Parkinson's London of the 1620s, in particular the flowering of the ornamental garden as a distinct and acceptable area of gardening, appear to have been absorbed into normal practice: as has been seen, Hanmer demonstrates an exclusive and unashamed pleasure in his ornamental flower garden. Exotic plants continued to be imported in ever increasing varieties and methods of caring for them had advanced, even if only through trial and error. As Parkinson had predicted, the importing of spring-flowering bulbs, and now more particularly the evergreens that both Evelyn and Hanmer were so taken with, 'make a Garden of delight even in the winter time'.[82] At the same time, Evelyn was introducing innovative elements into his garden, such as the French-inspired grove, with its axial walks and evergreen thickets or the Dutch-influenced lime tree avenue, pointing the way forward to features which became increasingly fashionable in English gardens towards the end of the century. It seems that by this time there were so many new ideas and influences that it was possible for the gardener or garden-owner simply to pick and choose those elements that took their fancy in order to incorporate them into their gardens.

10

THE PLANTS

Ever since the Romans brought leeks, parsley and grape vines to English shores, plants have been on the move. As John Parkinson points out:

> Those flowers that have beene usually planted in former times in Gardens of this King-dome…have by time and custome attained the name of English flowers, although the most of them were never naturall of this our Land, but brought in from other countries at one time or other, by those that tooke pleasure in them where they first saw them.[1]

It is now time to consider more fully the central, but ephemeral and therefore somewhat elusive, element of gardens and gardening, namely, the plants. How were plants – whether native or from across the seas – actually obtained by gardeners for their gardens? Where were they being bought? How much did they cost? How were they being exchanged?

This chapter will attempt to answer some of these questions by first exploring the growth of the plant trade through the range of networks that allowed the commercial and non-commercial exchange of native plants from medieval times to the early modern period. The focus here will be on indigenous plants, that is, native English garden plants, found growing naturally in the wild and which were brought into the garden for cultivation. Consideration will then be given to the nascent development of a more formal nursery trade, mostly centred on London, which came about as an inevitable consequence of the increased interest in, and demand for, rare and exotic plants from the New World and the Continent. The focus in this part of the chapter will therefore shift to an emphasis on the 'outlandish' or foreign plants which were beginning to grace the gardens of England and Wales.

By 1700, there were fifteen or so large-scale nurseries of some standing established in London, a result of the rise in the specialised trade of the nurseryman in cultivating, improving and distributing plants. The most comprehensive study of this subject so far was carried out by John Harvey in the early 1970s when he explored the available evidence for the burgeoning nursery trade during this period, identifying it as a development synonymous with the growing attraction of collecting and cultivating plants for pleasure. Noting the time-lag between new plants being introduced into the country during the time of Gerard, Parkinson and Tradescant at the beginning of the seventeenth century and the rise of more substantial nurseries by the end of the century, Harvey concluded that there was little in the way of an organised commercial plant trade in England prior to 1660.[2] Contrary to this assessment, however, as will be demonstrated in the following pages, there is a significant body of evidence to suggest that by this time nurserymen at home and abroad were already in the business of satisfying the demands of gardeners and plant enthusiasts alike.

Informal horticultural networks, enabling the buying and selling of plants and seeds, had been in existence since medieval times, the supply of plants being firmly in the hands of professional gardeners rather than commercial nurserymen.[3] Long before this specialised trade emerged, it was the gardener who had the expert knowledge of plants, who produced seeds, grafts and surplus seedlings from their plants, and who in turn required plants to furnish the gardens and orchards of their masters. During the reign of Edward I, records show that in 1275, William Gardiner was paid for a considerable variety of plants for the king's gardens and orchards, including cherry trees, oziers, quinces, peach trees and gooseberry bushes. It perhaps comes as no surprise to see that most of the purchases were of fruit trees, their role in supplying tasty and seasonal food for the tables of the aristocracy being as crucial as ever, but the shopping list also included lily bulbs and peony roots. Other payments to various individuals for plants and seeds indicate that there must have been some kind of significant plant trade in Westminster at this time.[4] In 1345, a petition was presented to the Mayor of London on behalf of the gardeners of the city, demanding that they 'may stand in peace in the same place where they have been wont in times of old...there to sell the garden produce of their said masters, and make their profit, as heretofore they have been in their wont to do'.[5] Although in later centuries the trade of the nurserymen, who sold living plants, became distinct from the trade of the market gardener, who sold garden produce, suffice it to say here that even in these early days there is evidence of a healthy and significant horticultural trade.

Moving into the early sixteenth century, detailed accounts relating to the gardens of Tudor London reveal records which not only indicate the purchase of plants for the king's garden at Hampton Court and Cardinal Wolsey's garden at York Place, but also the names of local suppliers.[6] More complicated transactions included the payment of 10s 8d to one Ed Gryffith who spent eight days riding to Buckinghamshire and back in order to purchase sixty-seven apple trees. These were later delivered to London at a further cost of 6d each. Further evidence suggests that by the early decades of the sixteenth century, gardeners were also working independently, hiring out their services for fixed periods of time as well as apparently selling seeds, herb and flower plants from their own gardens.[7] Payments for items such as billhooks, spades, knives and wheelbarrows indicate that there was clearly also a reliable source of specialist tools for the gardener. Although details are scant, this kind of anecdotal evidence points convincingly to an increasing commercialisation of horticulture during this time.

In the early modern period, similar evidence emerges from the documentary sources to indicate that much of the trade in plants, such as it was, continued to be carried out at a local level. Although there is a reasonable amount of evidence from accounts that plants and seeds were being purchased, however, details of who was supplying them and where they were being grown is more difficult to ascertain. The household accounts of the Earl of Sussex at Gorhambury in Hertfordshire, for instance, note a payment of 8s made in March 1638 for four hundred cabbage plants and another one-off payment of £1 7s 6d, later the same month, for 'garden seeds'. This is a large sum of money given that such purchases are normally counted in pennies but, as the majority of kitchen garden produce would have been sown in the spring, it is likely that this was probably the main supply of seeds for the year. We can safely assume that these seeds, although unspecified, were vegetable seeds, as the sum totals for the year itemise 'Diging the kitchen garden, seeds and plants £4 11s 6d'.[8] The household accounts of John Willoughby of Leyhill in Devon are a little more specific in their recording of payments for seeds: cucumber, carrot, turnip and mustard seeds are all purchased along with peas and beans for sowing, although, as at Gorhambury, cabbages were bought as plants, generally by the hundred. Cabbage plants also appear frequently in the somewhat sparse accounts of the Nunwell household, but such records still offer no clues as to where these items were being purchased.

The Halland House accounts, in contrast, are slightly more enlightening in this regard, as they offer additional information to the price paid. Cabbage plants and garden seeds are obtained from the nearby market town of Lewes, and in another entry a Mr Abel of Lewes has provided six rose plants. Thomas the gardener is paid for seeds he brought from London and on other occasions Mister Foster, Mr Ills, William Gardener and John Grove are all paid for seeds, cabbage and artichoke plants respectively. Mr Ills also supplied a garden spade for 4s.[9] Evidence such as this lends weight to the idea that common seeds, plants and garden tools were bought and sold locally through a network of gardeners working either independently or employed on estates such as Halland. The reference to Thomas the gardener fetching seeds from London suggests that it is the gardener's responsibility to source the supplies of seeds and plants. This idea is borne out in other evidence: in a letter to his estate steward Harry Rose, Sir Thomas Temple suggests he 'deale with Richard [the gardener] who both for peares & Apple stockes can best furnish me', although we later learn that this source of supply is not always reliable, as Richard wrote to advise Sir Thomas that he can no longer supply apricot trees as promised, because they had died.[10] On Sir John Oglander's Nunwell estate, payments are recorded in February 1629 'To Jacob for Gardeninge and seedes' and to 'Smyth for worke and plants', while at Llantrithyd, Sir Thomas Aubrey's estate in south Wales, there is a similar note of a payment 'To Jenkin for plants'.[11] At Trentham Hall the gardener, John Jarvis, is paid on a number of occasions for 'setts for the Court', osiers, willows and turnip seeds.[12] It is difficult to escape the conclusion here that Jacob, Smyth, Jenkin and Jarvis, all estate workers, were either raising these plants and

seeds themselves or obtaining them from a third party in order to sell them on to their employers.

Another side to this picture is presented by Richard Gardner of Shrewsbury who was the author of a little booklet first published in 1599 called *Profitable Instructions for the Manuring, Sowing, and Planting of Kitchin Gardens*. This is essentially a book about how to grow garden produce and seeds for sale, and his philanthropic motives for writing the book are set out clearly on the title page as being 'very profitable for the common-wealth and greatly for the helpe and comfort of poore people' (fig. 151). In it, Gardner is encouraging his peers to follow his example and grow vegetables, particularly roots such as carrots, parsnips and turnips, to sell at reasonable prices to the poor in times of hardship, 'when bread was wanting'.[13] This was a real solution to a real problem: between 1594 and 1597, England had suffered from four successive harvest failures, leading to severe and sustained price rises – the cost of flour increased by 190 per cent – inevitably resulting in a time of great hardship and famine for many of the population.[14] The vegetables Gardner chose to include in his book are those which he considers will 'provide sufficient victuals for the poore and greatest number of people, to relieve their hungrie stomackes'. He does not include what he calls 'dainty sallets'.[15]

As well as providing instructions on how to grow vegetables for sale, Gardner offers advice on growing crops in order to produce 'good seedes'. Growing vegetables for their seed requires a different procedure from growing them for consumption. They are not harvested when ripe but are left in the ground to flower and produce seed which is then carefully collected – Gardner offers meticulous instructions. The seeds thus produced could obviously be used to sow the next crop or, as was the case with the resulting produce, they could be sold. In the last chapter of his book, Gardner sets out what he considers a reasonable price to charge for both the produce and the seeds 'till the people may have store of their owne growing for their gardens'. The concept of helping the poor by enabling them to grow their own food rather than simply giving them handouts is an idea with which we are now familiar, but by urging reasonable prices and suggesting this kind of 'not-for-profit' set-up, Gardner was advocating a fairly radical notion for the time. Whether or not his advice was heeded by fellow citizens of Shrewsbury goes unrecorded by history but what this evidence offers is further credence to the notion that it was common practice for gardeners to raise seed in their own gardens specifically for sale.

Other plants which appear to have been in constant demand are quicksets, used mainly for hedging. In some cases, these were raised on the estate where they were required but, when purchased, they were generally supplied in vast quantities, usually priced by the hundred. At Trentham Hall over the winter of 1635, there are frequent references to payments for 'setts' at the rate of 6*d* per hundred. Some of these, as noted earlier, were supplied by Jarvis the gardener, but most payments were made to one Roger Whilton, who does not appear anywhere else in the accounts apart from this context of purchasing quicksets, so it could be assumed that he was an independent supplier. Thousands of quicksets and osiers were purchased and planted around the new garden and grounds at Trentham that winter. In the same year, at Llantrithyd a total of 3,600 plants and quicksets were purchased for planting on the estate for a total of 9s.[16] It might seem remarkable that such large numbers of plants were apparently so easily and cheaply available but for rural areas it is possible to conceive of enterprising gardeners gathering cuttings of easily rooting plants such as willow and hawthorn without much difficulty. A full-size stock tree or an existing hedge would have provided hundreds of cuttings or sets. All that the independent supplier would have required was a plot of land in which to root the cuttings and they would have been ready for selling on within the year, or he might have just supplied the cuttings as they were, to be rooted *in situ*. An alternative supply, as previously discussed, may well have been from the sale of surplus stocks from neighbouring estates. The records of Sir Thomas Temple and Richard Cholmeley, for instance, both contain numerous references to the sale of hedging, timber and brushwood.[17]

Evidence shows that there was also a demand for larger trees, particularly fruit trees, for the gardens of gentry estates. These trees, if not available locally, were apparently being transported long distances in order to grace the gardens of their owners. In 1645, the Halland household accounts reveal that Philip was paid the not inconsiderable sum of £2 for '23 trees that he bought at Pettworth', as well as a further 6s 6d 'for his charges going thether & back againe for those trees, and for his horses'.[18] More interesting, perhaps, is the purchase of fruit trees for the Llantrithyd estate of Sir Thomas Aubrey. On 6 March 1623, a payment of 3s 10d is recorded 'For carriage of the trees from London', followed by a further payment of 5s 'Geven unto Richard Herberts servant whome he sent hether to plant the trees that was sent from Londone'. A separate list of husbandry expenses for the same date indicates a total of 45s 6d paid for four nectarines, one cherry and twenty-two other trees. It must be assumed that these are the same trees sent from London.[19] That the trees bound for Llantrithyd must have been something unusual is emphasised by the fact that a particular gardener had to be drafted in to plant them, the resident gardener perhaps not having the necessary skill to undertake this task. We are not told how the trees were transported but, as the road from London to south Wales was neither short nor easy, it is likely that they will have been sent by sea, probably via the port of Bristol. At this time, moving goods by water was generally more efficient than bringing them overland – records also show that Sir Arthur Ingram had trees and roses shipped from London to Hull for his gardens at York and Sheriff Hutton – but still this operation would not have been either cheap or quick.[20] As this presumably was the only way to obtain such trees, apparently not available from local sources, it is indicative of the time, money and effort that people were prepared to expend in obtaining what they wanted for their orchards and gardens.

At the same time, for the early modern gardener concerned with growing vegetables, fruit and herbs for the household, one of the main ways of obtaining new plants for the garden was to raise them himself by collecting, saving and sowing seed, propagating cuttings (or 'slips' as they were known), grafting fruit trees and so on. These are skills and techniques that would have been familiar to gardeners of the day – John Parkinson even wonders if he needs to spend time setting down in writing something that 'is so well known unto all'.[21] John Evelyn had a large nursery garden at Sayes Court – he mentions growing eight hundred plants in it at one time – and the Halland House accounts also make several references to 'the nursery', an area clearly used for raising plants. Payments are noted to Clark for half a day 'grafting cheries in the nursery' and again to 'Clark for gathering of crabstocks and potting them in the nursery': these, presumably, were rootstocks destined for grafting apple trees in the orchard.[22] It seems from entries such as these that, far from being purchased, the crabstocks and quicksets were either being gathered from the countryside or possibly from stock trees on site – Temple specifically mentions keeping stocks for this purpose at Burton Dassett.[23] In the same way, on another occasion Pelham's gardener is paid 10d for the 'gathering of 100 honeysuckells for the garden', while weeding women are paid 5d a day for 'gathering of violetts and setting of them'.[24] This reminds us, as noted earlier, that many garden plants were simply gathered from the countryside and then planted, or 'sett', in the garden. Contemporary garden writers offered advice on the 'encrease' of flowers and plants by setting slips, rooted cuttings, offsets from bulbs and of course collecting and sowing seed: by these methods a gardener could populate his garden with many vegetables, fruits, herbs and flowers for free.

Other ways of obtaining free plants are hinted at in the Temple manuscripts which have many references to the acquisition of trees, grafts and cuttings from friends, relations and other acquaintances. Although these documents do not record such arrangements, it is difficult to imagine that they were not reciprocal and it is almost certain that this exchange of plants, with its inevitable accompanying recommendations and advice, was common practice – as it still is today – among gardeners and garden owners. Unfortunately, there is little actual evidence of this, because where money did not change hands, transactions were rarely recorded and this is one reason why Sir Thomas's correspondence is so valuable as a source of evidence. His letters regarding the collecting of vine cuttings from John Hall's garden at Stratford-upon-Avon, as recommended by Temple's sister-in-law, have already been discussed but, once again, they provide a case in point. News of Mr Hall's grapevine had travelled to Burton Dassett from Stratford via Mrs Peter Temple.[25] It is not clear whether or not Mr Hall and Sir Thomas were acquainted but ,whatever the case, Hall appears happy for Temple's gardener to take the cuttings. Here, then, is yet another reliable source of good plants – other people's gardens.

Sir Thomas also obtained fruit trees from a range of other sources, including many from the gardens of other Temple estates. One entry in his memorandum book, dated in the autumn of 1630, records the getting 'from Miles Temple my Sonn, walnut and quince trees of the best sorte; damsons from Bubnell; Russett apples from Prescott 2 trees, from Stow 2 trees, from Mr Peters orchard 2 trees, from Ball of Newport 2 trees'.[26] Ball of Newport appears to have been some kind of a nurseryman, being mentioned at least four times by Sir Thomas, both as a practitioner of grafting and as a supplier of fruit trees.[27] From evidence elsewhere in the manuscripts we know that James Prescott is a gentleman acquaintance,[28] but the rest of the trees are received from various relations and other Temple estates, including Bubbenhall and Stow. When Richard the gardener's promised apricot trees fail to materialise, Temple asks his daughter-in-law to get some alternative trees – presumably from her own garden – 'of the sorte that have good rootes'.[29] On another occasion, Sir Thomas instructs Harry Rose to arrange for the 'Abricott tree [that] is planted at Kingsters house to be removed. I would have it replanted at the Southend of my Parler'.[30] Whether this was a gift or an acquisition is impossible to ascertain.

Other evidence of the free exchange of plants between fellow gardeners is provided through examples of friends giving plants as opposed to receiving them. The keen gardener Lady Margaret Hoby, who we already know was a friend of William Lawson, noted in her diary: 'I went into the Garden, and gave some hearbes unto a good wife of Erley for his [sic] garden'.[31] And Robert Sidney's prolific garden has already been discussed: as well as gifts of fruit from his orchards, on one occasion he wrote to his wife that he had 'prom-

ised my Lady of Suffolk two Melicote trees, the one grafted, the other ungrafted, and one ungrafted to Sir Th. Monson', asking her to instruct the gardener to choose three of the best in the ground, to dig them up and 'send them hither'.[32]

It is clear, then, that well-established networks of plant exchange were in operation throughout rural England during this period. Informal networks existed between garden owners, who swapped plants, trees, cuttings and advice among themselves. At the same time, there is also evidence of some kind of commercial horticultural trade network, working mostly at a local level and generally carried out between gardeners acting either on behalf of their masters or independently for themselves. It seems likely that these kinds of arrangement had been carried on in some form for centuries and that, in rural areas at least, they continued to do so. The accompanying dissemination of gardening knowledge along similar lines must also be assumed. However, we have also seen evidence that during this period, specialist trees and plants were being purchased and brought from London, often over long and difficult routes, to furnish the gardens of wealthy gentry folk in England and Wales and, if the focus is now shifted to the capital, as it was then, a different picture of plant acquisition begins to emerge.

By 1600, London was the third largest city in Europe, its population had quadrupled in the past one hundred years and it was more than fifteen times larger than the next most populous cities in England and Wales. Its position on the River Thames ensured that it was of huge commercial importance, both as a centre of trade, a centre of consumption and the hub of all that was new and fashionable (fig. 153).

The East India Company, set up to facilitate access to Asian markets and commodities, was granted its first royal charter by Elizabeth I on 31 December 1600.[33] Expansion in world exploration and trade was bringing a range of exotic and luxury goods to England's shores through the City of London that had never been seen before and this of course included plants.[34] Their rarity made them objects of desire among plantsmen, garden enthusiasts and collectors alike and, in London at least, there is evidence of a burgeoning organised commercial nursery trade in the early seventeenth century that was meeting these demands.

It is known from a variety of sources that there were already commercial nurseries supplying fruit trees and other plants to gardeners in Elizabethan and early Stuart London. Parkinson, for instance, frequently refers to 'our Nursery Gardiners', although not always in particularly complimentary terms: 'scarce one of twentie of our Nurserie men', he writes, 'doe sell the right, but give one for another: for it is an inherent qualitie almost hereditarie with most of them, to sell any man an ordinary fruit for whatsoever rare fruit he shall ask

for: so little are they to be trusted'.[35] If we leave aside for the moment this somewhat scathing attack on an entire profession, his remarks nevertheless indicate that there were a significant number of nurserymen doing business in the London area with whom Parkinson was familiar, even if only by reputation. Elsewhere he comments that gentlemen who do not intend to keep a nursery themselves (such as that we have observed being maintained at Halland House and Sayes Court, for instance) must instead 'buy them already grafted to their hands of them that make their living of it', again implying a prevalence of such practitioners.[36] Lawson also mentions that some 'buy sets [of apple trees] already grafted', again reinforcing the view that there were those that made a living of it.[37]

Parkinson rarely actually names any nurserymen (perhaps because he has nothing good to say about them), but there are two notable exceptions. One is his reference to Master Ralph Tuggie, describing and illustrating two carnations named after him as 'the most beautiful that I ever did see' and referring to Tuggie himself as 'the most industrious preserver of all natures beauties' (see fig. 8).[38] Tuggie is again referred to as a 'Florist' in Thomas Johnson's 1633 revised edition of Gerard's *Herball*, coupling his name with both Parkinson and John Tradescant, while Tradescant himself notes in the back of his copy of Parkinson's *Par-*

adisi that he has in his garden '4 more Roses whearof Mr Tuggy Hathe two'. Not only was Ralph Tuggie clearly a renowned florist in his day but his reputation also lived on. In 1659, Hanmer refers to 'one Tuggey in Westminster' who raised some good auriculas bearing his name 'about thirty yeares since', and in 1665 John Rea lists in his *Flora* a number of auriculas that 'retain the names of those that raised them', including Tuggie among them.[39] Despite his reputation as a florist, though, Tuggie was not yet dealing with rarities from abroad, but only with established English garden flowers – carnations, roses and auriculas.

The other nurseryman that Parkinson picks out for special mention is 'Master John Millen, dwelling in Olde Streete, who from John Tradescant and all others that have had good fruit, hath stored himselfe with the best only, and he can sufficiently furnish any'.[40] It is a relief to discover that Parkinson did not regard all nurserymen as untrustworthy rogues! Again, Thomas Johnson agreed that for anyone who wanted gooseberry bushes, apricot, peach, pear, plum, apple or cherry trees for their garden, they were 'to be had with Mr John Millen in Old-street, in whose nursery are to be found the choisest fruits this kingdom yields'.[41] It seems, however, that this nursery had only recently been set up on this site. The 'Agas' map of Elizabethan London shows Old Street running east–west along the northern outskirts of the city, with just a few houses with large garden areas, surrounded on three sides by open fields (fig. 155). Seventy years later, in 1633, a 'Plan of an Estate in Old Street', drawn by Adam Bowen shows this same area, now clearly marked as 'Millians Land' (fig. 156; these variations in name spellings are to be expected – Johnson in his edition of Gerard's *Herball* refers to the same person in Old Street as John Milion).[42] Although mentioned by Parkinson and Johnson, this nurseryman does not appear in Gerard's original version of the *Herball* published in 1597, so it is reasonable to assume that the Old Street nursery established its reputation only after the beginning of the seventeenth century.

Gerard may not have known of John Millen but he did recommend several suppliers of fruit trees. In his chapter on pears, he mentions by name 'Master Henry Banbury of Toothill Street neere unto Westminster, an excellent graffer & painfull planter', 'Master Richard Pointer, a most cunning and curious graffer and planter of all manner of rare fruits, dwelling in…Twickenham' and 'Master Warnar, a diligent and most affectionate lover of plants neere Hors[l]ey downe by London', in whose ground 'all these before specified and many sortes more' will be found growing.[43] Henry Banbury's nursery business can be traced back

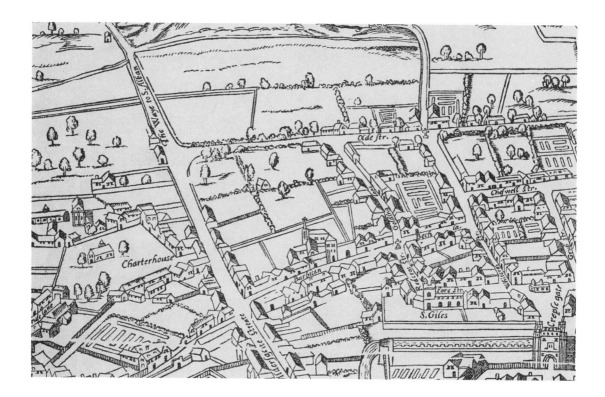

to the middle of the sixteenth century, to a basket-making business run by his father which required the growing of various types of willow. By the end of the century, Gerard is praising him for the wide variety of apples and pears which he stocked and by 1653 his son was dispatching fruit trees, including apricots, cherries, nectarines and peaches, to an address in Ireland.[44] There is evidence, then, that this nursery business was run by at least three generations of the same family from the address in Tothill Street on the western outskirts of Westminster, just south of St James's Park. Locating Tothill Street on a map of London dating from around 1643 reveals its proximity to 'Tutle Feilds', where a number of areas given over to the growing of orchards are clearly depicted (fig. 157). Westminster, we remember, is also where Ralph Tuggie maintained his garden.

Nothing further is known about Mr Warnar but, again, locating Horsey Down on the same London map shows a similar area on the outskirts of town, surrounded by a number of fields and orchard areas, but this time to the south-east, just across the river from the Tower of London (see fig. 159). Mr Pointer's nursery, as indicated by Gerard, was way up-river, beyond Richmond and Hampton Court, in 'a small village neere London called Twickenham'.[45]

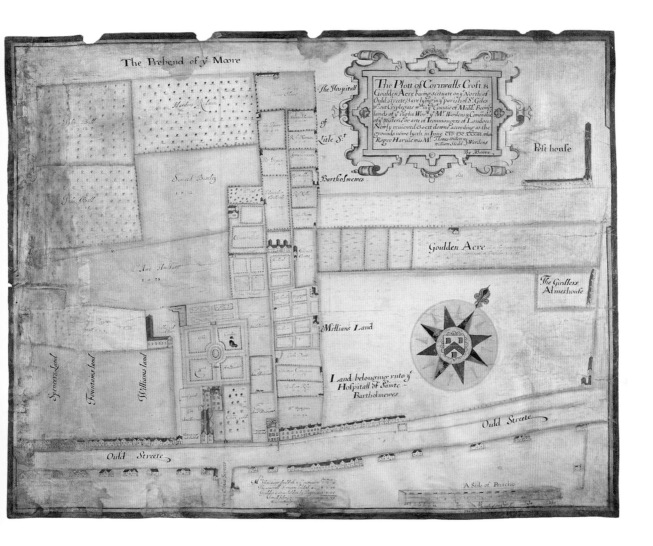

The contemporary writer John Stow, who produced his *Survey of London* in 1598, also backs up some of this information. He notes, with apparent regret, that a number of areas outside the city walls are 'now' made into 'garden-plots'. Stow's publication was the result of many years of living and compiling his work in London and much of it seems to be a wistful looking back to the days of his childhood. He mentions 'The Town Ditch without the wall', originally built for the defence of the city but which had become either a narrow, filthy channel or 'altogether stopped up for gardens planted'. He cites in particular an area along the Minories, just outside the city wall to the east, where the ditch is 'inclosed, and the banks thereof let out for garden-plots...whereby the city wall is hidden' and, indeed,

157 Detail from the Faithorne and Newcourt map of London, *c.*1643, showing Westminster, Tothill Street and Tutle Fields

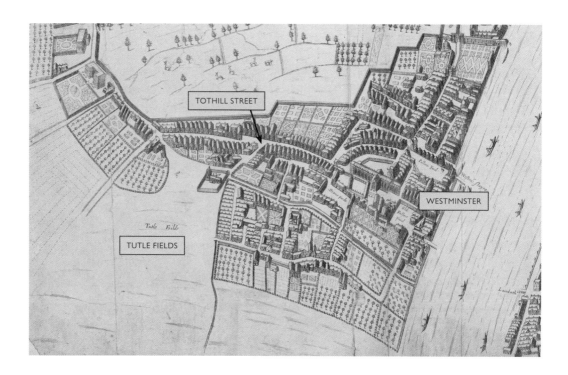

these very gardens can be seen depicted on the 'Agas' map of the city, all along the eastern stretch of the city wall between Posterngate and Aldgate (fig. 158).[46] Stow goes on to observe that Tower Hill was 'greatly diminished by building of tenements and garden-plots' and similarly, in the area around Spitalfields, which once comprised 'pleasant fields, very commodious for citizens', there was now 'continual building throughout of garden-houses and small cottages; and the fields on either sides to be turned into garden-plots'.[47] As it is clear that Stow does not view these changes as a good thing, it is safe to assume that these 'garden-plots' were not ornamental or pleasure gardens but were recently established commercial concerns spreading ever further round the outskirts of his city. These changes are made clear by comparing the 'Agas' map from the mid-sixteenth century to the Faithorne and Newcourt map of the same area in the mid-seventeenth century. The 'Spital Fyeld' and 'Goodmans Fields' are depicted at the earlier date as just that – open fields – but by the later date they are divided into garden plots and orchards which by this time, fifty years after Stow, extended a long way eastwards, down-river to Stepney and beyond (fig. 159).[48]

From these examples, it is evident that by the mid-seventeenth century the suburban areas of the city, whether north, south, east or west, appear to have been given over to large-scale gardening, gradually moving out as new housing extended well beyond the city

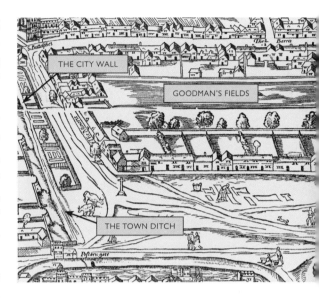

walls. Much of this is likely to have been market gardening, growing vegetables and herbs for sale in the London markets, but some of these areas at least must have been given over to the growing of plants and trees for sale.[49]

Although most of the examples cited here refer to suppliers of fruit trees, there was also clearly a market for the large-scale production of native hedging plants and trees, such as were supplied for the new garden at Gray's Inn Court laid out at the end of the sixteenth century under the direction of Sir Francis Bacon. The accounts indicate the purchase of a phenomenal number of hedging plants: 20,000 quicksets and 20,000 privet plants were bought at 3s 8d and 2s per thousand respectively, as well as 8 birch trees, 16 cherry trees and 66 elms. These were presumably full-size trees because they are sold for 18d, 12d and 9d each, as opposed to similar prices per hundred for the 3,700 eglantine plants or per thousand for the quicksets. Finally, there were 125 standard roses at 10s per hundred and 1600 woodbines (honeysuckle) at 6d per hundred.[50] Records such as these beg the question as to where it was possible to purchase so many

159   Detail from the Faithorne and Newcourt map of London,
showing the extent of gardens downriver to the east, c.1643

plants at one time in an area which was, relatively speaking, not rural. There are two possibilities to consider here. One is the likelihood, as discussed earlier, that in the London area at least, large-scale commercial nursery gardens were being set up and run in order to meet this kind of demand. The other is that goods such as these were being imported to London from the provinces to meet demand.[51] Furthermore, although in this instance flowering plants are being supplied, they are not particularly outstanding or unusual. Parkinson describes the eglantine rose as being 'not onely planted in Gardens...but growing wilde in many woods and hedges'. Honeysuckle likewise 'groweth wilde in every hedge'.[52] Plants such as these may well have been supplied by a nurseryman who, as noted in the case of quicksets, was taking cuttings from the countryside and growing them on his own land for sale. Whatever their source, however, a network of supply was clearly available to those who needed it.

It is also likely that London gardeners were able to buy their seeds and plants from shops. Although there is even less firm evidence for this than for the nursery business, there are enough clues to enable consideration of this possibility. Stow mentions a shop on the corner of Soper Lane and Cheapside 'wherein a woman sold seeds, roots and herbs';

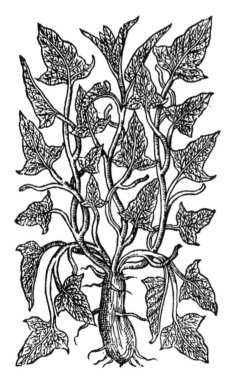

in July 1631, Robert Hill, a grocer 'dwelling at the three Angells in lumber [Lombard] streete' sold a large variety of garden seeds to John Winthrop on the eve of his setting sail for Massachusetts for the colony he was to establish there (the bill came to £1 6s) and John Gerard purchased his first specimen of a new potato plant from the Royal Exchange, although it 'perished and rotted' once he had planted it in his garden (fig. 160).[53]

How anyone could make a year-round living out of so seasonal an activity as seed sowing is difficult to see and it appears that, in the early days at least, the trade of selling seeds was carried out alongside other businesses. As just seen, Robert Hill the grocer was also a supplier of seeds. Another, slightly less obvious, example is of one William Lucas, the proprietor of a seedsman's business from which a trade catalogue survives, who describes himself in his will as a milliner. It is likely too that apothecaries such as John Parkinson, who used seeds and plant roots in the preparation of their medicines, would also have sold these from their shops for the garden.[54] It has also been speculated that

Parkinson sold a wider range of plants directly from his garden at Long Acre but, although plausible, there is little evidence for this.[55] Similar hypothesising which stands up to slightly tougher scrutiny is directed towards the John Tradescants, elder and younger, and the famous garden which they established at the property into which the family settled in South Lambeth in about 1629. We know from Parkinson himself that Tradescant the elder was in the business of supplying fruit trees to the nurseryman John Millen, but this must have been before he moved to the house and garden in Lambeth. This property, which became known as Tradescant's Ark, was filled with exotic rarities that the Tradescants had collected either themselves or indirectly via other travellers from around the globe: plants were displayed in the garden and 'curiosities' were displayed in the house.[56]

The Tradescant museum (which may have looked something like the depiction of a contemporaneous Danish cabinet of curiosities from Ole Worm's *Museum Wormianum* (1655; fig. 161), became famous and was visited both by those with a thirst for scientific knowledge and by the merely curious. It seems, from extant records at least, that this was the first garden to be opened to the public for the price of a fixed entrance fee, although whether or not plants were available for sale is more difficult to ascertain. On 2 May 1662, Sir Daniel Fleming's household accounts record details of a visit to Tradescant's Ark. As well as 1s for a coach from Whitehall, 2s for 'a Boat thither and back again' across the river from Westminster to Lambeth, and a further 2s for four entrance fees at 6d each, there is also an entry for 2s 6d 'spent at Jo. a Tradeskins'.[57] There is no further detail but it is reasonable to speculate that this may have been for plants from the garden and that by this date the Tradescants were also running a nursery from their premises. At the same time, and in the same way that John Evelyn was inspired by Morin's garden in Paris to attempt to recreate it in his own garden at Sayes Court, it is likely that visitors to the Tradescants' garden may also have left not just with plants but with ideas and inspiration for their own gardens.

Despite the anecdotal nature of much of this evidence, it is possible to draw some conclusions about the general picture of the plant trade in England in the early seventeenth century. In the provinces, these were likely to be informal arrangements, involving the purchase or free exchange of easily available native plants, while in London commercial nurseries were being established, who were already supplying keen gardeners not just in the capital but all over the country. It appears that those with sufficient means to overcome the difficulties of supply and transport were able to satisfy their needs through the existing trade networks. However, almost all the transactions referred to so far deal with the supply of fruit trees, native hedging plants and vegetables and herbs for the garden. What we have not yet come across, despite the increased interest in ornamental plants since the early years of the seventeenth century, are nurseries trading in the new range of flowering plants from abroad.

The time-lag between this new wave of plant introductions in the early seventeenth century and the establishment of an organised domestic plant trade has already been noted, so what was happening during these intervening years? How were new and exotic plants being acquired and distributed among gardeners and plant enthusiasts and what effect did this have on the way people viewed their gardens? We can start to consider these questions by looking in detail at the quintessential example of the rare and exotic being imported into England, namely, the tulip.

The unique place of the tulip in seventeenth-century garden history cannot be underestimated. It is difficult to imagine now what this common-or-garden plant represented in the minds of early seventeenth-century gardeners but at that time, the tulip, now characteristically Dutch, was 'a strang[e] and forraine flower'.[58] It was new, never having been seen before in this part of Europe; it was exotic, being brought to Europe through Constantinople from the Middle East; it was unpredictable in that it apparently changed its colour from one year to the next and, perhaps most importantly, it appeared, like Shakespeare's Cleopatra, in 'infinite variety'. A contemporary still life of tulips by Andries Daniels and Frans Francken the younger not only depicts this variety but also, by displaying them in a richly ornamented vase, emphasises the sense of ostentation, luxury and exoticism associated with these flowers (fig. 162). Tulips varied in colour, shape and form: they could be any shade of white, yellow, red or purple; they could be a single colour, variegated or striped; they could have pointed, rounded or feathered petals. And once the bulbs were planted, due to the accidental and unknown processes of cross-breeding, mutation and disease, they were quite likely to change and produce new and different flowers: a grower could never be entirely sure what they were going to get, but this of course only added to their mystery.[59] In 1597, Gerard describes just fourteen varieties in his *Herball* and it is likely that he first saw these tulips in the garden of his friend James Garret, an apothecary, originally from Flanders, who lived and worked in London. Gerard describes Garret as 'a curious searcher of simples', who had a particular interest in tulips. He had, according to Gerard, 'undertaken to find out... their infinite sorts, by diligent sowing of their seeds, and by planting those of his owne propagation, and by others received from his friends beyond the seas for the space of twenty years'.[60]

This suggests that tulips had been in England from at least 1577 and it is indeed likely that it was through Garret that they were introduced. A few years earlier, in 1571, Garret had received as a guest his fellow-countryman Carolus Clusius, the most famous botanist of his age and a central figure in horticultural activity in Europe. Clusius maintained a huge network of correspondents which facilitated the free exchange of botanical information, seeds and bulbs and this network was responsible, among other things, for much of the distribution of the tulip throughout Europe.[61] Recent research has identified an English 'outpost' of this Europe-wide network, a Protestant refugee community of naturalists, practising physicians and apothecaries who lived on Lime Street in London. This group included Garret, as well as the renowned physician and botanist Matthias de l'Obel (who eventually became Royal Botanist at the court of James I), his son-in-law, James Cole, and the Dutch consul Emmanuel van Meteran, who carried out the vital role of postmaster for the community, ensuring the distribution of their letters, knowledge and specimens across Europe, despite the political and religious disputes raging throughout the Continent.[62] Given that we know from this correspondence that Clusius possessed tulips as early as 1570, we know that he visited his correspondent, friend and fellow-botanist James Garret in 1571 and we know from Gerard that Garret had been growing and experimenting with

tulips in his own garden for at least twenty years, it seems a reasonable proposition that Clusius and Garret between them are strong contenders to take the credit for the introduction of the tulip into England.[63]

After his appointment as the director of the newly established botanical garden at the University of Leiden in 1593, Clusius planted more than six hundred varieties of tulip both in this garden and in his own, the latter being repeatedly robbed of many of his prized varieties. Although obviously a problem for Clusius, this highlights yet another of the tulip's distinctive characteristics: because they were rare, exotic and curious, they were also extremely expensive, making them collectable objects of desire among wealthy connoisseurs. And herein lies the essence of probably the best-known fact about the Dutch tulip trade, the short-lived phenomenon known as 'tulipmania' when, so the stories go, single bulbs of the prized variety *Semper Augustus* changed hands for the price of a house (fig. 163). For a brief period between the summer of 1636 and the spring of 1637 tulips were remarkably expensive. Because tulip bulbs spent most of the year out of sight beneath the ground, sales took the form of contracts for unseen and, as explained before, unknown goods – and the changes that could occur in the bulbs from one year to the next were not always for the better. Contracts were passed on for higher and higher sums, the potential for double-dealing was huge and when the time came, buyers could not pay and sellers could not deliver. Not surprisingly, the bottom quickly dropped out of this market. However, with the benefit of hindsight, it seems that the extremes of tulipmania have been vastly exaggerated, the known 'facts' being based on contemporary moralising propaganda.[64] That tulipmania happened is not disputed but it did not have the seismic effects on personal fortunes and the wider economy that we have been led to believe.

Aside from this note of caution, there are two more facts about tulipmania that must be borne in mind. One is that this was an economic phenomenon which had little to do with the desirability of the plants. The other is that it was a Dutch phenomenon which did not particularly affect the tulip trade in England. As observed in this chapter, the fascination with tulips began much earlier and continued long after the mid-1630s when this crisis occurred. After Gerard had described his fourteen tulips in 1597, thirty years later, Parkinson described more than a hundred varieties, occupying twenty-four folio pages of his book, with four full-page woodcuts illustrating thirty different kinds (fig. 164).[65]

Despite their place in Clusius's botanical garden, tulips had no medicinal purpose. Gerard, always anxious to attribute plants with uses and virtues, noted that 'There hath not been any thing set down of the antient or later Writers, as touching the Nature or Vertues of the *Tulipa*, but they are esteemed specially for the beauty of their flowers'.[66] And this is the essential point: as Gerard observed, tulips were grown for their beauty and for their

Semper Augustus.

ornamental value alone. This was their virtue and, as Parkinson noted, there were none that did not delight in them.[67] Another thirty years on and Sir Thomas Hanmer was continuing to extol the virtues of tulips 'whose flower is beautifull in its figure, and most rich and admirable in colours and wonderfull in variety of markings'.[68] Elsewhere, he was more specific, saying that 'the more colours there are in a flower the better, and the more unusuall and strange they are the more to bee esteemed, but it is necessary there bee either white or yellow stripes in every good Tulipe.'[69] There were now so many varieties of tulip available that they could be ranked within themselves, some more 'esteemed' than others.

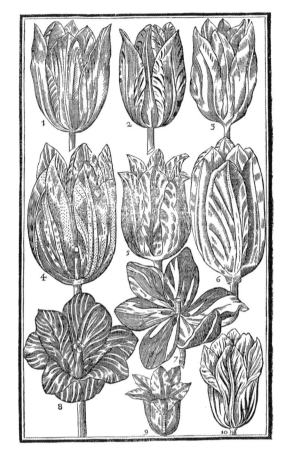

This points to one more of the tulip's many-faceted qualities which have assured its place in garden history to the present day. As well as the highly prized varieties based on particular colour and stripe combinations that were sought by connoisseurs who were prepared to pay high prices for their exclusivity, there were also less sought-after and less esteemed plain-coloured varieties, which could be produced more cheaply for the mass market. So, in effect, anyone could own a tulip and grow it in their garden and it was on this marketing potential – to be all things to all people – that the Dutch bulb trade grew and flourished.[70] As already noted, the gardener's love affair with the tulip far outlasted the temporary madness of tulipmania: it is known, for instance, that Hanmer exchanged bulbs with fellow tulip-fanciers such as John Rea, Sir John Trevor and General John Lambert, the last even being lampooned for his love of these flowers, appearing caricatured in a pack of cards as the 'Knight of the Golden Tulip'.[71] Even as it became more common, the tulip was still prized as a beautiful plant to be given pride of place in the ornamental garden. Although an extreme example, the tulip encapsulates the essence of what made these new plants so desirable: they were exotic, different, mysterious, bringing an element of a new world unknown to most people into their gardens. They were collectable, expensive and grown specifically for their beauty and ornamental value.

The tulip, however, was just one example of a flower, rare and exotic at the beginning of the seventeenth century, that eventually found its way into the generality of gardens of early modern England and there were a host of routes by which other such plants continued to arrive on English shores throughout the century. Plantsmen were sent to buy plants from markets on the Continent for their wealthy clients; travellers and adventurers journeyed across the globe, bringing back seeds and roots to be distributed among friends, acquaintances or simply those who might either be interested in them or even might know what to do with them. Plant-hunters were specifically commissioned to seek plants to bring back to England; others left these shores to collect plants for themselves, and those living in enforced or voluntary exile during the Civil Wars eventually returned to England with new ideas, plants and contacts.

One well-documented example of an Englishman doing business with overseas nurserymen early in the century was John Tradescant (fig. 165), who travelled extensively throughout the Low Countries and France during 1611 to buy plants on behalf of Robert Cecil, the first Earl of Salisbury, for the gardens at the newly acquired and rebuilt Hatfield House in Hertfordshire. Although nothing is known about Tradescant's early career, a letter of 1609 from Tradescant to the secretary at the British Embassy in Brussels, William Trumbell, regarding passports to travel on the Continent indicates that by this time he had been travelling abroad on behalf of other people, his familiarity with the bureaucracy involved suggesting that he had probably been doing so for a number of years.[72] Whether it was his expertise as a gardener or his experience as a businessman abroad that prompted him to be sent on a two-month plant-buying trip to Holland and France in September 1611 is open to debate, but clearly it was a winning combination for a successful shopping expedition. Extant detailed bills for this journey reveal not only the plants he purchased and the prices paid for them, but also the nurseries that he visited and details of how the plants were transported back to England.[73] His first ports of call were in Holland where he bought a wide variety of fruit trees from nurseries in Delft and Haarlem, rare roses and shrubs from Leiden and eight hundred tulip bulbs from a second nursery in Haarlem, for which he paid 10s a hundred. Although this was twenty years before the tulipmania which afflicted Holland in the 1630s, it is interesting that a healthy trade in tulip bulbs was clearly already established in that country and that bulbs were beginning to be brought back to England by plant enthusiasts such as Tradescant.

After leaving Holland, Tradescant continued his journey to Paris where (as noted in Chapter 6) he met the French king's renowned gardeners, the father and son team of Jean and Vespasien Robin. Whether this was the first time these gardeners had met is unknown, but it was a relationship that continued long after this visit: in his list of acquisitions written

in the back of his copy of Parkinson's *Paradisi in Sole*, published in 1629, Tradescant notes on three occasions plants he has procured from 'Mr Robine'.[74] During his visit in 1611, Tradescant took the opportunity to stock up on a wide variety of exotic rarities such as orange trees in pots, pomegranate trees, oleander trees, myrtle trees and 'manye other Rare Shrubs give me by master Robyns'.[75] Nearly twenty years later, Parkinson commented that pomegranates 'never beareth ripe fruit in this our Countrey', that myrtles similarly 'will not fructifie...nor yet abide without extraordinary care' and does not mention oleanders at all.[76] These were rare acquisitions indeed – it would be fascinating to know how they fared, if at all, at Hatfield (fig. 166).

This kind of shopping trip, of course, was not typical. Robert Cecil held one of the highest offices in the land, the gardens at Hatfield House were famous for their extravagance and Tradescant was both an extraordinary plantsman and, it appears, a well-travelled businessman, who was in the privileged position of being able to combine his knowledge and skill for the benefit of himself and his employer. What this example indicates, however, is that although as yet there is little evidence of an organised horticultural trade dealing with rare and ornamental plants in England, there clearly was a flourishing trade in such plants on the Continent; for those with sufficient means, it was possible to travel abroad and purchase plants that were not yet available at home.

Of greater significance perhaps were the plant-hunting adventures of his own that Tradescant embarked on after leaving the employ of the Earl of Salisbury. In June 1618, he joined a ship bound for Archangel on the northern coast of Russia under the command of Sir Dudley Digges, who had been sent by the king to negotiate the terms of a loan with the Russian Tsar in Moscow. Tradescant's official role on this expedition is unclear, but the fact that he kept an extremely detailed extant account of this journey suggests that he was taken along as a naturalist by appointment rather than joining the trip at his own instigation. Whatever the case, he certainly took advantage of any opportunity to go ashore and record the flora and fauna that he saw. While the ship was moored at Archangel and the ambassadorial party were engaged in their (unsuccessful as it happens) negotiations with the tsar, Tradescant spent three weeks being carried by boat 'from iland to iland to see what things growe upon them'. He sailed home a full month ahead of the main party, presumably anxious to ensure that his precious cargo of plant specimens did not deteriorate too much.[77] Two years later, Tradescant was off on his travels again, this time to North Africa. On this occasion, he returned, according to Parkinson, with many sorts of apricot trees and a wild pomegranate which had never before been seen in England, until John Tradescant, 'my very loving good friend brought it from the parts beyond the Seas and planted it in his Lords Garden at Canterbury' (fig. 167 and see fig. 102).[78]

Further opportunities to indulge his passion for collecting came when he entered the employ of George Villiers, the Duke of Buckingham, in 1624, which once again involved much Continental travel in a variety of roles. As well as visiting the Low Countries again to buy plants for his new employer, he also acted as a baggage-handler on the duke's journey to France for the proxy wedding of Henrietta Maria to King Charles and, less happily, as a ship's engineer on the duke's ill-conceived military intervention at La Rochelle in 1627, which resulted in a disastrous defeat.[79] But wherever he went, and for whatever purpose, Tradescant returned with plants and other curiosities, many well-chronicled, as has been seen, by his friend John Parkinson, who makes numerous references in his book to 'that worthy, curious, and diligent searcher and preserver of all natures rarities and varieties… John Tradescant'.[80]

Despite financial interests in the New World – he purchased two shares in the Virginia Company in 1617 – Tradescant the elder never travelled there himself, but his son made three attested visits to the Americas. The first was in 1637 when it is recorded in State Papers that the purpose of his visit was 'to gather up all raritye of flowers, plants, shells, etc.', and whence he brought back 'a couple of hundred plants hitherto unknown to our world'. We learn this from the correspondence of one John Morris, the inheritor of the London watermills built near London Bridge by his father in 1580, with his friend Johannes de Laet, a director of the Dutch West India Company in Holland.[81] Morris was an avid book collector and one of his particular interests was botany. He was a great admirer of the work of Parkinson, contributing no less than three dedications to Parkinson's 1640 *Theatrum Botanicum*. With the help and advice of Parkinson and after a thorough inspection of the material that Tradescant had brought back from this trip, a list of the plants and dried specimens was compiled and circulated among interested botanists the following year. Morris remarks that in addition there were 'many seeds which do not yet show of what species they are likely to be',[82] a perennial problem with packets of dried seeds from unknown sources and which of course made cataloguing them impossible. Tradescant's father had died in April 1638 while he was away on this trip, so on his return the son no longer had his father's knowledge to draw on and, presumably, this is why the task of identification and classification was left to others. Nevertheless, there was a notable concern to order and disseminate this new information to interested parties.

Although he never quite achieved the same horticultural reputation as his father, Tradescant the younger clearly took seriously his role in continuing his father's work and preserving his legacy. He contributed to the garden collection at the Ark by bringing back plants from Virginian voyages and in 1656 he published *Musaeum Tradescantianum*, a catalogue of the 'Collection of Rarities preserved at South-Lambeth neere London', listing all the 'naturall' and 'artificiall' materials in the museum and concluding with the 'Hortus Tradescantianus', a comprehensive list of the plants in his garden.[83] After much long and bitter legal wrangling following his death, the collection was eventually transferred, as he had wished, to Oxford University, as 'an honour to our Nation'. What is left of the collection can still be seen at the Ashmolean Museum in Oxford.

Between them, the Tradescants have been credited with the introduction of many new plant varieties into England but in fact many of these plants, recorded as being grown in the garden at South Lambeth, were either already growing in England or had come to them first through friends and other contacts from their travels abroad. Parkinson, for instance, describes and names a particular variety of spiderwort (other varieties of the plant being already known in England) as *Phalangium Ephemerum Virginianum Joannis Tradescant*, a 'Spider-wort of late knowledge, and for it the Christian world is indebted unto that painful industrious searcher…John Tradescant, who first received it of a friend, that brought it out of Virginia'.[84] The whole genus of spiderwort, including all seventy-five known varieties, is now classified as *Tradescantia*, even though, as Parkinson makes clear, all that can actually be attributed to Tradescant himself is that he took one variety of the genus from a friend (whose name remains unknown) who had brought it from abroad and cultivated it in his garden. Nevertheless, however much claims may have been overstated, the John Tradescants, particularly the elder, were pioneers in collecting plants from overseas and attempting to cultivate them in their native country. They did this in a garden that was open to the public so that anyone could see the results of their endeavours, and they were instrumental in the distribution of these plants among friends and colleagues, who then planted and grew them in their own gardens, thus starting a chain of distribution and dissemination of knowledge among the wider gardening community.

Due to their high-profile adventuring as well as to the extant and comprehensive catalogues of their plant collections, the John Tradescants deservedly earned their place in history as pioneering plant collectors of their age. But there were others. For instance, Parkinson mentions a Guillaume (or William) Boel who travelled to Spain in 1607 searching for rare plants. Parkinson makes many references to Boel, 'often before and hereafter remembered', describing the plants he had brought back for him. It seems from a later remark by Parkinson that he actually commissioned Boel to collect plants for him: he complains that some of the seeds collected by Boel, 'but to me of debt, for going into Spaine almost wholly on my charge', were then given by Boel to someone else.[85] How this relationship between commissioner and collector actually worked is as unclear to us as it obviously was to the parties involved at the time: it seems unlikely that Parkinson would have paid Boel to travel especially to Spain on his behalf to collect plants but perhaps Boel was making the journey anyway and Parkinson simply paid him to fetch him some plants while he was there. But, whatever Parkinson might have felt about the matter, Boel clearly did not feel that he had exclusive rights to the plants he had found. What is clear is that this was a commercial transaction, Boel being paid to seek plants on behalf of clients.

Both Gerard's and Parkinson's books abound with examples of plants and seeds received from 'beyond the seas' as gifts, directly or indirectly via friends and acquaintances returning from voyages abroad. Gerard receives new varieties of gilliflowers 'procured from Poland' by Mr Nicolas Leet, who also supplies beet seeds 'from beyond the seas'; he writes that 'a friend of mine' brought a Golden Thistle from Peru and on another occasion, he received the root of a ginger plant by way of 'our men who sacked Domingo in the [West] Indies [who] digged it up there in sundry places wilde'. At other times, he is less specific: he writes of a Persian Lily which grows naturally in Persia, but 'is nowe made by the industrie of travailers into those countries, lovers of plants, a denizon in some fewe of our London gardens'.[86] Already mentioned are the rare and exotic plants received by Parkinson, such as those from Boel and from his friend Tradescant, which he planted in his garden. Others arrived by even more circuitous routes, such as the Indian 'Yukka' plant, now flourishing in his garden, which was first brought to England from the West Indies (see fig. 79). Gerard had kept one for a long time in his garden and then sent one to the Parisian nurseryman Jean Robin, from whom he frequently records having received plants and seeds. As noted before, arrangements such as this were reciprocal: Robin's son Vespasien then sent one to Master John de Franqueville in London, who then passed it on to Parkinson.[87]

Parkinson cites many plants as coming from Spain, Portugal and Constantinople but which in fact originated from even further afield. In some cases the history was known: for instance, a 'double yellow Rose, which first was procured to be brought into England... from Constantinople, which (as we heare) was first brought thither from Syria'.[88] There must be many other examples where plants found in a particular place were assumed to be natives of that country but which would in fact have originated from other parts of the world. As noted at the beginning of this chapter, plants have been on the move for a very long time.

There is an abundance of evidence, then, that rare and exotic plants were reaching England from the beginning of the new century. The many examples found in the books of Gerard and Parkinson offer a lively picture of a thriving network of enthusiasts and acquaintances through whom new plants from all over the globe were being imported, distributed and exchanged. But this is only part of the story: in what other ways were these plants being distributed? And how did that change between 1608, when Parkinson was carefully nurturing exotic plants brought back from Spain with various degrees of success, and the end of the century, when there were at least fifteen established nurseries trading in London? What evidence is there that the trade in ornamental plants began to flourish on a more organised commercial basis?

These questions have already been examined from the viewpoint of the tradesman, using evidence such as catalogues of seeds and plants for sale, and the conclusion has been that there is little in the way of firm evidence for trading until after the Restoration in 1660.[89] If we now approach this question from the point of view of those who were being supplied with the plants, rather than the tradesmen supplying them, there is plenty of evidence to suggest that a commercial trade in flowering plants existed well before this date. Early references are scant but, for instance, in a letter dated 20 April 1609, John Chamberlain reports to his friend Dudley Carleton from Ware Park that 'we have now four or five flowers...that cost twelve pound', the inclusion of the purchase price indicating a business transaction.[90] In the early 1630s, Sir John Oglander notes in his memorandum book that he has purchased 'French Flowers' which cost him 10 shillings a root, as well as all sorts of tulips.[91] In 1649, a carrier is paid 3s 9d for bringing a box of flowers from London to Tavistock, the Devonshire home of the Earl and Countess of Bath.[92] The large sums being paid for these ornamental plants – compared to say, the 1s per hundred for the roses purchased for the new garden at Gray's Inn Court – indicate their rarity and value. However, while such anecdotes tell us that exotic and expensive plants were being purchased, they still offer no information as to where the plants were being obtained.

Among this paucity of evidence we are fortunate, then, that there is one valuable documentary source which sheds light on the trade in ornamental plants specifically during the decades of the mid-seventeenth century, and that is Sir Thomas Hanmer's previously discussed notebooks, compiled during the years 1654–7. These little books contain, among other things, a unique record of plants which Sir Thomas purchased from various nurserymen in London and in Paris, as well as plants he had given to and received from various friends and relatives.[93] Some of the lists are annotated with prices paid and the name and address of the suppliers. As already established, Hanmer was undoubtedly one of the leading plantsmen of his age, so information on who was supplying him with plants is clearly of exceptional interest.

Throughout the notebook, Hamner names more than thirty individuals, a number of them on several occasions, of whom twelve we know are in the business of selling plants because in every case, Hanmer indicates how much he has paid for plants from these people. A further three are likely to be nurserymen since addresses are supplied that indicate business premises and another two of the named individuals are identified as gardeners. Of the remaining people mentioned, some are clearly friends and acquaintances because, although plants are exchanged, no money ever appears to change hands. A handful are simply names about whom no more information is provided.

The first thing to note is that the networks of free exchange already discussed continued into the 1650s as one way in which new varieties of exotic flowers and plants were distributed. Of Hanmer's friends and acquaintances, some such as the Parliamentarian General John Lambert, are well-known figures. On two occasions, Lambert is noted as a recipient of Hanmer's generosity, receiving from him in June 1655 'a very great mother-root of [the tulip] Agate Hanmer' (see fig. 144) and more tulips in June 1656. The eponymously named Agate Hanmer was one of his best tulips: according to John Rea, it was introduced into Britain by Hanmer and was 'a beautiful flower' striped with 'three good colours: gredeline [a kind of purple], deep scarlet and pure white'.[94] This clearly represented a significant gift. Lambert is mentioned twice more by Hanmer, noting flowers he has particularly admired in his garden, also indicating Lambert's source for these flowers: 'yellow jasmine, the double striped pomegranate, many Narcissi' including one from 'Mr Bed[?ing]ton, a merchant'. There is no further information about Mr Bedington but the fact that he is described as a merchant and that he 'furnished Ld Lambert' with this variety indicate a business transaction rather than a gift.[95] On another occasion, Hanmer admires tulips in Lambert's garden 'from Moryn', the Parisian nurseryman we have come across before and will meet again. Lambert's love of gardening is well known: he had recently purchased Wimbledon House, the former home of Queen Henrietta Maria, and continued to tend its notable gardens, and while imprisoned at Castle Cornet on the island of Guernsey following the Restoration, he created a garden there which still bears his name (fig. 168).[96] This was a friendship between a displaced Royalist, Hanmer, and one of the most influential men in the new Cromwellian regime, General Sir John Lambert, to give him his full title: a love of gardening and plants apparently transcended even major political barriers during those troubled times.

Other friends and relatives are mentioned by Sir Thomas in a variety of contexts: there is a list of 'Tulips given by me to my cosin 1654', another of 'Gilliflowers given me by Mrs

Thurl. apr. 1656'; a purple and white iris is admired in the garden of 'Mrs Seely in Shooe Lane'; tulips are sent to Sir J Trevor, Mr Blackley, Mrs Thurloe and Mr Downton and 'beares eares' sent to Lady Pooley, who appears to be a neighbour in Lewisham. Clearly, networks of exchange of plants between fellow-gardeners continued to thrive, providing one means by which rare or exotic specimens were distributed. Once one person had obtained them, however it was achieved, then bulbs, offsets, cuttings and seeds were passed round the circle of flower enthusiasts for cultivating in their own gardens.[97]

Two individuals with whom Hanmer seems to have had a more ambivalent relationship were John Rose and John Rea. Rose is mentioned more times than any other individual in Hanmer's notebook, in a number of contexts including giving and receiving tulips – 'I promised him the best offset of Ag Hanmer…I am to have from him an offsett of the Dutchess of Venice' – and supplying gilliflowers. He also offers horticultural advice, all carefully recorded by Hanmer, on how to encourage reluctant seeds to germinate, how to sow auriculas, and how to over-winter tender plants. Rose is well known as a gardener, famously being appointed the king's gardener at St James's in 1661. At the time Hanmer knew him, it is likely that Rose was working for the Earl of Essex, Robert Devereux, at Essex House in London, where Hanmer appears to have visited Rose in 1654, admiring some of the plants that he saw in the garden there.[98] It is possible that Rose was in business as a nurseryman but, whether or not this was the case, he was clearly in a position to supply plants, and it appears on a number of occasions that he was acting as an intermediary between supplier and recipient. Hanmer notes that he 'left with Mr Rose...9 rootes which Tho. Turner delivered to him last wynter', the gift of the tulip bulb for Lord Lambert was 'sent him by Rose' (see fig. 144). Elsewhere, Hanmer writes that 'I left [London] September 1st, 42 star Anemones of Mr Downton and the 4 anemones from Mons. Picot to be set by Mr Rose for mee'. This last note implies the possibility that Rose might actually have worked for Hanmer, even if only on an occasional and independent basis.

The other individual with whom Hanmer had extensive dealings was his friend John Rea, who ran his own long-established nursery business at Kinlet, near Bewdley in Shropshire, which although not close to Bettisfield was probably no longer than a day's ride away; in this we have an example of a nursery well away from London, serving the provinces. Rea has already been mentioned as the author of *Flora: De Florum Cultura*, published in 1665, intended as an updated version of Parkinson's *Paradisi in Sole* and the first publication of its kind since 1629. It includes a dedicatory epistle to Hanmer in which Rea praises both Hanmer's superior knowledge of gardening and his generosity which has 'furnished me with many noble and new varieties' from his 'incomparable Collection'.[99] In his notebook, Hanmer records 'Tulipes which I gave Mr Rea 1654', listing about forty varieties. In the same year, he also mentions 'Reas good tulips' with which he filled a bed in the garden at Haulton. However, although Rea was in business, his dealings with Hanmer appear to have been only reciprocal and there is no record of money ever changing hands between them. It seems that, rather than being any kind of business arrangement, this was a friendship based on a mutual interest in gardening.

Of exceptional interest in these notebooks is the information provided about the commercial nurserymen with whom Hanmer did business, most of whom were based in London. Mr Moulart is mentioned on three occasions: twice as the supplier of flowers admired by Hanmer in others' gardens and once as a supplier to Hanmer (fig. 169).[100] Moulart has been identified as James Moullar (Mullar), a 'flowerist' of Spitalfields, who died in 1666.[101] From Hanmer's notes, he appears to have been a specialist supplier of recently introduced bulbs. Hanmer also spends considerably larger sums of money buying plants

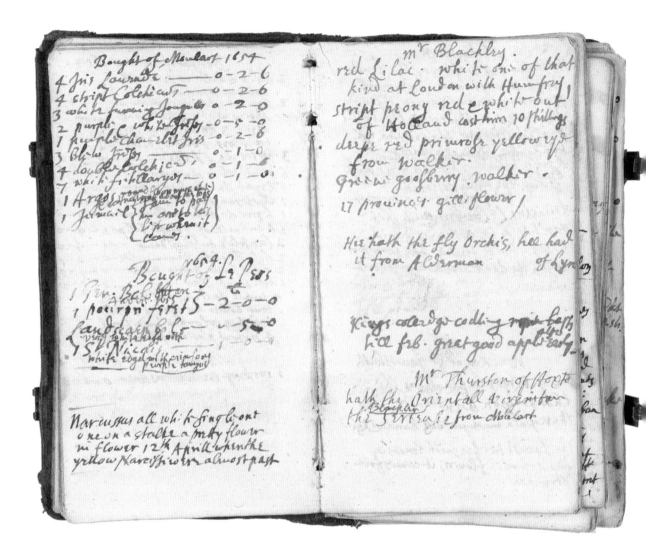

from 'Geldrop' in 1655. Although the notes indicate that this is a person ('I bought of him'), Geldrop is also the name of a town in Holland, which, if this is where Hanmer bought them from, would explain why they appear to be so expensive, the prices noted in pounds rather than shillings as elsewhere (fig. 170).[102]

Hanmer's fondness for 'beares eares' (auriculas) has already been noted, and his main supplier of these seems to have been 'Humphries of Woollstable in Westminster'. He bought several varieties in 1654 and took some of them to his garden at Haulton. Humphrey's reputation as a specialist in auriculas was also noted by John Rea in his *Flora* where

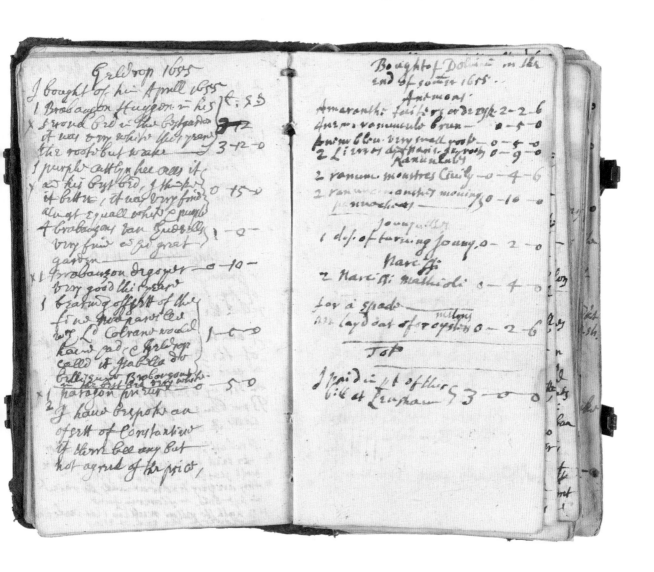

he mentions auriculas named after 'those that raised them' and includes Humphries in this list.[103] There is some evidence to suggest that by the end of the seventeenth century, this plant had become hugely popular: like the tulip, the infinite variety of colours and patterns on its petals were counted among its desirable attributes.[104]

Westminster has previously been noted as an area which attracted a number of nurseries: Ralph Tuggie and Henry Banbury both ran their businesses from there. Walker of St James, mentioned by Hanmer in his notebook as having many 'virginia plants', is also likely to have been located in this area. There is an extant plan of Woolstaple, where Humphries

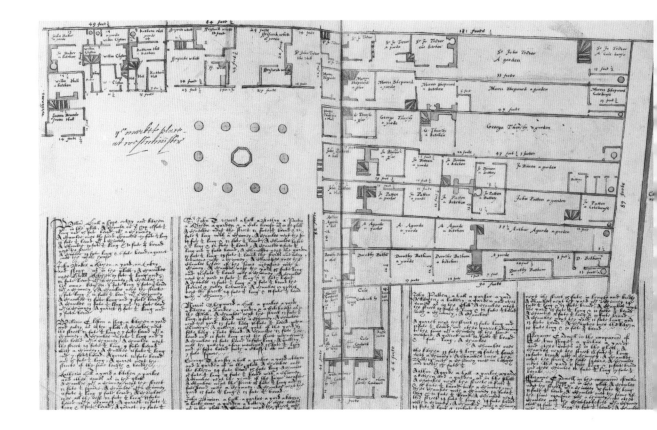

171   Ralph Treswell's plan of Woolstaple Yard, Westminster, *c.*1603

nursery was located, executed by Ralph Treswell in about 1603, which shows a number of small houses arranged along the eastern side of the market place at Westminster: although the houses are small, with a footprint of just one or two rooms, they all have reasonably large gardens, of between fifty and a hundred feet (fig. 171).[105] Clearly, this was an area of London in which it was possible to lease sufficient land to run a small nursery business. Its proximity to the market place may also be significant.

On the other side of town, Hanmer bought gilliflowers from Smyth of Greenwich: he paid 18*d* for each root and 2*d* each for pots to put them in. At the same time he bought a range of other plants to 'set in the border at Leusham' as well as '3 pannes of beares ears seed for 14 shill.' On another occasion he bought auricula plants from Smyth at 1*s* a root, again for the garden at Lewisham, which is just a mile or so from Greenwich.

Hanmer also dealt with another nurseryman on the doorstep in Lewisham. Unfortunately, his name is not clear from the manuscript but he supplied Hanmer with a wide variety of flowering plants, including hyacinths, narcissi, irises, anemones, ranunculus and

312

columbines. On one occasion he also provided a spade for 2s 6d. Hanmer must have had a particularly good relationship with this nurseryman, as it seems that not only did he buy a significant amount of goods from him but he also had them on account. In the summer of 1655, he notes at the bottom of another list of plants bought from here: 'I paid in part of their bill at Leusham £3 0s 0d'. Again, like Moulart, this nurseryman specialised in the new range of flowering bulbs and other plants.

From this overview of nurserymen known to Hanmer it is clear that, contrary to Harvey's assessment, there were a significant number of established nurseries in 1650s London. That they were reasonably prevalent can be inferred from the fact that Hanmer was apparently able to choose suppliers located either close to his house at Lewisham, well out to the east of London and south of the river, or otherwise located on the western outskirts of the city, more convenient for transporting plants to his home at Bettisfield in north Wales. The fact that Hanmer felt it necessary to deal with nurseries in London for the supply of these kinds of plants indicates that they were not available more locally and that trade, as was the case with all imported luxury goods, was centred on the capital. It seems too, from the scant information provided here, that some nurseries were quite specialised, dealing mainly in bulbs as in the case of Moulart, or auriculas in the case of Humphries. Smyth and the Lewisham nurseryman appear to have been slightly larger concerns, selling a wider variety of plants and also garden equipment such as pots and spades. What is absolutely clear, though, is that all these London nurseries were catering for a new and growing market for flowering plants in a way that simply had not been seen before.

At the same time, Sir Thomas continued to do business with nurserymen from abroad, specifically Picot and Pierre Morin, both from Paris.[106] The Morin brothers have been noted before as suppliers of plants to Tradescant.[107] Pierre Morin was also the inspiration for Evelyn's oval garden at Sayes Court. Not only did Evelyn visit Morin's garden but from his correspondence with his father-in-law Sir Richard Browne it is known that he also purchased plants from there long after his return to England.[108] Hanmer also spent time in Paris during the same period as Evelyn, so it is not surprising that an equally enthusiastic gardener and plantsman would have known of Morin's nursery and also continued to purchase plants from him once back in England.

As well as providing the usual list of plants purchased and prices paid, Hanmer's notes regarding Morin add further insight into his dealings with this nurseryman. There appears, for instance, to have been much negotiation, not to say disputing, over the prices charged. Hanmer notes: 'I desired these tulips of Moryn at a reasonable price but I wrote to [him]

172 Irises, from Crispin van den Passe's *Hortus Floridus*, *c.*1615

that this was way too deare'. In May 1656, Hanmer records prices he has 'offered' to Morin for a variety of plants, and on the next page he notes that 'Moryn demands 20 livres le cent for Irises mixt.'[109] Hanmer clearly thought Morin's prices were expensive but from these notes it is possible to conclude that prices were not fixed but open to negotiation. It also appears that the relationship between Hanmer and Morin was not always amicable. Having said that, Hanmer clearly respected the nurseryman's specialist knowledge: he noted advice from Morin about growing tulips and watering plants, as well as copying out in full into his notebook Morin's *Catalogue* of plants and flowers, published in 1651, which comprised lists of many varieties of tulips, irises, rananculus and anemones. Hanmer made use of this advice in his *Garden Book*, as well as referring there to Morin's 'printed Catalogue' on two separate occasions, once with reference to his collection of irises and again to his collection of anemones.[110]

The other Parisian nurseryman with whom Hanmer communicated was Monsieur Picot. He noted advice from him about growing tulips and anemones, which should 'be planted all before the 10th September English account', reminding us that foreign trade and communication involved not only different currencies but also a different calendar. French use of

the Gregorian calendar was adopted much earlier than in England and the result was that French dates would have been ten days ahead of English ones. In other words, 10 September would have fallen ten or eleven days earlier in France than in England and this crucial time difference was clearly thought worth mentioning by Picot with regard to planting anemones. Hanmer also notes that his wife has received some plants from Picot, including four anemones and eleven tulips.

Picot has not thus far appeared in any other records but his address, given fully by Hanmer as 'fauxbourg St Germain rue St Pere proche la charite A Paris', is exactly the same as the address given in Morin's *Catalogue* for the location of his nursery. It is of course possible that these two nurserymen were running their businesses side by side but it is also possible that Picot worked for Morin, and that on some occasions customers may have communicated directly with him rather than his employer. Morin's nursery was well established by this time and sufficiently renowned to admit the possibility of employing staff. As already mentioned, it seems likely that Hanmer would have met both Morin and Picot when he was living in France; that he continued to do business with them once he returned, despite the obvious difficulties, indicates loyalty and respect for these plantsmen, as well as a belief in the superiority of their plants, the varieties available and their expertise.

Hanmer's notebooks, in summary, provide unequivocal evidence that by the 1650s there was an established nursery trade centred on London, dealing in a wide range of rare and no longer so rare ornamental plants for the garden, responding to the increased interest in flower gardening for pleasure among the gentry of the land.

As has been amply demonstrated, from the late sixteenth century, new plants and ideas about gardening had been arriving in England in many ways – via plant collectors, adventurers, immigrants and travellers. Once they had arrived, they were then distributed and disseminated through the same kinds of networks of communication and trade that had been in existence in the country for centuries. Furthermore, there were also positive moves towards the development of an established commercial trade in ornamental plants for the garden in the first half of the seventeenth century.

It is also noteworthy that at the same time, expertise, advice and knowledge were also being disseminated through a similarly wide range of non-commercial networks. The intellectual community of horticulturists centred on the figure of Carolus Clusius has been mentioned, its influence reaching as far as the tight-knit group of naturalists living and working on Lime Street in London. The principles of the free exchange of intellectual ideas, botanical knowledge and methods of scientific study which underpinned this community continued into the new century, where they manifested themselves again in correspondence networks such as the Hartlib Circle, this time centred on Samuel Hartlib and primarily concerned with agricultural improvement. These somewhat difficult to define intellectual networks were eventually given permanence with the founding of the Royal Society in 1660.[111]

Alongside these scholars and intellectuals, at a much more local level gardeners and plant enthusiasts continued to share their knowledge and experience just as they had always done. Whether recommending varieties of apple tree to a neighbour, gathering information regarding the cultivation of new plants from books, nurserymen or fellow-gardeners, paying to view the spectacular display of curiosities in Tradescant's Ark or simply looking over the garden wall to see what the neighbours were up to, new ideas, inspiration and knowledge continued to spread among the gardeners of early modern England.

11
CONCLUSIONS

'A ffitt place for any Gentleman'

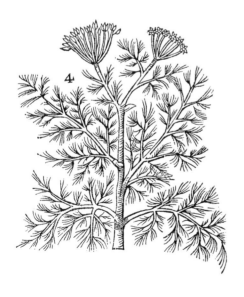

This book has discussed at length what the early modern garden may have looked like, with some account of the changes that occurred during the period and an attempt to identify the factors that brought about and facilitated these changes. It now remains to reflect on what the gardens themselves actually meant to those who created them, what they said about them and what role their gardens played in defining their social and cultural identity. We have considered the hierarchy of gardeners who were working in the gardens, from labourers to skilled gardeners at all levels, and the idea that some gentlemen were actively involved in the cultivation of their gardens. But, whoever had done the work, how, ultimately, did garden owners view what they had created? How did they use their gardens – as private spaces in which to spend time in solitude or with their families, or as a public arena in which to entertain their friends and offer hospitality to their neighbours (fig. 173)? How did their gardens contribute to defining their status?

For John Parkinson, status and gardens went hand in hand: the way a garden was laid out and the plants with which it was furnished made a statement about the owner's standing in society. He observed, as has been noted, that 'Gentlemen of the better sort and quality, will provide such a parcell of ground to bee laid out for their Garden...as may be fit and answerable to the degree they hold' and he makes frequent reference throughout his book to the gentility of his readers.[1] This is, in fact, concomitant with a similar concern among the gentry for building and improving their houses. According to recent surveys, more new country houses were built between 1570 and 1620 than in any other subsequent half-century, providing aspirants and new arrivals with the opportunity to proclaim their ambitions and display their gentlemanly status. At the same time, established members of the gentry set about renovating and rebuilding their ancestral homes in order to reassert their status above the newcomers.[2] In either case, a gentleman's house – and his garden – provided a prominent arena in which to demonstrate his wealth and standing in society. But still, how did this actually manifest itself in practice? How do we know, for instance, what impression these gardens had on those who saw them?

There are two sources which can help to answer these questions: one is in the written accounts of both the garden-owners and of those who visited them; the other is in the evidence that can be gleaned from the structure of the gardens themselves – further consideration of features such as walks, alleys, terraces and mounts reveals how the actual construction of the garden space lent itself to being displayed and viewed. In much the same way as the books considered in Chapter 1, a garden can only reach its full potential when it is actually used: in other words, when its occupants, whoever they may be, interact in some way with the space that surrounds them.

Anecdotal evidence gleaned from written accounts indicates that the practice of visiting other people's houses and gardens was well established in the sixteenth and seventeenth centuries. In the same way that members of the English gentry visited gardens on the near Continent in France, the Netherlands and Italy, so foreign noblemen arrived in England to embark on a similar tour of cultural highlights. Sources reveal that important visitors to London were taken on a tour, certainly of the royal residences such as Hampton Court, Nonsuch, Whitehall and Windsor. Theobalds in Hertfordshire was also included in the list, even when it still belonged to the Cecils, before it was taken over by James I in the early seventeenth century. The travel diaries of, for instance, Paul Hentzner, a German lawyer who visited in 1598, Thomas Platter, a Swiss physician who visited a year later in 1599, and the Moravian nobleman Baron Waldstein, who was received in 1600, all describe in detail the magnificent gardens they saw at these properties.[3] How these visits were arranged is more difficult to ascertain, although it is known, for instance, that Sir Robert Cecil received Baron Waldstein in London and secured his audience with the queen – presumably, arranging a sight-seeing trip round London for distinguished visitors was all in a day's work.[4] Hentzner records being admitted into the Presence Chamber at Whitehall Palace 'by an order Mr Rogers had procured from the Lord Chamberlain'. Clearly, it was – as ever – useful to have contacts.[5]

In addition, there is evidence of visits to private houses and gardens. For instance, Abram Booth, a representative of the Dutch East India Company who came to England in 1629 on diplomatic business, as well as taking time out to visit the royal residences just mentioned, also went to Arundel House on the Strand, Audley End in Essex, Caron House in South Lambeth and Wimbledon House in Surrey. He kept a journal in which he briefly described the houses and gardens that he visited.[6] In 1634, a party of travellers from Norfolk were shown round Sir Arthur Ingram's house in York where they gazed in admiration at his 'store of massie Plate, rich Hangings, lively Pictures and Statues, rich £150 pearle Glasses, fayre stately £500 Organ and other rich Furniture in every Roome'.[7] Unfortunately, they mention nothing about the garden but it is interesting that they felt qualified to put a value on Ingram's possessions. John Chamberlain writes on 22 April 1606 to his friend and correspondent Dudley Carleton, inviting him to come to Ware Park, the home of Sir Henry Fanshawe.[8] Why Chamberlain was in a position to invite his friend to someone else's home is unclear but it was a well-known garden, also mentioned by Sir Henry Wotton in his *Elements of Architecture*, observing that this garden, which he had clearly visited, was 'surely without parallel'. John Evelyn's many visits to gardens around Europe have already been discussed, but he continued to visit gardens on his return to England, noting in his diary, among others, 'Salisbury's Place at Hatfield; where the most considerable rarity besides the house…was the Garden & Vineyard rarely well water'd and planted'; 'his Majesties House and Garden at Theobalds'; 'my Lady Brooks gardens which was one of the neatest, & most celebrated in England' and 'Bedington that antient Seate of the Carews…famous for the first Orange garden of England, being now over-growne with trees'. Evelyn's own garden at Sayes Court was, of course, famously visited by Charles II in 1663.[9]

Although they provide us with little in the way of detail, all these examples serve to show that garden-visiting was a popular pastime among leisured folk. In some cases, it is possible that these visits were between friends, but it seems that visiting the houses and grounds of people they did not necessarily know was not uncommon. It is probable that strangers would be more likely to visit when the owners were not actually in residence: Hentzner visited Theobalds when the family were all away in London, attending the funeral of Lord Burghley.[10] There is evidence too that it was possible to gain admittance to a house by

tipping the servants. Once admitted, and perhaps depending on the size of the gratuity, visitors were given access not just to the public rooms but to the private areas as well. Presumably, the garden would have been included in the tour.[11] Again, such sight-seeing excursions were likely to have taken place in the absence of the owners. Whatever the circumstances, it is possible to conclude from evidence such as this that gardens were an important part of the owner's public display of his social standing, and that they were being seen and recorded as such by a wide variety of visitors.

On most occasions, however, the gentry received guests into their homes themselves. While the possibility of a cripplingly expensive royal visitation might have to be faced – we remember that Sir Richard Leveson had his entrance prepared for just such an event – for most of the time the gentry were entertaining their friends, peers and kinsmen, and their houses and gardens provided the perfect backdrop for their hospitality. On arrival, guests would have been impressed by a gatehouse or entrance displaying the family coat of arms (fig. 174), before being received into the buttery, hall or chamber, whichever was most appropriate to their degree.[12]

After receiving some refreshment, they are likely to have taken a stroll around the garden. Walks and alleys were ubiquitous features in all the gardens mentioned throughout this book and clearly they were there for a purpose – not just to divide up the quarters but to provide a space, 'enough for foure to walk a breast', through which to walk and admire the garden.[13] Walkways were often punctuated with seats and arbours – places to stop and rest in order to appreciate the colours and scents of the flowers more fully. Larger gardens boasted mounts and terraces, not only impressive features in themselves but also providing a raised vantage point from which to view the extent of the garden and its overall layout. The extant terrace at Lyveden New Bield provides an excellent example of this. This terrace, which traverses the middle of the garden, offers views to the north over the lower orchard and back down to the house, as well as to the south over the moated orchard with its concentric planting of fruit trees and roses and up towards the lodge at the

top of the garden. Ascending the mounts at the corners of the moated orchard would have enhanced this view.

Any geometric patterns or knots in the gardens would of course have been best viewed from above. The grandest houses and gardens may well have had a loggia, a permanent structure that provided a covered walkway round the garden, often at first-floor level, providing shade from the summer sun, protection from the winter cold and shelter from the rain at any time of year.[14] These were normally built on one of the walls facing the garden, often with no access from the house, although occasionally they were a separate building altogether. The remains of such a loggia can still be seen in the grounds of Campden Manor in Gloucestershire (fig. 175; see also fig. 128).

Similarly, a walk from the main house to the banqueting house located perhaps at the end of the garden would have involved traversing a route no doubt contrived to display the garden at its best. For instance, the banqueting house that can be seen in Evelyn's plan of Sayes Court (see figs 130, 132) is located at the end of the Long Promenade. The striking lodge at Lyveden New Bield can only be seen once the visitor has walked up the garden at least as far as the moated orchard (fig. 176). As well as the impressive layout, visitors would have had ample opportunities to view other examples of extravagant expenditure, such as the plants included in the garden. As has been noted, exotic flowers were a fine example of

a luxury item – defined as such by their cost, their rarity, their beauty and their purely orna-mental value – which could be fittingly displayed in the gardens of the gentry.

It should be remembered too that the high cost of plants comprised significantly more than just the initial sum paid for the bulb or root. For instance, much time and money were expended on their transport and, in some cases, the expertise required to tend exotic plants, which also had to be 'bought in'. In 1622, Sir Thomas Aubrey not only paid for the carriage of tender fruit trees from London to his home in south Wales but also for someone to plant them.[15] The cost of the plants purchased by Tradescant for Cecil was considerably increased by the cost of transporting them from many destinations around Europe to Hatfield House, not to mention the salary paid to Tradescant himself for under-taking this task over many months.[16] There is evidence too that French gardeners were employed by wealthy gentlemen, presumably because they had valuable knowledge of foreign plants and garden fashions that had not yet reached their English counterparts: this

too would have conferred a degree of status on their employers. The household accounts of Francis Carew of Beddington for 1570 include four references to French gardeners. In a postscript to a letter sent to Paris in September 1561, William Cecil asks for 'anything meet for the orchard or garden and an apt man for the same', and Robert Dudley, Earl of Leicester employed a French gardener at Kew, mentioned in the household accounts for 1599.[17] To have exotic plants growing in your garden signified your high standing in society, the consumption of luxury goods and show of extravagant expenditure, as in many other areas of life, giving 'visual expression to the social hierarchy'.[18]

Gardens also provided the ultimate interactive arena for other entertainment. As well as walking and enjoying the grounds, most gentry gardens incorporated a bowling alley, the apparent links with ancient Rome making it a fashionable and suitable sport for gentlemen. There is a bowling green seen on a plan of William Cecil's garden in the Strand; Sir Thomas Pelham paid a workman 1s 4d for two days mowing the bowling alley at Halland House; and a woodcut included in Thomas Hyll's *The Gardeners Labyrinth* clearly shows some kind of bowling area within the garden (fig. 177).[19] This image is reminiscent of the bowling green at Nunwell, which Sir John Oglander describes as being planted with a framework of vines and raspberries.

Oglander, along with many of his contemporaries, also mentions keeping the fish ponds in his garden well stocked with fish. Although the primary purpose for this would have been as a source of food, there is evidence that gentlemen also engaged in fishing as a leisure activity. Thomas Barker, in his compilation *The Country-mans Recreation*, includes a section on the 'Arte of Angling' along with other parts on planting, grafting and gardening. This book was published in 1654 and is highly likely to have been a response to the enormous popularity of Izaac Walton's discourse on fish and fishing, *The Compleat Angler*, produced in the previous year.[20] Written partly in order, as has been noted in other similar circumstances, to provide himself and his friends with some distraction during the years of political instability, the *Compleat Angler* ought to fit into the genre of ephemeral didactic literature, but time has shown it to be anything but, as it is still in print today. Nevertheless, its publication in 1653 reinforces this activity as another leisure pursuit considered fit for a gentleman.

Having said that, there was nothing particularly new about this pastime, as Sir Robert Sidney was preparing his ponds for a day's fishing with Sir Robert Wrothe and his friends at the beginning of the century. Sidney had left his estate manager, Thomas Golding, in charge of the arrangements but, as Golding described in a letter to Sidney, while he was away, two of Wrothe's men had been sent to 'make trial' of fishing in the river at Penshurst – presumably in advance of the impending visit by their master. Unfortunately, they discovered that the river was 'hard to be fished' and were not able to catch anything out of the ordinary such as carp, bream or pike. As a result, Golding had himself arranged for these big fish to be taken from the river and put into the pond in the orchard, presumably to ensure a good day's sport.[21] The provision of such recreation for friends and acquaintances was another important way in which a gentleman could ensure his standing among his peers.

Finally on this point, there is also to be considered the question of demonstrating 'good taste'. As gentlemen found themselves having to redefine their position above the rising middling class, the wealth required for the conspicuous accumulation of goods was no longer enough to affirm status: it now had to be accompanied by a capacity for discrimination, which was only possible through education and experience.[22] This is reminiscent of the distinction that was drawn by Evelyn between the intellectual gardener and middling practitioners, discussed in Chapter 5, and it seems that questions of taste were important throughout the period. Parkinson, for instance, offers to guide his readers in matters of taste, recognising that many do not know 'what to choose, or what to desire' and he will therefore select for them flowers for the garden that are 'fairest for shew'.[23] With the right advice, it was possible for the seventeenth-century gentleman to further establish his worth through the expression of his good taste.

By contrast, as well as for entertaining and recreation, gardens were used as places of solitude and spiritual refreshment. Immediately following his often quoted remark about spending too much money on flowers, Sir John Oglander continues: 'It was my Content, wearyed with studdye to solace my Selfe in the Garden and to see the spoorts of nature how in every several spetise [species] she sheweth her workmanshipp'. For him, his garden could be a place of retreat in which to contemplate the wonders of nature.[24] Lady Margaret Hoby takes herself into the garden 'after privat praier' to spend time on her own.[25] This search for privacy and solitude could also be extended to include close family and friends. Elsewhere, Oglander advises: 'Fitt up thei gardens, Orchards and Walkes handsome about thee that thou mayest give Content both to thei selve and wyfe to injoye the place', and Lady Hoby goes into the garden to talk with the local minister, Mr Rhodes, about personal spiritual matters.[26]

As we saw in the case of the enclosed medieval herber gardens and again in the privy gardens of the royal palaces, despite the many other considerations discussed earlier, these gardens were seen as places of escape and refuge from the outside world and were to be shared with no one except the closest of friends and relatives. The concept of the parlour garden has already been discussed in Chapter 6 and the examples of Sir Thomas Temple's 'little gardine at Dassett paled', John Evelyn's 'Private Garden of choice flowers', 'Sir Richard's Garden' at Trentham Hall and 'my Lady's garden' at Holme Lacy all point to a private space for leisure and contemplation.

This notion of the separation of the public and the private has already been discussed in a different context. In Chapter 2, we traced how the pursuit of private gain over working for the public good was gradually being acknowledged as an acceptable goal in life: private interests were being separated from the public. At a more pragmatic level, the same kind of change was occurring in the social structure of large households during this period. The idea of the central medieval hall in which the whole household, including servants, lived, ate and entertained guests was giving way to a new architectural style in which the living space was split into an increasing number of separate areas for dining and socialising. Servants were gradually banished to the upper quarters, or below stairs, and the family had their own private rooms – parlours – in which to eat and possibly entertain intimate friends. Grand and public entertaining now went on in the great chamber, usually an upper-floor room either over the parlour or what would have once been the great hall.[27]

It seems that this identifiable trend was also reflected in gardens: despite the demonstrable concern with public display and the apparent obligation to throw open the doors to all and sundry, gardens also had their private areas, which were not open to general access. Sir Thomas Hanmer expresses this clearly: 'All florists' – by florists he means gentlemen with flower gardens – 'have (besides their publicke grounds, wherein all people of quality are admitted to walke), a little private seminary or piece to sow and raise plants and trees in, and keep such treasures as are not to bee exposed to everyone's view'.[28]

Chapter 2 dealt with the 'profits and pleasures' of gardening as illuminated in contemporary literature, discussing in detail the moral, intellectual and spiritual contexts within which the evidence presented in this book should be viewed, and it is to this we now return. We recall, for instance, William Lawson's pleasure and delight in the results of his labours in his orchard and garden: 'And who can deny but the Principall end of an Orchard, is the honest delight of one wearied with the workes of his lawfull calling?'[29] Sentiments such as this can be interpreted in a number of ways. Sir John Oglander, as has been seen, takes a particular delight in spending time alone in his garden, as well as enjoying it with his wife. It is a place of refuge from the outside world in which they can admire, like Parkinson, the beauty of the plants and flowers for their own sake. There is no doubt that this is a garden of pleasure, possibly to be displayed, but primarily to be enjoyed.

The case for the garden of pleasure being simply that – a place for enjoyment – can be made by further consideration of Sir Thomas Temple's parlour garden at Burton Dassett. This little garden was clearly not about public display but to be able to indulge in creating an environment purely of sweet-smelling flowers, to produce such luxuries as grapes and apricots for the table or to be able to experiment with horticultural techniques, such as he did with his vine cuttings (irrespective of whether or not they were successful) – all this still represented an important assertion of Temple's gentlemanly status, which gave him the time and the opportunity to indulge in the pleasures of his garden.

Sir Thomas Hanmer took pleasure in both planning the layout of his garden and demonstrating a life-long interest in seeking out and collecting beautiful plants with which to furnish it. 'For these pleasures', wrote John Parkinson, 'are the delights of leasure'.[30] Sir Thomas could, surely, have only agreed with him.

For Lawson, there was pleasure in the labour as well as in the end result: 'View now with delight the works of your owne hands, your fruit trees of all sorts, loaden with sweet blossomes, and fruit of all tastes, operations and colours, your trees standing in comely order which way soever you look'.[31] As observed earlier in the cases of Wentworth, Oglander and Temple, he stressed the importance of actually doing some of the work oneself. Unlike many other recreational pursuits, gardening as a leisure activity seemed to occupy a unique and ambiguous position: although viewed as a pleasurable pastime, it was one which invariably involved an element of manual labour. Even today, digging the garden on a

Sunday afternoon is seen by some as a pleasurable contrast to a hard week sitting at a desk. This observation aside, what Lawson really seems to be commenting on is the satisfaction gained from creating order out of chaos: he mentions the delight of flowers 'comelily and orderly placed in your borders & squares'.[32]

This concern with orderliness is one which, we remember, was one of the major preoccupations of the age, reflected in gardens and garden-writing as well as anywhere else. It is reminiscent, for instance, of Parkinson's desire in *Paradisi in Sole* not only to divide 'beautiful flower plants' from the 'wilde and unfit' but also to rank them one against another:

> To satisfie therefore their desires that are lovers of such Delights, I took upon me this labour and charge, have selected and set forth a Garden of all the chiefest for choice, and fairest for shew, from among all the several Tribes and Kindreds of Natures beauty, and have ranked them as near as I could…in affinity to one another.[33]

What Parkinson was doing was much more than simply compiling a list of plant descriptions. He sought to distinguish the 'fit' from the 'unfit', to rank and order plants into a hierarchy according to their similarities and likenesses. In presenting readers with an ideal of an ordered and ranked garden, he was also presenting them with a perception, whether real or not, of an ordered, ranked and stable world.

This orderliness could be achieved through the art of gardening and it is difficult not to imagine that one of the roles of the gardener or the garden owner, in creating the garden itself, was to impose some order on unruly nature. In one small space that they could call their own, the gardener was in control, able to create an element of stability in an uncertain world. Oglander expressed this specifically when he wrote of his garden: 'Insomuch as of a rude Chaos I have now made it a ffitt place for any Gentleman'.[34]

So, after this long meander through the gardens of early modern England, what final conclusions can be drawn? Those in the higher echelons of society continued to enjoy their elaborate and extravagant showpiece gardens, just as they had always done; similarly, for those at the lower end of the social scale, their gardens remained as productive, utilitarian spaces to provide essential food and medicines for the household. However, for those who fell within the somewhat blurred boundaries of the gentry group, significant changes in the way they related to their gardens have been identified and demonstrated.

The main change, as exemplified by the work of John Parkinson, was the move from the utilitarian gardening of the sixteenth century to an increased interest in the ornamental pleasure garden. This has been amply demonstrated through detailed examination of the activities of the early modern gardener and garden owner, crucially linking them to corresponding changes that were happening in the society in which they lived. While, as has been shown, some aspects of gardens and gardening remained remarkably constant throughout the period, others did not. The opening years of the seventeenth century brought with them expanding horizons and new possibilities for the future. Inspired by foreign travel and influences, the expanding circulation of printed books and the ever-increasing availability of luxury goods, gentlemen, or those seeking to define themselves as such, sought new ways to assert and display their status. Filled with rare, exotic and expensive plants or embellished with statues, terraces and fountains, their gardens, like the houses to which they belonged, created a new arena in which to demonstrate the gentry's standing in society.

Through the evidence presented here, we have gained a rare and privileged glimpse into some of these gardens, enabling us to piece together a picture of what the early modern garden may have looked like and how it was used. What is more difficult to ascertain, though, from this disparate yet particular evidence is how typical these gardens were of the generality of early to mid-seventeenth-century gardens. Just because this extant evidence from a handful of gardens happens to be known to us, caution should be exercised in assuming that they are necessarily representative of the vast majority of gardens about which, of course, we know nothing at all.

What the study of these gardens clearly demonstrates, however, is a reflection of the personal tastes, experiences, interests, likes and dislikes of their owners. It has been seen, for example, that John Evelyn's garden reflected his travels in Holland and France and his well-documented interest in the new scientific methods, and that Sir Thomas Hanmer created his garden in order to display best the flowers that he loved and, although he was aware of costly embellishments, new fashions and elaborate designs, these were not his interest. Sir John Oglander indulged in expensive flowers and Sir Richard Leveson in an expensive remodelling, possibly inspired by other stylish gardens known to him. Sir Thomas Puckering built a new banqueting house, while Sir Thomas Temple preferred his old-fashioned parlour garden of sweet-smelling flowers.

Insights into these gardens have proved invaluable in enhancing our understanding of the early modern garden but, at the same time, it has been almost impossible to make generalisations about a typical garden of the time or to identify any unified style in English gardens of the period. As much as we would like to talk about Elizabethan, Renaissance, Jacobean or Caroline gardens, contemporary gardeners were clearly oblivious to these retrospective labels and simply acted according to their own inclinations. As Lawson observed: 'the form [of the garden] is so far neceesary as the owner shal think meet' and Parkinson agreed that 'everyman will please his owne fancie'.[35] This has been amply borne out in the gardens explored here which, as has been seen, were subject to enormous variations that were as much a result of individual taste and circumstance as of following any particular trend. It was only well into the eighteenth century that a truly 'English' style of gardening emerged, which became so widespread in its influence that it obliterated almost all evidence of everything that had gone before it.

This book set out to examine what early modern gardeners were doing in their gardens, attempting to understand their world from a contemporary point of view. Due perhaps to the essentially ephemeral nature of the activity of gardening, this important aspect of social and cultural life has thus far been largely neglected by historians. However, through close examination of a range of previously untapped primary sources, it has been possible to extend and challenge current knowledge of gardens across England and Wales during this period. While focussing on the gardens of the rural gentry, this analysis has at the same time sought to take the wider view, demonstrating and reflecting the concerns, anxieties, hopes and aspirations of people at the time, thereby contributing to a broader understanding of early modern society and its culture.

APPENDIX I

Bibliography of gardening literature published in English and significant related literature
c.1558–1660

Works are presented in chronological order and are all published in London unless otherwise stated. All details have been verified by the *English Short Title Catalogue* (ESTC), http://estc.bl.uk. FRBNF = Bibliothèque Nationale de France, Paris catalogue reference number, http://catalogue.bnf.fr.

Author	Title	Date	Reprints	Printer/Publisher	ESTC	Notes
Hyll, Thomas d. 1575?[1]	A most briefe and pleasaunte treatise, teachyng how to dresse, sowe, and set a garden	1558?		John Day	S92995	
			1563	Thomas Marshe	S115202	
Hyll, Thomas	The Proffitable Arte of Gardening, now the third tyme set fourth	1568		Thomas Marshe	S104094	Revised and enlarged version of the above publication. Seven editions.
			1572	Thomas Marshe	S104095	
			1574	Henrie Bynneman	S117236	
			1579	Henry Bynneman	S104101	
			1586	Robert Walde-grave	S120728	
			1593	Edward Allde	S104120	'third tyme set fourth' dropped from title.
			1608	Edward Allde [and H. Ballard]	S104123	'Proffitable' dropped from title.
Mascall, Leonard d. 1589	A Booke of the Arte and maner, howe to plant and graffe all sortes of trees	[1572]		Henrie Denham, for John Wight	S112379	Eight editions.
			1575	[Henry Denham and John Charlewood?], for John Wight	S112380	Reprinted anonymously as the first part of the *The Country-mans Recreation* in 1640 and 1654 and reprinted as *The country-mans new art of planting and graffing* in 1651, 1652 and 1656.
			1582	[John Kingston], for John Wight	S112419	
			1584	Henry Bynneman for John Wight	S1366	
			1590	T. Este, for Thomas Wight	S101426	
			1592	T. East, for Thomas Wight	S103380	
			1596	[Valentine Simmes]	S112422	
			1599	T. Este, for Thomas Wight	S2810	

1   The date of Hyll's death is unknown but F. R. Johnson, 'Thomas Hill: An Elizabethan Huxley', *HLQ*, 7:4 (August 1944), 338, surmised that it was 'not later than 1575'.

Author	Title	Date	Reprints	Printer/Publisher	ESTC	Notes
Scot, Reynolde d. 1599	*A Perfite Platforme of a Hoppe Garden*	1574	1576 1578	Henrie Denham Henrie Denham Henrie Denham	S103209 S116892 S116896	Three editions. Reprinted anonymously as the second part of the *The Country-mans Recreation* in 1640 and 1654.
Hyll, Thomas	*The Gardeners Labyrinth*	1577	1578 1586 1594 1608 1651 1652 1656 1660	Henry Bynneman Henry Bynneman John Wolfe Adam Islip Henry Ballard Jane Bell Jane Bell Jane Bell H[enry] Bell for Edward Brewster	S118782 S113279 S104113 S104115 S104118 R178161 R202411 R178162 R178163	Published after Hyll's death under the thinly disguised pseudonym of 'Dydymus Mountaine'. Nine editions.
Anon.	*A Short Instruction verie profitable and necessarie for all those that delight in gardening*	1592		John Wolfe	S2148	This book continued to be printed but always bound together with *The Orchard, and the Garden*.
Anon.	*The Orchard, and the Garden*	1594	1596 1597 1602	Adam Islip Adam Islip Adam Islip Adam Islip	S121003 S94531 S94532 S105739	Four editions (incorporating *A Short Instruction verie profitable and necessarie for all those that delight in gardening*). Reprinted as *The Expert Gardener* in 1640, and incorporated as the third part of *The Country-mans Recreation* in 1640 and 1654.

Author	Title	Date	Reprints	Printer/Publisher	ESTC	Notes
Gardner, Richard	*Profitable Instructions for the Manuring, Sowing, and Planting of Kitchin Gardens*	1599	1603	Edward Allde for Edward White Edward Allde for Edward White	S105694 S114902	Two editions.
Surflet, Richard d. 1606	*Maison Rustique, or The Countrie Farme*	1600	1606	Edm. Bollifant for Bonham Norton Arnold Hatfield for John Norton and John Bill	S101733	English translation of Charles Estienne's *L'agriculture et Maison Rustique*, reprinted numerous times in French between 1564 and 1689, q.v.
Plat, Hugh d. 1611?	*Floraes Paradise*	1608		H. L[ownes] for William Leake	S20798	Reprinted many years after Plat's death as *The Garden of Eden*, q.v. This book comprises a compilation of material ('secrets') gathered from many sources.
Markham, Gervase d. 1637	*The English Husbandman: The First Part*	1613		T[homas] S[nodham] for John Browne	S112063	'The Second Part of the First Booke' concerns the Art of Planting, grafting and gardening.
Markham, Gervase	*The Second Book of the English Husbandman*	1614	1615	T[homas] S[nodham] for John Browne T[homas] S[nodham] for John Browne	S112058 S112067	The Second Book concerns the ordering of the kitchen garden. The First and Second books were published together in 1635 as *The English Husbandman*; q.v.
Markham, Gervase	*Maison Rustique, or The Countrey Farme*	1616		Adam Islip for John Bill	S121357	A 'newly Reviewed' edition of Richard Surflet's translation of Estienne's *Maison Rustique*; q.v.

Author	Title	Date	Reprints	Printer/Publisher	ESTC	Notes
Lawson, William d. 1635	A New Orchard and Garden...with the Country Housewifes Garden	1618		Bar: Alsop for Roger Jackson	S106785	Thirteen editions, three printed after 1660 in 1665, 1676 and 1683.
			1623	I. H[aviland and G. Purslowe] for Roger Jackson	S108372	
			1626	I. H[aviland] for Francis Williams	S108391	Lawson's book was also incorporated in full in sixteen editions of Markham's A Way to get Wealth, published between 1623 and 1695.
			1631	Nicolas Okes for John Harison	S4739	
			1638	Edward [and Anne] Griffin for John Harison	S93434	
			1648	W. Wilson for John Harison	R25449	
			1653	W. Wilson for E. Brewster, and George Sawbridge	R23999	
			1656	W. Wilson for E. Brewster, [ditto]	R43360	
			1656	W. Wilson for E. Brewster, [ditto]	R43361	
			1660	W. Wilson for E. Brewster, [ditto]	R41543	
Anon.	Certaine excellent and new invented knots and mazes	1623		John Marriott	S108103	Illustrations of knots compiled from various sources. No text. Has been attributed to Gervase Markham but the printer's note signed 'I. M.' points to Marriott as the more likely compiler of this book.
Parkinson, John d. 1650	Paradisi in Sole, Paradisus Terrestris: or, A Garden of all Sorts of Pleasant Flowers	1629		Humphrey Lownes and Robert Young	S115360	Four editions. All identical apart from a new title page in the 1656 edition.
			1635	Tho. Cotes	S94613	
			1656	R. N.	R29251	
			1656	R. N.	R491318	

Author	Title	Date	Reprints	Printer/Publisher	ESTC	Notes
Markham, Gervase	*The English Husbandman*	1635	1635	[Augustine Mathewes and John Norton] for Henry Taunton [Augustine Mathewes and John Norton] for William Sheares	S112073 S112064	
Anon.	*The Expert Gardener*	1640		Richard Herne	S108876	Reprint of the anonymous *Orchard, and the Garden*.
Anon.	*The Country-mans Recreation*	1640		B. Alsop and T. Fawcet for Michael Young	S1108874	Anonymous reprint of Mascall's *Arte and maner*, Scot's *Perfite Platforme of a Hoppe Garden* and *The Expert Gardener*, q.v.
Plat, Hugh	*The Garden of Eden*	1653		William Leake	R181830	Revised and reprinted edition of *Floraes Paradise* (1608). Six further reprints and two revisions between 1653 and 1675.
Barker, Thomas fl. 1651	*The Country-mans Recreation*	1654		T. Mabb [and William Hunt] for William Shears	R207486	Barker seems to have appropriated the anonymous 1640 edition and added his own *The Arte of Angling*.
Bonnefons, Nicolas	*The French Gardiner*	1658	1658 1658	J[ames] C[otterell] for John Crooke J. C. for John Crooke for John Crooke	R170703 R28517 R209902	Seven editions, four printed after 1660 in 1669, 1672, 1675 and 1691. Translated into English by John Evelyn.
Hanmer, Thomas d. 1678	'The Garden Book'	1659		Unpublished manuscript		Hanmer never gave his book a title; it only became known as *The Garden Book* when the manuscript was finally published in 1933.
Evelyn, John d. 1706	'Elysium Britannicum'	c.1659		Unpublished manuscript		Eventually published in 2000, edited by John E. Ingram.

SIGNIFICANT RELATED LITERATURE

Author	Title	Date	Printer/Publisher	ESTC	Notes
Fitzherbert, John	The Boke of Husbandry	1534	Thomas Berthelet	S4300	First published in 1523 as A newe tracte or treatyse moost profytable for all Husbandemen. First book on husbandry in English.
Estienne, Charles	L'agriculture et Maison Rustique	1564	Paris: J. Du Puis	FRBNF 30407827	Revised and republished many times by his son-in-law Jean Liebault. Translated into English by Richard Surflet in 1600; q.v.
Tusser, Thomas	A hundreth good pointes of husbandrie	1557	Richard Totell, four editions	S101790	
Tusser, Thomas	Five hundred good points of husbandry	1573	Richard Totell, twenty editions before 1660	S118708	Husbandry – contains short section on gardening, directed at the housewife.
Heresbach, Conrad	Foure Bookes of Husbandry, Newly Englished and increased by Barnabe Googe	1577	Richard Watkins, seven editions	S103974	Husbandry – contains short section on gardening, directed at the housewife.
Lyte, Henry	A New Herbal of History of Plants	1578	Antwerp: Henry Loë, five editions	S126799	Herbal.
Gerard, John	The Herball, or Gererall Historie of Plantes	1597	Edm. Bollifont for [Bonham Norton and] John Norton	S122353	Herbal. Revised and reprinted by Thomas Johnson in 1633 and 1636.
Markham, Gervase	Cheape and Good husbandry	1614 1616	T. S. [nodham] for Roger Jackson	not listed S102892	The ESTC entry for this book only lists the 1616 edition, but notes that this is 'Another, enlarged edition of STC17336, pub. in 1614'. Numerous further editions were produced throughout the rest of the seventeenth century.

Author	Title	Date	Printer/Publisher	ESTC	Notes
Markham, Gervase	The English Huswife	1615	J[ohn] B[eale] for R. Jackson	S112047	Contains short section on gardening. First published as Book 2 of Countrey Contentments, then reprinted in various other publications, esp. The Way to Get Wealth.
Markham, Gervase	A Way to Get Wealth	1623	Roger Jackson, sixteen editions	S94121	Incorporating Lawson's A New Orchard and Garden.
Wotton, Henry	'Elements of Architecture'	1624	John Bill	S120324	Includes a chapter on gardens.
Bacon, Francis	'Of Gardens' from The Essayes or Counsels, civill and morall, of Francis Lo. Verulam, Viscount St. Alban	1625	John Haviland for Hanna Barret and Richard Whitaker	S124226	Essay on gardens. Forty-sixth essay in the collection.
Parkinson, John	Theatrum Botanicum: The Theater of Plants	1640	T. Cotes	S121875	Herbal.
Austen, Ralph	A Treatise of Fruit-trees	1653	Oxford: Leonard Lichfield for Tho: Robinson, two editions	R12161	Agricultural 'improvement' literature.
Hartlib, Samuel	His Legacie: A Discourse of Husbandry	1651	H. Hills for Richard Woodnothe	R202377	Collection of letters to Hartlib. Two further editions enlarged and reprinted in 1652 and 1655.
Mollet, André	Le Jardin de Plaisir	1651	Stockholm: H. Kayser		In French.
		1670	London: Thomas Newcomb for John Martyn	R7156	Translated into English by Mollet and published as The Garden of Pleasure.
Coles, William	The Art of Simpling	1656	J. G. for Nath: Brooke, two editions	R209440	Herbal.
Coles, William	Adam in Eden	1657	J. Steater for Nathaniel Brooke	R8275	Herbal.
Beale, John	Herefordshire Orchards: A Pattern for all England	1657	Roger Daniel	R4687	Agricultural 'improvement' literature.

APPENDIX 2

Transcript of Sir Thomas Hanmer's essay on gardening
National Library of Wales, Bettisfield MSS 1667

This document forms part of a bundle of unbound manuscripts held as part of the Bettisfield archive at the National Library of Wales in Aberystwyth. It is undated but, for the reasons discussed in Chapter 1, it is reasonable to assume that it was written around the same time as Hanmer was compiling his garden book in the 1650s. The manuscript is full of alterations, deletions and insertions and in places is extremely difficult to decipher. In 1876, a descendant of Sir Thomas Hanmer, John Lord Hanmer, transcribed this document, which was subsequently published in his book *A Memorial of the Parish and Family of Hanmer*.[1] This transcript is neither complete nor particularly accurate, John Hanmer simply leaving out the parts he could not read or adding his own interpretation. Nevertheless, his transcript was printed verbatim in the introduction to *The Garden Book of Sir Thomas Hanmer*, when the manuscript version of Sir Thomas's book was eventually published in 1933. This inaccurate transcript has inevitably been used and quoted ever since. Some of the shortcomings of John Hanmer's transcript have been noted by Ruth Duthie in an article of 1990, where an accurate transcription of a part of the manuscript has been reproduced.[2] What follows is the complete document, transcribed from Thomas Hanmer's original manuscript held in the Bettisfield archive. It offers a rare insight into contemporary gardening practice in England and in France, both within Hanmer's own experience, with his observations on how things had changed in recent years.

1 John Hanmer, *A Memorial of the Parish and Family of Hanmer in Flintshire* (London, 1877), pp. 95–8.
2 Ruth Duthie, 'The Planting Plans of Some Seventeenth-Century Flower Gardens', *GH*, 18:2 (1990), 83–8.

As soone as Peace hath introduc'd Plenty and Wealth into a Countrey, men quickly apply themselves to pleasures and by degrees indeavour to improve them to the height. Amongst the innocent ones, persons of quality and ingenuity have in all ages delighted themselves with beautifull Gardens, whose cheifest ornaments are choice Flowers, Trees and Plants. After which rarityes the French and Dutch have <del>/for some years past\[3] beene most diligent enquirers and collectors of as the Italians, and Germans before them, and <del> since our late Warr, many of this Nation.

The Rich amongst us are not now satisfied with good houses, Parkes, handsome avenues and issues <del>/to and from\ their dwellings, their ambition and curiosity extends /also\ to very costly embelishments of their Gardens Orchards and Walkes and some spare no <cost>/charge amongst other things\[4] in procuring the rarest flowers and plants to <del> /set them forth\ withall. Yet though this <del>/way of beautifying and divertisment\ comes apace into fashion, few know either how to choose well their materialls of this kind or to order and dispose of them and soe are at much charge in vaine [,] their gardiners being also for the most part very inexpert and dull. To remedy this in some measure this ensuing CATALOGUE[5] of choice plants (yet such as will beare our Climate) is exhibited to the publicke, with short directions for their preservation and encrease, not medling with their medicinall qualityes whereof soe many volumes have beene written. The tract is as little as may bee, the entention being only for a <del> tempory helpe to the Lovers of this <del> /way of delight\ foreseeing that <del> some perfecter thinges will come forth of this subject.

The method observed <del> /herein\ is First to treat of the best FLOWERS of all seasons /though to have some in all seasons //especially Annuals\\ some common ones must cover us. \[6] Then of such SHRUBS and TREES /whose leaves fall of yearly\ and may bee admitted into GARDENS and thirdly of <del> GREENES which are such plants whose VERDURE is PERPETUALL being never wholy uncloath'd of their sweet or beautifull leaves and therfore much esteem'd by us. What descriptions soever are given of <del> any of these, or directions concerning them are certainly agreable to truth and good iterated experiments[,] all fabulous secretts /for altering colors or other strange improvements in [three illegible words]\[7] which bookes and some mouths ar stuff withall

---

3   Sir Thomas Hanmer has deleted a word or phrase completely, inserting his correction above.

4   In this case the deletion is still legible, the correction inserted above.

5   Hanmer's use of capital letters is retained throughout.

6   This long phrase is squeezed in above another line, making both difficult to read.

7   Again, this long insertion between two lines is extremely difficult to read.

and whereby many are deluded to make tedious and costly trialls in vaine, being purposely omitted. To the maine,[8] thus much more is not unfitt to bee premised, that not only the whole designes or laying out of our garden grounds are much different from what our fathers used but the inward parts or workes also. The knotts <del>/or\ quarters are not hedgd about with privet, rosemary or other <del>/tall\ hearbes which <del> hide the prospect of the worke, and <del>/nourish\ hurtfull wormes and flyes, nor our standard fruit trees sufferd to grow soe high or thicke as to shadow our wyndowes, or cumber <del>and barren the soyle; but all is now commonly neere the house <del> layd <del> open and exposd to the view of the chambers, and the knotts and borders <del> /upheld\ only with very low colourd boards, stone or tile. <del>.[9] If the ground bee spatious, the /next\ adjacent quarters or PARTERRES as the french call them, are often of fine turfe, kept as low as any greene to bowle on, cut out curiously into EMBROIDERY of flowers, beasts birds or feuillages and the small alleys and intervalls filld with severall colord sands and dust with much art, with /but\ few flowers <del> in such knotts and those such as grow very low <del>for spoiling>[10] /least they debase\ the beauty of the embroidery from the eye. Most remote from the habitation are COMPARTIMENTS as they call them, which are knotts also <del> /and\ borders destind for flowers, yet sometimes entermixt with grasseworke, and on the outsides beautified with gilt flowers, potts on pedestells and /very\ dwarfe cypresses, firrs or other greenes which will endure the wynters cold / kept\ clipt in pyramides, globes or other figures <del> /placd\ discreetly and uniformly at reasonable distances from each other, and in these great growndes, beyond these compartments are either labyrinthes with hedges kept cut to a mans height or thicketts for birds <del> /cut through with severall straight or winding\ gravelly walkes, or <del> / you have\ variety of alleyes set with high trees as elms, limes, abells,[11] firrs, pines or <del> others, with Fountaines, /canalls, grottoes,\ statues, arbours, cabinettes /and allyes\ and seats different as the designe and nature of the place will admitt. These large grounds are commonly a third part longer than broad and cannot well bee lesse then two or three hundred yards in length, But it suffices most gentlemen to have only a <plott> square or oblong plott of fifty or three score yards with two or fower knotts of embroidery or

---

8   The whole of this paragraph up to this point was omitted by John Hanmer and has never appeared in ensuing reproductions.

9   A whole sentence is deleted.

10 These two words were not actually deleted by Hanmer but it is clear that this was his intention as indicated by the insertion above.

11 Abells are poplars: Duthie, 'Planting Plans', p. 84.

compartiments and handsome gravelle walkes of <five or> about five yards broad. <del> All florists have (besides their publicke grounds, wherein all people of quality are admitted to walke) a little private SEMINARY or piece to sow and raise plants and trees in, and keepe such treasures as are not to bee exposd to everyones view and [illegible word] adjoining to which they have a wynter house for shelter of tender plants in cold weather of which more hereafter.

ABBREVIATIONS

Bacon, 'Of Gardens'   Francis Bacon, 'Of Gardens' (1625), in *The Genius of the Place: The English Landscape Garden 1620–1820*, ed. John Dixon Hunt and Peter Willis (London: Paul Elek, 1975; repr. London: MIT Press, 1988), pp. 51–6

Bettisfield   Aberystwyth, National Library of Wales, Bettisfield Estate Records

BL   British Library, London

Diary   *The Diary of John Evelyn*, ed. E. S. de Beer, 6 vols (Oxford: Clarendon Press, 1955)

Evelyn, Add.   London, British Library, Evelyn Papers, Additional Manuscripts

Evelyn, *Elysium Britannicum*   John Evelyn, *Elysium Britannicum, or the Royal Gardens in Three Books*, ed. John E. Ingram (Philadelphia: University of Pennsylvania Press, 2000)

GH   *Garden History* (journal of the Garden History Society, now The Gardens Trust)

Gerard, *Herball*   John Gerard, *The Herball, or General Historie of Plantes* (London, 1597)

Hanmer, *Garden Book*   Thomas Hanmer, *The Garden Book of Sir Thomas Hanmer*, 'Now first printed from the MS volume of 1659 under the care of Ivy Elstob', intro. Eleanour Sinclair Rohde (London: Gerald Howe, 1933; repr. Mold: Clwyd County Council Library and Information Services, 1991)

HMC, *De L'Isle MSS*	Historical Manuscripts Commission, *Report on the MSS of Lord De L'Isle and Dudley at Penshurst Place*, 6 vols (London: Her Majesty's Stationery Office, 1925–66)
IOWRO, OG/AA/	Isle of Wight Records Office, Newport, Oglander Commonplace Books
Johnson, *Gerard's Herball*	*The Herball, or Generall Historie of Plantes*, ed. Thomas Johnson (London, 1633; 1636)
Lawson, *New Orchard and Garden*	William Lawson, *A New Orchard and Garden … with the Country Housewifes Garden* (London, 1618; facsimile edn, intro. Malcolm Thick, Totnes: Prospect Books, 2003)
LMA	London Metropolitan Archive
Markham, *English Husbandman*	Gervase Markham, *The English Husbandman: The First Part* (London, 1613)
O'Malley and Wolschke-Bulmahn	*John Evelyn's 'Elysium Britannicum' and European Gardening*, ed. Therese O'Malley and Joachim Wolschke-Bulmahn (Washington, DC: Dumbarton Oaks Research Library and Collection, 1998)
OED	Oxford English Dictionary, www.oed.com
ODNB	*Oxford Dictionary of National Biography*, www.oxforddnb.com
Parkinson, *Paradisi*	John Parkinson, *Paradisi in Sole, Paradisus Terrestris: or, A Garden of all Sorts of Pleasant Flowers* (London, 1629; facsimile edn, New York: Dover, 1976)
Pelham, Add.	London, British Library, Pelham Papers, Additional Manuscripts
SRO	Staffordshire Records Office, Stafford, Sutherland Collection
SBTRO	Shakespeare Birthplace Trust Records Office, Stratford-upon-Avon
Temple MSS	California, San Marino, Huntington Library, Stowe Archive, Temple Family Papers
WYAS	West Yorkshire Archive Service, Leeds

NOTES

INTRODUCTION

1 Parkinson, *Paradisi*, p. 3.

2 John N. D. Riddell, 'John Parkinson's Long Acre Garden 1600–1650', *GH*, 6:2 (1986), 112–24.

3 Parkinson, *Paradisi*, pp. 392, 388; R. T. Gunther, *Early British Botanists and their Gardens* (Oxford, 1922), p. 16; Gerard, *Herball*, e.g. p. 717; Riddell, 'John Parkinson's Long Acre Garden', p. 112; John Parkinson, *Theatrum Botanicum: The Theater of Plants* (London, 1640), Dedication.

4 Parkinson, *Paradisi*, p. 320.

5 Ibid., pp. 463, 7.

6 Ibid., pp. 8, 571.

7 Ibid., p. 24.

8 Ibid., p. 1.

9 One notable exception is the recent work of C. Paul Christianson, *The Riverside Gardens of Thomas More's London* (New Haven and London, 2005), which examines in detail the practicalities of gardening in the early sixteenth century. Also David Jacques, *Gardens of Court and Country: English Design, 1630–1730* (London, 2017) examines garden-making during this period, but unfortunately was published too recently to be taken into consideration here.

10 Parkinson, *Paradisi*, pp. 3, 1.

11 Thomas Hyll, *The Gardeners Labyrinth* (London, 1577), p. 2.

12 *The Holy Bible*, King James Version (1611), Genesis 2.15, 3.23.

13 Frank Crisp, *Mediaeval Gardens*, 2 vols (London, 1924), vol. 1, p. 2.

14 Gilles Clément cited in Danielle Dagenais, 'The Garden of Movement: Ecological Rhetoric in Support of Gardening Practice', *Studies in the History of Gardens & Designed Landscapes: An International Quarterly*, 4:4 (2004), 323. For more on this garden, see also Bernard St-Denis, 'Just what is a Garden?', *Studies in the History of Gardens & Designed Landscapes*, 27:1 (2007), 61–76.

15 Ralph Austen, *A Treatise of Fruit-trees* (Oxford, 1653), The Epistle Dedicatory.

16 Lawson, *New Orchard and Garden*, pp. 11–12. Unlike Parkinson, Lawson's main concern appears to be to prevent the fruit being stolen, as the neighbours may 'prove theeves'.

17 Ibid., p. 10.

18 The *OED* concurs, defining a garden as 'an enclosed piece of ground devoted to the cultivation of flowers, fruits or vegetables' and an orchard as 'Originally: a garden (freq. Enclosed), esp. for herbs and fruit trees. Now: an area of land, freq. enclosed, given over to the cultivation of fruit trees' and originating from the Latin *hortus*, meaning garden – ortus/ort + yard.

19 William Harrison, *The Description of England* (1587), ed. Georges Edelen (Washington, DC, and New York, 1994), p. 264.

20   The somewhat elusive role of women in the garden is discussed in Ch. 5.

21   Lyveden New Bield garden is currently owned by the National Trust and is discussed in more detail in Chs 3, 8 and 11.

22   These gardens will be discussed later in the text. For those interested in visiting these gardens where possible, the Parks and Gardens database is now available online, offering a comprehensive overview of historic gardens in the UK, including details of both those that are open to public and those that are not: www.parksand-gardens.org.

23   See e.g. Roy Strong, *The Renaissance Garden in England* (London, 1979); Paula Henderson, *The Tudor House and Garden* (New Haven and London, 2005). However, Strong is at pains to point out that his concern is solely with the gardens of the elite and Henderson widens her remit somewhat to include gardens of the lesser aristocracy.

24   *Aubrey's Natural History of Wiltshire*, intro. K. G. Ponting (Newton Abbot: David and Charles Reprints, 1969), p. 93.

25   Daniel Defoe, *A Tour Thro' the Whole Island of Great Britain* (1721–26), cited in David Jacques, 'Who knows what a Dutch Garden is?', *GH*, 30:2 (Winter 2002), 117.

26   David Marsh, 'The Gardens and Gardeners of Later Stuart London' (PhD thesis, University of London, 2004), p. 507.

27   These arguments were also rehearsed, in relation to the study of eighteenth-century landscapes, by Edward Harwood and Tom Williamson in their contributions to a paper delivered at the Society of Architectural Historians of Great Britain in 2006: Edward Harwood, Tom Williamson, Michael Leslie and John Dixon Hunt, 'Whither Garden History?', *Studies in the History of Gardens & Designed Landscapes*, 27:2 (2007), 91–112, esp. pp. 92, 97. I hope this book goes some way to address the many important issues raised in that paper.

28   SRO, D593/R/1/2. This garden is discussed in detail in Ch. 8.

29   Brent Elliot, 'Historical Revivalism in the Twentieth Century: A Brief Introduction', *GH*, 28:1 (Summer 2000), 29.

30   Influential examples included *Rei Rusticae Scriptores*, a compilation of writings on agriculture by Cato, Varro, Columella and Palladius, first published in Venice in 1470 and proving so popular that seventeen new editions had appeared by 1521. Equally popular was Xenophon's *Oeconomicus, or Of Household*: five editions were published in Latin translation between 1508 and 1526, before being translated into English six years later: Joan Thirsk, 'Making a Fresh Start: Sixteenth-Century Agriculture and the Classical Inspiration', in *Culture and Cultivation in Early Modern England*, ed. Michael Leslie and Timothy Raylor (Leicester, 1992), pp. 18–19.

31   Anna Parkinson, *Nature's Alchemist: John Parkinson, Herbalist to Charles I* (London, 2007), p. 288.

32   Thomas Hyll, *The Profitable Art of Gardening, now the third tyme set forth* (London, 4th edn, 1579), sig. Ci; Reynolde Scot, *A Perfite Platforme of a Hoppe Garden* (London, 1574), p. 50; Markham, *English Husbandman*, sig. A3v.

33   Parkinson, *Paradisi*, p. 3.

34   E.g., Lawson's *New Orchard and Garden* and Markham's *English Husbandman* are analysed in Judith Roberts, 'The Gardens of the Gentry in the Late Tudor Period', *GH*, 27:1 (1999), 89–108; Jennifer Munroe, *Gender and the Garden in Early Modern English Literature* (Aldershot, 2008), esp. ch. 1, examines these garden manuals to discuss gender and class in the early modern garden.

35   This argument also applies to other didactic manuals, e.g., Anna Bryson, *From Courtesy to Civility: Changing Codes of Conduct in Early Modern England* (Oxford, 1998), p. 6.

36   Parkinson, *Paradisi*, p. 307.

37   See e.g. Gerard, *Herball*, pp. 764–72.

38   Thomas Smith, *De Republica Anglorum* (London, 1583), p. 20; Harrison, *Description of England*, p. 94. For a full discussion on definitions of the gentry, see Felicity Heal and Clive Holmes, *The Gentry in England and Wales, 1500–1700* (Basingstoke, 1994), pp. 6–19.

39   Heal and Holmes, *Gentry in England and Wales*, p. 9. Sir Thomas Temple, under James I, acquired the titles of knight in 1603 and baronet in 1611. Edwin F. Gay, 'The Rise of an English Country Family: Peter and John Temple, to 1603', *Huntington Library Quarterly*, 1:4 (1938), 368, 390, cites the rise of the Temple family from tenant sheep-farmers to English landed gentry in the sixteenth century as an example of Tudor social mobility when 'new men broke through the stratifications of the existing order'. Much the same kind of story can be told for the

other gentlemen knights who appear in this book. Lawson has been identified as the vicar of the Yorkshire parish of Ormesby, a man of some learning and considerable land-holding: Lawson, *New Orchard and Garden*, intro. Malcolm Thick, p. 9.

40   E.g. Jan Woudstra and Sally O'Halloran, 'Sir John Reresby's Garden Notebook and Garden (1633–44) at Thrybergh, Yorkshire', *GH*, 36:1 (2008), 135–93; John Phillips and Nicholas Burnett, 'The Chronology and Layout of Francis Carew's Garden at Beddington, Surrey', *GH*, 33:2 (2005), 155–88.

41   IOWRO, The Oglander Collection; Temple MSS.

42   Pelham, Add.; SRO, D593/R/1/2; Mark Merry and Catherine Richardson, eds, *The Household Account Book of Sir Thomas Puckering of Warwick, 1620* (Stratford upon Avon, 2012); Lloyd Bowen, ed., *Family and Society in Early Stuart Glamorgan: The Household Accounts of Sir Thomas Aubrey of Llantrithyd, c.1565–1641* (Cardiff, 2006).

43   Evelyn, Add., esp. Add. 78610A–S.

44   Hanmer, *Garden Book*; Bettisfield, 1663, 1666, 1667.

45   HMC, *De L'Isle MSS*, vol. 3, Lord Sidney to Thomas Golding, 3 April 1605.

1   THE 'ARTE OF GARDENING'

1   Thomas Hyll, *The Proffitable Arte of Gardening now the third tyme set fourth* (London, 1568; rev. edn of *A briefe and pleasaunte treatise*, with new title), Preface to the Reader.

2   Reynolde Scot, *A Perfite Platforme of a Hoppe Garden* (London, 1574), sigs Bii, Biiv.

3   Hyll, *Profitable Art of Gardening* (1579 edn), sig. Aii, Dedication to Sir Henrie Seamer.

4   Julia Crick and Alexandra Walsham, *The Uses of Script and Print, 1300–1700* (Cambridge, 2004), pp. 6–7.

5   Natasha Glaisyer and Sara Pennell, eds, *Didactic Literature in England 1500–1800* (Aldershot, 2003), p. 4; Rebecca Bushnell, 'The Gardener and the Book', in ibid., p. 124.

6   Lynette Hunter, 'Books for Daily Life: Household, Husbandry, Behaviour', in *The Cambridge History of the Book in Britain*, vol. 4: *1567–1695*, ed. John Barnard and D. F. McKenzie (Cambridge, 2002), pp. 514–16.

7   Lawson, *New Orchard and Garden*, pp. 1–2.

8   For more on 'the middling sort', see Jonathan Barry and Christopher Brooks, eds, *The Middling Sort of People: Culture, Society and Politics in England, 1550–1800* (Basingstoke, 1994).

9   Leonard Mascall, *A Booke of the Arte and maner, howe to plant and graffe all sortes of trees* (London, 1572), sig. Av (hereafter, *Arte and maner*); Scot, *Perfite Platforme*, sigs Biiv, Biiiv.

10   Markham, *English Husbandman*; Lawson, *New Orchard and Garden*; *A Short Instruction verie profitable and necessarie for all those that delight in gardening* (London, 1592).

11   Richard Gardner, *Profitable Instructions for the Manuring, Sowing, and Planting of Kitchin Gardens* (London, 1599).

12   F. R. Johnson, 'Notes on English Retail Book Prices', *The Library*, ser. 5, 5 (1950), 104, 93.

13   See Ch. 5 for more on wages.

14   Gervase Markham, *The English Husbandman* (London, 1635), pp. 8–9.

15   Keith Thomas, 'The Meaning of Literacy in Early Modern England', in *The Written Word: Literacy in Transition*, ed. Gerd Baumann (Oxford, 1986), p. 99; Tessa Watt, *Cheap Print and Popular Piety* (Cambridge, 1991), p. 7.

16   William Sherman, *Used Books: Marking Readers in Renaissance England* (Philadelphia, 2008), p. xv; Thomas, 'Meaning of Literacy', p. 101.

17   John Heminge and Henrie Condell, 'To the great Variety of Readers', front matter to *The First Folio of Shakespeare* (London, 1623).

18   For more on literacy see David Cressy, *Literacy and the Social Order: Reading and Writing in Tudor and Stuart England* (Cambridge, 1980); Thomas, 'Meaning of Literacy'; Watt, *Cheap Print*.

19   Stephen Orgel, *The Reader in the Book: A Study of Spaces and Traces* (Oxford, 2015), p. 10; Heidi Brayman Hackel, *Reading Material in Early Modern England: Print, Gender, and Literacy* (Cambridge, 2005), p. 30.

20   Glaisyer and Pennell, *Didactic Literature*, p. 8.

21   Scot, *Perfite Platforme*, sig. Biiv; Mascall, *Arte and maner*, sig. Av.

22   Lawson, *New Orchard and Garden*, sig. A3v.

23   Watt, *Cheap Print*, p. 8.

24 Orgel, *Reader in the Book*, pp. 11–14.

25 Ibid., Sherman, *Used Books*.

26 Henry Peacham, *The Compleat Gentleman: fashioning him absolut* (London, 1622; facsimile edn, New York, 1968), p. 54.

27 Sherman, *Used Books*, p. 4.

28 Anna Parkinson, *Nature's Alchemist: John Parkinson, Herbalist to Charles I* (London, 2007), p. 271; Johnson, 'Notes on English Retail Book Prices', p. 102.

29 John Parkinson, *Paradisi in Sole*, Bodleian Library, Oxford, Antiq.c.E.1629; Jan Woudstra and Sally O'Halloran, 'Sir John Reresby's Garden Notebook and Garden (1633–44) at Thrybergh, Yorkshire', *GH*, 36:1 (2008), 135–93; Hanmer, *Garden Book*, p. 32.

30 John Parkinson, *Paradisi in Sole*, BL, Eve.b.49; Linda Peck, *Consuming Splendor* (Cambridge, 2005), p. 226; Caroline Spearing, 'Abraham Cowley's *Plantarum Libri Sex, 1662*', London Renaissance Seminar, 9 January 2016.

31 Parkinson, *Paradisi*, Epistle to the Reader.

32 Copies of original editions of these books are held in the Royal Horticultural Society Lindley Library, London, and the British Library, London.

33 Mascall, *Arte and maner*, sig. Aiiiiv; Blanche Henrey, *British Botanical and Horticultural Literature before 1800*, 3 vols (Oxford, 1975), vol. 1, pp. 63–4.

34 Hyll, *Profitable Art of Gardening* (1579), sig. Aaiii.

35 Thirty-eight titles, including reprints and editions, are listed on http://estc.bl.uk, the *English Short Title Catalogue*, as 'gathered' and 'Englished' by Hyll. For a short biography of his life with a bibliography of his known works, see F. R. Johnson, 'Thomas Hill: An Elizabethan Huxley', *Huntington Library Quarterly*, 7:4 (1944), 329–51.

36 Paula Findlen, 'Francis Bacon and the Reform of Natural History in the Seventeenth Century', in *History and the Disciplines*, ed. Donald Kelley (Woodbridge, 1997), pp. 239–60.

37 Deborah Harkness, *The Jewel House: Elizabethan London and the Scientific Revolution* (New Haven and London, 2007), p. 2.

38 Hyll, *Profitable Art of Gardening*, sig. Aaiii.

39 Markham, *English Husbandman*, sig. A.

40 Ibid., title page.

41 Markham, *Countrey Farme*, p. 156.

42 Joan Thirsk, 'Making a Fresh Start: Sixteenth Century Agriculture and the Classical Inspiration', in *Culture and Cultivation in Early Modern England: Writing and the Land*, ed. Michael Leslie and Timothy Raylor (Leicester, 1992), p. 27.

43 Lawson, *New Orchard and Garden*, dedication.

44 Ibid., introduction, p. 9.

45 Ibid., preface.

46 Ibid., p. 3.

47 Ibid., pp. 22–3.

48 Parkinson, *Paradisi*, p. 8.

49 Ibid., p. 22.

50 Whereas, as has been established, the practice of publishing other people's work was widely accepted, in the case of the *Herball*, Gerard committed the error of not acknowledging his source and passing the work off as his own. For more on the scandal surrounding this publication, see Marcus Woodward, *Gerard's Herball: The Essence thereof distilled* (London, 1971), pp. xv–xvii; also Harkness, *Jewel House*, pp. 15–18.

51 John Parkinson, *Theatrum Botanicum: The Theater of Plants* (London, 1640), p. 1108.

52 Parkinson, *Paradisi*, p. 24.

53 See Hunter, 'Books for Daily Life'.

54 John Rea, *Flora: De Florum Cultura, or A Complete Florilege* (London, 1665).

55 Bushnell, 'Gardener and the Book', p. 128.

56 Hanmer, *Garden Book*, 'A note on the text', p. xxxi.

57 Harold Love, *Scribal Publication in the Seventeenth Century* (Oxford, 1993); Peter Beal, *In Praise of Scribes: Manuscripts and their Makers in Seventeenth-Century England* (Oxford: Oxford University Press, 1998); Crick and Walsham, *Uses of Script*.

58 Love, *Scribal Publication*, p. 35; Crick and Walsham, *Uses of Script*, pp. 6–9; Hackel, *Reading Material*, p. 28.

59 Bettisfield, 1667; 21753B; see Ruth Duthie, 'The Planting Plans of Some Seventeenth-Century Flower Gardens', *GH*, 18:2 (1990), 101 n. 8 on the disappearance of this third manuscript. My own research would agree with her conclusion.

60 Hanmer, *Garden Book*, p. v.

61 Ibid., p. xxxi.

62 See e.g. Duthie, 'Planting Plans', p. 83; Hanmer, *Garden Book*, 'A note on the text', p. xxxi; Bettisfield, 1667. See Appendix 2 for full transcript of this essay.

63 Evelyn, Add. 78298.

64 Sir Thomas Hanmer, letter to John Evelyn, 1668, cited in Jenny Robinson, 'New Light on Sir Thomas Hanmer', *GH*, 16:1 (1988), 6.

65 Elstob, though (Hanmer, *Garden Book*, p. xxxii), states that the MS. she was looking at was 'scrawled' with corrections and insertions – more evidence, perhaps, that this was a third copy of the manuscript.

66 Nicolas Bonnefons, *The French Gardiner*, trans. John Evelyn (London, 1658).

67 The most recent and authoritative debate was the Dumbarton Oaks Colloquium on the History of Landscape Architecture, 1993, 'John Evelyn's *Elysium Britannicum* and European Gardening': see Therese O'Malley and Joachim Wolschke-Bulmahn.

68 John E. Ingram, 'John Evelyn's *Elysium Britannicum*: Provenance, Condition, Transcription', in ibid., p. 36.

69 Bonnefons, *French Gardiner*, sig. A2v.

70 Nathaniel Johnson cited in Michael Hunter, 'John Evelyn in the 1650s: A Virtuoso in Quest of a Role', in O'Malley and Wolschke-Bulmahn, p. 103.

71 John Dixon Hunt, 'Evelyn's Idea of a Garden: A Theory for all Seasons' in ibid., p. 270.

72 Evelyn, *Elysium Britannicum*, p. 5.

2 'PROFITS AND PLEASURES'

1 Thomas Hyll, *The Profitable Art of Gardening* (London, 1579), sig. Ci; Markham, *English Husbandman*, p. 33; Leonard Mascall, *Arte and maner*, sig. Aiv.

2 Ralph Austen, *A Treatise of Fruit-trees* (Oxford, 1653), 'To the Reader' [p. 3].

3 Ibid., p. 41.

4 Parkinson, *Paradisi*, title page.

5 Ibid., Epistle to the Reader.

6 Ibid., p. 461.

7 Lawson, *New Orchard and Garden*, p. 1.

8 Reynolde Scot, *A Perfite Platforme of a Hoppe Garden* (London, 1574), 'To the Reader'.

9 John Morrill, ed., *The Oxford Illustrated History of Tudor and Stuart Britain* (Oxford, 1996), pp. 174, 196; Keith Thomas, *The Ends of Life: Roads to Fulfilment in Early Modern England* (Oxford, 2009), pp. 15–20.

10 Quentin Skinner, *Visions of Politics*, 2 vols (Cambridge: Cambridge University Press, 2002), vol. 2, pp.

224–44; Margo Todd, *Christian Humanism and the Puritan Social Order* (Cambridge: Cambridge University Press, 1987), pp. 124–30.

11 Mascall, *Arte and maner*, sig. Aiv.

12 Ibid., sigs Aiiiiv, Bi.

13 Markham, *English Husbandman*, Epistle to the Reader.

14 Ibid., sig. A2.

15 Ibid., sig. A3. Although husbandry clearly covers a much wider range of activity than gardening, Markham includes the work of the gardener within the role of the husbandman.

16 Ibid., sig. A3v.

17 David Pennington, 'Beyond the Moral Economy: Economic Change, Ideology and the 1621 House of Commons', *Parliamentary History*, 25:2 (2006), 214–31; Paul Slack, *The Invention of Improvement: Information and Material Progress in Seventeenth-Century England* (Oxford, 2014), p. 5. By the end of the seventeenth century, England had become twice as rich as it had been at the beginning and per capita income had also significantly increased: Slack, *Invention of Improvement*, p. 14.

18 Thomas, *Ends of Life*, p. 29.

19 Sir Thomas Wilson, *The State of England* (1600), in *The Camden Society*, ser. 3, 52, Miscellany vol. 16, ed. F. J. Fisher (London, 1936), p. 18.

20 *The Orchard, and the Garden* (London, 1597), pp. 20–21.

21 Lawson, *New Orchard and Garden*, p. 52.

22 Ibid., p. 53.

23 Mascall, *Arte and maner*, sig. Aii.

24 Lawson, *New Orchard and Garden*, p. 53.

25 E.g., Columella, the Roman agricultural writer, was eloquent in his praise of the country life, setting it in stark contrast to what he considered to be a contemptible life spent seeking preferment at 'court': Joan Thirsk, 'Making a Fresh Start: Sixteenth-Century Agriculture and the Classical Inspiration', in *Culture and Cultivation in Early Modern England: Writing and the Land*, ed. Michael Leslie and Timothy Raylor (Leicester, 1992), p. 21. Even today, a wholesome country life is set in favourable contrast to the materialism of the city.

26 Richard Cust and Ann Hughes, eds, *Conflict in Early Stuart England: Studies in Religion and Politics, 1603–1642* (Harlow, 1989), p. 20.

27   Lawson, *New Orchard and Garden*, p. 53.

28   Linda Peck, *Consuming Splendor* (Cambridge, 2005), pp. 2–8; Thomas, *Ends of Life*, pp. 132–42. See also Lisa Jardine, *Worldly Goods: A New History of the Renaissance* (London: Macmillan, 1996); Keith Wrightson, *Earthly Necessities: Economic Lives in Early Modern Britain* (New Haven and London, 2000).

29   Thomas, *Ends of Life*, p. 113; Alice T. Friedman, 'Inside/Out: Women, Domesticity, and the Pleasures of the City', in *Material London, c.1600*, ed. Lena Cowen Orlin (Philadelphia, PA, 2000), p. 232.

30   Thomas Mun cited in Peck, *Consuming Splendor*, p. 7; Bishop Sprat cited in Thomas, *Ends of Life*, p. 139.

31   Parkinson, *Paradisi*, Epistle to the Reader.

32   Gerard, *Herball*, Epistle Dedicatorie.

33   Parkinson, *Paradisi*, Epistle to the Reader.

34   Ibid., pp. 27–9.

35   Ibid., Epistle to the Reader.

36   A few years earlier, in 1625, Francis Bacon in his essay 'Of Gardens' expressed much the same view: 'Indeed, it is the Purest of Humane Pleasures', he wrote, going on to describe a 'princely' garden, laid out with an abundance of fruit trees and ornamental flowers. He makes absolutely no mention of profits or labour.

3   SETTING THE SCENE

1   See e.g. William Gouge, *Of Domesticall Duties* (London, 1622), p. 18.

2   Conrad Heresbach, *Foure Bookes of Husbandry*, Newley Englished and increased by Barnabe Googe (London, 1577; facsimile, New York, 1971), p. 48.

3   For more on the history of Lyveden New Bield's garden, see Andrew Eburne, 'The Passion of Sir Thomas Tresham: New Light on the Gardens and Lodge at Lyveden' (hereafter, 'New Light'), *GH*, 36:1 (2008), 114–34; see also Brian Dix, 'The Archaeology of Some Renaissance Gardens', *Renaissance Studies*, 25:1 (February 2011), 170–73.

4   Markham, *English Husbandman*, p. 112.

5   Ibid., pp. 112–16.

6   Parkinson, *Paradisi*, p. 3.

7   Lawson, *New Orchard and Garden*, p. 11.

8   Parkinson, *Paradisi*, p. 3.

9   Lawson, *New Orchard and Garden*, p. 11.

10   Parkinson, *Paradisi*, p. 3.

11   Ibid., p. 5.

12   Timothy Mowl, *Elizabethan and Jacobean Style* (London, 1993), p. 177.

13   The seminal work on this remains Roy Strong, *The Renaissance Garden in England* (London, 1979).

14   Paula Henderson, *The Tudor House and Garden* (New Haven and London, 2005), p. 94; Paula Henderson, 'Clinging to the Past: Medievalism in the English "Renaissance" Garden', *Renaissance Studies*, 25:1 (2011), 42–69; Strong, *Renaissance Garden*, pp. 10, 14.

15   Sylvia Landsberg, *The Medieval Garden* (London, 1995), p. 13. For more on medieval gardens, see John Harvey, *Mediaeval Gardens* (London, 1981).

16   Albertus Magnus, 'On the planting of pleasure gardens' (c.1260), cited in Harvey, *Mediaeval Gardens*, p. 6.

17   Chris Dyer, 'Gardens and Garden Produce in the Later Middle Ages', in *Food in Medieval England*, ed. C. M. Woolgar, D. Sergeantson and T. Waldron (Oxford, 2006), p. 29.

18   Landsberg, *Medieval Garden*, p. 38; David Jacques, 'The *Compartiment* System in Tudor England', *GH*, 27:1 (Summer 1999), 32.

19   Strong, *Renaissance Garden*, p. 15.

20   A rare and early example of this concept being utilised in England in the 1580s was the building of Wollaton Hall, Nottinghamshire, the home of Sir Francis Willoughby, designed by the mason-architect Robert Smythson, whose extant drawings of his original design show clearly that the garden was to be incorporated along with the house into an overall geometrical and symmetrical order: Henderson, *Tudor House and Garden*, p. 21; see also Alice T. Friedman, *House and Household in Elizabethan England: Wollaton Hall and the Willoughby Family* (London, 1989).

21   Strong, *Renaissance Garden*, p. 15.

22   Jacques, '*Compartiment* System', p. 32.

23   Jacques Androuet du Cerceau, *Le premier volume des plus excellents bastiments de France* (Paris, 1576). For Château de Villandry, see www.chateauvillandry.fr, accessed 22 August 2017.

24   The so-called 'Agas' or 'Woodcut' map is an important record of sixteenth-century London. Made up of 8 wooden blocks, it extends more than 6 feet (183 cm) wide. Once attributed to the Elizabethan surveyor Ralph

Agas, this is now firmly refuted but it is still referred to as the 'Agas' map. It was produced some time between 1561 and 1570 and is largely based on the slightly earlier, more detailed Copperplate map, dated c.1557.

25 Eburne, 'New Light', p. 124. The exact arrangement envisaged seems not to have been entirely clear, as Tresham's keeper, John Slynn, wrote to him in 1604 that he and Mr George (the estate steward) 'differ in opinion of your directions'; they agree to leave things as they are until 'your worship come home': ibid. It is still possible to detect the concentric circles in which the fruit trees were to be planted (see fig. 30), although the current owners have interpreted the area as a grass labyrinth.

26 It is well known that the garden lodge at Lyveden New Bield incorporates much religious symbolism, which reflected Tresham's Catholic faith, but it is more difficult to transpose this symbolism to the garden itself, which seems to conform to recognised gardening practice of the day.

27 The title page of Hyll's first book, A most briefe and pleasaunte treatise, published c.1558, carries a woodcut of a square ornamental garden, replaced in a later publication, The Gardeners Labyrinth, with an image of gardeners working in a series of raised square or rectilinear beds, but as will be discussed in Ch. 7, illustrations in books were generally little to do with the author but were added by the printer from a variety of sources.

28 Thomas Hill [Hyll], The Gardener's Labyrinth, ed. Richard Mabey (Oxford, 1988), p. 48.

29 Lawson, New Orchard and Garden, p. 11.

30 Markham, English Husbandman, pp. 116–26.

31 Parkinson, Paradisi, p. 5.

32 Bacon, 'Of Gardens', p. 52.

33 Parkinson, Paradisi, p. 3.

34 The London Surveys of Ralph Treswell, ed. John Schofield (London Topographical Society, 1987).

35 William Harrison, The Description of England (1587), ed. Georges Edelen (Washington, DC, and New York, 1994), p. 253; Henderson, Tudor House and Garden, p. 14.

36 Francis Bamford, ed., A Royalist's Notebook: The Commonplace Book of Sir John Oglander (London, 1936), p. 203.

37 Ralph Austen, A Treatise of Fruit-trees (Oxford, 1653), p. 33. For more on hospitality and food as gifts, see Felicity Heal, Hospitality in Early Modern England (Oxford, 1990), and 'Food Gifts, the Household and the Politics of Exchange in Early Modern England', Past and Present, 199 (2008), 41–70.

38 Thomas Hyll, The Gardeners Labyrinth (London, 1577), pp. 29–30.

39 Ibid., pp. 36–7, 28.

40 Land in Stratford was divided into burgages 3½ × 12 perches (52 × 198 ft): Jeanne Jones, Family Life in Shakespeare's England (Stroud: Alan Sutton; Stratford-up-on-Avon: Shakespeare Birthplace Trust, 1996), p. 1.

41 Stratford-upon-Avon Inventories, vol. 1: 1538–1625, ed. Jeanne Jones (Stratford-upon-Avon: Dugdale Society in association with the Shakespeare Birthplace Trust, 2002), p. 123.

42 Harrison, Description of England, p. xxxv.

43 Ibid., p. 264.

44 John Harvey, 'Vegetables in the Middle Ages', GH, 12:2 (1984), 94; Richard Gardner, Profitable Instructions for the Manuring, Sowing, and Planting of Kitchin Gardens (London, 1599), sig. C4.

45 Gerard, Herball, pp. 762–78.

46 Ibid., p. 770.

47 Harrison, Description of England, p. 264.

48 Harvey, 'Vegetables in the Middle Ages'; Dyer, 'Gardens and Garden Produce', p. 28.

49 Harrison, Description of England, p. 265. Lay-stows, or leystalls, were communal areas where refuse and dung were collected.

50 Ibid., p. 269.

51 Calendar of Wynn (of Gwydir) Papers (National Library of Wales, 1926), 205, p. 37.

52 For more on food as gifts, see Heal, 'Food Gifts', 41–70. In this article, Heal questions why apples and pears seem to have been acceptable gifts but vegetables do not (p. 56). Perhaps one answer is that whereas vegetables are cheap and easy to grow, apples and pears were not so.

53 Lawson, New Orchard and Garden, p. 7.

54 The Memorandum Book of Richard Cholmeley of Brandsby 1602–1623, North Yorkshire County Record Office publications, no. 44 (Northallerton, 1988).

55 HMC, De L'Isle MSS, vol. 2, Sir Robert Sidney to Lady Sidney, 25 September 1595; vol 4, Viscount Lisle to Lady Lisle, 3 October 1608, 8 July 1609; vol. 5, Viscount Lisle to Viscountess Lisle, 15 June 1615.

56 Ibid., vol. 4, Thomas Golding to Viscount Lisle, 6 May 1611.

57 The so-called 'Little Ice Age' refers to a period much debated by historians, variously defined as somewhere between the years 1300 and 1850, but climaxing during the sixteenth and seventeenth centuries, when a marked cooling of the climate was observed and measured: Brian Fagan, *The Little Ice Age: How Climate made History 1300–1800* (New York: Basic Books, 2000), pp. 47–8; Herbert Lamb, *Climate, History and the Modern World* (London: Routledge, 1995), p. 202; Emmanuel Le Roy Ladurie, 'History and Climate', in *Economy and Society in Early Modern Europe*, ed. Peter Burke (London: Routledge and Kegan Paul, 1972), pp. 134–69.

58 Harrison, *Description of England*, p. 269.

59 HMC, *De L'Isle MSS*, vol. 1, p. 258, Accounts of Sir Henry Sidney, 1573–74.

60 John Phillips and Nicholas Burnett, 'The Chronology and Layout of Francis Carew's Garden at Beddington, Surrey', *GH*, 33:2 (2005), 157–8.

61 Evelyn, *Diary*, vol. 3, p. 221.

62 Markham, *English Husbandman*, p. 129.

63 John Gerard, *Catalogus arborum [fructium ac plantarum tam indigenarum, quam exoticarum, in horto Iohannis Gerardi nascentium]* (London, 1596), repr. 1599 with English plant names added to the Latin.

64 Gerard, *Herball*, p. 196.

65 Ibid., p. 273.

66 Ibid., p. 1220.

67 Strong, *Renaissance Garden*, p. 52.

68 Baron Waldstein, *The Diary of Baron Waldstein: A Traveller in Elizabethan England*, trans. G. W. Groos (London, 1981), p. 87; Paul Hentzner, *A Journey into England in the year 1598* (first printed in Latin, c.1598, trans. in part Strawberry Hill, 1757; repr. Reading, 1807), p. 28; Strong, *Renaissance Garden*, pp. 52–3.

69 Letter sent from Worcester, 20 August 1575, in R. J. P. Kuin, ed., *Robert Langham, A Letter* (Leiden, 1938), p. 70. There is some debate over the authorship of this letter, although Kuin identifies the writer as Robert Langham, 'Keper of the Councell Chamber' (p. 15). The 2009 reconstruction of this garden at Kenilworth Castle by English Heritage was based on the description given in this letter. For more on this, see Alexander Samson, '*Locus amoenus*: Gardens and Horticulture in the Renaissance', *Renaissance Studies*, 25:1 (2011), 22.

70 Harrison, *Description of England*, pp. 270–71.

71 Eburne, 'New Light', pp. 124, 130.

72 Roy Strong, *The Artist and the Garden* (New Haven and London, 2000), fig. 164, Anthony van den Wyngaerde, *View of the Privy Garden, Pond Garden and the Mount at Hampton Court*, 1558, and fig. 5, detail from *The Family of Henry VIII*, c.1545. This painting can also be viewed at www.royalcollection.org.uk/collection/405796/the-family-of-henry-viii (accessed 15 September 2017).

73 Kuin, *Robert Langham*, p. 69.

74 Strong, *Renaissance Garden*, p. 35, and *Artist and the Garden*, p. 19.

75 Lawson, *New Orchard and Garden*, pp. 13, 55. Whether Lawson is advocating the building of an artificial river or simply taking advantage of a natural one is unclear: as it is likely that Lawson's own land ran up to the south bank of the River Tees, the latter suggestion seems more probable; see John Harvey, 'William Lawson and his Garden', *Country Life*, 28 October 1982, 1340.

76 Henderson, *Tudor House and Garden*, p. 155.

77 Hyll, *Gardeners Labyrinth*, p. 45.

78 HMC, *De L'Isle MSS*, vol. 3, Thomas Golding to Viscount Lisle, 8 May 1607.

79 See Henderson, *Tudor House and Garden* for more on buildings in gardens, esp. ch. 5, 'The Architecture of the "Earthly Paradise"'.

80 C. Paul Christianson, *The Riverside Gardens of Thomas More's London* (New Haven and London, 2005), p. 167.

81 George Cavendish, *Metrical Visions* (c.1558), ed. A. S. G. Edwards (Colombia, SC: University of South Carolina Press for the Newberry Library, 1980). Cavendish was employed in the Wolsey household and wrote this verse tragedy some thirty years after Wolsey's death in 1530.

82 Christianson, *Riverside Gardens*, p. 169; Jacques, 'Compartment System', p. 42.

83 Jacques, 'Compartment System', p. 43.

84 Harrison, *Description of England*, pp. 269, 265.

4   CONTINUITIES

1 Mark Girouard, 'The Smythson Collection of the Royal Institute of British Architects, *Architectural History*, vol., 5 (1962), pp. 21–184. The plans can be viewed on

the RIBA website: www.architecture.com/image-library (accessed 24 November 2017).

2   Roy Strong, *The Artist and the Garden* (New Haven and London, 2000), p. 35, observes that the garden style recorded in Jacobean and Caroline painting 'is firmly late Elizabethan', and Tom Williamson, *Polite Landscapes: Gardens and Society in Eighteenth Century England* (Stroud, 1995), p. 19, wrote that a general gardening style until the Civil War draws no distinction between Tudor and early Stuart gentry gardens, portraying them as 'comparatively small spaces which were clearly separated from the surrounding world by high hedges, fences or walls. Their design was dominated by geometry'.

3   Lawson, *New Orchard and Garden*, p. 54.

4   IOWRO, OG/AA/29, fol. 27v; OG/AA/27, fols 31, 47.

5   Ibid., OG/AA/14, 'How Eastnunwell Came to the Oglanders 1619'.

6   Ibid., OG/AA/29, fol. 27v. 'Melecatoons' were any of several late-ripening varieties of peach; see melacoton peach, *OED*.

7   Nunwell's house and garden are still privately owned and are occasionally open to visitors: www.nunwellhouse.co.uk, accessed 28 September 2017.

8   Parkinson, *Paradisi*, p. 1.

9   Jan Woudstra and Sally O'Halloran, 'Sir John Reresby's Garden Notebook and Garden (1633–44) at Thrybergh, Yorkshire', *GH*, 36:1 (2008), 139.

10   Temple MSS, STT2308–2337, STT2143–2155, STT2276–2302, the majority of these letters sent from either Wolverton or Burton Dassett.

11   Temple MSS, STT CL&I Box 1, Inventory 16 October 1624: 'A booke of sundry parcells of household stuff Beddinge, victuals, etc. leaft by Sir Thomas and the Lady Temple at Stow when Sir Peter began housekeeping there, & Sr Thomas departed thence'. Note that Stow (now known as Stowe) is consistently spelled by Temple in this way throughout these manuscripts.

12   Temple MSS, STT2347.

13   Temple MSS, STT2288; ST38, fol. 19; STT2279; STT2347.

14   Temple MSS, STT2145, STT2287. I am grateful to Mairi MacDonald at the Shakespeare Birthplace Trust for first drawing my attention to photocopies of these two letters held at the SBTRO.

15   Hanmer, *Garden Book*, p. 161.

16   Parkinson, *Paradisi*, p. 598, gives the Latin name *Laurus* for the bay tree.

17   Temple MSS, STT2285.

18   Ibid., STT2286, STT2290.

19   *The Memorandum Book of Richard Cholmeley of Brandsby 1602–1623*, North Yorkshire County Record Office Publications, no. 44 (Northallerton, 1988), see e.g. p. 54.

20   Joan Thirsk, ed., *The Agrarian History of England and Wales*, vol. 4: *1500–1640* (Cambridge, 1991), p. 168.

21   Temple MSS, ST38, fol. 7; STT2143.

22   Mark Merry and Catherine Richardson, eds, *The Household Account Book of Sir Thomas Puckering of Warwick, 1620* (Stratford-upon-Avon, 2012), p. 94.

23   John Broad, *Transforming English Rural Society: The Verneys and the Claydons, 1600–1820* (Cambridge, 2004), pp. 134, 146.

24   John Fitzherbert, *The Boke of Husbandry* (1534), ed. the Rev. W Skeat (London: Trübner & Co. for the English Dialect Society, 1882), p. 27.

25   IOWRO, OG/AA/27, fols 75, 86.

26   *Memorandum Book of Richard Cholmeley*, p. 156.

27   IOWRO, OG/AA/26; Plan of Nunwell House, 1748; Temple MSS, ST38, fol. 11; SRO, D593/R/1/2; Merry and Richardson, *Household Account Book of Sir Thomas Puckering*, p. 308.

28   Temple MSS, STT2154, STT2296.

29   Ibid., STT2145, STT2154. A 'pryve house' is equivalent to an outdoor toilet in modern parlance. John Evelyn and the Trentham House accounts refer to the same facility as the 'house of office': Evelyn, Add. 78628A; SRO, D593/R/1/2, 2nd March 1638.

30   Malcolm Thick, *The Neat House Gardens: Early Market Gardening around London* (Totnes, 1998), pp. 61, 102; *OED*, see under 'leystall'.

31   Charles Welch, *The History of the Worshipful Company of Gardeners* (London, 1900), p. 28.

32   Broad, *Transforming English Rural Society*, p. 135.

33   Merry and Richardson, *Household Account Book of Sir Thomas Puckering*, p. 180: SRO, D593/R/1/2; Pelham, Add. 33147; IOWRO, OG/AA/28.

34   Temple MSS, STT2279; STT2299; STT2276.

35   Nathaniel Alcock, *Warwickshire Grazier and London Skinner, 1532–1555: The Account Book of Peter Temple and Thomas Heritage* (London, 1981), p. 176.

36   *Memorandum Book of Richard Cholmeley*, e.g. pp. 91, 95; Merry and Richardson, *Household Account Book of Sir Thomas Puckering*, p. 182. A quickset is a living hedging plant.

37   Temple MSS, ST38, fol. 11.

38   IOWRO, OG/AA/6.

39   Ibid., OG/AA/28, fol. 4.

40   A. M. Foster, *Bee Boles and Bee Houses* (Princes Risborough, 1988), p. 3; Landsberg, *Medieval Garden*, p. 44; IOWRO, OG/AA/28, fol. 4.

41   Charles Butler, *The feminine monarchie, or A treatise concerning bees* (Oxford, 1609), sig. Av. Thomas Hyll, 'A profitable instruction of the perfite ordering of Bees', in *The Profitable Arte of Gardening* (London, 1574), sig. Aaiii.

42   Conrad Heresbach, *Foure Bookes of Husbandry* (London, 1577).

43   Lawson, *New Orchard and Garden*, pp. 88, 85.

44   Conrad Heresbach, *Foure Bookes of Husbandry* (London, 1577), p. 182; Hyll, *Profitable Arte of Gardening* (1574), p. 3.

45   The word 'skep' was in fact a wider term, meaning a kind of woven basket for carrying anything from coal to corn: *OED*.

46   Lawson, *New Orchard and Garden*, p. 55.

47   Gervase Markham, *Cheape and Good Husbandry* (London, 1614), p. 153.

48   Lawson, *New Orchard and Garden*, p. 86.

49   Margaret Hoby, *The Private Life of an Elizabethan Lady: The Diary of Lady Margaret Hoby, 1599–1605*, ed. Joanna Moody (Stroud, 1998), p. 13. According to Lawson, p. 91, 'Taking of Bees' involves the removing of the bees from the hive either by smoking or drowning, before harvesting the honey. It seems clear that this is what Lady Hoby was doing.

50   Judith Spicksley, ed., *The Business and Household Accounts of Joyce Jeffreys, Spinster of Hereford 1638–1648* (Oxford, 2012), p. 285.

51   *Stratford-upon-Avon Inventories*, vol. 1: *1538–1699*, ed. Jeanne Jones (Stratford-upon-Avon, 2002), p. 127.

52   Hyll, 'A Profitable instruction of the perfite ordering of Bees', sig. Aaii.

53   Lawson, *New Orchard and Garden*, pp. 85, 55.

54   Timothy Raylor, 'Samuel Hartlib and the Commonwealth of Bees', in *Culture and Cultivation in Early Modern England: Writing and the Land*, ed. Michael Leslie and Timothy Raylor (Leicester, 1992), pp. 94–5. For more on the idea of agricultural 'improvement', see ibid.

55   Raylor, 'Samuel Hartlib', p. 103.

56   Evelyn, *Diary*, vol. 3, pp. 110, 354; www.pepysdiary.com/diary/1665/05/05/, accessed 29 August 2017.

57   See e.g. Pelham, Add. 33147, fols 61v, 96v, 97; SRO, DR593/R/3/3–4; Todd Gray, ed., *Devon Household Accounts, 1627–59, Part 1* (Exeter, 1995), p. 86; Lionel M. Munby, ed., *Early Stuart Household Accounts* (Cambridge, 1986), pp. 171, 193; Merry and Richardson, *Household Account Book of Sir Thomas Puckering*, p. 168.

58   See e.g. Gray, *Devon Household Accounts, Part 1*, pp. 9, 17.

59   Munby, *Early Stuart Household Accounts*, pp. 160, 162; Gray, *Devon Household Accounts, Part 1*, p. 39; Merry and Richardson, *Household Account Book of Sir Thomas Puckering*, p. 163.

60   Pelham, Add. 33147, fols 60v, 97, 101, 223.

61   Merry and Richardson, *Household Account Book of Sir Thomas Puckering*, p. 161.

62   Joan Thirsk, *Food in Early Modern England: Phases, Fads, Fashions 1500–1760* (London, 2007), pp. 171, 242.

63   Gerard, *Herball*, pp. 1041, 1046.

64   Richard Gardner, *Profitable Instructions for the Manuring, Sowing and Planting of Kitchin gardens* (London, 1599), sig. C3v.

65   Parkinson, *Paradisi*, pp. 521–2.

66   Gray, *Devon Household Accounts, Part 1*, pp. 124, 86.

67   E.g., ibid., pp. 11, 13, 127, 142, 145; IOWRO, OG/AA/27, fol. 47; *Memorandum Book of Richard Cholmeley*, pp. 129, 155.

68   Gardner, *Profitable instructions*, sigs A4–B3v.

69   Hyll, *Gardeners Labyrinth*, p. 90.

70   Pelham, Add. 33147, fols 78v, 120v, 125, 176v.

71   Parkinson, *Paradisi*, pp. 469, 504.

72   Mary Keeler, *The Long Parliament, 1640–1641: A Biographical Study of its Members* (Philadelphia, PA: American Philosophical Society, 1954), p. 301.

73   Pelham, Add. 33147, fol. 130; Munby, *Early Stuart Household Accounts*, p. 171; Spicksley, *Business and Household Accounts of Joyce Jeffreys*, p. 221.

74   Maggie Campbell-Culver, *The Origin of Plants* (London, 2004), pp. 30–31.

75   John Harvey, 'Garden Plants of around 1525: The Fromond List', *GH*, 17:2 (Autumn 1989), 122–34.

76   Gerard, *Herball*, pp. 991–3.

77   Parkinson, *Paradisi*, p. 520.

78   And apparently they still are – in 2010 the BBC Food website included a recipe for 'Braised thistle stem'.

79   *Memorandum Book of Richard Cholmeley*, p. 218.

80   Parkinson, *Paradisi*, p. 516. This vegetable is still known as a Jerusalem artichoke but is neither an artichoke (as Parkinson rightly says) nor a potato. *Helianthus tuberosus*, as it is now classified, is a type of sunflower, cultivated for its tuberous root.

81   Parkinson, *Paradisi*, p. 567.

82   Lloyd Bowen, ed., *Family and Society in Early Stuart Glamorgan: The Household Accounts of Sir Thomas Aubrey of Llantrithyd, c.1565–1641* (Cardiff, 2006), pp. 45, 52; Munby, *Early Stuart Household Accounts*, pp. 175–6.

83   *Calendar of Wynn (of Gwydir) Papers* (Aberystwyth, 1926), 851, p. 136; 1131, p. 182.

84   Ibid., 637, p. 101. It is unclear what 'meurtriers' refer to, although Wynn describes them as a fruit which differs from the orange both in taste and leaf.

85   Munby, *Early Stuart Household Accounts*, pp. 166, 174, 175.

86   HMC, *De L'Isle MSS*, vol. 4, Viscount Lisle to Lady Lisle, 24 September 1609; Temple MSS, ST38, fol. 31v; STT2285; STT2290.

87   Parkinson, *Paradisi*, p. 582.

88   IOWRO, OG/AA/29, fol. 27v; Temple MSS, STT2347; *Memorandum Book of Richard Cholmeley*, p. 190.

89   A 'pentisse' (penthouse) was a sloping roof or ledge placed against a wall or over a door or window to provide shelter from the weather: *OED*.

90   Markham, *English Husbandman*, p. 129.

91   Ibid., p. 131.

92   Gervase Markham, *The Countrey Farme* (London, 1616), p. 298.

93   *Calendar of Wynn Papers*, 637, p. 101.

94   Markham, *Countrey Farme*, pp. 300–01. Although the practice of lighting fires under fruit trees to protect them from spring frosts was carried out in plum orchards in the Vale of Evesham until the 1950s, orange trees are far less hardy than plum trees and therefore less likely to respond favourably to this treatment.

95   Parkinson, *Paradisi*, pp. 551.

96   As opposed to the apparatus that heats it, a 'stove' at this time referred to the building or structure which was used as a heated house for protecting plants; from the Icelandic *stofa*, meaning an enclosed, usually heated, room: *OED*.

97   Parkinson, *Paradisi*, pp. 584, 25.

98   Ibid., p. 553.

99   Markham, *English Husbandman*, p. 131.

100   Lawson, *New Orchard and Garden*, p. 8.

101   Gray, *Devon Household Accounts, Part 1*, p. 14; OG/AA/29; Temple MSS, STT2287; Evelyn, Add. 78220.

102   For more on seventeenth-century climate change, see Ch. 3 n. 57 above.

103   Parkinson, *Paradisi*, pp. 552.

5   THE GARDENERS

1   Lionel M. Munby, ed., *Early Stuart Household Accounts* (Cambridge, 1986), pp. xix, 199, 200.

2   Charles Welch, *The History of the Worshipful Company of Gardeners* (London, 1900), p. 17.

3   Thomas Hyll, *The Profitable Art of Gardening* (London, 1579), sig. C.

4   Markham, *English Husbandman*, p. 105.

5   Lawson, *New Orchard and Garden*, pp. 1–2.

6   Pelham, Add. 33147, fols 37, 43, 61v, 89.

7   Munby, *Early Stuart Household Accounts*, p. 160; Lloyd Bowen, ed., *Family and Society in Early Stuart Glamorgan: The Household Accounts of Sir Thomas Aubrey of Llantrithyd, c.1565–1641* (Cardiff, 2006), p. 74 (hereafter, *Household Accounts of Thomas Aubrey*).

8   David Whitehead, 'Some Connected Thoughts on the Parks and Gardens of Herefordshire before the Age of Landscape Gardening', *Transactions of the Woolhope Naturalists' Field Club*, 48:2 (1995), 217.

9   Pelham, Add. 33147, e.g. fols 89, 125; 122; Todd Gray, ed., *Devon Household Accounts, 1627–59, Part 1* (Exeter, 1995), p. 124; Margaret Hoby, *The Private Life of an Elizabethan Lady: The Diary of Lady Margaret Hoby, 1599–1605*, ed. Joanna Moody (Stroud, 1998), p. 142 (hereafter, *Diary of Lady Margaret Hoby*).

10   Munby, *Early Stuart Household Accounts*, p. 166; SRO, D593/R/1/2; Temple MSS, ST452, pp. 75, 84.

11   Lawson, *New Orchard and Garden*, p. 4.

12   SRO, D593/R/1/2; Pelham, Add. 33147, fol. 6v. A perch measured approx. 16 ft (5 m).

13   Bowen, *Household Accounts of Thomas Aubrey*, p. 135.

14   Bower Marsh and John Ainsworth, eds, *Records of the Worshipful Company of Carpenters, V: Warden's Account Book 1571–1599* (Oxford, 1937); SRO, D593/R/1/2.

15   Pelham, Add. 33147, fol. 10; Whitehead, 'Some Connected Thoughts', p. 217; Judith Spicksley, ed., *The Business and Household Accounts of Joyce Jeffreys, Spinster of Hereford 1638–1648* (Oxford, 2012), pp. 198, 216.

16   Temple MSS, ST452.

17   Hanmer, *Garden Book*, p. 159.

18   Temple MSS, STT2279, STT2284, STT2296, STT2347.

19   Ibid., STT2284, STT2285, STT2287, STT2296.

20   Ibid., STT2296.

21   Tessa Watt, *Cheap Print and Popular Piety* (Cambridge, 1991), p. 7. See Ch. 1 above for more on literacy in early modern England.

22   Temple MSS, STT2282.

23   Melvyn Barnes, *Root and Branch: A History of the Worshipful Company of Gardeners of London* (London, 1994), p. 31.

24   Welch, *History of the Worshipful Company of Gardeners*, p. 22.

25   Parkinson, *Paradisi*, p. 571.

26   Christopher Brooks, 'Apprenticeship, Social Mobility and the Middling Sort, 1550–1800', in *The Middling Sort of People: Culture, Society and Politics in England, 1550–1800*, ed. Jonathan Barry and Christopher Brooks (Basingstoke, 1994), p. 54.

27   Prudence Leith-Ross, *The John Tradescants: Gardeners to the Rose and Lily Queen* (London, 1984), pp. 78, 82, 116.

28   The role of the professions in early modern England has been discussed at length by modern historians, with the general conclusion that, outside the three recognised and established professions of the clergy, law and medicine, the distinctions between profession, trade and craft were blurred indeed, the concepts having by this time 'acquired a convenient breadth and ambiguity': Wilfred Prest, ed., *The Professions in Early Modern England* (London: Croom Helm, c.1987), p. 12. See also Geoffrey

Holmes, *Augustan England: Professions, State and Society, 1680–1730* (London: George Allen & Unwin, 1982); Rosemary O'Day, *The Professions in Early Modern England 1480–1800* (Harlow, Pearson Education, 2000).

29   Gerard, *Herball*, p. 1091.

30   *ODNB*, from which further information on Gerard and Tradescant comes, unless otherwise specified.

31   Gerard, *Herball*, Epistle Dedicatorie.

32   Hyll, *Profitable Art of Gardening* (1579), Epistle to Sir Henrie Seamer, sigs Aii–Aiiv.

33   Evelyn, *Elysium Britannicum*, p. 34.

34   For more on freemen defined as professionals and gentlemen, see Kenneth Charlton, 'The Professions in Sixteenth-Century England', *University of Birmingham Historical Journal*, 12 (1969), 20–41; Richard Cust and Steve Rea, Court of Chivalry website www.court-of-chivalry.bham.ac.uk, Case 367, Leming v Clopton, accessed 1 July 2011; Steve Rappaport, *Worlds within Worlds: Structures of Life in Sixteenth-Century London* (Cambridge, 1989), pp. 258–9.

35   William Hazlitt, *The Livery Companies of the City of London* (New York, 1969), p. 84; Brooks, 'Apprenticeship, Social Mobility', p. 60; Barnes, *Root and Branch*, p. 22.

36   The Gardeners' Company, once established, was a minor company, ranked 66th in order of precedence; in fact, although the ordinances provided for a livery, it was never actually granted by the Court of Aldermen. Neither did it ever possess a hall: Barnes, *Root and Branch*, p. 22; Welch, *History of the Worshipful Company of Gardeners*, p. 29.

37   Anna Parkinson, *Nature's Alchemist: John Parkinson, Herbalist to Charles I* (London, 2007), pp. 15–16.

38   Ibid., p. 176; Cecil Wall, *The History of the Worshipful Society of Apothecaries* (London, 1963); John Parkinson, *Theatrum Botanicum: The Theater of Plants* (London, 1640), To the Reader.

39   Leith-Ross, *John Tradescants*, p. 100.

40   Despite the fact that the Tradescants blatantly displayed their coat of arms, as seen e.g. on their tomb (see fig. 73), they were not actually entitled to do so: ibid., p. 105.

41   Holmes, *Augustan England*, p. 21; Keith Thomas, *The Ends of Life: Roads to Fulfilment in Early Modern England* (Oxford, 2009), p. 131.

42   Evelyn, *Elysium Britannicum*, p. 35.

43   Holmes, *Augustan England*, p. 8.

44   Evelyn, *Elysium Britannicum*, pp. 84–91.

45   Ibid., p. 35.

46   Lawson, *New Orchard and Garden*, p. 2.

47   Henry Peacham, *The Compleat Gentleman: fashioning him absolut...a noble gentleman* (London, 1622); see also Ch. 1 above.

48   Parkinson, *Paradisi*, p. 538.

49   IOWRO, OG/AA/29, fols 29v, 34.

50   Oglander was appointed Deputy Governor of Portsmouth in 1620, Deputy Governor of the Isle of Wight in 1624, sat in the Parliaments of 1625, 1626 and 1628–9 and was Commissioner and then Sheriff of Hampshire in 1635–9: *ODNB*.

51   IOWRO, OG/AA/27, fol. 80.

52   Ibid., OG/AA/28, n.p.

53   Jan Woudstra and Sally O'Halloran, 'Sir John Reresby's Garden Notebook and Garden (1633–44) at Thrybergh, Yorkshire', *GH*, 36:1 (2008), 160.

54   Temple MSS, STT2284, STT2296.

55   Evelyn, *Elysium Britannicum*, p. 35.

56   Gervase Markham, *The English Housewife* (London, 1615), ed. Michael Best (Montreal and Kingston, Ontario, 1986), pp. 8, 60.

57   Conrad Heresbach, *Foure Bookes of Husbandry*, trans. Barnabe Googe (facsimile edn, New York, 1971), p. 48v.

58   Thomas Hill, *The Gardener's Labyrinth* (1652), ed. Richard Mabey (Oxford, 1988), p. 25.

59   Malcom Thick, intro. to Lawson, *New Orchard and Garden*, p. 21.

60   Mark Merry and Catherine Richardson, eds, *The Household Account Book of Sir Thomas Puckering, 1620* (Stratford-upon-Avon, 2012), pp. 44–5, 248; Spicksley, *Business and Household Accounts of Joyce Jeffreys*, pp. 90, 86.

61   *Diary of Lady Margaret Hoby*, e.g. pp. 18, 29, 65, 79.

62   Lawson, *New Orchard and Garden*, p. 55.

6   NEW ASPIRATIONS

1   Gerard, *Herball*, sig. A1v, pp. 55, 116, 123, 285, 780.

2   Parkinson, *Paradisi*, Epistle to the Reader.

3   John Parkinson, *Theatrum Botanicum: A Theater of Plants* (London, 1640), p. 889. Spignel is the common name for *Meum athamanticum*, a herbaceous perennial with small white flowers, similar to cow parsley.

4   Ibid., p. 1064.

5   Ibid., dedication by John Harmar.

6   In ibid., p. 609, Parkinson refers specifically to 'my garden in Long acre'.

7   John N. D. Riddell, 'John Parkinson's Long Acre Garden 1600–1650', *Journal of Garden History*, 6:2 (1986), 113.

8   Ibid.

9   Parkinson, *Theatrum Botanicum*, p. 1091: 'if in my former dayes I had thought to have published the fruits of my Garden, I had then beene more curious to have taken descriptions of a number of Plants, which have perished with me and now I want'.

10   Parkinson, *Paradisi*, p. 23.

11   Mark Merry and Catherine Richardson, eds, *The Household Account Book of Sir Thomas Puckering of Warwick, 1620* (Stratford-upon-Avon, 2012), p. 94.

12   Parkinson, *Paradisi*, p. 22.

13   William Harrison, *The Description of England* (1577; 1587), ed. Georges Edelen (Washington, DC, and New York, 1994), p. 265.

14   Parkinson, *Paradisi*, pp. 22–5.

15   Ibid., p. 22.

16   Ibid., pp. 23, 24.

17   Ibid., p. 25.

18   Although Parkinson could not have known it, it was only another thirty years or so before the Royal Society was established in 1660, formally embracing scientific method and practical experiment as a legitimate source of knowledge.

19   Parkinson, *Paradisi*, p. 23. Many of the phenomena being observed and recorded by Parkinson were processes that occur accidentally in nature, but they were not ones that were necessarily understood by early modern gardeners. For instance, we now know that cross-pollination of flower varieties and species naturally brings about variations in colour, size and so on, and this is even more likely to occur in a garden situation where flowers and plants that would not normally be found growing in the same place are planted close to one another. And it was not understood until as late as the twentieth century that the much admired variegation in tulip colours is caused by a viral disease: Parkinson put this natural occurrence

down to rogue gardeners digging up the bulbs and swapping them for ones of a different colour (p. 13).

20   Ibid., p. 24.

21   Rebecca Bushnell, *Green Desire: Imagining Early Modern English Gardens* (New York, 2003), p. 58.

22   Parkinson, *Paradisi*, p. 18.

23   Ibid., pp. 17–22.

24   Ibid., p. 21.

25   Ibid., p. 463.

26   Ibid., p. 21.

27   Ibid., pp. 6–7.

28   Ibid., p. 607.

29   Ibid., p. 6.

30   Ibid.

31   Ibid., p. 7. The delightful La Seigneurie Gardens, Sark, are open to the public every day during the summer: www.laseigneuriegardens.com, accessed 5 September 2017.

32   Ibid., p. 7.

33   Ibid., pp. 11–12.

34   Ibid., p. 8.

35   Dutch gardeners apparently had the opposite problem: their obsession with growing tulips left them without flowers and colour in their gardens in the summer: Anne Goldgar, *Tulipmania: Money, Honor, and Knowledge in the Dutch Golden Age* (Chicago and London, 2008), p. 50.

36   Parkinson, *Paradisi*, p. 14.

37   Ibid., p. 9. Parkinson often appeals specifically to 'gentlewomen', perhaps in deference to Queen Henrietta Maria to whom his book is dedicated.

38   Ibid., p. 13.

39   Ibid., p. 8 The Flemish physician Matthias de l'Obel in his 1576 *Stripium Observationes* (Antwerp) had also included plants solely for their decorative value and there is evidence that Parkinson was heavily influenced by this man's work, his copy of the book being heavily annotated with notes of his own: Anna Parkinson, *Nature's Alchemist: John Parkinson, Herbalist to Charles I* (London, 2007), p. 71. However, de l'Obel was not a gardener or a garden writer, but a physician and botanist. Neither were any of his books, including this one, published in English.

40   C. Paul Christianson, *The Riverside Gardens of Thomas More's London* (New Haven and London, 2005), pp. 9, 41, 58.

41   Richard Surflet, *Maison Rustique, or the Countrie Farme* (London, 1600), p. 300.

42   Ibid., pp. 300–01.

43   Lawson, *New Orchard and Garden*, pp. 79, 77.

44   Parkinson, *Paradisi*, p. 1.

45   Ibid., p. 461.

46   In the early 1660s, the French garden designer André Mollet, in his English translation of his best-seller *Le Jardin de Plaisir*, or *The Garden of Pleasure* (Stockholm: 1651; trans. London, 1670), p. 4, recognised the necessity of incorporating a place for the kitchen garden within the whole, but by then recommended that this 'deformity may be hid by high Palissado's; for we do not allow that the Garden of Pleasure should admit of common Herbes.'

47   Parkinson, *Paradisi*, p. 461.

48   Keith Thomas, *The Ends of Life: Roads to Fulfilment in Early Modern England* (Oxford, 2009), p. 140.

49   All quotations from this essay are taken from Bacon, 'Of Gardens'.

50   Paula Henderson, 'Sir Francis Bacon's Essay "Of Gardens" in Context', *GH*, 36:1 (2008), 59; Hassell Smith, 'The Gardens of Sir Nicholas and Sir Francis Bacon', in *Religion, Culture and Society in Early Modern Britain*, ed. Anthony Fletcher and Peter Roberts (Cambridge: Cambridge University Press, 1994), pp. 125–60.

51   Markham, *English Husbandman*, p. 112.

52   This idea of incorporating the countryside into the garden anticipates the great landscape designers of the following century such as 'Capability' Brown and William Kent, who 'leaped the fence and saw that all nature was a garden': Horace Walpole, 'The History of the Modern Taste in Gardening' (1771/80), in *The Genius of the Place: The English Landscape Garden 1620–1820*, ed. John Dixon Hunt and Peter Willis (London and Cambridge, Mass., 1988), p. 313.

53   Henry Wotton, 'The Elements of Architecture' (1624), in ibid., pp. 48–9.

54   John Chamberlain, *The Letters of John Chamberlain*, ed. Norman McClure, 2 vols (Philadelphia, 1939), vol. 1, p. 227.

55   Ann Fanshawe, *The Memoirs of Ann, Lady Fanshawe* (London, 1907), p. 9.

56   Roy Strong, *The Artist and the Garden* (New Haven and London, 2000), p. 149; fig. 184. Newburgh Priory was

the seat of the Belasyse family, one of whom we know had an interest in gardens and gardening as he appears to be the 'Sir Henry Belloses' to whom Lawson dedicates his *New Orchard and Garden*, mentioning Sir Henry's 'delightfull skill in matters of this nature' (sigs A2, A2v).

57   See ibid., pp. 149–52.

58   R. T. Gunther, *Early British Botanists and their Gardens* (Oxford, 1922), pp. 348–51; Jan Woudstra and Sally O'Halloran, 'Sir John Reresby's Garden Notebook and Garden (1633–44) at Thrybergh, Yorkshire', *GH*, 36:1 (2008), 159–92.

59   The plant lists were published in R. T. Gunther, 'The Garden of Rev. Walter Stonehouse', *Gardeners' Chronicle*, 15 May 1920.

60   Gunther, *Early British Botanists*, p. 272.

61   Woudstra and O'Halloran, 'Sir John Reresby's Garden Notebook', p. 137. This article contains a full transcription of Reresby's Notebook.

62   John Tradescant, *Plantarum in Horto* (1634). Although he lists 750 plants growing in his garden, we have no idea how they were planted or how the garden was laid out.

63   John Cartwright, ed., *The Memoirs of Sir John Reresby of Thrybergh, 1634–1689 written by himself* (1875).

64   Woudstra and O'Halloran, 'Sir John Reresby's Garden Notebook', pp. 137–9.

65   Cartwright, *Memoirs of Sir John Reresby*, p. 14.

66   Ibid., p. 78. See Ch. 8 here for more on summerhouses.

67   Parkinson, *Paradisi*, p. 461.

68   Temple MSS, ST452.

69   The term 'parlour' also defies precise definition but at this time it tended to be an informal sitting or eating room, off the main hall, on the ground floor, used by the family for private conversation or dining: Mark Girouard, *Life in the English Country House* (New Haven and London: Yale University Press, 1978), pp. 103–4.

70   Temple MSS, ST452, STT2279, STT2288; Merry and Richardson, *Household Account Book of Sir Thomas Puckering*, p. 304; Evelyn, Add. 78628A; Bettisfield 1667.

71   IOWRO, OG/AA/29, fol. 27v; OG/AA/27, fols 47–49. Other secondary sources have transcribed and perpetuated this figure as 10 pence a root, an amount hardly worthy of comment. However, examination of the original documents confirms the figure as 10 *shillings* a root.

72   Chamberlain, *Letters*, p. 290.

73   IOWRO, OG/AA/29, fol. 25.

74   Ibid., OG/AA/26; OG/AA/29, fol. 6.

75   Ibid., OG/AA/26.

76   John Tradescant quoted in Prudence Leith-Ross, *The John Tradescants: Gardeners to the Rose and Lily Queen* (London, 1984), pp. 32, 37–8.

77   Bettisfield 1663.

78   See e.g. Linda Peck, *Consuming Splendor* (Cambridge, 2005), p. 13; Anna Bryson, *From Courtesy to Civility: Changing Codes of Conduct in Early Modern England* (Oxford, 1998), pp. 75–6.

79   See e.g. Anne Goldgar, *Tulipmania: Money, Honor, and Knowledge in the Dutch Golden Age* (Chicago and London, 2007); Anna Pavord, *The Tulip* (London, 2000); Simon Schama, *The Embarrassment of Riches* (London, 1991). See also Ch. 10 here.

80   Parkinson, *Paradisi*, p. 8.

81   David Jacques, 'The *Compartment* System in Tudor England', *GH*, 27:1 (Summer 1999), 39.

82   Temple MSS, STT2287, STT2284, STT2271, STT2301.

7   THE KNOTTY PROBLEM OF KNOTS

1   Roy Strong, *The Artist and the Garden* (New Haven and London, 2000), p. 13; C. Paul Christianson, *The Riverside Gardens of Thomas More's London* (New Haven and London, 2005), p. 169.

2   Markham, *English Husbandman*, p. 120.

3   Roy Strong, *The Renaissance Garden in England* (London, 1979), p. 40.

4   Temple MSS, ST452, p. 75; Judith Spicksley, ed., *The Business and Household Accounts of Joyce Jeffreys, Spinster of Hereford 1638–1648* (Oxford, 2012), p. 200; OG/AA/29, fol. 27v; Rebecca Roberts, '"Two meane fellows grand projectors": The Self-Projection of Sir Arthur Ingram and Lionel Cranfield, Earl of Middlesex, 1600–1645, with particular reference to their houses' (PhD thesis, Teeside University, 2012), p. 39; Temple MSS, ST2347.

5   Bettisfield 1667; see App. 2.

6   David Jacques, 'The *Compartment* System in Tudor England', *GH*, 27:1 (Summer 1999), 43; Strong, *Artist and the Garden*, p. 31.

7   E.g. Markham, *English Husbandman*, p. 112; Lawson, *New Orchard and Garden*, p. 54; André Mollet, *Le Jardin de Plaisir*, or *The Garden of Pleasure* (Sweden, 1651; trans. London, 1670), p. 4; Evelyn, *Elysium Britannicum*, p. 123.

8   Comparison between Charles Estienne, *L'agriculture et Maison Rustique* (Paris, 1598) and Richard Surflet, *Maison Rustique, or the Countrie Farme* (London, 1600), pp. 331–42.

9   Surflet, *Countrie Farme*, p. 327.

10   Strong, *Artist and the Garden*, esp. pp. 28–35.

11   Ibid., p. 31. Sir Thomas More, counsellor to Henry VIII, then Lord Chancellor in 1529–32, was executed for refusing the sign the Oath of Supremacy recognising Henry as the head of the Church in England.

12   Ibid., p. 33.

13   L. G. Wickham Legg, ed., 'A Relation of a short survey of the Western Counties made by a Lieutenant of the Military Company in Norwich, 1635', in *Camden Miscellany*, 3rd ser., vol. 52, cited in Prudence Leith-Ross, *The John Tradescants: Gardeners to the Rose and Lily Queen* (London, 1984), p. 45.

14   Conversation between the (now retired) Head Gardener, Barry Locke, and the author, 18 February 2010.

15   Ernest Law, *Shakespeare's Garden* (Stratford-up-on-Avon: Shakespeare Head Press, 1922), p. 21.

16   An information board indicates that this is a re-creation of Law's twentieth-century design, but by virtue of its location in the garden of William Shakespeare, the numerous visitors who flock to see this attraction could be forgiven for assuming that they are looking at a representation of a Tudor knot garden.

17   R. J. P. Kuin, ed., *Robert Langham, A Letter* (Leiden, 1938).

18   Private correspondence with David Jacques, who designed the gardens at Kenilworth. Jacques comments that in turn, the French architect Androuet du Cerceau, who we have come across before (see pp. 62–4), derived his style from Serlio.

19   See Ch. 1 above for more on the derivative nature of contemporary literature; see also App. 1. Examination of several of the British Library's *Maison Rustique* editions reveals that although the 1572 reprint does not contain any information about the making of knots, the 1598 edition does and it seems that this edition was the basis of the English translations.

20   E.g. Surflet, *Countrie Farme*, p. 323.

21   Arthur M. Hind, *An Introduction to a History of Woodcut* (New York: Dover, 1963), p. 16; Kenneth Lindley, *The Woodblock Engravers* (Newton Abbot: David & Charles, 1970), p. 90; Tessa Watt, *Cheap Print and Popular Piety* (Cambridge, 1991), p. 242.

22   Thomas Hyll, *The Gardeners Labyrinth* (1577), p. 25.

23   Thomas Hyll, *The Proffitable Arte of Gardening* (1568), pp. 10–11, 15–16. Mazes in this context seem to have simply been one possible element of an ornamental knot design: see e.g. Wyngaerde's drawing of Richmond Palace, du Cerceau's plans of the Jardin de Valleri and Montargis or Sir Thomas Tresham's 'labyrinth' at Lyvedon New Bield (see figs 46, 24, 23, 30).

24   Markham, *English Husbandman*, p. 112–23.

25   Ibid., p. 124. This was in 1613, before Markham's own edition, *The Countrey Farme*, was published in 1616.

26   Ibid., p. 126.

27   *The Trevelyon Miscellany of 1608*, ed. Heather Woolf (Seattle: University of Washington Press, 2007; facsimile of Folger Shakespeare Library MS. V.b.232), p. 7.

28   F. R. Johnson, 'Notes on English Retail Book Prices', *The Library*, 5th ser, 5 (1950), 84, 90.

29   See Ch. 1 above for comparative book prices.

30   Parkinson, *Paradisi*, p. 5.

31   Lawson, *New Orchard and Garden*, sig. A3v.

32   Ibid., p. 70.

33   Mollet, *Le Jardin de Plaisir*, p. 9.

34   French visitor cited in David Jacques and Arend Jan van der Horst, *The Gardens of William and Mary* (London, 1988), p. 26.

35   Mollet, *Le Jardin de Plaisir*, p. 9.

36   Bettisfield 1667; also App. 2. Hanmer is unlikely to be describing anything he has seen in England but, rather, gardens he has seen in France. See Ch. 9 here.

37   Helen Leach, *Cultivating Myths: Fiction, Fact and Fashion in Garden History* (Auckland: Random House, 2000), p. 174.

38   The Hampton Court reconstruction is based on contemporary plans and illustrations of the garden from the late seventeenth century: Todd Longstaffe-Gowan, 'Fruit in Historic Gardens', Garden History Society conference, Hampton Court Palace, 15 November 2008.

39   Perhaps, as indicated by the contemporary portraits, the making of intricate knot gardens was the preserve of the upper elite but, even then, evidence is scant.

40   Some people clearly preferred not to make knots at all. In October 1606, John Chamberlain reported in a letter to his friend Dudley Carleton that Sir Henry Fanshaw was building a fort, complete with ramparts and bulwarks, in the middle of his garden at Ware Park, 'in steede of a knot': John Chamberlain, *The Letters of John Chamberlain*, ed. Norman McClure, 2 vols (Philadelphia, 1939), vol. 1, p. 235.

8   ARTIFICIAL ORNAMENT IN THE GARDEN

1   Parkinson, *Paradisi*, title; Lawson, *New Orchard and Garden*, pp. 52–4; Bettisfield 1667.

2   Roy Strong, *The Renaissance Garden in England* (London, 1979), p. 18; see also fig. 22 above.

3   For more on Hatfield and Wilton House's gardens, see ibid. and Paula Henderson, *The Tudor House and Garden* (New Haven and London, 2005), passim.

4   John Aubrey, *The Natural History of Wiltshire*, Pt II, Ch. II, Project Gutenberg EBook https://archive.org/details/thenaturalhistor04934gut, accessed 14 September 2017. For more on the science and technology involved in the rainbow fountain at Wilton, see Paige Johnson, 'Proof of the Heavenly Iris: The Fountain of Three Rainbows at Wilton House, Wiltshire', *Garden History* 35:1 (2007), pp. 51–67.

5   Henderson, *Tudor House and Garden*, pp. 182–4.

6   J. C. Louden, ed., *An Encyclopaedia of Plants* (London: Longman, Rees, Orme, Brown and Green, 1829), cited by Elisabeth Whittle, *The Historic Gardens of Wales* (London, 1992), pp. 27–8.

7   Roy Strong, *The Artist and the Garden* (New Haven and London, 2000), p. 127.

8   Andrew Thrush and John Ferris, *The House of Commons, 1604–1629*, vol. 5 (Cambridge, 2010), pp. 107–8. The background to and development of Trentham Hall during this period are discussed in Richard Wisker, 'The First Trentham Hall', *Staffordshire History*, 24 (1996), 6–14. This house was demolished in the late seventeenth century.

9   SRO, D593/R/1/2. All quotations from the Trentham accounts in this chapter are from this document,

unless otherwise stated. I am grateful to Helen Smith for first drawing my attention to this document.

10   Robert Plot, *The Natural History of Staffordshire* (Oxford, 1686), whose engravings were executed by the Dutch engraver Michael Burghers: see *Bryan's Dictionary of Painters and Engravers*, 5 vols (4th edn rev. George Williamson, London: Bell, 1903), vol. 1, p. 216.

11   Lloyd Bowen, ed., *Family and Society in Early Stuart Glamorgan: The Household Accounts of Sir Thomas Aubrey of Llantrithyd, c.1565–1641* (Cardiff, 2006), p. 100 (hereafter, *Household Accounts of Thomas Aubrey*).

12   Temple MSS, STT2347; HMC, *De L'Isle MSS*, vol. 3, Thomas Golding to Viscount Lisle, 8 May 1607; Mark Merry and Catherine Richardson, eds, *The Household Account Book of Sir Thomas Puckering of Warwick, 1620* (Stratford-upon-Avon, 2012), p. 164.

13   David Whitehead, 'Some Connected Thoughts on the Parks and Gardens of Herefordshire', *Transactions of the Woolhope Naturalists' Field Club*, 48:2 (1995), 217.

14   Lionel M. Munby, ed., *Early Stuart Household Accounts* (Cambridge, 1986), e.g. pp. 166, 176; SRO, D593/R/1/3.

15   Although it is impossible to know how accurate these depictions of Trentham were, among the illustrations of gentry houses in Staffordshire in Plot's overview, most simply focus on the building with only a few including the garden as well. The fact that Plot included two views of Trentham in his *History*, one specifically showing the layout of the garden, indicates that he considered it noteworthy and it would be fair to assume that the illustration, even if not particularly detailed, offers at least an impression of the garden created at Trentham Hall.

16   Rebecca Roberts, '"Two meane fellows grand projectors": The Self-Projection of Sir Arthur Ingram and Lionel Cranfield, Earl of Middlesex, 1600–1645, with Particular Reference to their Houses' (PhD thesis, Teeside University, 2012), p. 388; WYAS, WYL100/EA/13/9, TN/SH/F3/1.

17   Anthony Fletcher, *A County Community in Peace and War: Sussex 1600–1660* (London, 1975), p. 43.

18   Henderson, *Tudor House and Garden*, pp. 155, 156, fig. 177.

19   Whitehead, 'Connected Thoughts on the Parks and Gardens of Herefordshire', p. 219; HMC, *De L'Isle MSS*, vol. 3, Thomas Golding to Viscount Lisle, 8 May 1607,

p. 375; Pelham, Add. 33145, fol. 68; Merry and Richardson, *Household Account Book of Sir Thomas Puckering*, p. 164.

20 Cheshire Records Office, Chester, DHC/H/199.

21 Parkinson, *Paradisi*, p. 5.

22 John Broad, *Transforming English Rural Society: The Verneys and the Claydons 1600–1820* (Cambridge, 2004), p. 119; CRO, DHC/H/199; Henderson, *Tudor House and Garden*, p. 183.

23 Germaine Warkentin, *The Queen's Majesty's Passage and Related Documents* (Toronto: Victoria University, 2004), p. 108; WYAS, WY100/EA/13/9.

24 HMC, *De L'Isle MSS*, vol. 11, 8 May 1607, p. 374; Pelham, Add. 33147, fol. 68.

25 Merry and Richardson, *Household Account Book of Sir Thomas Puckering*, p. 164.

26 Lawson, *New Orchard and Garden*, pp. 53, 55.

27 Robert Cecil quoted in Andrew Eburne, 'The Passion of Sir Thomas Tresham: New Light on the Gardens and Lodge at Lyveden', *GH*, 36:1 (2008), 121.

28 Whitehead, 'Connected Thoughts on the Parks and Gardens of Herefordshire', p. 219.

29 Bowen, *Household Accounts of Thomas Aubrey*, pp. 22–3.

30 Temple MSS, ST38, fol. 7.

31 Ibid., STT2302, 2279, 2282.

32 Lawson, *New Orchard and Garden*, p. 13.

33 Temple MSS, STT2329.

34 WYAS, WYL178/4.

35 Bacon, 'Of Gardens', p. 54.

36 Strong, *Artist and the Garden*, pp. 47–8; David Howarth, *Lord Arundel and his Circle* (New Haven and London: Yale University Press, 1985), p. 63; Edward Charney, ed., *The Evolution of English Collecting: The Reception of Italian Art in the Tudor and Stuart Periods* (New Haven and London: Yale University Press, 2003), pp. 40–41.

37 Strong, *Artist and the Garden*, pp. 48, 49, fig. 52. See also Ch. 7 here.

38 *Peacham's Compleat Gentleman 1634*, ed. G. S. Gordon (Oxford, 1906), p. 107.

39 See Ch. 3, n. 72.

40 R. Malcolm Smutts, 'Howard, Thomas, fourteenth earl of Arundel (1585–1646)', *ODNB*, May 2015; *Peacham's Compleat Gentleman*, pp. 108–9.

41 SRO, D593/R/1/2; Bowen, *Household Accounts of Thomas Aubrey*, p. 87; IOWRO, OG/AA/31.

42 Henderson, *Tudor House and Garden*, p. 197.

43 Roberts, '"Two meane fellows grand projectors"', p. 396.

44 Joanna Moody, ed., *The Private Life of an Elizabethan Lady: The Diary of Lady Margaret Hoby 1599–1605* (Stroud, 1998), p. 27.

45 Merry and Richardson, *Household Account Book of Sir Thomas Puckering*, p. 32.

46 Judith Spicksley, ed., *The Business and Household Accounts of Joyce Jeffreys, Spinster of Hereford 1638–1648* (Oxford, 2012), pp. 175, 258.

47 Bowen, *Household Accounts of Thomas Aubrey*, pp. 20, 87–8.

48 For more see Eburne, 'Passion of Sir Thomas Tresham', pp. 114–34; Mary Elizabeth Finch, *The Wealth of Five Northamptonshire Families, 1540–1640* (Oxford: Northamptonshire Record Society, 1956), pp. 72–91.

49 Roberts, '"Two meane fellows grand projectors"', p. 413.

50 Campden Manor's two banqueting houses have recently been restored by the Landmark Trust.

51 Merry and Richardson, *Household Account Book of Sir Thomas Puckering*, pp. 74–7 for full analysis of the building of Warwick Priory's banqueting house.

52 Ibid., pp. 158, 161, 163, 164, 169, 178.

53 Roberts, '"Two meane fellows grand projectors"', pp. 419–20; WYAS, WYL178/4.

54 Parkinson, *Paradisi*, p. 3.

55 Thrush and Ferris, *House of Commons*, vol. 5, p. 108.

56 Merry and Richardson, *Household Account Book of Sir Thomas Puckering*, p. 20; Thrush and Ferris, *House of Commons*, vol. 3, p. 507.

57 The gardens at Stowe, created by Temple's descendents, became renowned as one of the finest examples of eighteenth-century landscape gardens in England and are still extant.

9 WAR AND PEACE

1 John Evelyn, 1651, cited by John Ingram in Evelyn, *Elysium Britannicum*, intro., p. 3.

2 John Evelyn, *Diary*, vol. 2, p. 79.

3   Francis Bamford, ed., *A Royalist's Notebook: The Commonplace Book of Sir John Oglander* (London, 1936), p. 105.

4   *Memoirs of the Verney Family during the Seventeenth Century*, comp. Frances and Margaret Verney, 2 vols (London: Longmans, Green & Co., 1925), vol. 1, p. 291.

5   For more on the impact of the Civil Wars on the gentry, see John Broad, *Transforming English Rural Society: The Verneys and Claydons, 1600–1820* (Cambridge, 2004), pp. 27–9; Felicity Heal and Clive Holmes, *The Gentry in England and Wales, 1500–1700* (Basingstoke, 2002), pp. 214–26; Ann Hughes, *Politics, Society and Civil War* (Cambridge: Cambridge University Press, 1987), pp. 255–90.

6   Heal and Holmes, *Gentry in England and Wales*, p. 224.

7   Broad, *Transforming English Rural Society*, p. 30.

8   Sir Ralph Verney, 1653, in *Memoirs of the Verney Family*, vol. 2, p. 1.

9   Claydon House and gardens have been rebuilt, renovated and restored over the years (open to the public: www.claydonestate.co.uk or www.nationaltrust.org.uk/claydon both accessed 19 September 2017).

10   Broad, *Transforming English Rural Society*, p. 43; *Memoirs of the Verney Family*, vol. 1, pp. 524, 535, 438; vol. 2, p. 121; Susan Whyman, 'Verney, Sir Ralph, first baronet (1613–1696)', *ODNB*.

11   Ian Atherton, 'Scudamore, John, first Viscount Scudamore (1601–1671)', *ODNB*; Evelyn cited in David Whitehead, 'Some Connected Thoughts on the Parks and Gardens of Herefordshire', *Transactions of the Woolhope Naturalists' Field Club*, 48:2 (1995), 216.

12   Jan Woudstra and Sally O'Halloran, 'Sir John Reresby's Garden Notebook and Garden (1633–44) at Thrybergh, Yorkshire', *GH*, 36:1 (2008), 154–5.

13   Hanmer, *Garden Book*, intro. Eleanour Sinclair Rohde, p. xi.

14   *Diary*, vol. 2, p. 81.

15   E.g. Evelyn, Add. 15858, fols 11, 13, 14.

16   *Diary*, vol. 3, pp. 191, 193.

17   Ibid., p. 80.

18   Evelyn, Add. 15857, fol. 78, Christopher Browne to Richard Browne, February 1642.

19   Evelyn, Add. 78220, fol. 50, ibid., November 1643.

20   Evelyn, Add. 15857, fol. 80, ibid., March 1642.

21   Evelyn, Add. 78221, fol. 60, John Evelyn to Sir Richard Browne, February 1652.

22   *Diary*, vol. 2, pp. 60, 46.

23   Timothy Mowl, *Gentlemen and Players: Gardeners of the English Landscape* (Stroud, 2000), p. 36.

24   All the following information about this garden is taken from Evelyn's plan and his annotations, unless otherwise stated.

25   *Diary*, vol. 3, p. 80.

26   Parkinson, *Paradisi*, pp. 5, 3.

27   Prudence Leith-Ross, 'A Seventeenth-Century Paris Garden', *GH*, 21:2 (1993), p. 152; *Diary*, vol. 2, p. 133.

28   Evelyn, Add. 78221, fols 61, 63; fol. 56, Evelyn to Sir Richard Browne, September 1652.

29   Gillian Darley, *John Evelyn: Living for Ingenuity* (New Haven and London: Yale University Press, 2006), p. 41.

30   Mowl, *Gentlemen and Players*, p. 42.

31   Evelyn, Add. 78221, fol. 65, Evelyn to Browne, October 1656.

32   Evelyn, 1657, cited in Leith-Ross, 'A Seventeenth-Century Paris Garden', p. 153. However, gardeners change their minds and gardens can be easily altered in a season or two. By 1685, the oval garden had been replaced by a large semicircular bowling green, surrounded by cherries and pears, underplanted with gooseberries and strawberries, bordered on the north, east and south by fruit trees such as apples, damson, apricots, peaches, vines and figs, a salutary reminder of the dangers of trying to date gardens too precisely: Evelyn, Add. 78628B, 'Plan by John Evelyn of part of the south-west portion of the garden at Sayes Court, with a list of fruit trees planted there, February 1685'.

33   Evelyn, Add. 78221, fol. 63, Evelyn to Browne, January 1653.

34   For a brief summary of the features of French garden style, see John Dixon Hunt and Peter Willis, eds, *The Genius of the Place: The English Landscape Garden 1620–1820* (Cambridge, Mass., and London, 1988), p. 7. For more on French gardens see Kenneth Woodbridge, *Princely Gardens: The Origins and Development of the French Formal Style* (London: Thames & Hudson, 1986). For contemporary French garden designs see André Mollet, *Le Jardin de Plaisir*, or *The Garden of Pleasure* (Stockholm, 1651; trans. London, 1670).

35 Evelyn, Add. 78221, fol. 63, Evelyn to Browne.

36 Evelyn, Add. 78613, fols 22–23, agreement between Evelyn and Matthew Blissett, January 1652.

37 Evelyn, Add. 78221, fol. 56, Evelyn to Browne, September 1652.

38 Evelyn, Add. 78221, fol. 65, Evelyn to Browne. Naomi Sheeter, 'Harnessing Nature: Gardens and Science in John Evelyn's England, 1650–1710' (MPhil thesis, University of Birmingham, 2000), has explored in detail this important aspect of Evelyn's life, concluding that there was much interplay between gardening and science at this time, as manifested by the work of the Hartlib circle, of which Evelyn was a member; it seems likely that at the same time as making trials of new horticultural techniques, he was also using his existing knowledge of gardens and gardening as a means of furthering scientific experiment.

39 *Diary*, vol. 1, pp. 154, 496, 561; vol. 4, p. 558. Michael Charlesworth, 'A Plan by John Evelyn for Henry Howard's Garden at Albury Park Surrey', in O'Malley and Wolschke-Bulmahn, pp. 289–90.

40 *Diary*, vol. 2, p. 4.

41 See Felicity Heal, 'The Idea of Hospitality in Early Modern England', *Past and Present*, 102 (1984), 68. This style of writing is also reminiscent of the country-house poems of Jonson, Carew and Marvel (with which Evelyn was surely familiar) which celebrated an idealised view of rural life. For more on that poetry, see Raymond Williams, *The Country and the City* (London: Chatto and Windus, 1973).

42 *Diary*, vol. 1, intro. E. S. de Beer, p. 46.

43 Evelyn, Add. 78610A.

44 *Diary*, vol. 3, p. 60.

45 Evelyn, Add. 78610B.

46 *Diary*, vol. 2, p. 81.

47 Evelyn, Add. 78610C.

48 Evelyn, Add. 78303, from which all quotations from George Evelyn's letters come, unless otherwise stated.

49 *Diary*, vol. 2, p. 551.

50 Ibid., vol. 2, pp. 394–7, 418.

51 Ibid., vol. 1, intro., pp. 46, 85.

52 Evelyn, Add. 78610G, H, F.

53 Evelyn explains the complexities of the engineering involved here in his *Diary*, vol. 3, p. 61.

54 Ibid., vol. 2, pp. 4–5.

55 Ibid., vol. 3, pp. 154, 496.

56 Ibid., p. 561.

57 These trade and exchange networks are examined more fully in Chapter 10 here.

58 Bettisfield 1667, also discussed in Ch. 1 above.

59 This view is endorsed by Roy Strong, *The Artist and the Garden* (New Haven and London, 2000), p. 156, who suggests that Hanmer was describing elements of the French garden style that became the dominant influence in England after 1660; see also Ruth Duthie, 'The Planting Plans of Some Seventeenth-Century Flower Gardens', *GH*, 18:2 (1990), 83, 85.

60 John Rea cited in Duthie, 'Planting Plans', p. 82; Parkinson, *Paradisi*, p. 3.

61 Thomas Hanmer to John Evelyn, 1668, cited in Jenny Robinson, 'New Light on Sir Thomas Hanmer', *GH*, 16:1 (1988), 6.

62 Both these MSS are part of Bettisfield 1667. For a transcript of the list see Hanmer, *Garden Book*, intro. Eleanour Sinclair Rohde, pp. xxi–xxiv.

63 Bettisfield 925.

64 Bettisfield 1663.

65 Ibid.

66 Hanmer, *Garden Book*, p. 23.

67 Ibid., pp. 16, 15.

68 Ibid., p. 9.

69 Hanmer's essay on gardening, Bettisfield 1667.

70 Bettisfield 21753 B.

71 Hanmer, *Garden Book*, p. 9. All the following references to the over-wintering of plants come from this section of that book.

72 Bettisfield 1663.

73 Thirty years later Evelyn was still addressing this problem. He too recognised that plants needed to breathe ('as I presume to call it', he adds in parenthesis, clearly unsure of the correct term) and came up with an ingenious method of keeping a constant supply of fresh warm air circulating in a glasshouse, using an external stove and pipes to transfer the heat inside: Mark Laird, 'The Greenhouse and the Great Storm of 1703 in the Life of John Evelyn and his Contemporaries', *GH*, 34:2 (2006), 158. In the meantime, Hanmer's doors and windows went some way towards solving this problem.

74 Again, it was Evelyn who appears to have been the first to recognise this, noting in his *Kalendarium Hort-*

ense (1691) that 'Light itself, next to Air, is of wonderful importance'. The essential process of photosynthesis, and the linking of sunlight to that process, was not discovered by scientists until the end of the following century.

75   Bettisfield 1667.

76   Ibid.

77   Hanmer, *Garden Book*, intro., p. xxi, pp. 79, 52, 38; Pierre Morin, *Catalogues de quelques Plantes à Fleurs qui sont de présent au jardin de Pierre Morin le jeune, dit Troisième; Fleuriste* (Paris, 1651).

78   Hanmer, *Garden Book*, p. 18.

79   Ibid., p. 19.

80   Bettisfield 1667; 925; 1165.

81   Hanmer to Evelyn, 1668, cited in Robinson, 'New Light on Sir Thomas Hanmer', p. 6.

82   Parkinson, *Paradisi*, p. 8.

10   THE PLANTS

1   Parkinson, *Paradisi*, p. 11.

2   John Harvey, *Early Gardening Catalogues* (London, 1972); John Harvey, *Early Nurserymen* (London, 1974), esp. pp. 7, 5.

3   Harvey, *Early Nurserymen*, p. 27.

4   Ibid., p. 40.

5   Petition to the Lord Mayor of London, 1345, cited in Charles Welch, *The History of the Worshipful Company of Gardeners* (London, 1900), p. 18.

6   C. Paul Christianson, *The Riverside Gardens of Thomas More's London* (New Haven and London, 2005), p. 111.

7   Ibid., pp. 111–12, 118.

8   Lionel M. Munby, ed., *Early Stuart Household Accounts* (Cambridge, 1986), pp. 167, 168, 194.

9   Pelham, Add. 33147, fols 16, 89, 10, 17, 71, 89, 78v, 130, 89.

10   Temple MSS, STT2289, STT2296.

11   IOWRO, OG/AA/28; Lloyd Bowen, ed., *Family and Society in Early Stuart Glamorgan: The Household Accounts of Sir Thomas Aubrey of Llantrithyd, c.1565–1641* (Cardiff, 2006), p. 73 (hereafter, *Household Accounts of Thomas Aubrey*).

12   SRO, D593/R/1/2.

13   Richard Gardner, *Profitable Instructions for the Manuring, Sowing, and Planting of Kitchin Gardens* (London, 1599), sig. D2v.

14   M. J. Power, 'London and the Control of the "Crisis" of the 1590s', *History*, 70:230 (October 1985), 371.

15   Gardner, *Profitable Instructions*, sig. D2.

16   SRO, D593/R/1/2; Bowen, *Household Accounts of Thomas Aubrey*, p. 124.

17   E.g. Temple MSS, STT2276; *The Memorandum Book of Richard Cholmeley of Brandsby 1602–1623* (Northallerton: North Yorkshire County Records Office Publications, no. 44, 1988).

18   Pelham, Add. 33147, fol. 141v.

19   Bowen, *Household Accounts of Thomas Aubrey*, pp. 55, 60.

20   M. D. G. Wanklyn, 'The Severn Navigation in the Seventeenth-Century: Long-Distance Trade of Shrewsbury Boats', *Midland History*, 13:1 (1988), 34–58; John Chartres, *Internal Trade in England 1500–1700* (London: Macmillan, 1977), p. 42; WYAS, WYL178/4, Sir Arthur Ingram to John Matteson, 29 October 1622.

21   Parkinson, *Paradisi*, p. 18.

22   Evelyn, Add. 78221, John Evelyn to Sir Richard Browne, September 1652, fol. 56. Pelham, Add. 33147, fols 141v, 163v. A rootstock is the lower part of a plant used in grafting onto which the upper part, or scion, is grafted.

23   E.g. Temple MSS, STT2143, STT2282.

24   Pelham, Add. 33147, fols 141v, 122.

25   Temple MSS, ST2287.

26   Ibid., ST38, fol. 31v.

27   Ibid., fols 18v, 30v, 31v.

28   E.g. ibid., STT2146, STT2148, STT2300.

29   Ibid., STT2296.

30   Ibid., STT2289.

31   Margaret Hoby, *The Private Life of an Elizabethan Lady: The Diary of Lady Margaret Hoby 1599–1605*, ed. Joanna Moody (Stroud, 1998), p. 14.

32   HMC, *De L'Isle MSS*, vol. 4, Viscount Lisle to Lady Lisle, 31 October 1610.

33   Huw Bowen, '400 Years of the East India Company', *History Today*, 50:7 (July 2000), 47.

34   David Sacks, 'London's Dominion', in *Material London, c.1600*, ed. Lena Cowen Orlin (Philadelphia,

2000), p. 22; Frederick J. Fisher, *London and the English Economy, 1500–1700*, ed. P. J. Corfield and N. B. Harte (London, 1989), pp. 105–6.

35 Parkinson, *Paradisi*, pp. 574, 571. Parkinson's is the first recorded use of the term 'nurseryman', indicating perhaps the relatively recent specialisation of this aspect of the horticultural trade.

36 Ibid., p. 538.

37 Lawson, *New Orchard and Garden*, p. 17.

38 Parkinson, *Paradisi*, pp. 312–14.

39 Johnson, *Gerard's Herball*, pp. 161, 589, 785; Tradescant's copy of Parkinson, *Paradisi* (1629), Bodleian Library, Oxford, Antiq.c.E.1629.1; Hanmer, *Garden Book*, p. 80; see Harvey, *Early Nurserymen*, p. 43.

40 Parkinson, *Paradisi*, p. 575.

41 Johnson, *Gerard's Herball* (1633), pp. 1324, 1448, 1456, 1496, 1506.

42 Ibid., p. 481.

43 Gerard, *Herball*, p. 1269.

44 Harvey, *Early Nurserymen*, pp. 40–41.

45 Gerard, *Herball*, p. 1269.

46 John Stow, *A Survey of London written in the year 1598* (repr. Stroud, 2005), pp. 39, 122–3.

47 Ibid., pp. 122–5.

48 Harvey, *Early Nurserymen*, p. 45.

49 For more on the growth of market gardens, see Fisher, *London and the English Economy*, pp. 67–9; Malcolm Thick, *The Neat House Gardens: Early Market Gardening around London* (Totnes, 1998).

50 David Jacques, '"The Chief Ornament" of Gray's Inn: The Walks from Bacon to Brown', *GH*, 17:1 (1989), 45.

51 Fisher, *London and the English Economy*, p. 65.

52 Parkinson, *Paradisi*, pp. 418, 404.

53 Stow, *Survey of London*, p. 236; Ann Leighton, *Early English Gardens in New England: 'for meate or medicine'* (London, 1970), p. 190; Gerard, *Herball*, p. 780. This is not the same as the newly arrived Potato of Virginia (not from Virginia at all, but South America) which Gerard describes on p. 781, saying they prospered as well in his garden as in their native land.

54 Harvey, *Early Nurserymen*, p. 4; Anna Parkinson, *Nature's Alchemist: John Parkinson, Herbalist to Charles I* (London, 2007), p. 177.

55 A. Parkinson, *Nature's Alchemist*, p. 111.

56 Prudence Leith-Ross, *The John Tradescants: Gardeners to the Rose and Lily Queen* (London, 1984), pp. 89–90.

57 Daniel Fleming household accounts, cited in ibid., pp. 89–91.

58 Gerard, *Herball*, p. 116.

59 Anna Pavord, *The Tulip* (London, 2000), p. 8.

60 Gerard, *Herball*, p. 177.

61 Deborah Harkness, *The Jewel House: Elizabethan London and the Scientific Revolution* (New Haven and London, 2007), p. 26; Anne Goldgar, *Tulipmania: Money, Honor, and Knowledge in the Dutch Golden Age* (Chicago and London, 2008), pp. 22, 34.

62 Harkness, *Jewel House*, 'Living on Lime Street', pp. 15–56.

63 For more on the introduction of the tulip into Europe see Goldgar, *Tulipmania*, esp. pp. 34–6.

64 Ibid., p. 6.

65 Parkinson, *Paradisi*, pp. 45–67.

66 Gerard, *Herball*, p. 120.

67 Parkinson, *Paradisi*, p. 9.

68 Hanmer, *Garden Book*, p. 18.

69 Sir Thomas Hanmer, insert 'On Tulips', reproduced in Evelyn, *Elysium Britannicum*, p. 445.

70 Simon Schama, *The Embarrassment of Riches* (London: Fontana, 1988), p. 351.

71 Bettisfield 1663; W. H. Dawson, *Cromwell's Understudy: The Life and Times of General John Lambert* (London: Hodge, 1938), p. 456.

72 Leith-Ross, *John Tradescants*, pp. 26–8; Sonia Anderson, 'The Elder William Trumbull: A Biographical Sketch', *British Library Journal*, 19 (1993), 115–32.

73 Leith-Ross, *John Tradescants*, pp. 28–40.

74 Parkinson, *Paradisi*, Bodleian, Antiq.c.E.1629.1.

75 John Tradescant cited in Leith-Ross, *John Tradescants*, p. 37.

76 Parkinson, *Paradisi*, pp. 428, 427.

77 See Leith-Ross, *John Tradescants*, where Tradescant's diary is reproduced in full.

78 Parkinson, *Paradisi*, p. 430. By 1620, Tradescant was working for Edward, Lord Wotton, who lived at the former monastery of St Augustine in Canterbury.

79 Leith-Ross, *John Tradescants*, pp. 78, 82.

80 Parkinson, *Paradisi*, p. 346.

81   J. Bekkers, *Correspondence of John Morris with Johannes de Laet (1634–1649)* (Assen: Van Gorcum, 1970); *ODNB*.

82   Leith-Ross, *John Tradescants*, p. 102.

83   Transcribed in ibid., pp. 227, 231.

84   Parkinson, *Paradisi*, p. 152.

85   John Parkinson, *Theatrum Botanicum: The Theater of Plants* (London, 1640), p. 1064.

86   Gerard, *Herball*, pp. 251, 994, 55, 152.

87   Parkinson, *Paradisi*, p. 434.

88   Ibid., *Paradisi*, p. 420.

89   Harvey, *Early Gardening Catalogues*, p. 7. The earliest known trade catalogue, produced by William Lucas to advertise the wide range of seeds, plants and roots available from his shop by the sign of 'the Naked Boy near Strand Bridge, London', is thought to have been published *c.*1677: Harvey, p. 15.

90   John Chamberlain, *The Letters of John Chamberlain*, ed. Norman McClure (Philadelphia, 1939), vol. 1, p. 290.

91   IOWRO, OG/AA/29, fol. 27v.

92   Todd Gray, ed., *Devon Household Accounts, 1627–59, Part 2: Henry, fifth Earl of Bath, and Rachel, Countess of Bath, of Tawstoc* (Exeter, 1996), p. 79.

93   Bettisfield 1663, from which the following information comes unless otherwise stated.

94   John Rea, *Flora: De Florum Cultura, or A Complete Florilege* (London, 1665), pp. 65–6.

95   Although Lambert was never formally created a peer, Hanmer consistently refers to him throughout his notebook as 'Lord Lambert'.

96   General Lambert's garden at Castle Cornet on Guernsey is open to the public. It is laid out in a 17th-century pattern and contains medicinal herbs and flowers that would have been used at the time: www.visitguernsey.com/castle-cornet, accessed 20 September 2017.

97   Bulbs naturally reproduce themselves by growing offsets (baby bulbs) from the base of the main bulb. These can be removed by the gardener and planted to produce a new plant. It is an easier and more reliable way of propagating flowering bulbs than the alternative method of collecting seed.

98   Bettisfield 1663.

99   Rea, *Flora*, sig. B2.

100   Bettisfield 1663.

101   Harvey, *Early Nurserymen*, p. 43.

102   Bettisfield 1663.

103   Rea, *Flora*, p. 153.

104   According to Elspeth Thompson, 'Stalls or Circle?', *The Garden* (April 2010), 236, 'by the end of the 17th century, auricula fancying was on a par with tulipomania'.

105   John Schofield, ed., *The London Surveys of Ralph Treswell* (London, 1987), p. 146.

106   All Hanmer's references to these Paris nurserymen come from Bettisfield 1663.

107   Tradescant also notes plants received from Morin in 1629 and from Pierre's elder brother, René, in 1631, in his list at the back of his copy of Parkinson's *Paradisi*, Bodleian, Antiq.c.E.1629.1.

108   Evelyn, Add. 78221.

109   It is difficult to ascertain meaningful currency conversions for this period, not least because the value of the French livre fluctuated depending on time and place, but the consensus suggests that £1 was worth approx. 13 livres: *OED*, www.oed.com; www.pierre-marteau.com/currency/converter/eng-fra.html; accessed 20 September 2017.

110   Hanmer, *Garden Book*, pp. 38, 59; Pierre Morin, *Catalogues de quelques Plantes à Fleurs qui sont de présent au jardin de Pierre Morin le jeune, dit Troisième; Fleuriste* (Paris, 1651).

111   Michael Hunter, *Establishing the New Science: The Experience of the Early Royal Society* (Woodbridge, 1989), p. 4.

11   CONCLUSIONS

1   See Introduction above and Parkinson, *Paradisi*, e.g. pp. 7, 8, 9.

2   Felicity Heal and Clive Holmes, *The Gentry in England and Wales, 1500–1700* (Basingstoke, 2002), p. 298.

3   Paul Hentzner, *A Journey into England in the year 1598*, ed. Horace Walpole (Strawberry Hill, 1757; repr. Reading, 1807); *Thomas Platter's Travels in England* (1599), trans. and ed. Clare Williams (London: Jonathan Cape, 1937); Baron Waldstein, *The Diary of Baron Waldstein: A Traveller in Elizabethan England* (1600), trans. G. W. Groos (London, 1981).

4   Waldstein, *Diary*, p. 82.

5   Hentzner, *Journey into England*, p. 25.

6   H. J. Louw, 'Some Royal and Other Great Houses in England: Extracts from the Journal of Abram Booth', *Architectural History*, 27 (1984), 503–9.

7   J. T. Cliffe, *The Yorkshire Gentry from the Reformation to the Civil War* (London: Athlone Press, 1969), pp. 278–9.

8   John Chamberlain, *The Letters of John Chamberlain*, ed. Norman McClure (Philadelphia, 1939), vol. 1, p. 227.

9   Henry Wotton, 'The Elements of Architecture' (1624), in *The Genius of the Place: The English Landscape Garden 1620–1820*, ed. John Dixon Hunt and Peter Willis (Cambridge, Mass., and London, 1988), p. 48; Evelyn, *Diary*, vol. 2, 11 March 1642, 19 April 1643; vol. 3, 8 May 1654, 27 September 1658, 30 April 1663.

10 Paula Henderson, *The Tudor House and Garden* (New Haven and London, 2005), p. 84.

11 Keith Thomas, *The Ends of Life: Roads to Fulfilment in Early Modern England* (Oxford, 2009), p. 116.

12 Heal and Holmes, *Gentry in England and Wales*, p. 284.

13 Francis Bacon, 'Of Gardens' (1625), in Hunt and Willis, *Genius of the Place*, p. 54.

14 For more on loggias see Henderson, *Tudor House and Garden*, pp. 153–4.

15 Lloyd Bowen, ed., *Family and Society in Early Stuart Glamorgan: The Household Accounts of Sir Thomas Aubrey of Llantrithyd, c.1565–1641* (Cardiff, 2006), p. 55.

16 Prudence Leith-Ross, *The John Tradescants: Gardeners to the Rose and Lily Queen* (London, 1984), p. 35.

17 See John Phillips and Nicholas Burnett, 'The Chronology and Layout of Francis Carew's Garden at Beddington, Surrey', *GH*, 33:2 (2005), pp. 159, 161.

18 Thomas, *Ends of Life*, p. 118. For more on this, see Ch. 2 above.

19 Henderson, *Tudor House and Garden*, p. 10; Pelham, Add. 33147, fol. 6v.

20 Thomas Barker, *The Country-mans Recreation* (London, 1654); Izaac Walton, *The Compleat Angler* (London, 1653).

21 HMC, *De L'Isle MSS*, vol. 5, Thomas Golding to Viscount L'Isle, 20 May 1612.

22 Thomas, *Ends of Life*, pp. 129–31.

23 Parkinson, *Paradisi*, Epistle to the Reader.

24 IOWRO, OG/AA/29, fol. 25.

25 Margaret Hoby, *The Private Life of an Elizabethan Lady: The Diary of Lady Margaret Hoby 1599–1605*, ed. Joanna Moody (Stroud, 1998), p. 157.

26 IOWRO, OG/AA/28, fol. 3; Hoby, *Private Life of an Elizabethan Lady*, p. 10.

27 Mark Girouard, *Life in the English Country House* (New Haven and London: Yale University Press, 1978), pp. 102–4.

28 Bettisfield 1667.

29 Lawson, *New Orchard and Garden*, p. 52.

30 Parkinson, *Paradisi*, p. 65.

31 Lawson, *New Orchard and Garden*, p. 54.

32 Ibid.

33 Parkinson, *Paradisi*, Epistle to the Reader.

34 OG/AA/29, fol. 27v. The transcription by Francis Bamford in *A Royalist's Notebook: The Commonplace Book of Sir John Oglander* (London, 1936), p. 84, states that the garden was made of a 'rude chase', an expression that has been perpetuated in secondary sources. However, it is clear that Sir John's use of the biblical word 'Chaos', as well as being unmistakeable, is also deliberate in that it serves to put his own description of what he has achieved on a much more elevated plane.

35 Lawson, *New Orchard and Garden*, p. 13; Parkinson, *Paradisi*, p. 3.

SELECT BIBLIOGRAPHY

MANUSCRIPT SOURCES

British Library, London
  Evelyn Papers, Additional Manuscripts
  Pelham Papers, Additional Manuscripts
Huntington Library, San Marino, California. Temple
  Family Papers, Stowe Archive
Isle of Wight Records Office, Newport. Oglander
  Collection
London Metropolitan Archive
  'Agas' map of London
  Copperplate map of London
  Records of the Worshipful Company of
    Gardeners
  Records of the Worshipful Company of
    Ironmongers
National Library of Wales, Aberystwyth. Bettisfield
  Estate Records
Staffordshire Records Office, Stafford. Sutherland
  Collection
West Yorkshire Archive Service, Leeds. Temple
  Newsam MSS

PRIMARY PRINTED SOURCES

Austen, Ralph, *A Treatise of Fruit-trees* (Oxford,
  1653)
Bacon, Francis, 'Of Gardens' (1625), repr. in Hunt
  and Willis, *Genius of the Place*, pp. 51–6
Bamford, Francis, ed., *A Royalist's Notebook: The
  Commonplace Book of Sir John Oglander* (London:
  Constable, 1936)
Barker, Thomas, *The Country-mans Recreation*
  (London, 1654)
Bonnefons, Nicolas, *The French Gardiner*, trans. John
  Evelyn (London, 1658)
Bowen, Lloyd, ed., *Family and Society in Early Stuart
  Glamorgan: The Household Accounts of Sir Thomas
  Aubrey of Llantrithyd, c.1565–1641* (Cardiff: South
  Wales Record Society, 2006)
Butler, Charles, *The feminine monarchie, or A treatise
  concerning bees* (Oxford, 1609; facsimile edn,
  Amsterdam and New York: Da Capo Press, 1969)
Calendar of Wynn (of Gwydir) Papers (Aberystwyth:
  National Library of Wales, 1926)
Cartwright, John, ed., *The Memoirs of Sir John Reresby
  of Thrybergh, 1634–1689 written by himself*
  (London: Longmans, Green and Co., 1875)

Certaine excellent and new invented knots and mazes (London, 1623)

The Country-mans Recreation (London, 1640)

Chamberlain, John, *The Letters of John Chamberlain*, ed. Norman McClure, 2 vols (Philadelphia: American Philosophical Society, 1939)

du Cerceau, Jacques Androuet, *Le premier volume des plus excellents bastiments de France* (Paris, 1576; repr. Westmead, England: Gregg International, 1972)

Estienne, Charles, *L'agriculture et Maison Rustique* (Paris, 1564; 1572; 1598)

Evelyn, John, *The Diary of John Evelyn*, ed. E. S. de Beer, 6 vols (Oxford: Clarendon Press, 1955)

—, *Elysium Britannicum, or the Royal Gardens in Three Books*, ed. John E. Ingram (Philadelphia: University of Pennsylvania Press, 2000)

The Expert Gardener (London, 1640)

Fanshawe, Lady Ann, *The Memoirs of Ann, Lady Fanshawe* (repr. from the original MS., London: John Lane, Bodley Head, 1907)

Gardner, Richard, *Profitable Instructions for the Manuring, Sowing, and Planting of Kitchin Gardens* (London, 1599)

Gerard, John, *The Herball, or Generall Historie of Plantes* (London, 1597)

—, *The Herball, or Generall Historie of Plantes*, ed. Thomas Johnson (London, 1633; 1636)

Gray, Todd, ed., *Devon Household Accounts, 1627–59, Part 1: Sir Richard and Lady Lucy Reynall of Forde (1627–48), John Willoughby of Leyhill (1644–6) and Sir Edward Wise of Sydenham (1655–9)* (Exeter: Devon and Cornwall Record Society, 1995)

—, *Devon Household Accounts, 1627–59, Part 2: Henry, fifth Earl of Bath, and Rachel, Countess of Bath, of Tawstoc* (Exeter: Devon and Cornwall Record Society, 1996)

Hanmer, Thomas, *The Garden Book of Sir Thomas Hanmer*, 'Now first printed from the MS volume of 1659 under the care of Ivy Elstob', intro. Eleanour Sinclair Rohde (London: Gerald Howe, 1933; repr. Mold: Clwyd County Library and Information Service, 1991)

Harrison, William, *The Description of England* (1577; 1587), ed. Georges Edelen (Washington, DC: Folger Shakespeare Library, and New York: Dover, 1994)

Hentzner, Paul, *A Journey into England in the year 1598*, ed. Horace Walpole (Strawberry Hill, 1757; repr. Reading: T. E. Williams, 1807)

Heresbach, Conrad, *Foure Bookes of Husbandry*, Newely Englished and increased by Barnabe Googe (London, 1577; facsimile edn, New York: Da Capo Press, 1971)

Historical Manuscripts Commission, *Report on the MSS of Lord De L'Isle and Dudley at Penshurst Place*, 6 vols (London: Her Majesty's Stationery Office, 1925–66)

Hill, Thomas, *The Gardener's Labyrinth* (1652), ed. Richard Mabey (Oxford: Oxford University Press, 1988)

Hoby, Margaret, *The Private Life of an Elizabethan Lady: The Diary of Lady Margaret Hoby 1599–1605*, ed. Joanna Moody (Stroud: Sutton, 1998)

The Holy Bible (King James Version) (1611; London: Eyre and Spottiswoode, 1862)

Hyll, Thomas, *A most briefe and pleasaunte treatise, teachyng how to dresse, sowe, and set a garden* (London, [c.1558]; 1563)

—, *The Gardeners Labyrinth* (London, 1577; 1578; 1651)

—, *The Proffitable Arte of Gardening, now the third tyme set fourth* (London, 1568; 1579)

Josselin, Ralph, *The Diary of Ralph Josselin, 1616–1683*, ed. Alan MacFarlane (Oxford: Oxford University Press, 1991)

Kuin, R. J. P., ed., *Robert Langham, A Letter* (Leiden: Brill, 1938)

Lawson, William, *A New Orchard and Garden... with the Country Housewifes Garden* (London, 1618; facsimile edn, intro. Malcolm Thick, Totnes: Prospect Books, 2003)

Markham, Gervase, *The English Housewife* (London, 1615), ed. Michael Best (Montreal and Kingston, Ontario: McGill-Queen's University Press, 1986)

—, *Cheape and Good Husbandry* (London, 1614)

—, *The English Husbandman: The First Part* (London, 1613)

—, *The English Husbandman* (London, 1635)

—, *Maison Rustique, or the Countrey Farme* (London, 1616)

—, *The Second Book of the English Husbandman* (London, 1614)

Marsh, Bower, and John Ainsworth, eds, *Records of the Worshipful Company of Carpenters, V: Warden's Account Book 1571–1599* (Oxford: Oxford University Press, 1937)

Mascall, Leonard, *A Booke of the Arte and maner, howe to plant and graffe all sortes of trees* (London, [1572])

The Memorandum Book of Richard Cholmeley of Brandsby 1602–1623, North Yorkshire County Records Office Publications, no. 44 (Northallerton, 1988)

Merry, Mark, and Catherine Richardson, eds, *The Household Account Book of Sir Thomas Puckering of Warwick, 1620* (Stratford-upon-Avon: Dugdale Society in association with the Shakespeare Birthplace Trust, 2012)

Mollet, André, *Le Jardin de Plaisir*, or *The Garden of Pleasure* (Stockholm: H. Kayser, 1651; trans. London, 1670; facsimile edn Uppsala, Sweden: Gyllene Snittet, 2006)

Morin, Pierre, *Catalogues de quelques Plantes à Fleurs qui sont de présent au jardin de Pierre Morin le jeune, dit Troisième; Fleuriste* (Paris, 1651)

Munby, Lionel M., ed., *Early Stuart Household Accounts* (Cambridge: Hertfordshire Record Society, 1986)

The Orchard, and the Garden (London, 1594)

Parkinson, John, *Paradisi in Sole, Paradisus Terrestris: or, A Garden of all Sorts of Pleasant Flowers* (London, 1629; facsimile edn, New York: Dover, 1976)

—, *Paradisi in Sole, Paradisus Terrestris: or, A Garden of all Sorts of Pleasant Flowers* (London, 1629; facsimile edn, London, Methuen, 1904)

—, *Paradisi in Sole, Paradisus Terrestris: or, A Garden of all Sorts of Pleasant Flowers* (London, 1629; copy annot. John Tradescant, Bodleian Library, Oxford, Antiq.c.E.1629)

—, *Theatrum Botanicum: The Theater of Plants* (London, 1640)

Peacham, Henry, *The Compleat Gentleman: fashioning him absolut in the most necessary and commendable qualities concerning minde or bodie that may be required in a noble gentleman* (London, 1622; facsimile edn, New York: Da Capo Press, 1968)

Peacham's Compleat Gentleman 1634, ed. G. S. Gordon (Oxford: Clarendon Press, 1906)

Plot, Robert, *The Natural History of Staffordshire* (Oxford, 1686)

Rea, John, *Flora: De Florum Cultura, or A Complete Florilege* (London, 1665)

Schofield, John, ed., *The London Surveys of Ralph Treswell* (London: London Topographical Society, 1987)

Scot, Reynolde, *A Perfite Platforme of a Hoppe Garden* (London, 1574)

Spicksley, Judith, ed., *The Business and Household Accounts of Joyce Jeffreys, Spinster of Hereford 1638–1648* (Oxford: Oxford University Press, 2012)

Stow, John, *A Survey of London written in the year 1598* (repr. Stroud: Sutton Publishing, 2005)

Stratford-upon-Avon Inventories, vol. 1: *1538–1699*, ed. Jeanne Jones (Stratford-upon-Avon: Dugdale Society in association with the Shakespeare Birthplace Trust, 2002)

Surflet, Richard, *Maison Rustique, or the Countrie Farme* (London, 1600; 1606)

The Trevelyon Miscellany of 1608, ed. Heather Woolf (Seattle: University of Washington Press, 2007; facsimile of Folger Shakespeare Library MS. V.b.232)

Waldstein, Baron, *The Diary of Baron Waldstein: A Traveller in Elizabethan England* (1600), trans. G. W. Groos (London: Thames & Hudson, 1981)

Woodward, Marcus, ed., *Gerard's Herball: The Essence thereof distilled* (London: Minerva, 1971)

Wotton, Henry, 'The Elements of Architecture' (1624), in *Reliquiae Wottonianae* (London, 1654), pp. 269–71; repr. in Hunt and Willis, *Genius of the Place*, pp. 48–50

SECONDARY SOURCES

Alcock, Nathaniel, *Warwickshire Grazier and London Skinner, 1532–1555: The Account Book of Peter Temple and Thomas Heritage* (London: Oxford University Press, 1981)

Barnard, John, and D. F. McKenzie, eds, *The Cambridge History of the Book in Britain: Vol. 4, 1567–1695* (Cambridge: Cambridge University Press, 2002)

Barnes, Melvyn, *Root and Branch: A History of the Worshipful Company of Gardeners of London* (London: Worshipful Company of Gardeners, 1994)

Barry, Jonathan, and Christopher Brooks, eds, *The Middling Sort of People: Culture, Society and Politics in England, 1550–1800* (Basingstoke: Macmillan, 1994)

Broad, John, *Transforming English Rural Society: The Verneys and the Claydons, 1600–1820* (Cambridge: Cambridge University Press, 2004)

Bryson, Anna, *From Courtesy to Civility: Changing Codes of Conduct in Early Modern England* (Oxford: Oxford University Press, 1998)

Bushnell, Rebecca, *Green Desire: Imagining Early Modern English Gardens* (New York: Cornell University Press, 2003)

—, 'The Gardener and the Book', in Glaisyer and Pennell, *Didactic Literature in England*, pp. 118–36

Christianson, C. Paul, *The Riverside Gardens of Thomas More's London* (New Haven and London: Yale University Press, 2005)

Cressy, David, *Literacy and the Social Order: Reading and Writing in Tudor and Stuart England* (Cambridge: Cambridge University Press, 1980)

Crick, Julia, and Alexandra Walsham, *The Uses of Script and Print, 1300–1700* (Cambridge: Cambridge University Press, 2004)

Crisp, Frank, *Mediaeval Gardens*, 2 vols (London: John Lane, Bodley Head, 1924)

Cust, Richard, and Ann Hughes, eds, *Conflict in Early Stuart England: Studies in Religion and Politics, 1603–1642* (Harlow: Longman, 1989)

'A Document concerning Shakespeare's Garden', *Huntington Library Bulletin*, 1 (1931), 199–201 (no author attributed)

Duthie, Ruth, 'The Planting Plans of Some Seventeenth-Century Flower Gardens', *GH*, 18:2 (1990), 77–102

Dyer, Chris, 'Gardens and Garden Produce in the later Middle Ages', in *Food in Medieval England*, ed. C. M. Woolgar, D. Sergeantson and T. Waldron (Oxford: Oxford University Press, 2006), pp. 28–40

Eburne, Andrew, 'The Passion of Sir Thomas Tresham: New Light on the Gardens and Lodge at Lyveden', *GH*, 36:1 (2008), 114–34

Findlen, Paula, 'Francis Bacon and the Reform of Natural History in the Seventeenth Century', in *History and the Disciplines*, ed. Donald Kelley (Woodbridge: University of Rochester Press, 1997), pp. 239–60

Fisher, Frederick J., *London and the English Economy, 1500–1700*, ed. P. J. Corfield and N. B. Harte (London: Hambledon Press, 1989)

Fletcher, Anthony, *A County Community in Peace and War: Sussex 1600–1660* (London: Longman, 1975)

Foster, A. M, *Bee Boles and Bee Houses* (Princes Risborough: Shire Publications, 1988)

Friedman, Alice T., *House and Household in Elizabethan England: Wollaton Hall and the Willoughby Family* (London: University of Chicago Press, 1989)

Gay, Edwin F., 'The Rise of an English Country Family: Peter and John Temple, to 1603', *Huntington Library Quarterly*, 1:4 (1938), 367–90

—, 'The Temples of Stowe and their Debts: Sir Thomas and Sir Peter Temple, 1603-1653', *Huntington Library Quarterly*, 2:4 (1939), 399–438

Girouard, Mark, *Robert Smythson and the Elizabethan Country House* (New Haven and London: Yale University Press, 1983)

Glaisyer, Natasha, and Sara Pennell, eds, *Didactic Literature in England 1500–1800* (Aldershot: Ashgate, 2003)

Goldgar, Anne, *Tulipmania: Money, Honor, and Knowledge in the Dutch Golden Age* (Chicago and London: University of Chicago Press, 2008)

Gunther, R. T., *Early British Botanists and their Gardens* (Oxford: Oxford University Press, 1922)

Hackel, Heidi Brayman, *Reading Material in Early Modern England: Print, Gender, and Literacy* (Cambridge: Cambridge University Press, 2005)

Hanmer, John, 1st Baron, *A Memorial of the Parish and Family of Hanmer in Flintshire* (London: Chiswick Press, 1877)

Harkness, Deborah, *The Jewel House: Elizabethan London and the Scientific Revolution* (New Haven and London: Yale University Press, 2007)

Harvey, John, *Early Gardening Catalogues* (London: Phillimore, 1972)

—, *Early Nurserymen* (London: Phillimore, 1974)

—, *Mediaeval Gardens* (London: Batsford, 1981)

—, 'William Lawson and his Garden', *Country Life*, 28 October 1982, 1338–40

—, 'Vegetables in the Middle Ages', *GH*, 12:2 (1984), 89–99

Harwood, Edward, et al., 'Whither Garden History', *Studies in the History of Gardens and Designed Landscapes*, 27:2 (2007), 91–112

Heal, Felicity, 'Food Gifts, the Household and the Politics of Exchange in Early Modern England', *Past and Present*, 199 (2008), 41–70

—, *Hospitality in Early Modern England* (Oxford: Clarendon Press, 1990)

—, 'The Idea of Hospitality in Early Modern England', *Past and Present*, 102 (1984), 66–93

— and Clive Holmes, *The Gentry in England and Wales, 1500–1700* (Basingstoke: Macmillan, 1994; repr. 2002)

Henderson, Paula, *The Tudor House and Garden* (New Haven and London: Yale University Press, 2005)

—, 'Clinging to the Past: Medievalism in the English "Renaissance" Garden', *Renaissance Studies*, 25:1 (2011), 42–69

Henrey, Blanche, *British Botanical and Horticultural Literature before 1800*, 3 vols (Oxford: Oxford University Press, 1975), vol. 1, *The Sixteenth and Seventeenth Centuries: History and Bibliography*

Hunt, John Dixon, 'Evelyn's Idea of a Garden: A Theory for all Seasons', in O'Malley and Wolschke-Bulmahn, pp. 269–88

—, and Peter Willis, eds, *The Genius of the Place: The English Landscape Garden 1620–1820* (London: Paul Elek, 1975; repr. Cambridge, Mass., and London: MIT Press, 1988)

Hunter, Lynette, 'Books for Daily Life: Household, Husbandry, Behaviour', in *The Cambridge History of the Book in Britain*, vol. 4, *1567–1695*, ed. John Barnard and D. F. McKenzie (Cambridge: Cambridge University Press, 2002), pp. 514–30

Hunter, Michael, *Establishing the New Science: The Experience of the Early Royal Society* (Woodbridge: Boydell Press, 1989)

—, 'John Evelyn in the 1650s: A Virtuoso in Quest of a Role', in O'Malley and Wolschke-Bulmahn, pp. 79–106

Ingram, John, 'John Evelyn's *Elysium Britannicum*: Provenance, Condition, Transcription', in O'Malley and Wolschke-Bulmahn, pp. 35–56

Jacques, David, '"The Chief Ornament" of Gray's Inn: The Walks from Bacon to Brown', *GH*, 17:1 (1989), 41–67

—, 'The *Compartiment* System in Tudor England', *GH*, 27:1 (Summer 1999), 32–53

—, 'Who knows what a Dutch Garden is?', *GH*, 30:2 (Winter 2002), 114–30

—, and Arend Jan van der Horst, *The Gardens of William and Mary* (London: Christopher Helm, 1988)

Johnson, F. R., 'Thomas Hill: An Elizabethan Huxley', *Huntington Library Quarterly*, 7:4 (1944), 329–51

—, 'Notes on English Retail Book Prices', *The Library*, ser. 5, 5 (1950), 83–178

Landsberg, Sylvia, *The Medieval Garden* (London: British Museum Press, 1995)

Leith-Ross, Prudence, *The John Tradescants: Gardeners to the Rose and Lily Queen* (London: Peter Owen, 1984)

—, 'The Garden of John Evelyn at Deptford', *GH*, 25:2 (1997), 138–52

—, 'A Seventeenth-Century Paris Garden', *GH*, 21:2 (1993), 150–57

Leslie, Michael, and Timothy Raylor, eds, *Culture and Cultivation in Early Modern England: Writing and the Land* (Leicester: Leicester University Press, 1992)

Lindahl, Goran, 'André Mollet, Le Jardin de Plaisir', Reviews, *GH*, 32:2 (2004), 286–9

Love, Harold, *Scribal Publication in the Seventeenth Century* (Oxford: Clarendon Press, 1993)

—, 'Oral and Scribal Texts in Early Modern England' in *The Cambridge History of the Book in Britain, Vol. 4: 1567–1695*, ed. John Barnard and D. F. McKenzie (Cambridge: Cambridge University Press, 2002), pp. 97–121

Marsh, David, 'The Gardens and Gardeners of Later Stuart London' (PhD thesis, University of London, 2004)

Morrill, John, ed., *The Oxford Illustrated History of Tudor and Stuart Britain* (Oxford: Oxford University Press, 1996)

Mowl, Timothy, *Elizabethan and Jacobean Style* (London: Phaidon, 1993)

—, *Gentlemen and Players: Gardeners of the English Landscape* (Stroud: Sutton, 2000)

Munroe, Jennifer, *Gender and the Garden in Early Modern English Literature* (Aldershot: Ashgate, 2008)

O'Malley, Therese, and Joachim Wolschke-Bulmahn, eds, *John Evelyn's 'Elysium Britannicum' and European Gardening* (Washington, DC: Dumbarton Oaks Research Library and Collection, 1998)

Orgel, Stephen, *The Reader in the Book: A Study of Spaces and Traces* (Oxford: Oxford University Press, 2015)

Orlin, Lena Cowen, ed., *Material London, c.1600* (Philadelphia: University of Pennsylvania Press, 2000)

Parkinson, Anna, *Nature's Alchemist: John Parkinson, Herbalist to Charles I* (London: Frances Lincoln, 2007)

Pavord, Anna, *The Tulip* (London: Bloomsbury, 2000)

Peck, Linda, *Consuming Splendor* (Cambridge: Cambridge University Press, 2005)

Pennington, David, 'Beyond the Moral Economy: Economic Change, Ideology and the 1621 House of Commons', *Parliamentary History*, 25:2 (2006), 214–31

Phillips, John, and Nicholas Burnett, 'The Chronology and Layout of Francis Carew's Garden at Beddington, Surrey', *GH*, 33:2 (2005), 155–88

Rappaport, Steve, *Worlds within Worlds: Structures of Life in Sixteenth-Century London* (Cambridge: Cambridge University Press, 1989)

Riddell, John N. D., 'John Parkinson's Long Acre Garden 1600–1650', *GH*, 6:2 (1986), 112–24

Roberts, Judith, 'The Gardens of the Gentry in the Late Tudor Period', *GH*, 27:1 (1999), 89–108

Roberts, Rebecca, '"Two meane fellows grand projectors": The Self-Projection of Sir Arthur Ingram and Lionel Cranfield, Earl of Middlesex, 1600–1645, with Particular Reference to their Houses' (PhD thesis, Teeside University, 2012)

Robinson, Jenny, 'New Light on Sir Thomas Hanmer', *GH*, 16:1 (1988), 1–7

Samson, Alexander, '*Locus amoenus*: Gardens and Horticulture in the Renaissance', *Renaissance Studies*, 25:1 (2011), 1–23

Sherman, William, *Used Books: Marking Readers in Renaissance England* (Philadelphia: University of Pennsylvania Press, 2008)

Slack, Paul, *The Invention of Improvement: Information and Material Progress in Seventeenth-Century England* (Oxford: Oxford University Press, 2014)

Small, Carola, and Alastair Small, 'John Evelyn and the Garden of Epicurus', *Journal of the Warburg and Courtauld Institutes*, 60 (1997), 194–214

Strong, Roy, *The Artist and the Garden* (New Haven and London: Yale University Press, 2000)

—, *The Renaissance Garden in England* (London: Thames and Hudson, 1979)

—, 'The Renaissance Garden in England Reconsidered', *GH*, 27:1 (1999), 2–9

Thick, Malcolm, *The Neat House Gardens: Early Market Gardening around London* (Totnes: Prospect Books, 1998)

Thirsk, Joan, *Food in Early Modern England: Phases, Fads, Fashions 1500–1760* (London: Hambledon Continuum, 2007)

—, ed., *The Agrarian History of England and Wales*, vol. 4: *1500–1640* (Cambridge: Cambridge University Press, 1991)

—, 'Making a Fresh Start: Sixteenth-Century Agriculture and the Classical Inspiration', in *Culture and Cultivation in Early Modern England: Writing and the Land*, ed. Michael Leslie and Timothy Raylor (Leicester: Leicester University Press, 1992), pp. 15–34

Thomas, Keith, *The Ends of Life: Roads to Fulfilment in Early Modern England* (Oxford: Oxford University Press, 2009)

—, *Man and the Natural World* (London: Penguin, 1984)

—, 'The Meaning of Literacy in Early Modern England', in *The Written Word: Literacy in Transition*, ed. Gerd Baumann (Oxford, Clarendon, 1986), pp. 97–131

Thrush, Andrew, and John Ferris, *The House of Commons 1604–1629*, 5 vols (Cambridge: Cambridge University Press, 2010)

Wall, Cecil, *The History of the Worshipful Society of Apothecaries* (London: Oxford University Press for the Wellcome Historical Medical Museum, 1963)

Watt, Tessa, *Cheap Print and Popular Piety* (Cambridge: Cambridge University Press, 1991)

Welch, Charles, *The History of the Worshipful Company of Gardeners* (London: Blades, East & Blades, 1900)

Whitehead, David, 'Some Connected Thoughts on the Parks and Gardens of Herefordshire', *Transactions of the Woolhope Naturalists' Field Club*, 48:2 (1995), 193–223

Whittle, Elisabeth, *The Historic Gardens of Wales* (London: HMSO, 1992)

Williamson, Tom, *Polite Landscapes: Gardens and Society in Eighteenth Century England* (Stroud: Sutton, 1995)

Wisker, Richard, 'The First Trentham Hall', *Staffordshire History*, 24 (1996), 6–14

Woudstra, Jan, and Sally O'Halloran, 'Sir John Reresby's Garden Notebook and Garden (1633–44) at Thrybergh, Yorkshire', *GH*, 36:1 (2008), 135–93

Wrightson, Keith, *Earthly Necessities: Economic Lives in Early Modern Britain* (New Haven and London: Yale University Press, 2000)

—, 'Sorts of People in Tudor and Stuart England', in *The Middling Sort of People: Culture, Society and Politics in England, 1550–1800*, ed. Jonathan Barry and Christopher Brooks (Basingstoke: Macmillan, 1994), pp. 28–51

LIST OF ILLUSTRATIONS

NOTE: *Tradescant's Orchard* (see p. viii and figs 38, 48, 52, 65, 154) is a series of sixty-six watercolours of garden fruits attributed, probably incorrectly, to Tradescant, although it is possible that his reputation as a gardener and grower of fruit trees may at least have inspired this collection; see https://treasures.bodleian.ox.ac.uk/treasures/tradescants-orchard/ (accessed 1 September 2017).

Endpapers   Title page (detail) from John Gerard, *The Herball, or Generall Historie of Plantes* (London, 1597). Linda Hall Library of Science, Engineering & Technology.

Chapter vignettes all from Parkinson, *Paradisi in Sole*: (p. 1) Virginia potatoes, p. 517; (p. v) Apple blossom, p. 403; (p. xii) Jonquil, p. 93; (p. 22) Anemone, p. 291; (p. 42) Walnut, p. 597; (p. 54) Garden peas, p. 523; (p. 92) Horseradish, p. 511; (p. 126) Common sage, p. 475; (p. 150) Fritillary, p. 41; (p. 182) Apple rose, p. 419; (p. 210) Apple, p. 585; (p. 236) Hellebore, p. 343; (p. 276) Raspberry, p. 559; (p. 316) Dill, p. 493.

Frontispiece   Jacques le Moyne, *French Rose and Privet Hawk Moth*, 1585. © Trustees of the British Museum. All rights reserved.

p. vi   Gardener at work, from Thomas Hyll, *The Gardeners Labyrinth* (London, 1577), title page.

p. viii   'The Red Gousebery', from *Tradescant's Orchard* c.1620. MS. Ashmole 1461, fol. 013r. The Bodleian Library, University of Oxford.

p. x   Bird's-eye view of Conwy Castle, c.1600, detail. Hatfield House, CMP 1/62. By courtesy of the Marquess of Salisbury.

INTRODUCTION

1   Portrait of John Parkinson, from his *Paradisi in Sole, Paradisus Terrestris: or, A Garden of all Sorts of Pleasant Flowers* (London, 1629), facing p. 1.

2   Attributed to Ambrosius Bosschaert, *Large Bouquet in Gilt-Mounted Wan-Li Vase*, c.1620. © Norton Simon Art Foundation, Gift of Mr. Norton Simon.

3   Ralph Austen, *A Treatise of Fruit-trees* (Oxford, 1653), detail from title page.

4   Early modern gardeners at work, from Thomas Hyll, *The Gardeners Labyrinth* (London, 1577), p. 25. The Bodleian Library, University of Oxford.

5   Spiral mount at Lyveden New Bield, Northamptonshire, 2015. Photograph: the author.

6   The renovated garden (2016) at Shakespeare's New Place, Stratford-upon-Avon, 2017. Photograph: the author.

7   Elizabethan Garden, from Thomas Hyll, *The Gardeners Labyrinth* (London, 1577), p. 41. The Bodleian Library, University of Oxford.

8   Carnations and gilliflowers, from Parkinson, *Paradisi in Sole*, p. 313.

1 THE 'ARTE OF GARDENING'

9 Title page from Thomas Hyll, *A most briefe and pleasaunte treatise* (London, c.1558).

10 Leonard Mascall, 'The booke unto the Reader', from *A Booke of the Arte and maner, howe to plant and graffe all sorts of trees* (London, [1572]), sig. A^v.

11 *Francis Bacon, 1st Viscount St Alban*, after 1626. Engraving after Simon de Passe. © National Portrait Gallery, London.

12 Title page from Gervase Markham, *Maison Rustique, or the Countrey Farme* (London, 1616). © British Library Board. All rights reserved / Bridgeman Images.

2 'PROFITS AND PLEASURES'

13 Title page from Ralph Austen, *A Treatise of Fruit-trees* (Oxford, 1653).

14 Title page from John Parkinson, *Paradisi in Sole, Paradisus Terrestris* (London, 1629).

15 Crown Imperial, from Parkinson, *Paradisi in Sole*, p. 29.

3 SETTING THE SCENE

16 'The manner of watering a garden with a pump', from Thomas Hyll, *The Gardeners Labyrinth* (London, 1577), p. 53. The Bodleian Library, University of Oxford.

17 Representation of Hull, 1539. BL, Cotton Augustus 1.i.83. © British Library Board. All rights reserved / Bridgeman Images.

18 Lyveden New Bield, Northamptonshire, viewed from the north, 2017. Photograph: Lyndon Griffith.

19 A 'Plaine square' divided into four quarters, from Gervase Markham, *The English Husbandman* (London, 1613), p. 113.

20 'The Garden of Pleasure', from Guillaume de Lorris and Jean de Meun, *Le Roman de la Rose, c.1500*. BL, Harley MS. 4425, f. 12v. © British Library Board. All rights reserved / Bridgeman Images.

21 Map of Wilton, Wiltshire, c.1565. Wiltshire and Swindon History Centre, Wilton Estate Archives, 2057/S/3. By kind permission of the Earl of Pembroke and the Trustees of Wilton House Trust, Wilton, Salisbury.

22 Etienne DuPérac, *Tivoli Palace and Gardens*, 1573. http://commons.wikimedia.org.

23 *Montargis*, from Jacques Androuet du Cerceau, *Le premier volume des plus excellents bastiments de France* (Paris, 1576).

24 *Jardin de Valleri*, from Jacques Androuet du Cerceau, *Le premier volume des plus excellents bastiments de France* (Paris, 1576).

25 View of the Renaissance-style kitchen gardens at Château de Villandry, France, re-created c.1918 after du Cerceau, 2017. Photograph: the author.

26 Detail from the 'Agas' map of London, c.1561. London Metropolitan Archives, City of London.

27 Detail from the 'Agas' map of London, c.1561. London Metropolitan Archives, City of London (annotated by the author).

28 Moorfields map image made from the Copperplate map of London, c.1559. Museum of London (annotated by the author).

29 Toddington Manor, Bedfordshire, survey by Ralph Agas, 1581. BL, Add. 38065FH. © British Library Board. All rights reserved / Bridgeman Images.

30 Moated orchard at Lyveden New Bield, Northamptonshire, 2017. Photograph: Lyndon Griffith.

31 Clothworkers' Hall, Mincing Lane, London, detail from Ralph Treswell, *Survaye of all the Landes and Tenements belonginge to the Worshipfull Company of the Clothworkers of London*, 1612, fol. 12r. Clothworkers' Company Archive, London, CL/G/7/1.

32 Sir Edward Darcy's garden, 12–14 Billiter Street, London, detail from Treswell, *Survaye*, fols 15v–16r. Clothworkers' Company Archive, London, CL/G/7/1.

33 Mr Beastney's garden under the City walls, Monkwell Street, London, detail from Treswell, *Survaye*, fol. 29r. Clothworkers' Company Archive, London, CL/G/7/1.

34 Robert Wood's garden, 4–18 Lower East Smithfield, London, detail from Treswell, *Survaye*, fol. 20r. Clothworkers' Company Archive, London, CL/G/7/1.

35 A still, from Hyll, *The Gardeners Labyrinth*, 'The seconde parte' (London, 1577), p. 12. The Bodleian Library, University of Oxford.

36   Garden tools, from Leonard Mascall, *A Booke of the Arte and maner, howe to plant and graffe all sorts of trees* (London, [1572]), sig. Ciiii.

37   Melons, from John Gerard, *The Herball, or Generall Historie of Plantes* (London, 1597), p. 771.

38   'The Tradescant cherry', from *Tradescant's Orchard*, c.1620. MS. Ashmole 1461, fol. 025r. The Bodleian Library, University of Oxford.

39   Title page from John Gerard, *The Herball, or Generall Historie of Plantes* (London, 1597). Linda Hall Library of Science, Engineering & Technology.

40   Obelisk in the re-created Elizabethan garden, Kenilworth Castle, Warwickshire, 2017. Photograph: the author. Reproduced by kind permission of English Heritage.

41   White bears and marble fountain in the re-created Elizabethan garden, Kenilworth Castle, Warwickshire, 2017. Photograph: the author. Reproduced by kind permission of English Heritage.

42   Anthonis van den Wyngaerde, *Whitehall Stairs, View of Whitehall Palace and the Great Garden*, 1540–50. WA.Suth.C.4.99.1. © Ashmolean Museum, University of Oxford.

43   Detail from the 'Agas' map of London, c.1561. London Metropolitan Archives, City of London.

44   Detail from the 'Agas' map of London, c.1561. London Metropolitan Archives, City of London.

45   Small garden with an arbour, from Nicholas Goodman, *Holland's Leaguer* (London, 1632), frontispiece.

46   Anthonis van den Wyngaerde, *The River Front of Richmond Palace and Privy Gardens* (detail), 1540–50. WA.Suth.L.4.11.1. © Ashmolean Museum, University of Oxford.

4   CONTINUITIES

47   Plan of a garden, from William Lawson, *A New Orchard and Garden […] with the Country Housewifes Garden* (London, 1618), p. 12.

48   'The Apricooke', from *Tradescant's Orchard*, c.1620. MS. Ashmole 1461, fol. 090r. The Bodleian Library, University of Oxford.

49   Detail from a map of Nunwell, Isle of Wight, 1748. Drawing: Jonathan Paull, from a copy held at the Isle of Wight Archaeological Centre.

50   Nunwell House, Isle of Wight, 2017. Photograph: Lyndon Griffith.

51   Conjectural view of Sir Thomas Temple's new garden, Burton Dassett, Warwickshire. Drawing: Jonathan Paull.

52   'The smalle Reson grape', from *Tradescant's Orchard*, c.1620. Ms. Ashmole 1461, fol. 143r. The Bodleian Library, University of Oxford.

53   Dove house, seventeenth century, Wichenford, Worcestershire. Photograph: the author. By kind permission of the National Trust.

54   Cheapside Market, from *A Caveat for the citty of London*, 1598. Folger MS. V.a.318, fol. 15r. By permission of the Folger Shakespeare Library.

55   Detail of fig. 130.

56   Beehives in a garden, from Thomas Hyll, *The Gardeners Labyrinth* (London, 1577), p. 53. The Bodleian Library, University of Oxford.

57   Frontispiece from John Levett, *The Ordering of Bees* (London, 1634).

58   Bee boles at Packwood House, Warwickshire, 2017. Photograph: Matthew Paull. By kind permission of the National Trust.

59   Pieter Bruegel the elder, *The Beekeepers* (*Die Imker*), c.1568. © bpk / Kupferstichkabinette, SMB / Jörg P. Anders.

60   'Description of a transparent beehive', from John Evelyn, *Elysium Britannicum*, 1650. BL, Add. 78342, fol. 212v. © British Library Board. All rights reserved / Bridgeman Images.

61   Gardeners and a selection of tools, from Thomas Hyll, *The Gardeners Labyrinth* (London, 1651), p. 54. © British Library Board. All Rights Reserved / Bridgeman Images.

62   Cabbages and coleworts, from John Parkinson, *Paradisi in Sole, Paradisus Terrestris* (London, 1629), p. 505.

63   Globe and thistle artichokes, from Parkinson, *Paradisi in Sole*, p. 519.

64   'The perfecte form of an Apple tree', from Lawson, *A New Orchard and Garden*, p. 38.

65 'The Graunde Cornation Peach', from *Tradescant's Orchard*, c.1620, MS. Ashmole 1461, fol. 111r. The Bodleian Library, University of Oxford.

66 British (English) School, *Sir Thomas and Lady Lucy with Seven of their Children*, c.1624. Charlecote Park, Warwickshire. © National Trust Images / Derrick E. Witty.

67 Gardener at work, from Leonard Mascall, *A Booke of the Arte and maner, howe to plant and graffe all sorts of trees* (London, [1572]), title page.

5 THE GARDENERS

68 Gardeners at work, from William Lawson, *A New Orchard and Garden [...] with the Country Housewifes Garden* (London, 1618), title page.

69 Gardener pruning a fruit tree, from *The Orchard, and the Garden* (London, 1594), p. 7.

70 Coat of arms of the Worshipful Company of Gardeners (as sketched in 1616). By kind permission of the Worshipful Company of Gardeners.

71 Portrait of John Gerard, from his *Herball, or Generall Historie of Plantes* (London, 1597), facing p. 1. Linda Hall Library of Science, Engineering & Technology

72 Attributed to Thomas de Critz, *John Tradescant the Younger as a Gardener*, 1648–53. © Ashmolean Museum, University of Oxford.

73 Tomb of the John Tradescants, c.1662. Garden Museum, London, 2010. Photograph: the author.

74 Illustration of garden tools, from John Evelyn, *Elysium Britannicum*, 1650. BL, Add. 78342, fols 57v–58. © British Library Board. All rights reserved / Bridgeman Images.

75 Grafting tools and techniques, from John Parkinson, *Paradisi in Sole, Paradisus Terrestris* (London, 1629), p. 543.

76 John Lavorgne, *Thomas Wentworth, grandfather of the Earl of Stafford, and his wife, Margaret Gascoigne*, c.1575 (possibly a seventeenth-century copy). Reproduced by kind permission of Lady Juliet Tadgell.

77 Portrait of Susan Hanmer, c.1702. From Margaret Willes, *The Making of the English Gardener* (London and New Haven, 2011), p. 236. Photograph: A.C.Cooper.com, London.

6 NEW ASPIRATIONS

78 Title page from William Lawson, *A New Orchard and Garden [...] with the Country Housewifes Garden* (London, 1618).

79 Yucca plant, from John Parkinson, *Paradisi in Sole, Paradisus Terrestris* (London, 1629), p. 435.

80 Double-flowered narcissus, from Crispin van den Passe, *Hortus Floridus* (Utrecht, c.1615).

81 Jacques le Moyne, *Madonna Lily*, 1585. © Trustees of the British Museum. All rights reserved.

82 Jacques le Moyne, *Clove Pink*, 1585. © Trustees of the British Museum. All rights reserved.

83 Box hedging clipped into a knot, Kenilworth Castle, Warwickshire, 2017. Photograph: the author. Reproduced by kind permission of English Heritage.

84 Stone-bordered beds, La Seigneurie gardens, Sark, Channel Islands, 2010. Photograph: the author.

85 Jacques le Moyne, *Columbine and Ladybird*, 1585. © Trustees of the British Museum. All rights reserved.

86 Beehives in a garden, c.1600, from Frank Crisp, *Mediaeval Gardens*, 2 vols (London: John Lane Bodley Head, 1924), vol. 1, fig. 109.

87 Varieties of hyacinths, from Parkinson, *Paradisi in Sole*, p. 125.

88 Jacques le Moyne, *Strawberry Plant*, 1585. © Trustees of the British Museum. All rights reserved.

89 The Rev. Walter Stonehouse, 'A Modell of my Garden at Darfield, 1640'. Magdalen College Library, MS. No. 239, fol. 40. By kind permission of the President and Fellows of Magdalen College, Oxford.

90 Re-creation of a knot garden at Moseley Old Hall, Staffordshire, 2017. Photograph: the author. By kind permission of the National Trust.

91 Fritillaria, from Parkinson, *Paradisi in Sole*, p. 41.

92 Jacques le Moyne, *Dog Rose and Small Tortoiseshell Butterfly*, 1585. © Trustees of the British Museum. All rights reserved.

7 THE KNOTTY PROBLEM OF KNOTS

93 Interlacing knot design, from *The Orchard, and the Garden* (London, 1594), p. 45.

94 Rowland Lockey, after Holbein, *Sir Thomas More and Family*, 1594. © Victoria and Albert Museum, London.

95 Detail of fig. 94.

96 Bird's-eye view of Conwy Castle, *c*.1600, detail. Hatfield House, CMP 1/62. By courtesy of the Marquess of Salisbury.

97 Detail of fig. 66.

98 Cornelius Johnson, *Arthur, 1st Baron Capel and his Family*, *c*.1640. © National Portrait Gallery, London.

99 Unknown artist, *Lettice Newdigate, aged Two*, 1606. Arbury Hall, Warwickshire. By kind permission of Lord Daventry.

100 Unknown artist, *Jane Shirley, Baroness Holles of Ifield*, *c*.1625–30. Longleat House, Collection No. 9124. © Reproduced by permission of the Marquess of Bath, Longleat House, Warminster, Wiltshire.

101 Hovenden's map of All Souls College, Oxford, *c*.1586–1605, detail. Codrington Library, University of Oxford. By kind permission of the Warden and Fellows of All Souls College, Oxford.

102 Detail of garden from plan of St Augustine's, Canterbury, *c*.1642. Canturbury Cathedral Archives, CAA-Map/123. Reproduced courtesy of the Chapter of Canterbury.

103 Elizabethan garden re-created in 2009 at Kenilworth Castle, Warwickshire, 2011. Photograph: the author. Reproduced by kind permission of English Heritage.

104 Knot designs, from Thomas Hyll, *The Gardeners Labyrinth* (London, 1578), last page. The Bodleian Library, University of Oxford.

105 Detail of fig. 101.

106 Detail of fig. 99.

107 Detail of fig. 31.

108 Four knot designs, from John Parkinson, *Paradisi in Sole, Paradisus Terrestris* (London, 1629), p. 4.

109 Girolamo Porro, plan of the botanical garden at Padua University, *Horto dei semplici di Padova* (Venice, 1591). http://commons.wikimedia.org.

110 'A Proper Knotte', from Thomas Hyll, *The Gardeners Labyrinth* (London 1577), p. 80. The Bodleian Library, University of Oxford.

111 The knot garden at Sudeley Castle in Gloucestershire, 2017. Photograph: Sudely Castle, Winchcombe.

112 Lucas de Heere, *Allegory of the Tudor Succession*, *c*.1572, detail. By kind permission of Sudely Castle, Winchcombe.

113 Designs for knots, from William Lawson, *A New Orchard and Garden [...] with the Country Housewifes Garden* (London, 1618), pp. 81–2.

114 'Knot in Embroidery', from André Mollet, *Le Jardin de Plaisir* (London, 1670), fol. 3.

115 'Compartment of Turff', from André Mollet, *Le Jardin de Plaisir* (London, 1670), fol. 4.

116 Leonard Knyff, *Hampton Court from the East* (detail), *c*.1702–14. Royal Collection Trust © Her Majesty Queen Elizabeth II 2017.

8 ARTIFICIAL ORNAMENT IN THE GARDEN

117 Salomon de Caus, design for a Mount Parnassus, from *Les Raisons des forces mouvantes* (Paris, 1615).

118 Unknown artist, *Llannerch, Denbighshire, Wales*, *c*.1667. Yale Center for British Art, Paul Mellon Collection (B1976.7.115).

119 Trentham Hall, from Robert Plot, *The Natural History of Staffordshire* (Oxford, 1686). Cadbury Research Library: Special Collections, University of Birmingham, DA670.S69, pl. 24.

120 Detail of fig. 119.

121 Trentham Hall, from Plot, *The Natural History of Staffordshire*, pl. 23. Photograph: David Jacques.

122 Detail of fig. 118.

123 Inigo Jones's design for a fountain, *c*.1633, from John Harris and Gordon Higgot, *Inigo Jones: Complete Architectural Drawings* (London: Philip Wilson, 1989), p. 215.

124 Daniel Mytens, *Althea Talbot, Countess of Arundel, sitting before the Picture Gallery of Arundel House*, 1618, detail. © National Portrait Gallery, London.

125 The moat and spiral mount at the south-west corner of the orchard at Lyveden New Bield, Northamptonshire, 2017. Photograph: Lyndon Griffith. By kind permission of the National Trust.

126   Daniel Mytens, *Thomas Howard, Earl of Arundel*, *c*.1627, detail. Private collection.

127   Elizabethan garden at Kenilworth Castle, Warwickshire, 2017. Photograph: the author. Reproduced by kind permission of English Heritage.

128   Two banqueting houses at either end of the raised terrace at Campden Manor, Gloucestershire, 2017. Photograph: Lyndon Griffith.

129   Ingestre Hall, from Plot, *The Natural History of Staffordshire*, 1686, pl. 26. Photograph: David Jacques.

9   WAR AND PEACE

130   John Evelyn, plan of Sayes Court, Deptford, *c*.1653. BL, Evelyn Papers, Add. 78628A. © British Library Board. All rights reserved / Bridgeman Images.

131   Detail of fig. 130.

132   Detail of fig. 130.

133   Richard Symonds, the garden of Pierre Morin, 1649. BL, Harley MS 1278 f. 81v. © British Library Board. All rights reserved / Bridgeman Images.

134   Detail of fig. 130.

135   Detail of fig. 130.

136   John Evelyn, 'A Rude dra[u]ght of Wotton Garden', 1640. BL, Evelyn Papers, Add. 78610A © British Library Board. All rights reserved / Bridgeman Images.

137   John Evelyn, 'Prospect of the old house at Wotton', 1640. BL, Evelyn Papers, Add. 78610B. © British Library Board. All rights reserved / Bridgeman Images.

138   The portico at Wotton House, Surrey, 2017. Photograph: the author. By kind permission of De Vere Wotton House Hotel.

139   John Evelyn, 'Wotton in Surrey, The house of Geo: Evelyn Esq.', 1653. BL, Evelyn Papers, Add. 78610G. © British Library Board. All rights reserved / Bridgeman Images.

140   John Evelyn, view of Wotton with the garden, grotto and environs, *c*.1650s. BL, Evelyn Papers, Add. 78610H. © British Library Board. All rights reserved / Bridgeman Images.

141   John Evelyn, 'This Designe of a Garden I made for the Duke of Norfolk at his house at Albury in Surrey...', *c*.1680, from *The Miscellaneous Writings of John Evelyn, Esq. F.R.S.*, ed. William Upcott (London, 1825), extra-illustrated copy. Image kindly provided by the Harry Ransom Center, University of Texas at Austin.

142   The 'crypta' at Albury Park, Surrey, 2017. Photograph: the author. By kind permission of the Trustees of the Albury Estate.

143   Sir Anthony van Dyck, *Sir Thomas Hanmer*, *c*.1638. Weston Park, Shropshire. Courtesy of the Weston Park Foundation.

144   Two pages from Sir Thomas Hanmer's notebook, *c*.1654–7. Bettisfield 1663. Supplied by Llyfrgell Genedlaethol Cymru / National Library of Wales. By kind permission of Sir Guy Hanmer, Bt.

145   Anemones, from Crispin van den Passe, *Hortus Floridus* (Utrecht, *c*.1615).

146   Page from Hanmer's notebook, 'My flowers at Haulton', September 1654. Bettisfield 1663. Supplied by Llyfrgell Genedlaethol Cymru / National Library of Wales. By kind permission of Sir Guy Hanmer, Bt.

147   Page from Hanmer's notebook, 'Lewsh.', 11 October 1656. Bettisfield 1663. Supplied by Llyfrgell Genedlaethol Cymru / National Library of Wales. By kind permission of Sir Guy Hanmer, Bt.

148   Cyclamen, from Crispin van den Passe, *Hortus Floridus* (Utrecht, *c*.1615).

149   Auriculas, or 'beares eares', from Crispin van den Passe, *Hortus Floridus* (Utrecht, *c*.1615).

150   Jacques le Moyne, *Daffodil*, *c*.1585. © Trustees of the British Museum. All rights reserved.

10   THE PLANTS

151   Title page from Richard Gardner, *Profitable Instructions for the Manuring, Sowing, and Planting of Kitchin Gardens* (London, 1599).

152   Jacques le Moyne, *Apple*, *c*.1585. © Trustees of the British Museum. All rights reserved.

153   C. J. Visscher, *Panorama of London*, 1616, detail. London Metropolitan Archives, City of London.

154   'The red Gousbery', from *Tradescant's Orchard*, *c*.1620. MS. Ashmole 1461, fol. 013r. The Bodleian Library, University of Oxford.

155   Detail from the 'Agas' map of London, c.1561. London Metropolitan Archives, City of London.

156   Adam Bowen, 'Plan of an Estate in Old Street', 1633. London Metropolitan Archives, City of London. By kind permission of the Worshipful Company of Ironmongers.

157   Detail from the Faithorne and Newcourt map of London, c.1643. © Trustees of the British Museum. All rights reserved (annotated by the author).

158   Detail from the 'Agas' map of London, c.1561. London Metropolitan Archives, City of London (annotated by the author).

159   Detail from the Faithorne and Newcourt map of London, c.1643. © Trustees of the British Museum. All rights reserved (annotated by the author).

160   Potato plant, from John Gerard, *The Herball, or Generall Historie of Plantes* (London, 1597), p. 780.

161   A Danish museum of curiosities, 1655. Frontispiece to Ole Worm, *Museum Wormianum* (1655). http://commons.wikimedia.org.

162   Andries Daniels and Frans Francken the younger, *Vase with Tulips*, c.1625. Bilbao Museum of Fine Art. http://commons.wikimedia.org.

163   Unknown artist, Tulip *Semper Augustus*, seventeenth century. Norton Simon Art Foundation.

164   Tulips, from John Parkinson, *Paradisi in Sole, Paradisus Terrestris* (London, 1629), p. 59.

165   Attributed to Emanuel de Critz, *John Tradescant the Elder*, 1638–65. © Ashmolean Museum, University of Oxford.

166   Broad-leafed myrtle, from Parkinson, *Paradisi in Sole*, p. 429.

167   The smaller wild pomegranate tree, from Parkinson, *Paradisi in Sole*, p. 429.

168   General Lambert's Garden, Castle Cornet, Guernsey, 2014. Photograph: Chris George.

169   Two pages from Sir Thomas Hanmer's notebook, 1654. Bettisfield 1663. Supplied by Llyfrgell Genedlaethol Cymru / National Library of Wales. By kind permission of Sir Guy Hanmer, Bt.

170   Two pages from Sir Thomas Hanmer's notebook, 1655. Bettisfield 1663. Supplied by Llyfrgell Genedlaethol Cymru / National Library of Wales. By kind permission of Sir Guy Hanmer, Bt.

171   Plan of Woolstaple Yard, Westminster, c.1603, from Ralph Treswell, *Christ Hospital Evidence Book*, c.1603–9, ref. CLC/210/G/A/004 /MS12805. London Metropolitan Archives, City of London. By kind permission of Christ's Hospital.

172   Irises, from Crispin van den Passe, *Hortus Floridus* (Utrecht, c.1615).

11   CONCLUSIONS

173   Gentlemen at leisure in the garden, from Thomas Hyll, *The Gardeners Labyrinth* (London, 1577), facing p. 80. The Bodleian Library, University of Oxford.

174   Gateway to Hellens Manor, Much Marcle, Herefordshire, 1998. Photograph: Richard Surman.

175   Campden Manor, Gloucestershire, 2017. Photograph: Lyndon Griffith.

176   Lodge at Lyveden New Bield, Northamptonshire, 2015. Photograph: the author.

177   Detail of fig. 4.

INDEX

NOTE: Page numbers in italics refer to illustrations.

account books as documentary source 18, 19
  beekeeping costs 111
  gardeners' status and pay 127, 129–30, 177, 183, 279, 282
  gardeners' tools and equipment 114, 279, 313
  ornamental and structural features 105, 213, 214–16, 217–18, 219, 220–21, 227, 229, 231
  purchase and cost of plants 176, 177–8, 279, 281–2, 306, 309–15
    owners' lack of interest in plants 231–2
    unrecorded gifts of plants and fruit 119, 283
    for vegetable garden 74, 79, 115, 116
  vine cultivation 124
Adam and Garden of Eden 5, 47–50
Addams, Timothy (labourer) 129
'Agas' map of London 63, 64–5, 66, 87, 87, 90, 188, 290, 291
  Olde Street 287, 288
agriculture and gardening 104, 108, 114–15
air and survival of plants 269–70
Alaternus hedging 246, 247
Albertus Magnus 59
Albury Park, Surrey
  and Evelyn 8–9, 240, 251, 257–9, 257–8
    'crypta' 257, 258, 258

All Souls College, Oxford 193, 194, 198, 204
alleys see paths, alleys and walks
America: Tradescant the younger in 303, 304
Androuet du Cerceau, Jacques see du Cerceau
anemones 38, 178, 265, 266, 271, 314
angling as leisure activity 324
animal statues: heraldic beasts 86, 225–6, 227, 228
Anne of Denmark, queen of Scotland and England 211
annotations in gardening books 28–9, 30, 41
apple trees 71, 74, 118, 239, 249, 282, 283, 284, 286
  see also orchards and fruit trees
apprenticeships in gardening 133
apricot trees 81–2, 96, 97, 98, 122, 132, 279, 283
arbours 88, 89, 211, 320
Aristotle 32
Ark see Tradescant's Ark
arrangement and layout of gardens
  aesthetical considerations 69–70
  changes over generations 176, 184, 240, 260, 264
  earlier influences on garden design 59–68
  Elizabethan gardens 55–71, 93, 186–7, 250
  Hanmer on 265, 340–41
  and identity and status of owners 317, 320–21
  and individual taste 57, 58, 234–5, 240, 328–9
  'knot' and arrangement of beds 185
  limitations of available plot 70–71, 99, 243, 246
  literature on 57–8, 68–71
  marking pattern for knot gardens 160

medieval gardens 59–62
order and symmetry in layout 55–68, 70–71, 90–91, 93–5
parlour gardens and proximity to house 176–7, 250
position of ornamental flower garden 165–7
structural features of compartmentalised gardens 216–18, 340–41
Temple's 'Parlour gardine' 100–01, *101*, 102, 131, 145, 184
see also beds; order and symmetry in gardens
artichokes 116–18, *117*
artificial ornament see ornamental features
Arundel, Countess of 221, *222*
Arundel, Thomas Howard, Earl of 225, 228, 258
Arundel House, London 221, *222*, 225, *226*, 258, 319
Aubrey, John: *Natural History of Wiltshire* 10, 211
Aubrey, Sir Thomas 19, 119, 129, 130, 216, 224, 227, 228, 229, 232, 279, 322
auriculas ('beares eares') 38, 266, 271, *272*, 287, 310–11
Austen, Ralph: *A Treatise of Fruit-trees* 6, 7, 43, 44, 74, 81, 337
avenues: Evelyn's lime walk 244–5, 275

Bacon, Francis *33*, 50, 136
  'Of Gardens' 70, 168–70, 337
  pools in gardens 225
  purchase of plants for Gray's Inn Court garden 291–2, 306
  scented plants on paths 21, 70, 169–70
  scientific approach to natural world 32, 34, 36, 152, 156
Banbury, Henry (nurseryman) 287–8, 311
banqueting houses and rooms 9, 169, 211, 228–35, 249, 321
Barber-Surgeons' Company 134, 135, 136
Barker, Thomas: *The Country-mans Recreation* 324, 335
'bayslip' cuttings 103
Beale, John: *Herefordshire Orchards* 337
beans 103–4, 114–15, 116
beauty
  aesthetics of garden layout 69–70
  see also ornamental flower gardens
Beddington, Surrey 82–3, 122, 157, 319, 323
beds
  in ornamental flower garden 165
  size and layout 68, 199, 265
  use of 'knot' as term 184
bees and beehives *108–9*, 109–14, *111–13*, 147, 165, *166*, 250

Bettisfield, Flintshire 19, 184, 240, 272, 313
  notebooks on gardening during Civil Wars 260, *262–3*, 265; see also Hanmer, Sir Thomas
Bible: Adam and Garden of Eden 5, 47–50
Blissett, Matthew (gardener) 249
blood as fertiliser 103, 105
Boel, Guillaume (William) 36, 304–5
Bolsover Castle, Derbyshire 220
bones to mark out knot gardens 160
Bonnefons, Nicolas: *The French Gardiner* (trans. by Evelyn) 31, 40, 335
books on gardening see literature on gardening
Booth, Abram 319
Bosschaert, Ambrosius: *Large Bouquet in Gilt-Mounted Wan-Li Vase* (attrib.) 4
botanists 295, 297, 303, 315
  Parkinson as as *Botanicus Regius* 1, 133, 136, 167
  see also herbals
Bowen, Adam: plan of Old Street 287, *289*
bowling greens 95, 97, 98, 245, 253, 255, 323, *323*
box as edging plant 159–60, *160*
Bradwell, John (labourer) 220
Brandsby, Yorkshire 81, 104, 105, 108
bridges 224
Brossard, Davy: *L'Art & maniere de semer, faire pepiniers des sauvageaux* 31
Broughton, Henry (gardener) 130–31
Brown, Lancelot Capability 9
Browne, Christopher 124, 243, 247
Browne, Mary (*later* Evelyn) 241
Browne, Sir Richard 241, 243–4, 246, 250, 313
Bruegel, Pieter, the elder: *The Beekeepers 112*
Buckingham, George Villiers, 1st Duke of 137, 303
buildings see banqueting houses and rooms; glass-houses; lodges; summerhouses
bulbs 246, 265, 271, 278
  extension of flowering season 162, 164, 275
  price of bulbs from France 313–14
  see also tulips
Bulkley, Sir Richard 81, 119
Burghley, Lord see Cecil, William
Burton Dassett, Warwickshire 18, 99–104, 107–8, 110, 132, 222, 224
  Temple's 'Parlour gardine' 100–01, *101*, 102, 131, 145, 177, 179, 181, 184, 234, 325, 326
Butler, Charles: *The feminine monarchie* 109–10

cabbages 116, *117*, 279
cabinet de verdure 247, 249
Campden Manor, Gloucestershire 9, 230, *230*, 231, 238
    loggia 321, *321*
canals 219, 222, 223, 224
    see also water features
candles and beekeeping 109
Capel, Arthur, 1st Baron Capel of Hadham 189, *190*, 221
Carew, Sir Francis 82–3, 122, 157, 319, 323
Carleton, Dudley 306, 319
carnations *see* gilliflowers (carnations/pinks)
Castle Cornet, Guernsey: General Lambert's Garden 307,
    308
cats: Hanmer's advice on deterrents 269
cauliflower 116
Caus, Isaac de 211–12
Caus, Salomon de 211–12
Cecil, Robert, 1st Earl of Salisbury 134, 211, 223, 300, 302,
    319, 322
    see also Hatfield House
Cecil, William, 1st Baron Burghley 1, 85, 133, 135, 319, 323
    see also Theobalds, Hertfordshire
Cerceau, Jacques Androuet du *see* du Cerceau
Certaine excellent and new invented knots and mazes
    (anonymous book) 199, 334
Chamberlain, John 170, 177–8, 306, 319
Charlecote Park, Warwickshire 121, *121*, 189, *189*, 192–3
Charles I, king of England 1, 133, 136, 206, 215, 226, 237,
    303
Charles II, king of England 10, 113, 206
cherries and cherry trees *80*, 81–2, 121–2, *121*, 239
Chetwynd, Sir Walter 232
Cholmeley, Richard 81, 105, 108, 110, 118, 281
Christian values and gardening 45–50, 168
Christianson, C. Paul 183
citrus fruit *see* lemons; orange trees and orange-houses
Civil Wars 19, 172–3, 237–75
    gardens during 240–75
Clark, Robert, the elder (labourer) 129
Clark, Robert (labourer) 129
classical texts and gardening 13, 31, 32, 34, 35, 40, 109
Claydon House, Buckinghamshire 104, 220, 238–9
Clément, Gilles 5–6
climate
    climate change and decline in viticulture 124
    cultivation of tender plants
        fruit trees 81, 82, 97–8, 118–24, 265, 322

protection from climate 122, 123–4, 269–70, 275, 341
    and gardening literature 31–2, 34–5
Clothworkers' Hall, London 71, *72*, 193, *198*, 204
Clusius, Carolus 295, 297, 315
coats of arms 58, *58*, 320, *320*
Cole, James 295
Coles, William
    Adam in Eden 337
    The Art of Simpling 337
coleworts 116, *117*
columbines 162, *163*
Columella (Lucius Junius Moderatus) 5
'common wealth' world view 45–6, 47, 110, 151, 325
commonplace books 18–19, 95, 97, 176
Company of Gardeners 132–3, *133*, 135–6, 137
compartments (compartiments/*compartimenti*)
    Evelyn's enclosed gardens 247, 249
    in French gardens 264
    in Renaissance gardens
        influence in England 62–3, *63–7*, 64–5, 70, 207–8
        and use of 'knot' as term 185
    seventeenth-century gardens 216–18, 340–41
compost 104
conduits *see* fountains (conduits)
conspicuous consumption
    display of status 323
    growth in luxury goods 50–51, 52, 151, 168, 178
    ornamental and structural features of gardens 231–4
    tulips and 'tulipmania' 294–9
Conwy Castle *x*, 90, 188, *189*
Copperplate map of London 65, *67*, 87
correspondence as documentary source 11, 18–19, 99–100
cost *see* prices
country houses
    building and remodelling and status 317
    visiting houses and gardens 20, 234–5, 317, 318–24
Cowley, Abraham: *Plantarum Libri Sex* 29
Cranfield, Lionel, 1st Earl of Middlesex 184
Crisp, Sir Frank 5
crocuses and saffron 17, 148, 151, 162
Cromwellian regime *see* Parliamentarian regime
crop rotation 104
Crown Imperial 52, *52*, 271
'crypta' at Albury Park 257 258, *258*
cucumbers 17, 75, 77
cut-turf knots 189, 206–7, *207*, 209, 340
cuttings *see* propagation

cyclamen 265, 271, *271*
cypress trees as ornamental feature 246, 254

daffodils *see* narcissus
Daniels, Andries: *Vase with Tulips* (with Francken) 295, *296*
Darcy, Sir Edward and garden 71, *73*, 88
Darfield, south Yorkshire 172–3, *173*, 193, 195
Davies, Mutton 212, 259
de Beer, E. S. 251
Defoe, Daniel 10
design books and complex knot designs 203, 208
design of gardens *see* arrangement and layout of gardens
Dianthus see gilliflowers (carnations/pinks)
diaries 11, 318, 319
    women and gardens 110–11, 148, 283
    see also Evelyn, John: *Diary*
didactic texts 23–4, 27, 30–31
Digges, Sir Dudley 302
ditching 106, 107, 129
doors in gardens 216, 217, 221
double-flowered plants 156, *156*
doves
    dovecotes 74, 105, *105*, 109, 114
    dung as fertiliser 104, 105
du Cerceau, Jacques Androuet: *Bastiments de France* 62–3,
    64, *64*, 201
Dudley, Robert, Earl of Leicester 323
dung 104–5, 106, 249–50, 270
Dutch East India Company 319
Dutch gardens *see* Holland
Duthie, Ruth 338

East India Company 285
Edington Priory, Wiltshire 219
Edward I, king of England 218
eglantine roses 291, 292
Elizabeth I, queen of England 85, 88, 157, 197, 203, *203*,
    221
Elizabethan gardens 55–91
    food production 71, 74–83, 97
    lack of information on flowers in 83, 85–6
    lasting influence 102, 250
    layout 55–71, 90–91, 93, 186–7
    ornamental features 86–90, 225–6, 228
Elstob, Ivy: *The Garden Book of Sir Thomas Hanmer* 37, 38

Ely Palace, London 65, *66*, 101
embroidery patterns and knot designs 201, *202–3*, 203, 340
enclosure of gardens 55, 57, 93, *94*, 100, 173, 216–17
    as defining feature 5, 7, 58
    hedging 34–5, 59, 62, 100, 106–7, 108, 189, 243, 247,
        340
    medieval pleasure gardens 59, 60
    variety of materials in Evelyn's garden 243, 246
    see also compartments
Estienne, Charles: *L'agriculture et Maison Rustique* 31, 165,
    185, 198–9, 201, 204, 336
Evelyn, George (John's brother) 19, 251, 252, 253, 254–5
Evelyn, George (John's cousin) 253–4, 255
Evelyn, John 17–18, 19, 21, 29, 167
    on Beddington oranges 82–3, 319
    correspondence with Hanmer 38–9, 241, 264–5, 274
    Diary 82–3, 113, 240–41, 243, 245–7, 251–5, 257–8
    Elysium Britannicum 17, 37, 39–41, 237, 260, 335
        Hanmer's contribution 38–9, 40
        requirements of a professional gardener 135, *138–9*,
            140, 141, 146
        revisions and annotations 41
        transparent beehive 113, *113*
    exile during Civil Wars 238, 240–41, 328
    as gardener 124, 145–6
        fertiliser for garden 106
        private garden 109, 177, 250
        understanding of science 328
        visits and reports on gardens 319
    gardening during Civil Wars 240–60
        Albury Park garden design 240, 251, 257–9, *257–8*
        Sayes Court garden 237, 240, 241–50, 259, 274, 319,
            321, 325
        Wotton House garden design 240, 251–7, *252–3*,
            255–6, 258, 274
    influence of Italian gardens on 212, 254–5, 256–7, 258,
        274
    translation of *The French Gardiner* 31, 40
    use of 'knot' as term 185
Evelyn, Mary (née Browne) 241
evergreen plants 4, 246, 250, 254, 269, 270, 275, 339
    see also hedging
exchange of plants *see* gifts
exotic plants
    expansion of garden varieties 4, 52, 151, 161–2, 275,
        300, 302–6, 328
    exploration and introduction of 4, 20, 83, 85, 285, 300

fruit trees 81–3, 95, 97–8, 118–24, 173, 265, 302, 322
    and increase in global trade 20, 151, 285–6, 300
        trade in tulips 294–9, 300, 313–14
    protection from cold 269–70, 275, 341
    and status of owners 177–9, 297, 321–2, 323
        fashion for rare plants 274, 285
    travels of plant hunters and plant collectors 300, 302–6
    wide range of tulips 179, 295, 299
Expert Gardener, The see *Orchard and the Garden, The*

Fairfax, Sir Thomas 118
Faithorne and Newcourt map of London 290, *290–91*
Fanshawe, Lady Ann 170, 172
Fanshawe, Sir Henry 170, 172, 177–8, 319
farming *see* agriculture and gardening
fashions in gardening
    elite fashions and adoption by gentry 212, 213–14,
        218–19, 227–8
    endurance of knot gardens 183, 184, 208–9
    Hanmer on new fashions in mid-seventeenth century
        260, 264–5, 272, 274
    Parkinson on 159–60
fencing (paling) 57, 93, *94*, 100, 108, 131, 179, 243, 246
    enclosure as defining feature of gardens 5, 7, 58
fertilisers 104–5
    see also dung
fig trees 81, 97, 118, 122
fish ponds 74, 88, 104, 109, 114, 211, 224, 245, 324
fishing as leisure activity 324
Fitzherbert, John: *The Boke of Husbandry* 13, 104–5, 336
florists as suppliers of plants 286–7, 309
flowers
    cost of plants 176, 177–8, 306, 322
    and layout of garden 70, 165–7
    nurserymen and advice on growing 314
    ornamental value of tulips 297, 299
    owners' interest in 232
    as rare practice in medieval garden 70
    types of flowers in gardens 100, 102
        Bacon's recommendations 169–70
        Hanmer's lists of flowers 265–6, *267*, 270–74, 275
        in knot gardens 85, 95, 97, 176, 177, 193, 195, 202
        lack of information on 83, 85–6, 197
        Parkinson's advice on growing 161–4
        seventeenth-century expansion in varieties 161–2,
            169–70, 173, 175, 178, 179, 275, 328

    in utilitarian garden 75, 79
    see also ornamental flower gardens
food and food production
    Elizabethan gardens 71, 74–83, 97, 98
    Evelyn's garden at Sayes Court 243, 249–50
    gifts of food as sign of wealth 74, 81, 118, 119, 121–2
    and purchase of plants for gardens 278
    see also banqueting houses and rooms; vegetable
        (kitchen) gardens
Forde, Devon 114, 115, 124
fountains (conduits) 95, 169
    Elizabethan gardens 86–8, *86*
    medieval gardens 59
    seventeenth-century gardens 211 212, *212*, 219–20,
        221–2, *222*, 240, 250, 255
fragrance *see* scents in garden
France
    and complex knot designs 198–9, 201, 202, 206–7, *207*,
        208
    garden design and influence on British gardens 240, 241,
        246, 249, 259, 264, 265, 275
        French gardeners as status symbol 322–3
        French landscape designers and English gardens 211–12
        visits to French gardens 318
    nursery trade and sales to British gardeners 178, 241,
        246, 250, 260, 266, 313–15
        tulip varieties 271–2, 307, 313–14
    source of exotic plants in seventeenth century 178, 305,
        307
    Tradescant's visits and plant collecting 300, 302
    see also Renaissance gardens
Francken, Frans, the younger: *Vase with Tulips* (with Daniels)
    295, *296*
Franklin, Lady 29
French beans and soil improvement 103–4
fritillaries *174*, 271
fruit trees *see* orchards and fruit trees

Garden of Eden 5, 47–50
garden houses and lodges 229, 321, *322*
    see also banqueting houses and rooms
'garden of movement' 5–6
gardeners and labour in gardens 7, 19, 125, *125*, 127–49,
    128
    apprenticeships 133
    duties and areas of work 130–32

eminent gardeners 133–40
essential qualities 128, 140
garden owners and gardeners and gardening skills 131–2,
141–6, 179
gardening as profession 132–3, 135, 136, 137
French gardeners in England 322–3
specialist skills and knowledge 130, 131–2, 140, 142,
282, 314, 315, 322–3
status and pay 127, 129–30, 132–3, 136, 141, 177, 183,
279, 282
structural features and labourers' pay 216, 217–18,
220–21, 224
and trade in plants and horticultural equipment 279–80,
281, 285
informal exchange of plants 278, 283
'weeding women' 127, 129, 282
Gardeners' Company 132–3, *133*, 135–6, 137
gardening
changes in early modern period 3, 4–5, 10
descriptions and definitions 5, 7
lack of documentary evidence on early modern period
9–10, 184
manuscript sources of information 18, 37–9
see also propagation
gardening manuals *see* horticultural manuals; literature on
gardening
gardens
defining features 5–7
lack of surviving early modern gardens 7–9
piecemeal development 11
Gardiner, William (gardener) 278
Gardner, Richard: *Profitable Instructions for…Kitchin Gardens*
26, 77, 114, 280, *280*, 333
Garret, James 295
gatehouses and coat of arms 320, *320*
Geddes, Walter: *Book of Sundry Draughtes* 203
Geldrop (nurseryman) 309–10, *311*
Genesis: Adam and Garden of Eden 5, 47–50
gentry
adoption of elite fashions 212, 213–14, 218–19, 227–8
financial and personal costs of Civil Wars 237–8
gardening as acceptable activity 14, 17–18, 326–7
as readers of gardening literature 25, 26, 30, 38–9,
40–41, 141–2, 167, 274
specialist skills and knowledge 142–6, *143*
Hanmer on fashions in mid-seventeenth century 260,
264–5, 272, 274

identity and status and gardens 74, 317–29
interest in gardening 170–81
relationship with gardeners 131–2, 141–6, 179
varying reasons for creating gardens 231–2
leisure activities 323, 324
professional status of gardeners and social mobility 136,
137, 140
geometrical layout and use of squares 55–8, 69, 70–71,
90–91, 93–5, 98
Evelyn's 'Private garden' at Sayes Court 250
More family portrait garden 186-7 *187–8*
Stonehouse's garden at Darfield 172, *173*
Temple's new garden at Burton Dassett 100, 101, *101*
Tresham's Lyveden New Bield 55, *57*, 64, 65, 68
and use of 'knot' as term for layout of beds 185
viewed from above 321
see also knots and knot gardens
Gerard, John 114
background and career as surgeon 134, 135–6
catalogue of garden plants 83
demand for services as plantsman 83, 85, 133, 135, 137
friends' gifts of plants and seeds 305
The Herball, or Generall Historie of Plantes 1, 28, 36, 51,
77, *78*, 83, *84*, 117, 271, 336
exotic plants 151, 179
Johnson's expanded edition 13, 154, 286, 287
nurserymen in London 287, 288
portrait of Susan Hanmer 148, *149*
potato plant and portrait with 134, *134*, 135, 292, *292*
tulip varieties 295, 297, 299
Gervace, William (labourer) 217
gifts
exchange of plants between friends 118, 119, 260, 269,
278, 283, 285, 299, 304, 305, 307–9
gifts of food as sign of wealth 74, 81, 118, 119, 121–2
landowners' gift of fertiliser to tenants 104
gilliflowers (carnations/pinks) 15, *16*, 17, 95, 162, 176, 177,
265, 305
Parkinson's propagation advice 158–9
ginger plants 151, 305
glass-houses 82–3, 122, 123, 269–70
global trade and exotic plants and goods 20, 151, 178, 269,
285–6, 300, 302–3, 304–6
trade in tulips 294–9, 300, 313–14
globe artichokes 116–18, *117*
Golding, Thomas (estate manager) 21, 82, 324
Goodman, Nicholas: *Holland's Leaguer* 89

Goodyer, John 154
Googe, Barnabe: *Foure Bookes of Husbandry* 13, 55, 146, 336
Gorhambury, Hertfordshire 116, 119, 129, 169, 238, 279
gourds 75, 77
grafting
    as gentlemanly skill 142, 143–4, *143*
    ready grafted trees 286
grapes *see* vines
grass *see* bowling greens; turf knots
Greatbatch, Thomas (labourer) 216, 220
greenhouses *see* glass-houses
Griswell, Thomas (labourer) 216
Grocers' Company 136
grottoes 211, 240, 253, 254
Gwydir, Wynn family of, Conwy 119

Hall, John 102–3, 283
Halland House, Sussex 19, 219, 222, 229, 232, 282
    bowling alley 323
    cost of purchasing and transporting fruit trees 281
    gardeners' and labourers' pay 106–7, 129, 130, 221
    record of seeds and sundries purchases 279
    vegetable growing 116
Hampton Court, Surrey 85, 89, 165, 206, 207, *208*, 209, 278, 318
Hanmer, John, Lord 338
Hanmer, Susan 148, *149*
Hanmer, Sir Thomas 19–20, 167, 189, 207, 209, 211, 212, *261*, 326
    on contemporary fashions in gardens 260, 264–5, 272, 274
    contribution to Evelyn's *Elysium Britannicum* 38–9, 40
    correspondence with Evelyn 38–9, 241, 264–5, 274
    exile in France during Civil Wars 240, 241
    The Garden Book ('Of a Flower Garden') 20, 29, 37, 38–9, 103, 131, 266, 269, 270, 274, 314, 335
        essay MS of 38, 260, 264–5, 338–41
    garden notebooks 39, 260–75, *262–3*
    as gardener 124, 145–6, 177, 178, 184, 287, 328
    gardening during Civil Wars 237, 260–75, 274–5
        at Bettisfield 240, 241, 260, *262–3*, 265, 272
        at Haulton 19, 240, 265–6, *267*, 272
        at Lewisham 19–20, 240, 241, 265, 266, *268*, 312–13
        fondness for flowers and lists of plants 265–6, *267*, 270–74, 275

plant lists 260, 265–6, *267–8*, 270–74, 275
    on private spaces within gardens 325–6, 341
    suppliers and cost of plants 306–15, *310–11*
    on tulips 299, 309, 313–14
Harrison, William 7, 74, 77, 79, 81, 82, 85–6, 91, 117, 156
Hartlib, Samuel and circle 250, 315, 337
    The Reformed Commonwealth of Bees 113
Harvey, John 277, 313
Hatfield House, Hertfordshire 127, 130, 183, 211
    Tradescant the elder's garden 134, 137, 178, 322
    plant-collecting trips to Continent 300, 302
Haulton, Flintshire: Hanmer's garden 19, 240, 265–6, *267*, 272, 309, 310
heating and hot-houses 82–3, 122, 123, 270
hedging
    as enclosure 34–5, 59, 62, 100, 106–7, 179, 216–17
        dead hedges 108
        Evelyn's garden at Sayes Court 243, *244*, 246, 247
    in knot gardens 159–61, *160*, 184, 189, 195, 340
    labour for 129
    plants from France 246
    and supply of wood 107–8
    topiary in gardens 86, 169
    trade in quicksets 232, 281, 291
Hellens Manor, Herefordshire *320*
Henrietta Maria, queen consort of Charles I 136, 147, 167, 206, 303
Henry VIII, king of England 165, 225–6
Hentzner, Paul 318, 319
heraldic beasts statuary 86, 225–6, *227*, 228
herbals 13, 28, 36, 51, 83, *84*, 148
    see also Gerard, John
herber garden in medieval period 59
Heresbach, Conrad: *Foure Bookes of Husbandry* 13, 55, 146
Hicks, Sir Baptist 230, 231
Hill, Robert (supplier of garden seeds) 292
hives *108–9*, 109, 110, 111, *111–13*, 113, 165, *166*, 250
Hoby, Lady Margaret 110–11, 148, 228, 283, 325
Holbein, Hans, the younger 186
Holland
    bulb trade 299, 300
    Dutch gardens as influence 209, 241, 244–5, 259, 275
    English visitors to Dutch gardens 318
    Tradescant's travels and plant collecting 300
holly as hedging 243, *244*, 246–7
Holme Lacy, Herefordshire 129, 130, 217, 219, 222, 224, 229, 239, 325

Holt, Goodyeare (labourer) 216, 221
honey production 109, 110–11, 112–13
honeysuckle 291, 292
horticultural manuals 10, 12–14, 15, 23–6, 27, 29–30
    advice on beekeeping 109–10, 147
    advice on layout of gardens 57–8
    see also literature on gardening
'Hortus Tradescantianus' 304
hospitality
    display of gardens and houses for visitors 20, 234–5,
        317–24
    gifts of food and wealth 74, 81, 118, 119, 121–2
    provision of exotic fruit 81, 118
Hostler, John (labourer) 129
hot-houses 82–3, 122, 123, 270
household accounts see account books as documentary
    source
houses in gardens 229
    see also banqueting houses and rooms; summerhouses
housewife and gardens 146–7
'how-to' manuals 23–4, 27, 30–31
Howard, Henry, 6th Duke of Norfolk 240, 251, 257, 258–9
Howard, Thomas see Arundel, Thomas Howard, Earl of
Hull, Yorkshire: gardens in 55, 56
human manure 105–6
Humphries of Woollstable (nurseryman) 310–11, 311–12,
    313
Hunt, William (labourer) 217, 218
hyacinth family 169, 170
Hyll, Thomas 5, 14, 31, 34
    The Gardener's Labyrinth 8, 14, 23, 26, 56, 75, 90, 101,
        115, 220, 332
        beehives in garden plan 108, 109
        bowling area 323, 323
        identity and status and gardens 318
        and knot gardens 196, 197, 197, 199, 201, 201
        plants for vegetable garden 74–5, 116
        women and gardens 146–7
    on layout of gardens 68, 185
    A most briefe and pleasaunte treatise 13, 14, 17, 23, 24,
        26, 30, 41, 331
    The Profitable Arte of Gardening 43, 135, 331
        importance of gardeners 128
        instruction on beekeeping 109, 112, 113
        mazes 201

illustrations in gardening books 27, 28, 184
    and complex knot designs 198–202, 200–01, 208
    printers' use of stock illustrations 199, 201, 203–4
individual taste and gardening 20–21, 57, 58, 228, 234–5,
    240, 328–9
informal exchange of plants 118, 119, 260, 269, 278, 283,
    285, 299, 304, 305, 307–9
information see knowledge
Ingestre Hall, Staffordshire 232, 233
Ingram, Sir Arthur 184, 218–19, 221, 225, 229, 231, 282,
    319
    statues of heraldic beasts 228, 232, 234–5
Ingram, John 40
irises 38, 169, 271, 308, 314, 314
islands 249, 249
Italian gardens
    travel and influence on British gardens 239, 241, 300, 318
        Evelyn's garden designs 212, 254–5, 256–7, 258, 274
    see also Renaissance gardens

Jacques, David 62
Jarvis, John (gardener) 279, 281
Jauncy, Richard (gardener) 130
Jeffreys, Joyce 111, 116, 130, 148, 183, 228–9
Jerusalem artichokes 118
Johnson, Cornelius: Arthur, 1st Baron Capel and his Family
    189, 190, 221
Johnson, Nathaniel 40
Johnson, Thomas 1, 13, 154, 286, 287
Jones, Inigo 221, 222, 226
Josselyn, Ralph 111

Kempsall, Michaell (labourer) 129
Kenilworth Castle, Warwickshire 85, 85–6, 183
    recreated Elizabethan garden 160, 196–7, 196
    white bear statues 86, 197, 226, 227
kitchen gardens see vegetable (kitchen) gardens
knots and knot gardens 19, 69, 88–90, 98, 147, 160, 181,
    183–209, 264
    Bacon's dislike of 169
    complex designs and lack of evidence for execution
        184–5, 185, 190, 191, 192, 193, 195, 195–209
        execution in turf 189, 206–7, 207, 209
        origin in embroidery and pattern books 201, 202–3,
            203, 206, 208

edging and layout 201–2, 340
  hedges 159–61, *160*, 184, 189, 195, 340
  materials to mark layout 160
  Parkinson's advice on 159–61, 183–4
flowers in 85, 95, 97, 176, 177, 193, 195, 202
and geometrical layout of gardens 71, 93, 95, *173*, 208–9
as historical garden style 183
literature on and illustrations of 195–206, 208, 340
range of styles in seventeenth century 189–92, 208–9
  portraits and plans as unreliable depictions 192–3, 204,
    208
recreations at historic sites *160*, *173*, 183, 184, 195–7, *196*
uncertain meaning of 'knot' 15, 89–90, 183, 184–6
view from above 321
knowledge
  botanists and exchange of knowledge 295, 297, 315
  gentleman gardeners and specialist skills 142–6
  limited knowledge of bees 110, 113
  public sharing of knowledge 32, 50, 315
    information exchange of amateur gardeners 20, 315
    plant collectors and new and exotic plants 303, 304
    see also literature on gardening

La Seigneurie gardens, Sark *161*
labour see gardeners and labour in gardens
labyrinths see mazes and labyrinths
Laet, Johannes de 303
Lambert, General Sir John 299, 307, 309
landowners see gentry
landscape gardeners: emergence of 24, 137, 211–12, 329
Langham, Robert 85, 86, 196–7, 226
Latin texts on gardening 13
Law, Ernest 196
Lawson, William 7, 9, 17–18, 34, 68, 69, 152
  Margaret Hoby as neighbour 148
  A New Orchard and Garden 23, 27, 35, 41, 43, 79, 81, *118*,
    124, *153*, 211, 334
    beekeeping 109, 110, 113, 147
    Country Housewifes Garden appendix 26, 109, 147–8,
      166, 204–5, *205*
    flowers in orchards 165–6
    gardeners 25, 128, *128*, 129, 141
    gentlemen gardeners as target readership 26, 141–2,
      143
    individual taste in gardens 57, 328
    and knot gardens 185, 196, 204–6, *205*

layout of a garden 57, 58, 93, *94*, 109, 113, 185, 220
  ornamental features 86, 88
  pleasure and satisfaction from gardens 47–8, 326–7
  ready grafted trees 286
  structural and water features 222–3, 224–5
layout of gardens see arrangement and layout of gardens;
  order and symmetry in gardens
le Moyne, Jacques
  Apple 284
  Clove Pink 158
  Columbine and Ladybird 163
  Daffodil 273
  Dog Rose and Small Tortoiseshell Butterfly 180
  Madonna Lily 158
  Strawberry Plant 171
Le Nôtre, André 249
Leet, Nicolas 305
lemons 119
letters as documentary source 11, 18–19, 99–100
Leveson, Sir Richard 11, 19, 146, 214, 215, 217, 231–2, 320,
  328
  see also Trentham Hall
Levett, John: *The Ordering of Bees* 109, *109*
light and survival of plants 123–4, 269, 270
lilies *158*, 169, 305
Lime Street, London: network of botanists 295, 315
Linnaeus, Carl 15
literacy in early modern period 26–9, 132
literature on gardening 12–15, 17, 18–20, 23–41
  arrangement of garden layout 57–8, 68–71
  aspirational nature of texts 25, 30–31
  beekeeping advice and manuals 109–10, 147
  bibliography of 330–37
  derivative and translated texts 31–2, 34–5, 37, 147, 185
    as origin of complex knot garden designs 198–9, 201,
      202, 206–7, 208
  and introduction of ornamental flower garden and plants
    151–70
  knot gardens 195–206
    contemporary illustrations and twentieth-century
      recreations 196–7, *196*
    lack of clear instruction 201–2, 204–6, 208
  literacy and reader's relationship with text 26–9
  manuscripts and readership 37–8, 37–9, 40–41
  practical experience
    Hanmer's practical advice 266, 269, 272
    importance of record keeping 266

and layout of gardens and beds 68, 199
    Parkinson's practical advice 35–6, 157–8, 176–7
    and scientific methods and knowledge 32–6, 39–41,
        151, 152, 154–7, 314
    target readership 25–6, 30, 38–9, 40–41, 141–2, 167, 274
        men as target readership 26
        women as readers 26, 147–8
Llannerch, Denbighshire
    painting of house and garden 212–13, 213, 225, 259
        structural features in garden 217, 219, 219, 221, 229–30
        windows in walls 216
Llantrithyd Place, Wales 8, 19, 119
    payments for work in garden 129, 130, 224, 227, 229
    purchase of plants 279, 281–2
L'Obel, Matthias de 1, 154, 295
local conditions and garden design 99, 101–2
Lockey, Rowland: Sir Thomas More and Family (after
    Holbein) 186–7, 187–8
lodges 229, 321, 322
loggias and view of garden 321, 321
London 286
    Cheapside Market 106
    gardens
        medieval gardens and 'Agas' map 63, 64–5, 66, 87, 87,
            90, 188, 287, 290, 291
        Stow's Survey of London 289–90
        Treswell's surveys 71, 72–3, 193, 312, 312
    Hanmer's Lewisham garden 19–20, 240, 241, 265, 266,
        268, 312–13
    market gardens
        expansion in early modern period 289–91, 291, 292
        historical trade in London 278
        supply of human manure 105–6
    nursery trade 277, 285–94, 306
        growth in commercial nurseries 289–91, 291, 292,
            309–13, 315
        Old Street nursery 287, 288–9
        tulips 294–9, 306
    shops for sale of seeds and plants 292
    see also Arundel House; Long Acre; Sayes Court,
        Deptford; Whitehall Palace
Long Acre, London: Parkinson's garden 1, 154, 162, 292–3
Lovatt, Hugh (labourer) 129
Lucas, William (supplier of garden seeds) 292
Lucy, Sir Thomas: portrait with family 121–2, 121, 189, 189,
    192–3
luxury goods see conspicuous consumption

Lyte, Henry: A New Herbal of History of Plants 336
Lyveden New Bield, Northamptonshire 8, 9, 58, 86
    garden lodge 229, 321, 322
    geometrical arrangement 55, 57, 64, 65, 68
    moated orchard 55, 65, 68, 69, 222–4, 223
    terrace and views 320–21

Maison Rustique see Estienne, Charles; Markham: Maison
    Rustique, or the Countrey Farme; Surflet, Richard
manuals see horticultural manuals; literature on gardening
manure as fertiliser 104–5, 249–50
manuscripts 18, 37–8, 37–9
maps and plans and knot garden designs 193, 194–5, 198,
    198, 204
marginalia in gardening books 28–9, 30, 41
market gardens
    growth in London 289–91, 291, 292, 312
    historical trade in London 278
    human manure 105–6
Markham, Gervase 128, 152, 185
    Cheape and Good Husbandry 109, 110, 336
    The English Housewife 146, 147, 196, 337
    The English Husbandman 14, 26, 43, 333, 335
        and knot gardens 183, 199, 201–2, 206
        layout of garden 57, 58, 58, 68, 69–70, 93
        practical advice from various sources 34–5
        profitability of gardening 46
        protection of tender fruit trees 83, 122
    Maison Rustique, or the Countrey Farme 34–5, 34, 122–3,
        124, 199, 333
    A Way to Get Wealth 23, 337
Marriott, John 199
Mascall, Leonard
    A Booke of the Arte and maner, howe to plant and graffe
        25, 25, 27, 31, 41, 48, 79, 125, 331
        gardener's tools 75, 76, 140
        profitability of gardening 43, 45–6
Mason, Goodman (labourer) 129
mazes and labyrinths 86, 88, 90, 201, 264
    see also knots and knot gardens
mead and beekeeping 109, 113
medicinal uses of plants 3, 75, 75, 135, 155
    medieval gardens 59
    publication of herbals 13
    women's knowledge of 148
    see also herbals

medieval gardens 59–62, 165
melons 17, 75, 77, 82, 97, 122, 249, 254
memorandum books *see* notebooks and memorandum
    books
Meteran, Emmanuel van 295
Middlesex, Lionel Cranfield, 1st Earl of 184
'middling' classes and gardening literature 25, 30
Millen, John 287, 293
    Old Street nursery 287, *288–9*
Moare, Richard (labourer) 129, 216
moats 86, 88, 95, 219–20
    Evelyn's garden at Sayes Court *248*, 249
    Evelyn's garden at Wotton House 251, 252, *253*, 256
    moated orchard at Lyveden New Bield 55, *57*, 65, 68, *69*,
        222–4, *223*
Mollet, André 249
    Le Jardin de Plaisir 185, 206–7, *207*, 209, 337
monastic tradition and gardens 59, 109, 124
moral values and gardening 45–50, 151, 168, 327
More (Sir Thomas) family portrait 186–7, *187–8*
Moreton, Richard (labourer) 216
Morgan, Cadwallider (gardener) 127
Morgan, Owen (gardener) 130
Morin, Pierre ('Moryn'; nurseryman) 29, 178, 271, 307
    Hanmer's purchases from 313–15
    oval garden design 246, *247*, 313
    printed catalogue of plants 314
Morin, René (nurseryman) 29
Morris, John 303
Moseley Old Hall, Staffordshire *173*, 195
Moullar, James ('Mr Moulart'; nurseryman) 309, *310*, 313
mounts 9, 68, 86, *94*, 169, 217, 222–3, *223*, 320, 321
    Evelyn's garden designs 243, *244*, 246–7, *248*, 256
Mun, Thomas 51
myrtles 302, *302*
Mytens, Daniel: *Thomas Howard, Earl of Arundel* 225, *226*

names of plants: lack of standard system 15, 17, 77
narcissus (daffodil) *156*, 265, 271, *273*
natural history and empirical evidence 32, 34
nature: gardeners' attempts to change 155–7, 270
Netherlands *see* Holland
New Place, Stratford-upon-Avon *12*, 102–3, 183, 196
Newburgh Priory, Yorkshire 172
Newdigate, Lettice 190, *191*, *198*, 204
night soil 105–6

Nonsuch Palace, Surrey 85–6, 318
notebooks and memorandum books 39, 95, 100, 144–5,
    173, 175, 260
    see also account books as documentary source;
        commonplace books as documentary source; diaries;
        Hanmer: garden notebooks
Nunwell estate, Isle of Wight 18, 97–9, *98–9*, 217, 222, 279
    bowling green 95, 98, 323
    food from garden 74, 105, 108–9
    Oglander's planting of fruit trees 95, 97, 122, 144–5
    ornamental flower garden 176–9, 181, 184, 234, 306, 328
    statue 227, *228*
nursery trade 20, 151
    in France 178, 241, 246, 250, 260, 266, 271–2, 307,
        313–15
    informal origins 278–85, 306–9
    in London 277, 285–94, 306, 309–13, 315
    Parkinson on 133, 285–6, 287
    trade in tulips 294–9, 306, 313–14

Oglander, Sir John 107, 110, 124
    on beekeeping 109, 113
    commonplace books 18–19, 95, 97, 176
    and costs of Civil Wars 237
    inheritance of estate 95
    pigeon dung as fertiliser 105
    planting of fruit trees at Nunwell 95, 97, 144–5
    solace from garden 325, 326
    statue in garden 227, *228*
    see also Nunwell estate, Isle of Wight
Old Street nursery, London 287, *288–9*
oleander trees 83, 302
orange trees and orange-houses 82–3, 119, 122–3, 270,
    302, 319
Orchard and the Garden, The (anonymous text) 31, *130*, 185,
    199, 204, 332, 335
orchards and fruit trees 6–7, 35, 47, 79–83, 86, 93, 100, 172
    beehives in 113
    Evelyn's garden at Sayes Court 243, 249
    exotic fruit trees 81–3, 95, 97–8, 118–24, 173, 265, 302,
        322
    flowers in orchards 165–6
    food production as purpose of gardens 71, 74, 97, 98,
        121–2, 167
    gardeners' skills and pay 130, 131, 279, 282, 322
    gentleman gardeners and hands-on skills 142, 143–5, *143*

Hanmer's orchards and lists of fruit trees 265, 272
medieval orchard garden 59
moated orchard 55, *57*, 65, 68, *69*, 222–4, *223*
Oglander's orchard at Nunwell 95, 97, 144–5
ornamental features 223–4, 229
purchase of trees for 278, 279, 281–2, 283, 287
   Bacon's mass order 291–2
   nurserymen and supply of trees in London 287–8
Scudamore's orchard in Herefordshire 239
seventeenth-century gardens 172, 173
as sign of wealth 79, 81, 118, 322
women's management of 148–9
see also Austen: *A Treatise of Fruit-trees*; Lawson: *A New
   Orchard and Garden*; *Orchard and the Garden, The*
order and symmetry in gardens 14, 43, 44, 47, 327
analogy with social and familial order 55
layout of Elizabethan gardens 55–68, 90–91, 93, 186–7
Renaissance gardens and compartmentalisation 62–3,
   63–7, 64, 70, 91, 185, 207–8, 340–41
seventeenth-century gardens 172, *173*, 216–18
see also geometrical layout and use of squares
ornamental features 86–90, 169, 320
painting and colouring for effect 221
seventeenth-century gardens 211–35
   Evelyn's garden at Wotton 252, 253, 254
and utilitarian gardens 114, 224, 249
see also knots and knot gardens; walls
ornamental flower gardens 3, 5, 14, 19, 29, 39, 50, 74, 95,
  98, 151
beehive in 113, 114, 165, *166*
emergence in seventeenth century 165–81
Evelyn's 'Ovall garden' at Sayes Court 245–6, *245*, 313
Evelyn's 'Private garden' at Sayes Court 109, 177
extended flowering season 162, 164, 169, 275
Hanmer on edging methods 265, 340
Hanmer's list of suppliers 306–15
Hanmer's lists of flowers in 265–6, *267*, 270–74, 275
lack of information on types of flowers 83, 85–6
in medieval gardens 165
owners' interest in 170–81
Parkinson's advice on new flowers 161–4
planting styles 162, 164, 170
for pleasure of owners 51–3, 165, 166–7, 168–70, 181, 234
position in garden layout 165–7, 176–7
rarity in Elizabethan gardens 86, 162
records of plants in seventeenth-century gardens 154–5,
   161–4, 169–70, 175, 178, 179, 265–6

Temple's 'Parlour gardine' 100–01, *101*, 102, 131, 145,
   177, 179, 181, 184, 234, 325, 326
tulips as ornamental flowers 297, 299
see also flowers; knots and knot gardens
owners see gentry

Packwood House, Warwickshire *111*
Padua, University of 241
   knots in botanical garden 199, *200*
paintings see portraits and paintings
paling see fencing (paling)
Paradise see Garden of Eden
Parkinson, John 1–3, 5, 14, 21, 39, 68, 69, 137
and Boel 36, 304–5
as *Botanicus Regius* to Charles 11, 133, 136, 167
career as apothecary 134–5, 136, 155, 292
experience as foundation for works 34, 35–6, 152, 154–64
Long Acre garden 1, 154, 162
   sale of plants 292–3
on nurserymen 133, 285–6, 287
Paradisi in Sole, Paradisus Terrestris 1, 2, 18, 28–30, 35–7, 41
   arrangement of gardens 70–71, 93, 166–7, 176–7, 246,
     264
   Crown Imperial 52, *52*
   flowers for ornamental gardens 161–4, *170*, 175, 274,
     275
   folly of attempts to change the nature of plants 155–7
   gentleman gardeners and specialist skills 142, *142*, 143
   gilliflowers 15, *16*, 17, 158–9
   grapes (vines) in British climate 124
   individual taste in gardens 57, 328
   and knot gardens 159–61, 183–4, 197, 199, *200*, 204,
     205–6
   need for observation and experiment 152, 154–9
   notable owners of 28–9, 167, 300–01
   orderliness in garden and wider world 327
   origins of 'English' plants 277
   pleasure and ornamental gardens 43, 51–3, 165,
     166–7, 168, 211, 326
   practical advice to gardeners 157–8
   protection for orange trees 123
   provenance of plants 305
   purchase price 28, 204
   selection of flowers for good taste 324
   social and religious context 48, *49*, 50, 51–3, 121
   survival rates of exotic plants 302

tulips 179, 297, 299, *299*
useful and ornamental gardens 43
varieties of plants 151
vegetable growing 114–15, 116, 117, *117*, 118
water features 220
women as readers 147–8
status and garden's reflection of 317
Theatrum Botanicum 13, 28, 152, 154, 303, 337
on Tradescant's plant collection and travels 302–4
wild flowers for gardens 292
Parliamentarian regime 237, 238, 307
parlour gardens 176–7, 250, 325
Temple's 'Parlour gardine' 100–01, *101*, 102, 131, 145,
177, 179, 181, 184, 234, 325, 326
see also ornamental flower gardens; privy (private)
gardens
Parson, John (labourer) 216
parterres 98, 185, 206, 240, 245–6, 264, 340
Passe, Crispin van den: *Hortus Floridus 156, 266, 271, 272,
314*
paths, alleys and walks 58, 68, 69, 71, 93, 100, 199, 211
Evelyn's garden at Sayes Court
the Grove 247, *248*, 275
lime walk 244–5, 275
'Ovall garden' 245–6, *245*
promenade *248*, 249, 321
fragrant plants for walking on 21, 70, 169–70
structural features in compartmentalised gardens 217,
340–41
visitors and display of garden 320–22
see also wooded walks
pattern books and complex knot designs 203, 208
Peacham, Henry: *The Compleat Gentleman* 28, 141, 225, 226
peaches and peach trees 81–2, 119, *120–21*, 121–2
peas 104, 114–15, 116
pebbles to mark pattern in knot gardens 160
Pelham, Sir Thomas 19, 116, 146, 218–19, 232, 282, 323
Penshurst, Kent 81–2, 86, 88, 148–9, 216, 219, 221, 324
'pentisses' 83, 122
Pepys, Samuel 113
personal taste *see* individual taste and gardening
pest control 114, 159, 269
see also weed control techniques
Picot, Monsieur (nurseryman) 178, 266, 309, 313, 314–15
pigeons
dung as fertiliser 104–5
pigeon houses 74, 105, 114, 211, 252

pinks *see* gilliflowers (carnations/pinks)
plant collectors and exotic plants 52, 151, 162, 274, 297,
299, 300–06
Tradescants' travels 300–04
plant-hunters 36, 300–06
Tradescant's trips 302–3
plants 20, 277–315
expansion of available varieties 4, 52, 151, 161–2, 328
experiments with new plants in seventeenth century
154–7
Hanmer's lists and notebooks 260, 265–6, *267–8*,
270–74, 275, 306–315
lack of standardised names 15, 17, 77
limited knowledge in early modern gardens 83, 85–6
trade in plants 277–315
informal exchange of plants 118, 119, 260, 269, 278,
283, 285, 299, 304, 305, 307–9
nursery trade in London 277, 285–94, 306–13, 315
tulips 294–9, 300, 306, 309, 313–14
Tradescants' plant-collecting travels 300–04
transporting plants and trees 269, 281–2, 313, 322
types of plants in utilitarian gardens 74–5, 77–9, 95, 97,
114–24, 238–9
varying degrees of owners' interest in 231–2
see also bulbs; exotic plants; flowers; trees
Plat, Hugh
Floraes Paradise 333
The Garden of Eden 335
Platter, Thomas 318
pleasure from gardens and gardening 43, 45, 46–8, 50, 151,
168–70, 181, 326–7
Parkinson's promotion of ornamental gardens 39, 43,
51–3, 165, 166–7, 168
see also ornamental flower gardens
pleasure park in medieval period 59–60, *60*
Pliny: *Natural History* 32
Plot, Robert: *Natural History of Staffordshire 214–15, 215,
218, 218,* 232, *233*
plum trees 81, 82
Pointer, Richard (nurseryman) 287, 288
pomegranate trees 302, *303*
pompions (pumpkins) 17, 75, 77
ponds and pools 169, 219–20, 222, 224–5, 252, 256
fish ponds 74, 88, 104, 109, 114, 211, 245, 324
pools *see* ponds and pools
Porcher, Monsieur: knot designs 199
Porro, Girolamo 199

porticos 255, *255*, 256–7
portraits and paintings
  gardeners in family portraits 127
  gardens as feature in 18, 63–4, 74, 86
    fountains 221, *222*
    fruit production and status of sitters 121–2, 192–3
    knot gardens 186–93, *187–92*, 198, *198*, 208
    statuary 225–6, *226*
    unreliable picture of real gardens 192–3, 204, 208, 212–13
  gentleman gardeners and specialist skills 143–4, *143*
potash 104
potato plants 134, *134*, 135, 151, 292, *292*
Prescott, James 283
Price, Thomas (carpenter) 265
prices
  books 26, 28, 204
  plants 116, 176, 177–8, 239, 278, 306–7, 312, 322
  trees for Bacon's London garden 291
  trees for Edward I's orchard 278
  tulip bulbs 297, 300, 313–14
primroses 162
print *see* publishing and print culture in England
privy (private) gardens 165, 325–6, 341
  Evelyn's garden at Sayes Court 109, 177, 250
  see also ornamental flower gardens; parlour gardens
profit from gardening 43, 45, 167
  spiritual benefits 48, 50
propagation
  Evelyn's nursery garden 250, 282
  free material from countryside 282
  gardeners' sale of plants 278, 279–80, 281, 285
  grafting 142, 143–4, *143*, 286
  Hanmer on private garden for 341
  hedges and trees for wood 107–8
  and informal exchange of plants 278, 282, 305
  Parkinson on gilliflowers 158–9
  setting vine cuttings 102–3, 105, 283
  and tulip varieties 295, 297
  Verney's cherry tree cuttings 239
  see also nursery trade; seeds
protection of plants
  tender exotic plants 269–70, 275, 341
  fruit trees 122, 123–4
  trees as 5, 122
  windbreaks 159
  see also enclosure of gardens

pruning as specialist skill 131
public good
  'common wealth' world view 45–6, 47, 110, 151, 325
  public sharing of knowledge 32, 50, 303, 304
publishing and print culture in England 23–4, 151
  role of manuscript texts 37–8
  use of stock illustrations 199, 201, 203–4
Puckering, Sir Thomas 19, 111, 146, 148, 155, 177, 219, 221, 228, 238
  wealth and display of 231, 234, 328
pumpkins *see* pompions (pumpkins)
Purefoy, Anne 29

quarters *see* geometrical layout and use of squares
quicksets for hedging plants 34, 232, 281
Quickswood, Hertfordshire 127, 130

rabbit warrens 74, 109
Rea, John 299, 307, 308, 309
  Flora: De Florum Cultura 37, 39, 264, 287, 309, 310–11
recreation and restoration of historic gardens
  doubtful historical accuracy 12, 184
  knot gardens *160*, *173*, 183, 184, 195–7, *196*
religion
  Christian values and gardening 45–50, 168
  and garden houses 229
remodelling of gardens 214–16
Renaissance gardens and influence in England 59–60, 62–3, *63*–7, 70, 91, 165, 197
  Evelyn's garden designs 254, 256–7, 258, 259, 274
  structural and ornamental features 211, 212, 225, 232
Reresby, Sir John (father) 29, 99, 145, 167, 172, 173, 175–6, 181, 231, 234, 239–40
Reresby, Sir John (son) 175, 239–40
Restoration, The 237, 259
restoration *see* recreation and restoration of historic gardens
retreat *see* privy (private) gardens
Reynall family of Forde in Devon 114, 115, 124
Richard of Weston (gardener) 100, 102, 103–4, 131–2, 133, 179, 279
Richmond Palace, Surrey 90, *90*, 185, 188
rivers and streams 86, 88, *94*, 95, 222
Robin, Jean and Vespasien (nurserymen) 29, 178, 300, 302, 305

Rock Savage, Cheshire 220, 221, 229
Rolfe, Goodwife (wife of estate worker) 129
Rose, Harry (estate manager) 99, 107–8
    Temple's correspondence with 100, 101, 102, 103, 107,
        131–2, 145, 179, 181, 279, 283
Rose, John 266, 270, 308–9
roses 100, *180*, 291, 292, 305, 306
Rowley (Trentham labourer) 220
Royal Society 10, 259, 315
Rushton Hall, Northamptonshire 229

saffron 17, 148, 172
St Augustine's Abbey, Canterbury: knot garden 193, *195*,
    204
St Augustine's Friary, London: fountain 87–8, *87*
St Gall Monastery, Switzerland 62
St Mary's Spital, London 65, *67*, 88, 101
Savage, Sir Thomas 220
Sayes Court, Deptford, London 19, 20, 40, 124, 212
    Evelyn's creation of garden during Civil Wars 237, 240,
        241–50, 259, 274, 319, 321, 325
    beehives 109, 113, *113*, 250
    'Elaboratorie' 250
    food production 243, 249–50
    the Grove 247, *248*, 249, 275
    nursery garden and propagation 250, 282
    'Ovall garden' 245–6, *245, 247*, 313
    plan of garden 106, *107*, 241, 242, 244–5, 247
    private garden 109, 177, 250
    walks and promenades 244–5, *248*, 249, 275, 321
scents in garden
    flower garden 165, 166
    paths 21, 70, 169–70
    vegetable garden 167
Schofield, John 71
science and scientific methods
    Bacon 32, 34, 36, 152, 156
    Evelyn 250, 259, 328
    gardening literature 32–6, 39–41, 151, 152, 154–7, 314
Scot, Reynolde 14, 25–6, 27, 40
    Perfite Platforme of a Hoppe Garden 23, 45, 332
scribal publication 37–9
Scudamore, John, 1st Viscount Scudamore 217, 239
seats 86, 88, 211, 219, 221, 320
seeds 115–16
    Evelyn's seeds from France 246, 254

experiments with new plants in seventeenth century
    154–6, 303
as gifts from friends' travels 305
plants grown for seed collection 116, 280–81
trade in seeds 278, 279, 280–81, 292, 300
self-interest and morality 46–7, 50, 168
self-sufficiency of estates 107–9
Semper Augustus tulip 297, *298*
Serlio, Sebastiano: *Tutte l'opere d'architettura et prospetiva* 197
Shakespeare, William 102–3
Shakespeare's New Place, Stratford-upon-Avon *12*, 102–3,
    183, 196
sheep bones to mark pattern in knot gardens 160
Sheriff Hutton Hall, Yorkshire 218, 228, 282
Shirley, Jane, Baroness Holles of Ifield *192*
shops for sale of seeds and plants 292
Shyrley, John (labourer) 129
Sidney, Lady 148–9
Sidney, Sir Henry 82
Sidney, Sir Robert 21, 81–2, 86, 119, 283, 285, 324
size of gardens 264
skeps for bees 110
Slater, Francis 136
Smyth of Greenwich (nurseryman) 312, 313
Smythson, Robert 63, 93
social order and cultivation of gardens 10, 14, 17, 55
    aspirational literature on gardening 25, 30–31
    elite fashions and adoption by gentry 212, 213–14,
        218–19, 227–8
    and food production 71, 97
        beekeeping and degree of prosperity 111–12
        higher status vegetables and fruits 116, 118, 121–2,
            192–3
        orchards and fruit trees as sign of wealth 79, 81
        similar plants across social order 74–5, 77, 79, 115–16
    gardeners' status and pay 127, 129–30, 132–3, 136, 183,
        279, 282
    professional gardener's higher status 137, 140–41
    range of readers of gardening literature 25, 26, 30, 167
    social and moral context for gardens 43–53, 151, 168,
        326–7
        changing values and social order 47
        display of gardens and houses and status of owners 74,
            317–29
        gardens during Civil Wars 237–75
    types of medieval garden 59
    see also gentry; status symbols

Society of Apothecaries 136
soil improvement methods 103–5
spider-wort 304
spiritual benefits of gardening 48, 50, 325
Sprat, Bishop Thomas 51
squares see geometrical layout and use of squares
Starre, Goodwife (wife of estate worker) 129
statuary in gardens 86, 211, 212, 225–8, 226–7, 232, 256
status symbols
    gardens as 3, 5, 14, 50–51, 74, 192–3, 317–29
    orchards and fruit trees 79, 81, 118, 322
    ornamental features in seventeenth-century gardens 211,
        228–35, 320–21
    ornamental flower gardens 168, 177–9, 321–2
    rare plants 285
        tulips and 'tulipmania' 294–9
        vegetables and fruits 116, 118, 121–2, 192–3
steps 211, 217–19, 256
stills and still houses 75, 94
Stone, Nicholas 228
Stonehouse, Revd Walter 172–3, 173, 181, 193, 195
stoves 83, 123, 270
Stow, John: Survey of London 289–90
Stow(e), Buckinghamshire 9, 129, 130–31, 177, 183, 225, 234
Stratford-upon-Avon, Warwickshire 75, 77, 111
    Shakespeare's New Place 12, 102–3, 183, 196
strawberry plants 170, 171
streams see rivers and streams
Strong, Sir Roy 62, 86, 183, 186, 192
structural features see ornamental features
styles of gardening
    difficulty of classification 11
    elite fashions and adoption by gentry 212, 213–14,
        218–19, 227–8
    Hanmer on fashions in mid-seventeenth century 260,
        264–5, 272, 274
    individual practices and tastes 20–21, 57, 58, 228, 234–5,
        328–9
        changes over generations 176, 184, 240, 260, 264
    and introduction of new plants in seventeenth century
        164
    see also landscape gardeners
Sudeley Castle, Gloucestershire 202–3, 203
summerhouses 211, 229, 240
sundials 212, 246
Surflet, Richard: The Countrie Farme 31, 34, 165, 199, 202,
    333

Sussex, Earl and Countess of 119, 238, 279
Sutton, Raphe (carpenter) 105
swans 114, 224–5, 249
Sweet William (Sweet John) 1, 3, 134
symmetry see order and symmetry in gardens
Symonds, Richard 246

taste
    advice on good taste 324
    see also individual taste and gardening
taxation and Civil Wars 237–8
Temple, Sir Peter 130, 177
Temple, Sir Thomas 17–18, 18–19, 99–104, 110, 119, 122,
    124, 231
    account of setting vine cuttings 102–3, 105, 283
    correspondence with Harry Rose 100, 101, 102, 103,
        107, 145, 179, 181, 279, 283
        respect for gardeners' skills and knowledge 131–2
    new 'Parlour gardine' ('paled Gardine') 100–01, 101, 102,
        131, 145, 177, 179, 181, 184, 216, 234, 325, 326, 328
    pools in garden 224
    rates of pay for labourers 130
    sale of surplus plants and timber 281
    on swans 224, 225
Temple Newsam, Yorkshire 221, 225, 228, 229, 232
terminology
    interchangeable terms 17, 77
    uncertain meaning of 'knot' 15, 89–90, 183, 184–6
terraces 98, 211, 212, 217–19, 246–7, 255, 255, 256,
    320–21
Theobalds, Hertfordshire 83, 86, 133, 318, 319
thistle artichokes 116, 117, 117
Thrybergh, Yorkshire 29, 145, 172, 173, 175–6, 239–40
Toddington Manor, Bedfordshire 65, 68
tools for gardening 115, 250
    in accounts and inventories 75, 76, 114, 279, 312, 313
    early trade in horticultural products 278, 279, 312, 313
    Evelyn on tools of professional gardener 138–9, 140
    grafting tools 142–3, 143–4
topiary in gardens 86, 169
Tothill Street nursery, London 288, 290
Tower of London 165
trade see global trade; nursery trade; plants: trade in plants
Tradescant, John, the elder 1, 29, 133–4, 135, 137, 137,
    167, 293, 301
    garden at Hatfield House 133, 137, 178, 300, 302, 322

on London plant suppliers 286–7

supply of plants from garden 294

travels and plant collecting 300, 302–3

Tradescant, John, the younger 133, 134, *134*, 135, 137, *137*, 293

   Musaeum Tradescantianum 304

   travels and plant collecting 302–4

Tradescant's Ark (museum and garden), London 293–4, 304

Tradescant's Orchard 80, 96, *102*, *120*, 287

translated texts on gardening 31–2, 185

   as origin of complex knot garden designs 198–9, 201, 202, 206–7, 208

transport of plants and trees 269, 281–2, 313, 322

travel and influence on gardens at home 212, 226, 239, 328

   experiences in exile during Civil Wars 240–41, 249, 254–5, 300

   plant collectors and plant hunters 300–06

trees

   Bacon's mass order for Gray's Inn Court garden 291–2

   Evelyn's garden at Sayes Court 244–5, 246, 247, *248*, 249

   Evelyn's seeds for Wotton House 254

   and geometric layout *94*

   Hanmer's lists of plants 270, 339

   for protections of plants 5, 122

   and supply of wood 107–8, 249

   transporting fruit trees to provinces 281–2

   see also orchards and fruit trees; wooded walks

Trentham Hall, Staffordshire 9, 11, 19, 105, 106, 325

   gardeners' and labourers' status and pay 129, 130, 279

   purchase of plants 281

   remodelling of house and garden in 1630s 214–16, *214–15*, 217–18, *218*, 231–2

      financial cost 233–4

      statuary 227

      waterworks 219, 220–21

Tresham, Sir Thomas 8, 55, 58, 65, 68, 86, 88, 224, 229

   see also Lyveden New Bield

Treswell, Ralph

   London Surveys 71, *72–3*, 193

   Woolstaple Yard 311–12, *312*

Trevelyon, Thomas: *Trevelyon Miscellany of 1608* 203

Trevor, Sir John 299

Tudor, Thomas (gardener) 127, 130

Tuggie, Ralph (nurseryman) 286–7, 288, 311

tulips 20, 85, 95, 102, 151, 162, 173, 175, 176, 177, 296, *298–9*

   Hanmer on price of bulbs from France 178, 313–14

Hanmer's breeding of and gifts to friends 307

Hanmer's flower lists 265, 266, 271–2, 309

supply of plants in early modern England 294–9, 300, 306, 313–14

'tulipmania' phenomenon 297

variety of colour and form 164, 179, 295, 299

turf knots 189, 206–7, *207*, 209, 340

turf seats 88

Turner, William: *New Herbal* 13

Tusser, Thomas: *A hundreth good pointes of husbandrie* 13, 336

'Tutle Fields' nursery, London 288, *290*

Upfold, Goodwife (wife of estate worker) 129

uses of plants 43

   Parkinson's aesthetic focus 51–2

   see also food and food production; herbals; medicinal uses of plants

utilitarian gardens

   flowers in 75, 79, 93, 95, 165–6, 167

   food production as purpose of garden 71, 74–83, 95, 97, 98, 108–9, 167, 243, 249

   introduction of ornamental garden 151, 165–7, 327–8

   medieval gardens 60, *61*, 62

   and ornamental features 114, 224, 249

   see also medicinal uses of plants; orchards and fruit trees; vegetable (kitchen) gardens

van Dyck, Sir Anthony: *Sir Thomas Hanmer* 261

Vaughan, William (labourer) 221

vegetable (kitchen) gardens 93, 95, 100

   Evelyn's garden at Sayes Court *248*

   flower garden separate from 165, 166–7

   food production as purpose of garden 71, 74–5, 77–9, 97, 98, 108–9, 167, 243, 249

   gardeners and labour in 129

   instructive literature on 280–81, *280*

   medieval gardens 60

   plants grown for seed collection 280

   purchase of plants and seeds 115, 116, 279, 280–81

   seeds from travels abroad 305

   size and layout of beds 68

   types of plants grown 74–5, 77–9, 95, 114–18, 243, 249, 279–80

Ventris, Thomas and son (stonemasons) 228

Verney, Sir Ralph 104, 106, 238–9, 241
views and vistas 169, 256, 320–21
Villa d'Este gardens, Tivoli 62, *63*, 254
Villiers, George, 1st Duke of Buckingham 137, 303
vines 81, 95, 97, 98, *102*, 122
    climate change and decline in viticulture 124
    propagation by cuttings 102–3, 105, 283
    pruning by skilled gardeners 131
violets 162, 271
Virgil: *Georgics* 34
visiting gardens and status of owners 20, 234–5, 317–24, *318*
vistas and views 169, 256, 320–21

Waldstein, Baron 318, 319
Walker (nurseryman) 311
walks *see* paths, alleys and walks; wooded walks
walls
    as enclosing device 58, 59, 62, 173, 216–17, 243, 246
        walled gardens 82, 97–8, 122, 250
    as ornamental feature *214–15*, 215–16
Walton, Izaac: *The Compleat Angler* 324
Ware Park, Hertfordshire 170, 172, 306, 319
Warnar, Master (nurseryman) 287–8
Warwick Priory 114, 177, 219, 222, 234
    banqueting house 231, 328
    hedging plants 108, 232
    painted doors in garden 216, 221
    staff and garden labour 104, 105, 106
water features 86–8, *94*, 95, 114, 169, 211
    elaborate systems in seventeenth century 212, *212*, 219–25, *222–3*
    Evelyn's directions for Wotton House 252, 254, 255, 256
    and fresh water supply 224
    painting and colouring for effect 221
    pumping systems and use of gravity 220
    see also fountains (conduits); ponds and pools
waterfowl 114, 224–5, 249
wealth
    exotic flowers as sign of 177–9, 297, 321–2, 323
    gifts of food as sign of wealth 74, 81, 118, 119, 121–2
    Hanmer on fashionable gardens in seventeenth century 260, 264–5, 274
    ornamental features in seventeenth century 211, 228–35
    profit and early modern morality 45–7, 167
        changing values and social order 47, 151

and types of vegetables grown 116
    see also conspicuous consumption; status symbols
weather *see* climate
weed control techniques 103–4
weeding women 127, 129, 282
Wentworth, Thomas 127, 143–4, *143*, 145, 187–8
Wentworth Woodhouse, south Yorkshire 144, 187–8
Westminster nursery businesses 288, *290*, 310, 311–12, *312*
Whately, Alderman 77, 111
Whilton, Roger (supplier of quicksets) 281
Whitehall Palace, London 86–7, *87*, 165, 225–6, 318, 319
Wilkins, Dr John 113
Willoughby, John 115, 279
Wilton House, Wiltshire 60, *61*, 62, 64–5, 74
    ornamental features 211, 220
Wimbledon House, Surrey 93, 319
windbreaks for protection 159
windows in gardens 216, 229
Winthrop, John 292
Winwood, Sir Rafe 177–8
Wolsey, Cardinal Thomas 89, 183, 278
Wolverton, Buckinghamshire 99, 103, 130, 131
women and gardening 146–9
    diaries 110–11, 148, 283
    and gardening literature 26, 147–8
    'weeding women' and other garden tasks 127, 129, 282
woodcut illustrations and knot designs 199, 203–4
wooded walks 93, *94*
Worshipful Company of Gardeners 132–3, *133*, 135–6, 137
Wotton, Lord and Lady 193
Wotton, Sir Henry 170, 319, 336
Wotton House, Surrey 8–9, 19, 40, 212
    Evelyn's remodelling of garden 240, 251–7, *252–3*, *255–6*, 258, 259, 274
Wren, Christopher 113
Wrothe, Sir Robert 324
Wyngaerde, Anthonis van den 63
    Richmond Palace and Privy Gardens 90, *90*, 185, 188
    View of Whitehall Palace and the Great Garden 86–7, *87*
Wynn, Sir John of Gwydir 81, 119, 123

York: Ingram's house and garden 218, 225, 228, 232, 282, 319
yucca *155*, 305

Willms Rog.